ASIAN-CAJUN FUSION

AMERICA'S
THIRD
COAST

Carl A. Brasseaux and Donald W. Davis, series editors

University Press of Mississippi / Jackson

ASIAN-CAJUN FUSION

Shrimp from the Bay to the Bayou

Carl A. Brasseaux and Donald W. Davis

Foreword by Rex H. Caffey

This contribution has been supported with funding provided by the Louisiana
Sea Grant College Program (LSG) under NOAA Award # NA14OAR4170099.
Additional support is from the Louisiana Sea Grant Foundation. The funding
support of LSG and NOAA is gratefully acknowledged, along with the matching
support by LSU. Logo created by Louisiana Sea Grant College Program.

The University Press of Mississippi is the scholarly publishing agency of
the Mississippi Institutions of Higher Learning: Alcorn State University,
Delta State University, Jackson State University, Mississippi State University,
Mississippi University for Women, Mississippi Valley State University,
University of Mississippi, and University of Southern Mississippi.

www.upress.state.ms.us

The University Press of Mississippi is a member
of the Association of University Presses.

Original maps and artwork by Robert Ray

First printing 2022
∞

Library of Congress Control Number: 2021948554
Hardback ISBN 978-1-4968-3822-3
Epub single ISBN 978-1-4968-3823-0
Epub institutional ISBN 978-1-4968-3824-7
PDF single ISBN 978-1-4968-3825-4
PDF institutional ISBN 1-4968-3826-1

British Library Cataloging-in-Publication Data available

In memory of cherished friends and colleagues
taken before their time:
Jerome P. Voisin, 1953–2015
Sherwood M. "Woody" Gagliano, 1935–2020
Len Bahr, 1940–2019
Ming K. "MK" Wong, 1937–2020
Lisa G. Pond, 1963–2020
A. Otis Hebert, 1930–1976
Robert A. Nash, 1915–1976
Michael W. "Mike" Quin 1941–2021

And in joyful appreciation
of enduring friendships:
Chuck Wilson
Roland and Lou Anna Guidry
William Clifford Smith

CONTENTS

ACKNOWLEDGMENTS

The historical roots of Louisiana's shrimp industry extend to the nineteenth century. The commercialization and subsequent globalized distribution of this indigenous marine product is a fascinating, but largely forgotten, saga that links the people of south Louisiana's bayous to Old World Chinese communities via San Francisco as well as to American consumers nationwide. Our examination of the industry's evolutionary trajectory—a coast-to-coast research effort—has required substantial help and guidance from a broad spectrum of institutions and individuals. Library and archival professionals consistently went the proverbial extra mile to locate obscure manuscripts, ledgers, photos, maps, legal instruments, and other items in dusty boxes, bags, filing cabinets, and assorted containers. To these unsung investigative heroes, we extend a heartfelt thank-you.

As researchers who have collectively spent more than one hundred years sifting through documentary, photographic, and artifactual treasures variously found in libraries, attics, barns, sheds, and businesses scattered throughout the Louisiana coastal plain, we have developed a deep respect for the coastal region's denizens, whom we readily recognize as the real experts. We have genuinely treasured the warm hospitality and abiding generosity of the area's residents, who readily opened their homes and shared their experiences and insights with us. The informants' irrepressible candor, observational skills, and deductive abilities are truly inspirational.

We also acknowledge a debt of gratitude to our Louisiana Sea Grant colleagues for their unwavering support and assistance. Established in 1968, the Louisiana Sea Grant Program is charged with improving the public's understanding of the nation's coastal and marine resources through research, education, and extension services. We are particularly grateful for the encouragement and assistance of Robert Twilley, director emeritus of the Louisiana Sea Grant College Program, Matthew Bethel, DeWitt Braud Jr., Thu Bui, Rex Caffey, Leslie Davis, Anne Dugas, Emily S. Maung-Douglass, Julie Falgout, Carol Franze, Albert "Rusty" Gaudé, Thomas Hymel, Roy Kron, Brian LeBlanc, Julie Lively, Nicole Lundberg, Earl Melancon, Lyndsay Rushing, Kevin Savoie, Mark Shirley, and James Wilkins.

The authors also wish to extend their heartfelt thanks to Edmond Mouton, Louisiana Department of Wildlife and Fisheries; M. K. Wong, Chinese American entrepreneur; Bill Wong, president, Wong Association, San Francisco, CA; Pam Wong, Chinese Historical Society of America, San Francisco, CA; Larry Yee, executive secretary, Chinese Consolidated Benevolent Association, San Francisco, CA; Andrew S. C. Tam, businessman, San Francisco, CA; the staff of the Maritime and Seafood Industry Museum, Biloxi, MS; Farrell C. Latour, president, J. H. Menge and Company, New Orleans, LA; the staffs of the Jefferson and Lafourche Parish Clerks of Court, Gretna and Thibodaux, LA; the staff of Morgan City Archives, Young Sanders Center, Morgan City, LA; Dr. Florent Hardy Jr., former archivist, Louisiana State Archives, Baton Rouge, LA; the staff of Gulf Coast Supply, Cameron, LA; Monique L. McCleskey, Special Projects, Laitram Company, Harahan, LA; Tom Strider, registrar, and his staff, Louisiana State Museum, New Orleans, LA; Dr. Christopher Cenac, Houma, LA; Roland and Lou Anna Guidry, Cut Off, LA; Melissa Fox, Louisiana Department of Wildlife and Fisheries, Baton Rouge, LA; Gina Bardi, reference librarian, San Francisco Maritime National Historical Park Research Center, San Francisco, CA; Kathleen Correia, supervising librarian, California State Library, Sacramento, CA; Clifton Theriot, Archives and Special Collections, Ellender Memorial Library, Nicholls State University, Thibodaux, LA; Billy Talbot, A. F. Davidson Hardware and Supply, Houma, LA; Tommy Chauvin, Chauvin Brothers Hardware, Chauvin, LA; Daniel Alario Sr. and his wife and daughters, Alario Marine Supplies, Westwego, LA; Barbara Rust, archivist, National Archives, Ft. Worth, TX; Clay Skaggs, archivist, National Archives, San Francisco, CA; Debra Kaufman, California Historical Society, San Francisco, CA; Jane Pratt, head of reference, Richmond Public Library, Richmond, CA; Laura Callahan, Larkspur Library, Larkspur, CA; Jason Theriot, historian, Houston, TX; Mark Schleifstein, environmental reporter, NOLA.com/*Times-Picayune*, New Orleans, LA; Joseph Rodriquez, president, Rodriquez Shipyard, Bayou La Batre, AL; Andrew Gibson, president, Tidelands Seafood Company, Dulac, LA; Lance Authement, president, Hi Seas of Dulac, Dulac,

LA; Lynn Abbott and Kevin Williams, Special Collections, How-ard-Tilton Memorial Library, Tulane University, New Orleans, LA; F. C. Felterman Jr. and family, Patterson, LA; Nick Deonas, community historian, Fernandina Beach, FL; and Wayne Olson, reference librarian (retired), National Agricultural Library, Beltsville, MD.

Our names appear on the cover of this volume, but in all honesty, our spouses, Glenda and Karen, should appear on the byline, as they have always given us encouragement, support, reassurance, and forbearance for our perpetually distracted comportment. Even when we were frustrated and annoyed at our slow "progress," they always knew what to say to ease our concerns. They have always been in the wings but deserve much more than praise. They have never wavered from our desire to follow our passions—regardless of the hardships. They know we will get it done and insist we do it our way, regardless of the financial or professional consequences. We are driven, but it is our wives who have insisted we push hard to keep our intellectual fires burning. We love them dearly.

PREFACE

The research project that engendered this publication was inspired by the Louisiana shrimp industry's monumental challenges of the past quarter century—travails that directly threaten the very existence of North America's most productive decapod fishery. Shrimping has directly or indirectly impacted the lives of every resident of Louisiana's coastal plain. Yet the shrimping industry's contributions are either unappreciated or underappreciated by locals and outlanders alike. This apathy is compounded by a lack of grassroots knowledge of the industry's origins and the root causes of the ongoing crises—foreign imports and possible resultant demise of the wild-caught shrimp fishery. This work is an attempt to bring these causative threads to light.

The Louisiana fishing community's remarkable resilience is the most significant of these threads. Residents of Louisiana's working coast typically share a can-do, never-give-up mindset that has permitted physically isolated communities to endure hurricanes, oil spills, coastal subsidence, and erosion—as well as state and national politicians' apathy and condescension. Over the course of the past 150 years, they have simply adapted in the wake of successive calamities. It is folly to discount their tenacity and grit in the face of present challenges.

FOREWORD
—Rex H. Caffey

Modern-day accounts of America's love affair with shrimp typically center on the primary themes of commerce and culture. Ample evidence of these themes is available through a variety of sources, ranging from mass media to technical reports. In one iconic movie, a US soldier bound for Vietnam waxes wistfully on his Gulf Coast home, on his desire to return there after the war and become a shrimp boat captain, and on the culinary versatility of shrimp—describing it as "fruit of the sea." That now famous 1960s-era monologue includes an impressive litany of twenty-one shrimp preparations. But a cursory web search conducted today on the term *shrimp recipes* returns more than eight million hits—far more than any other type of seafood. And while the consumption of shrimp dates back ages, its recent surge in gastronomic popularity has been fueled by advancements in aquatic husbandry—advancements that have allowed these delectable decapods to evolve into a global commodity.

Reporting by Food and Agriculture Organization (FAO) indicates that the total volume of capture fisheries harvested from wild stocks reached an apparent peak nearly forty years ago. Since then, nearly all increases to the world's seafood supply have been derived from aquaculture. Shrimp farming, in particular, has emerged as a major industry. From initial production trials in the 1960s, the industry has grown into an economic juggernaut, with an annual volume approaching five million tons. Most of this production derives from countries of the Asian Pacific Rim, and for decades the primary importer has been the United States. This influx of product has led to a near doubling of the US per capita consumption. Americans now eat more shrimp than tuna and salmon combined.

Without question, the globalization of seafood has contributed to economic downturns in many fishing-dependent communities of the United States. Commoditization of the global shrimp market has been especially problematic for Louisiana, the cultural origin of the American shrimp trade. While Louisiana continues to be the national leader in shrimp landings, dockside prices have averaged $1.50 per pound for nearly four decades. Adjusted for inflation, this

To appeal to discriminating consumers, roadside retailers offer wild-caught, "fresh off the boat" shrimp. This type of business can be found throughout the state's working coast from a cluster of retailers at the Westwego Seafood Market to the Direct Seafood business at the Port of Delcambre, roadside stands along Bayous Lafourche, Terrebonne, Grand Caillou, Du Large, and elsewhere. In some cases, shrimp are sold directly off the boat at a captain's personal wharf. (Photo from the authors' collections, 2018.)

stagnation equates to a 70 percent reduction in the real price of shrimp paid to Bayou State harvesters since 1980.

Competitive pressures from imports have been exacerbated by rising input costs and a series of natural and man-made disasters. Hurricanes, oil spills, and now pandemics have added insult to injury. As a result of these factors, the number of active shrimp harvesters in the state is less than half of what it was just twenty years ago. The remnant fleet is working to differentiate itself from the commodity market through the development of value-added products, direct sales, niche marketing, and quality enhancement initiatives. While such efforts might appear novel, they are consistent with the industry's long record of survival through adaptation.

In *Asian-Cajun Fusion: Shrimp from the Bay to the Bayou*, Carl A. Brasseaux and Donald W. Davis take the deepest dive yet into the history of this storied American fishery. Whereas contemporary accounts tend to focus on the wild versus farmed shrimp conflict of the late twentieth century, Brasseaux and Davis start the story much earlier. This is no Gumpian narrative.

Beginning with subsistence consumption in the mid-1700s, the authors describe in detail how the capture and sale of Louisiana shrimp gradually expanded into increasingly broader waters and markets over the span of two centuries. The innovation that fueled that expansion is meticulously documented, with large portions of the book dedicated to developments in harvesting vessels and gear; advances in processing via drying, canning, and refrigeration; and the establishment of global supply chains and branded advertising. From a commerce perspective, readers will learn how trade routes, established as early as the mid-nineteenth century, sent Louisiana shrimp across the continental US by rail and to markets abroad by ship. From a cultural perspective, the book documents the contributions of numerous immigrant communities, and especially the Chinese, Cajun, and Vietnamese entrepreneurs whose efforts have commercialized Louisiana shrimp on an international scale.

As one of the nation's foremost colonial historians, Carl A. Brasseaux has published approximately fifty books on Louisiana's Acadian and Creole cultures. Donald W. Davis, a cultural geographer, has produced more than six hundred lectures and symposia pertaining to coastal Louisiana. In their second contribution to the Third Coast series, they serve up a trove of archival images and interviews to chronicle the commercial and cultural evolution of the Louisiana shrimp industry. The book is a testament to the industry's past resilience against many of the same challenges it faces today in terms of disasters, technology, labor, and competition. In an era in which globalization threatens the economic viability of domestic harvesting, readers are left with a sense that we have been here before—and that as long as there is a resource and human innovation, there will be a fishery.

ASIAN-CAJUN FUSION

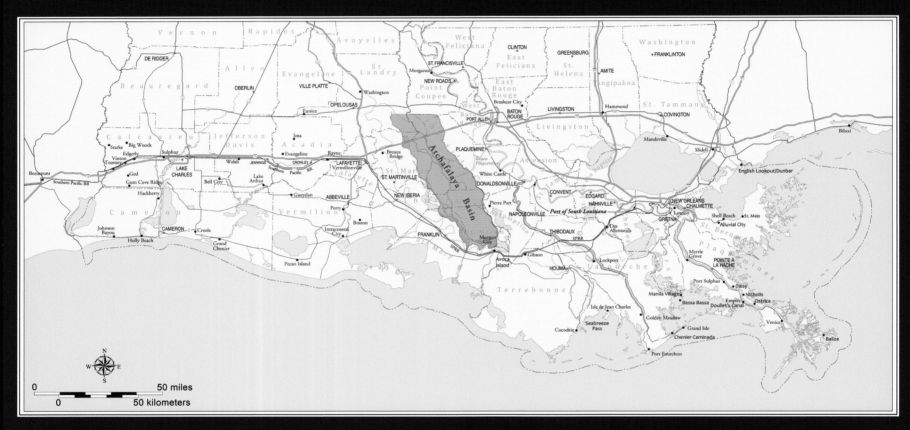

Louisiana's Coastal Communities. (Map designed by
Lisa Pond, Louisiana Geological Survey, and updated
by Robert Ray, Louisiana Sea Grant College Program.)

INTRODUCTION

Once a national fisheries juggernaut, the northern Gulf Coast shrimp industry is presently under siege, for fully 90 percent of all shrimp consumed by Americans—approximately 1.25 billion pounds annually—are imported from foreign, primarily Asian, aquafarms. As Paul Greenberg notes in *American Catch* (2014), the domestic shrimp industry is largely a victim of its own initial success. Once a sidebar item available primarily in "ethnic" restaurants, shrimp have become a popular, almost universal culinary staple throughout the United States. Greenberg observes that "a decade ago [ca. 2004] shrimp surpassed canned tuna as the most popular seafood in the United States and now the average American eats more than four pounds of it a year—roughly equivalent to the U.S. per capita consumption of the next two most popular seafoods—tuna and salmon—combined. If they didn't eat shrimp, most Americans today wouldn't eat any seafood at all" (91–92).

America's increasingly insatiable appetite for the diminutive shellfish rapidly outstripped the domestic fishery's ability to meet demand. For centuries, the nation's shrimpers have harvested wild (i.e., ocean-caught) shrimp, and as late as the 1960s, nearly three-fourths of all shrimp sold in the United States were caught in America's coastal waters, primarily in the Gulf of Mexico. However, the annual domestic catch is ultimately a finite resource, and as America's demand exploded, wholesale food distributors supplemented domestic shrimp species with their Asian and South American pond-raised cousins—to the point where the once ubiquitous American commodity is virtually again a niche product, despite its inherent gastronomic superiority. And yet America's domestic shrimping industry endures, thanks to the tenacity, resilience, and resourcefulness of its shrimpers.

Louisiana's shrimpers, unquestionably the most beleaguered in the nation, exhibit these traits in spades. Like their counterparts throughout the United States, these fishermen have faced not only persistently cheap and largely environmentally unregulated global competition, gradually falling dockside prices (roughly 50 percent between 1978 and 2013—with 2020 regarded as "the worst in forty years"), fluctuating and sporadically crippling fuel

Cajun cuisine is a product of the 1900s—with accelerated growth in the later part of the twentieth century. Cross-cultural fusion is an important component of south Louisiana's cooking traditions. The term has been widely appropriated by outsiders as witnessed by this Canadian "Famous Cajun Grill," which is actually a Chinese restaurant. (From the authors' collections, 2011.)

The shrimp boat *Heavy Metal* and a shrimper's plea for increased public consumption of domestically harvested shrimp. (Shrimp boat *Heavy Metal* from Images of New Orleans: The Donn Young Photograph Collection, Louisiana Digital Library, Baton Rouge, LA, https://www.louisianadigitallibrary.org/islandora/object/lsu-sc-dyp%3A225.)

Hurricanes have been the bane of the Louisiana shrimping industry since its inception. Tidal surges destroyed wooden platform villages, while winds and waves claimed untold boats and their crews. Most recently, Hurricanes Laura and Delta (2020) decimated Cameron's fishing fleet and destroyed its processing plants. (From *The Times*, December 27, 2004.)

prices, and unpredictable harvests but also unprecedented natural and man-made disasters of biblical proportions. Between 2005 and 2020, generational benchmark hurricanes, the Deepwater Horizon/Macondo oil spill, and epic freshwater flooding in the lower Mississippi River collectively confronted the Pelican State's fishermen with a litany of critical environmental and economic concerns: fishermen faced the loss of boats and equipment. Communities had to write off wharves, warehouses, and other vital fisheries infrastructure. The latest setback occurred in September 2020, when Laura, the strongest hurricane to ever make landfall in the United States, devastated southwestern Louisiana. The media prominently showcased these surface issues but largely ignored irreparable damage to estuaries that sustain the industry. Shrimpers, burdened by loans and the need to support their families, have found it difficult to rebound economically as their home parishes struggle to recover from successive historic catastrophes and restore essential services, which are often interdependent. Many areas impacted by Hurricane Laura, for example, were without electricity for several weeks to three months. Loss of electrical services is particularly calamitous. In the wake of Hurricane Rita (2005), for example, damage to the local electrical grid disabled the local ice factories, which in turn immobilized the shrimp fleet regardless of the availability of boats. This scenario reoccurred in the fall of 2020. The dearth of active boats forces processors to shutter their plants and lay off their workforces, thus adversely

Friends Don't Let Friends Eat Imported Shrimp. (Image and announcement created by authors.)

affecting the supply chain. In a shrimping town, virtually no one makes money when the boats are not operating.

Despite the widespread economic dislocation and staggering toll in human misery wrought by these myriad disasters, the national electronic and print media have largely overlooked the enduring plight of Louisiana's coastal communities, particularly those supporting the regional shrimp industry. Only a handful of important, but obscure, nonfiction works—notably Greenberg's *American Catch: The Fight for Our Local Seafood* (2014), Jill Ann Harrison's *Buoyancy on the Bayou: Shrimpers Face the Rising Tide of Globalization* (2012), and Christopher Hallowell's *People of the Bayou: Cajun Life in Lost America* (1979)—have provided outsiders with sporadic eyewitness glimpses of Louisiana shrimpers' daily struggles.

Even less well understood are the historic, economic, and environmental factors that led to the industry's meteoric rise to national prominence in the late nineteenth century and its successful maturation in the early to mid-twentieth, milestones that ironically contributed to the persistent threat of imports in the early twenty-first. Indeed, even families who have drawn their livelihoods from the Pelican State's bountiful coastal waters for generations are mistakenly convinced that the industry's origins and early evolution are permanently lost to the mists of time.

This investigation pierces this lingering veil of obscurity and, drawing on a long-ignored superabundance of documentary evidence, reveals for the first time the industry's origins and circuitous evolutionary track from its inception circa 1875 to the onset of the Vietnamese influx circa 1975 and the subsequent reincarnation of the regional fishery. Tracking the Louisiana fishery's evolutionary trajectory is greatly complicated by the industry's unique bifurcated nature: from its inception, the shrimp industry has consisted of two

Relentless downward price pressure, compounded by widespread environmental and economic damage wrought in Louisiana's prime shrimp nurseries by natural and man-made disasters bookended by Hurricanes Katrina and Rita (2005) and Laura, Delta, and Zeta (2020), along with the Deepwater Horizon disaster (2010), have forced many long-established Cajun shrimpers to abandon their fishing traditions. In April 2019, Louisiana shrimp landings for the month were reported to be the lowest in eighteen years, and this downward trend continued in 2020, partially because of the disruptions born of Hurricanes Laura, Delta, and Zeta. The surviving shrimpers have no defense against falling prices.

This scenario is not limited to families that have contributed to the Louisiana shrimp industry for generations. Following the collapse of South Vietnam in 1975, many boat people who transplanted to coastal Louisiana quickly carved an enduring niche for themselves in the shrimp industry. Their notable success was due in large part to the fact that Vietnamese shrimping operations were family enterprises in which extended families pooled their labor and financial resources. A generation later, however, many young, college-educated Vietnamese have joined the ranks of coastal Louisiana's professional classes, and Vietnamese shrimping families can no longer automatically draw on familial labor pools to sustain their operations as first-generation immigrants succumb to the ravages of age and infirmity. The availability of deckhands is a persistent problem. Traditionally, family members provided support labor. This is no longer the case.

As the region's fishing fleet shrinks, shrimp-related family-owned businesses in coastal communities face imminent closure, adding additional impetus to a growing void in the regional industry's infrastructure. The future of Louisiana shrimping is thus increasingly uncertain, particularly as the continued use of H-2A and H-2B visas, which have provided the seafood industry in Texas and Louisiana with low-cost immigrant seasonal workers, faces growing political resistance.

Vermilion Bay, located in south central Louisiana, is noted for its prodigious white shrimp harvest. White shrimp have a sweeter flavor than brown shrimp. (Image provided by the Louisiana Sea Grant College Program.)

distinct, yet inextricably linked, halves catering respectively to the very different demands of domestic and foreign marketplaces. One initially focused on American consumers in the eastern United States, the other on Asian—primarily Cantonese—buyers in the Far East. During the early decades of the fishery's existence, these dual entities were also differentiated by very different investors, workforces, administrations, and product lines. This industrial amalgam—composed, like Frankenstein's monster, of seemingly incompatible components—would intuitively seem to have been inevitably predestined to failure, yet it emerged as an American fisheries colossus, whose economic presence and culinary influence was, to paraphrase Aristotle, far greater than the sum of its disparate parts. This is the story of the Louisiana shrimp industry's improbable rise to prominence.

Louisiana's prodigious annual shrimp catches were once the stuff of American maritime fisheries lore. The state's shrimpers have traditionally harvested three species of these popular crustaceans: white shrimp (*Penaeus setiferus*), brown shrimp (*Penaeus aztecus*), and seabobs (*Xiphopenaeus kroyeri*). White and brown shrimp have dominated the commercial marketplace. White shrimp, the physically largest and most commercially valuable species, are staples of the restaurant and frozen seafood industries, while brown shrimp, smaller in size—and thus less valuable—are usually available commercially as either peeled tail meat or as fresh, heads-on shellfish. *Xiphopenaeus kroyeri* are the lifeblood of the dried shrimp trade.

Composite chart showing the varieties of marketable-size shrimp most common to each regional Gulf fishery. (Artwork by Robert Ray, art director, Louisiana Sea Grant College Program.)

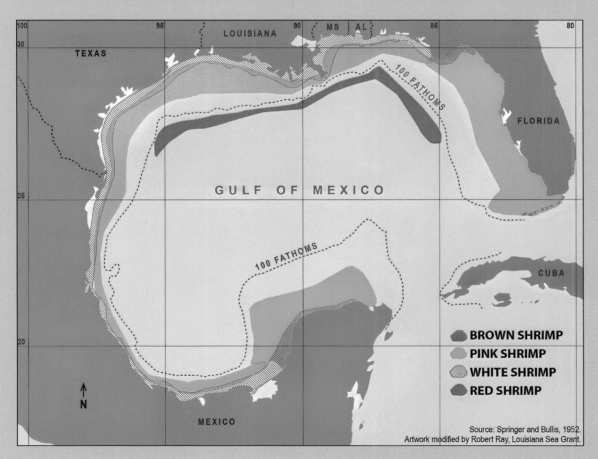

BROWN SHRIMP
PINK SHRIMP
WHITE SHRIMP
RED SHRIMP

Source: Springer and Bullis, 1952.
Artwork modified by Robert Ray, Louisiana Sea Grant.

CHAPTER 1

Three shrimp species account for about 98 percent of the nation's commercial catch. The white and brown varieties constitute the backbone of Louisiana's shrimp fishery, which has led the nation in the harvest of wild-caught shrimp since 2000. Another member of the Penaeidae family, pink shrimp is also a staple of the United States fishery, but this variety, found from the southern Chesapeake Bay to the Florida Keys and in the southeastern Bay of Campeche, is only rarely harvested in Louisiana waters. American shrimpers also catch the smaller "seabob" (a corruption of the French *six barbes*, meaning *six beards*), but they are of minor commercial importance and are harvested commercially only in Louisiana for the dried shrimp industry.

Each shrimp species has a distinct appearance. White shrimp can be identified by ten slender, relatively long "walking" legs and five pairs of swimming legs. They are not grooved, are a light gray, boast greenish tails, and have a yellow abdominal band. They have longer antennae than other shrimp—from two and a half to three times longer. Further, they have a short life span, usually less than two years. White shrimp spawn offshore, and the newly hatched shrimp travel to their estuary habitats in April and early May. Once in the estuaries, the larvae feed on plankton, while juvenile and adult shrimp are omnivorous and feed on bottom detritus, plants, microorganisms, and small fish. The Louisiana season generally opens from mid-August to mid-December; some waters stay open into January. Permits are required to harvest white shrimp in federal waters, which are generally open year-round.

Brown shrimp are similar to their larger cousins and also have ten slender walking legs and five pairs of swimming legs. However, they are grooved on the shell's surface and have a tail marked with a purple to reddish-purple band as well as green or red pigmentation. Like their cousins, they also have a life span of about two years, but they spawn in relatively deep water. Peak spawning is in spring and summer. By February and March, the larvae have settled in their nursery habitats to feed and mature. The juveniles and adults feed on plankton and are omnivorous, feeding on worms, algae, microscopic animals, and various types of organic debris. The brown shrimp season in Louisiana, inside estuarine waters, generally runs from May to July.

Seabobs, which are not dependent on estuaries, congregate along Louisiana's beaches and passes to feed on nutrients found in association with these geomorphic features. They have long recurved carapaces, and their last walking legs are extremely long and slender. Their legs are slightly pink or a yellow-orange. They also have especially long, reddish antennae. Their body color is whitish or grayish, with a yellowish front; they are occasionally completely yellow. They are bycatch harvested with the three main commercial shrimp species from North Carolina through the Gulf of Mexico and into the Caribbean Sea. Unlike the other three crustaceans, seabobs spend their entire life cycle in offshore waters and most likely spawn between July and December in the Gulf of Mexico. They have become the de facto species used in the shrimp-drying business and have been a part of this industry since its inception in Louisiana. This small shrimp is a target species during the fall and early winter months—October through December. Off the Cameron Parish coast is one the largest seabob harvest sites in the Gulf of Mexico.

A fifth shrimp variety, Royal Red, was first discovered in the Gulf of Mexico in 1950 by the United States Fish and Wildlife Service vessel *Oregon*, but it has never been a component of Louisiana's commercial fishery. Found at great depths off the Alabama coast, red shrimp are harvested by only a few licensed Bayou La Batre shrimpers specifically for distribution to restaurants along the eastern Gulf Coast.

Because of the ever-popular crustaceans' enduring commercial value in the national and international marketplaces, the Louisiana shrimp industry has been the mainstay of the state's nationally significant coastal fisheries since the establishment of the northern Gulf Coast's first shrimp cannery in New Orleans in 1867. In fact, Louisiana's domination of America's domestic shrimp industry was so complete that, by the mid-twentieth century, these shellfish became virtually synonymous in the nation's popular imagination with the Pelican State's coastal parishes—witness the early 1950s Top 40 standard "Shrimp Boats" and *Thunder Bay*, a 1953 movie starring James Stewart. That conditioned mental association has endured, thanks to the region's continuing dominance of the domestic industry. The National Marine Fisheries Service's official database of shrimp landings for the period from 1962 to 2018 (the most comprehensive and authoritative records available) indicates that Louisiana shrimp boats netted at least 50 percent of the national white shrimp catch in forty-six of the forty-eight years (95.83 percent) for which federal statistics are available. In addition, Louisiana's bounty accounted for 47.95 percent of the gross value of all white shrimp taken in United States waters.

Because it was a publicly denigrated minor commercial fishery, few contemporary verbal and graphic depictions exist for France's eighteenth-century shrimp fishery. These woodcuts from Denis Diderot's famous *Enycyclopédie* are perhaps the best surviving illustrations. (*Encyclopédie des arts et des métiers (1751–1780)*, *Pesches de Mer* [Maritime Fisheries] series.)

In the postbellum era, river shrimp were an easily accessible source of protein for the working poor in an era of widespread economic distress. (Lithograph from *Frank Leslie's Popular Monthly*, 1878.)

Two ancient tools—nets and fishing baskets—were easily crafted from local material to catch various edible crustaceans. (Lithograph from *Hearth and Home Magazine*, April 6, 1872.)

IN THE BEGINNING

However, saltwater shrimp did not figure prominently in early Louisiana's economy, in large part because of negative French attitudes toward the crustacean. First settled in 1699, the French colony's Gallic pioneers transplanted to the New World the prejudices of the Old World motherland, where consumption of the crustaceans was popularly associated with society's poorest and most disreputable elements, particularly alcoholics. In fact, in the provinces bordering the Atlantic Ocean, residents commonly referred to shrimp as "drunkards' food," and contemporary literature sometimes described shrimpers as troglodytes living in coastal caves. It is thus unsurprising that in 1702 a French administrator looked askance at the diet of the French Canadians in the colonial garrison at Biloxi: "It takes a lot to feed these hardy Canadians. They supplement their menus with [fish and shellfish] . . . [;] they deploy submerged trap nets baited with game to catch 'drunkard's meat,' in other words shrimp, which are enormous."

Following the establishment of New Orleans in 1718, colonists and soldiers reportedly began to drag seines through the shallows of Lake Pontchartrain in search of supplementary protein sources. The ethnographer, historian, and naturalist Antoine-Simon Le Page du Pratz, who resided in lower Louisiana from 1718 to 1732, provides the most authoritative account:

> For several years they [settlers] have brought fishing nets from France for use in Lake St. Louis [now Pontchartrain], [the bed of] which is level enough to permit fishing up to a league [approximately 2.5 miles] offshore. . . . One finds in the lake all sorts of saltwater fish, such as soles, plaices [flounders], mullets, rays, goatfishes, and others; just as there are freshwater fish, like carps, pikes [garfish], bowfins, and the like.

*1774 edition, p. 158, translation by the authors.

Le Page du Pratz then provides his readers with a lengthy homage to Lake Borgne's bountiful oyster reefs.

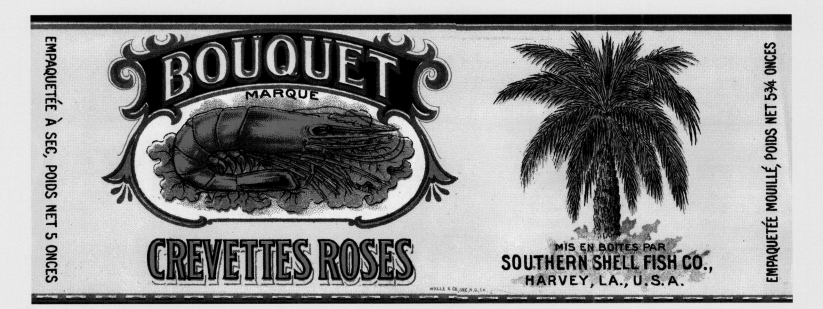

EMPAQUETÉE À SEC, POIDS NET 5 ONCES

BOUQUET
MARQUE

CREVETTES ROSES

MIS EN BOITES PAR
SOUTHERN SHELL FISH CO.,
HARVEY, LA., U.S.A.

WALLE & CO, INC, N.O., LA.

EMPAQUETÉE MOUILLÉ, POIDS NET 5¾ ONCES

In the early 1750s, while discussing river shrimp, former Louisiana colonist Dumont de Montigny noted that "in France, around La Rochelle and in various other cities or seaports, they commonly refer to this fish [i.e., shrimp] as drunkard's meat. This is particularly true of European shrimp which are quite small" (translation by the authors).

Although Louisiana's rural Francophones continue to use the eighteenth-century term *chevrette* to identify maritime decapods, the Bayou State's seafood processors have had to employ the now linguistically standard metropolitan term *crevette* for shrimp exported to foreign French-speaking markets. (Label from the Louisiana Historical Center, Louisiana State Museum, New Orleans, LA, date unknown.)

Hi-Seas' Blue Chip brand is marketed in the United States and several French-speaking countries. (Photo from the authors' collections, 2019.)

10/5 LB. (80 OZS.-2.27 kg) CARTON   PERMIT NO. LA. 23
PRODUCT OF U.S.A.
PRODUIT DES É.U.A.
WILD CAUGHT

BLUE CHIP
BRAND

FROZEN HEADLESS SHELL ON
SHRIMP
EN CARAPACE ÉTÊTÉES CONGELÉES
CREVETTES

HI-SEAS OF DULAC, INC. • 6576 GRAND CAILLOU ROAD • DULAC, LA 70353
(985)-563-7183

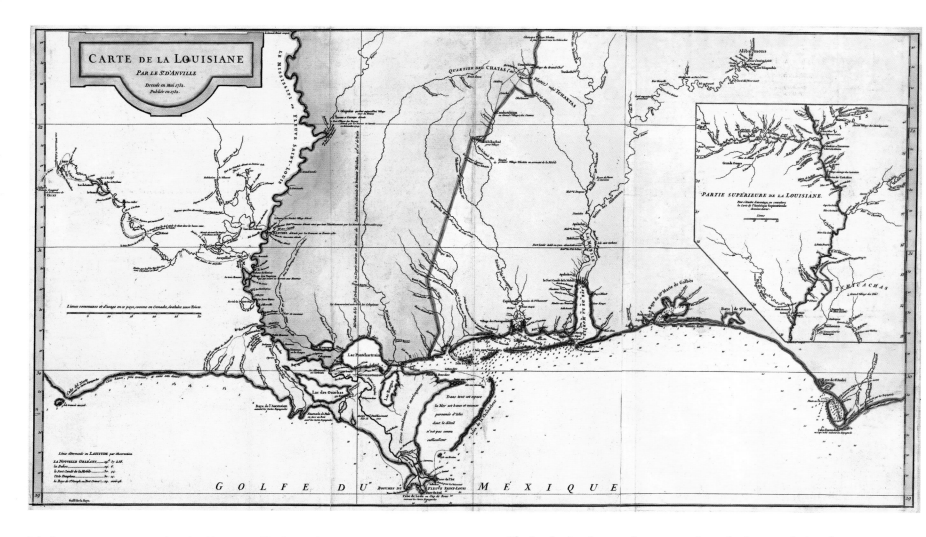

Lake Borgne was a remote southern Louisiana coastal backwater, but it served as the colony's initial gateway to the then seemingly inexhaustible aquatic resources of the Mississippi delta's estuaries. (Anville, *Carte de la Louisiane par le Sieur d'Anville, 1752*. From the David Rumsey Map Collection, David Rumsey Map Center, Stanford Libraries.)

Glaring by its absence is any mention of saltwater shrimp harvesting. This omission is, in fact, shocking, for during the French domination of Louisiana (1699–1763), the colony experienced long intervals—some extending years—during which its crucial supply line to France was severed, usually by British naval blockades. During these interludes, settlers faced calamitous shortages of traditional foodstuffs, and they were compelled to live off the land and consume readily available protein sources—regardless of their national gastronomic prejudices.

Much later in his chronicle, Le Page du Pratz provides a tantalizing clue to this perplexing mystery. He notes that French transplants had discovered the indigenous freshwater prawn that they dubbed *chevrette*—the common French Atlantic coast idiom for shrimp—because of its vague physical resemblance to the saltwater decapod. The chronicler's detailed description of this crustacean delineates the species:

Shrimp are diminutive crawfish; they are ordinarily no bigger than one's little finger and no longer than two or three inches; they carry their eggs like crawfish; when cooked, they never become redder than light pink. They have a more agreeable taste than crawfish; and, although the sea is their normal abode in other countries, in Louisiana, they are seen in the sea and in the river in large numbers a hundred leagues [250 miles] upstream.

They [lower Louisiana colonists] also catch big, beautiful shrimp in the St. Louis [i.e., Mississippi] River by means of sack-cloth fashioned into the form of a night-cap, enhanced at the top with a small wooden hoop, into which they insert meat or corn bran at the bottom, and [then] immerse [it] in the water.

River (freshwater) shrimp were once a dietary staple of the laboring population along the banks of the Mississippi River. (Courtesy of Darrell Felder, University of Louisiana at Lafayette.)

Little had changed by the early nineteenth century, when various eyewitness observers documented freshwater prawns' importance to Louisiana residents' diet. The anonymous author of *Mémoires sur la Louisiane et la Nouvelle-Orléans* (1804), for example, noted that

As this 1764 map by Jacques Nicolas Bellin clearly indicates, New Orleans, capital of French Louisiana, was sparsely populated, even by modest colonial North American standards. The census of 1763 documents a population of approximately three thousand. (J. N. Bellin, *Plan De La Nouvelle Orléans*, 1764, from the authors' collections.)

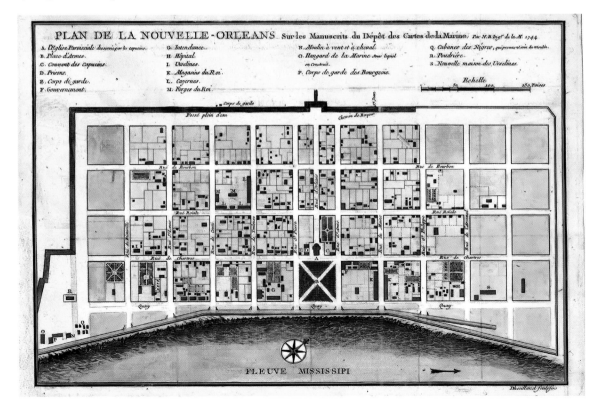

Charles Etienne Arthur Gayarré, one of Louisiana's pioneer historians, was the scion of a prominent Spanish colonial family. The former Gayarré plantation is now New Orleans's famed Audubon Park. (Lithograph from the authors' collections.)

"in the months of June, July, and August, the whole colony could derive its subsistence from this single comestible." This assertion is corroborated by pioneer Louisiana historian Charles Etienne Gayarré, who, in the postbellum era (1865–ca. 1898), recorded his recollections of his grandfather's plantation, situated at the current location of New Orleans's Audubon Zoo, around the turn of the nineteenth century. Gayarré noted that "fish and shrimps ... caught in the river" by plantation residents were essential sources of protein.

Freshwater prawns would remain a staple of the working poor's diet well into the twentieth century, but in middle- and upper-class households, Gulf shrimp established a foothold as new culinary traditions emerged in the early 1800s. The emergence of these new traditions roughly coincided with the massive 1809 influx of Saint-Domingue refugees, who literally doubled the size of New Orleans's population in approximately six months. The refugees, fleeing the

In 1809, after a sojourn in Oriente Province, Cuba, the largest contingent of these refugees made their way to New Orleans, where they doubled the size of the city's population in a six-month period. This woodcut depicts the refugees' flight from Cap-Français (now Cap-Haïtien). (From the Library Company of Philadelphia, *Incendie du Cap. Révolte général des Nègres. Massacre des Blancs*, 1815.)

Incendie du Cap.

servile revolution in present-day Haiti, consisted of approximately equal numbers of whites, free persons of color, and enslaved Black domestics, the overwhelming majority of whom were cooks. The cash-poor white enslavers almost immediately sought and found a new source of steady income by renting their slaves, particularly cooks, to more affluent New Orleans neighbors, and the result was a culinary revolution.

So widespread was the immigrant cooks' influence that, within a generation, their contributions became synonymous with New Orleans Creole cuisine. For example, the Crescent City tradition of eating red beans and rice is almost certainly a cultural artifact of the Saint-Domingue influx. It is also perhaps not coincidental that the Crescent City's large-scale consumption of seafood—eventually including shrimp—also dates from this culinary transitional period. M. E. Descourtilz, a French naturalist who produced a five-hundred-page study of the fauna and flora encountered by the refugees as they migrated across the northern Caribbean rim, repeatedly reported coastal crustacean harvesting. Caribbean seafood dishes quickly found favor with New Orleanians.

Development of a commercial shrimping operation to satisfy the growing urban demand for shrimp required creation of sustainable harvesting, transportation, and marketing infrastructures.

Saint-Domingue (present-day Haiti) was the jewel of the first French empire. In 1791, reports of the French Revolution set in motion a series of events that precipitated the colony's servile insurgency, bringing an end to both slavery and colonial rule. White slave owners, many free persons of color, and Black slaves fled the island in a series of migrations. The last exodus, begun in 1799, resulted in the establishment of an expatriate colony in Oriente Province, Cuba. This settlement thrived until 1809, when, in response to Napoleon's invasion of the Iberian Peninsula, Spanish Cuban authorities summarily expelled the Francophone immigrants, who migrated en masse to New Orleans.

In the first half of the twentieth century, Creole cookbooks—whether issued as books or as recipe collections syndicated in regional newspapers—were hugely popular and influential throughout south Louisiana. Although intended to promote New Orleans as a culinary tourist destination, these publications had the effect of promoting the northern Gulf Coast's shrimp and oyster industries through their seafood-centric recipes. (Advertisement from *Harper's Weekly*, September 9, 1905.)

A CREOLE COOK-BOOK
"COOKING IN OLD CREOLE DAYS"
By CÉLESTINE EUSTIS

This book gives recipes for all of the famous old Creole dishes—many of them having never before appeared in print—and explicit but clear directions are given for their preparation. The book includes as well a number of quaint old Creole songs in praise of famous dishes. The recipes are also given in French.

Charmingly Illustrated. Decorative Paper Sides, Cloth Back, $1.50

(*Imprint of R. H. RUSSELL*)

HARPER & BROTHERS. PUBLISHERS, FRANKLIN SQUARE, N. Y.

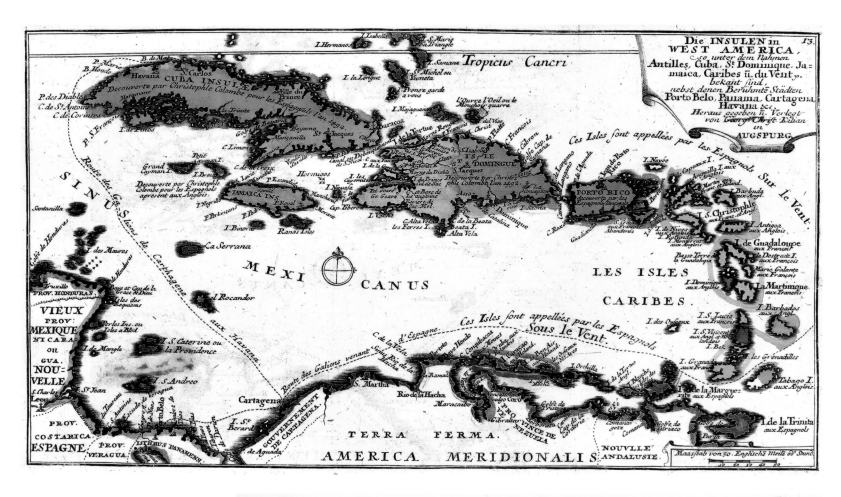

Saint-Domingue's economy was based on sugar and coffee production, both of which were labor-intensive industries. During the eighteenth century, Saint-Domingue was one of Louisiana's principal trade partners, and there were strong economic and familial ties between New Orleans and the Caribbean colony's principal cities. (Christian Friedrich von der Heiden, *Die Insulen in West America*, 1760. Courtesy of the Barry Lawrence Ruderman Map Collection, Stanford University Libraries.)

IN THE OLD FRENCH MARKET, NEW ORLEANS.—DRAWN BY JOHN W. ALEXANDER.—[SEE PAGE 39.]

For multiple generations, open air markets were the epicenters of New Orleans' gastronomic and culinary worlds. The most famous of these markets is the still-surviving French Market in the Vieux Carré (in its nineteenth century heyday). (Lithograph from *Harpers Weekly*, January 21, 1882.)

Establishment of a marketing infrastructure was the least problematic. Beginning around 1736, Louisiana's French colonial authorities—acting only at the behest of their superiors in France—begrudgingly launched sporadic efforts to establish public meat and produce markets in New Orleans as a means of both weaning the Crescent City from its dependence on imported European goods and simultaneously encouraging the development of local farm-to-market and commercial hunting operations. The government's feeble initial efforts were, not surprisingly, largely unsuccessful.

Following Louisiana's transfer to Spanish rule in 1763, the new colonial regime began to impose reforms designed to bring the Spanish empire's newest constituent territory into line with economic policies already in place with its sister colonies. This transition began in earnest in September 1769, when Governor Alejandro O'Reilly, shocked to find Louisiana's economy "in disarray" upon his arrival, established a cabildo (municipal council) in New Orleans and endowed it with the power to establish and regulate public markets as a means of ensuring a stable source of provisions for the municipality's residents. A mature public market system nevertheless did not emerge until the 1790s, and even then, the institutions' focus remained on beef and produce from the rural parishes in New Orleans's economic orbit. However, persistent difficulties in ensuring a steady beef supply from the Attakapas and Opelousas districts west of the Atchafalaya River created an opening for local commercial hunters and fishermen to sell their wares to the city's consumers. An American visitor to the Crescent City reported in early December 1803 that "the market is supplied with wild fowl and poultry of every kind, at the proper seasons several kinds of fish, oysters, which are passable, and beef, veal, pork, and mutton . . . as well as vegitables [sic] of every description." Shrimp, a glaring omission, would soon make their appearance after the 1809 Saint-Domingue influx.

In the late antebellum era, Charles Gayarré recalled that Spanish and Italian immigrant fishermen residing along Bayou Bienvenue, "a mile and a half from its entrance into Lake Borgne," had begun transporting their daily catch to the Crescent City by boat around the

The Attakapas district encompassed the present civil parishes of Lafayette, Vermilion, St. Martin, Iberia, and St. Mary. The Opelousas district consisted of all or parts of modern St. Landry, Evangeline, Acadia, Allen, Jefferson Davis, Beauregard, Calcasieu, and Cameron.

The feluccas (traditional wooden sailboats used in the eastern Mediterranean) pictured here were the initial mainstays of the San Francisco Bay and Louisiana fishing industries. Featuring centuries-old Mediterranean lateen sail designs, these vessels were fast, light, and maneuverable. (Lithography from *Frank Leslie's Illustrated Newspaper*, May 24, 1879.)

Over the course of the nineteenth century, feluccas were supplanted by luggers, shallow-draft vessels that could carry larger cargoes than their predecessors. (Postcard from the authors' collections, ca. 1900.)

time of the War of 1812; circumstantial evidence suggests that these deliveries included shellfish—that is, shrimp and oysters—from the Lake Borgne–area estuaries. By 1817, Louisiana fishermen had also discovered the "vast quantity of shell fish" in the Barataria Bay area.

Transportation of so-called "lake shrimp" (immature white shrimp) from coastal waters beyond Bayou Bienvenue to New Orleans was highly problematic because of the extreme perishability of the catch as well as the lack of effective local preservation technologies. Modern Louisiana shrimpers estimate that, during the months currently allotted to commercial seasons, their early nineteenth-century counterparts had less than five hours to transport newly caught crustaceans to New Orleans markets before summer heat, high humidity, and bacteria rendered their catch inedible. Given the sluggish speed of the sail-powered boats—primarily feluccas (small sailing vessels identified with Mediterranean origins) and, later, luggers (round-hulled, wooden, sail-powered folk boats)—then in use in coastal Louisiana as well as the markets'

BRINGING IN THE CATCH

Red sails in the sunset. Louisiana fishermen dyed their sails with tannin, a natural preservative derived from tree bark, which gave their sails a reddish hue. (Image from Schoonover, 1911:80.)

This lithograph, published in Louisiana's nineteenth-century German-language print media, shows a lugger making its way from Lake Pontchartrain to the Crescent City Basin's lugger docks via Bayou St. John and the Carondelet Canal. (Lithography from Frank Leslie's *Illustrirte Zeitung*, September 1867.)

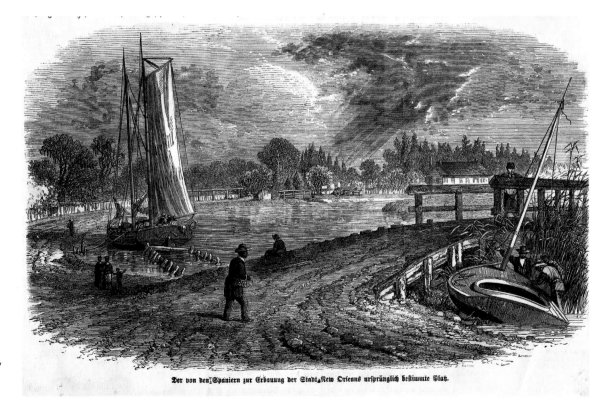

Der von den Spaniern zur Erbauung der Stadt New Orleans ursprünglich bestimmte Platz.

Luggers anchored at Spanish Fort along New Orleans's Bayou St. John. (Photo from LSU Libraries Special Collection, No. 116, Bayou View, Spanish Fort, George François Mugnier, New Orleans Scenes.)

limited hours of operation, the period's logistical imperatives effectively limited commercial shrimping to the marshes bordering eastern Lake Pontchartrain. Even within this highly circumscribed operating radius, commercial shrimping was an extremely risky enterprise. Reliable accounts of pioneer shrimping operations do not exist for the pre–Civil War era, but circumstantial evidence leads inevitably to that conclusion.

Quite simply, the nearest, consistently productive shrimping grounds were on the very edge of commercial accessibility, given the severe limitations of the period's transportation technology. The region's first shrimpers would have used feluccas—luggers by the late antebellum era—which, based on contemporary mariners' accounts, would have had a typical operational speed of about six knots when fully laden. The prolific shrimping grounds around Chef Menteur Pass lay approximately forty miles from New Orleans's Carondelet Canal's turning basin, the principal offloading site for coastal boats delivering seafood for Crescent City markets. Under ideal sailing conditions, contemporary shrimp boats would have required around five hours to reach the mouth of Bayou St. John. The crew then would have had to row or cordelle the boats four miles to the turning basin, a process that would have entailed at least two additional hours of travel. Shrimp boat crews then had to offload the cargo and transport it to its final destination. Because of the lack of refrigeration, the shrimp in the boats' holds would have been exposed to direct sunlight and intense heat for at least nine hours. This sustained exposure is in addition to the time—multiple hours if crews employed seining—required to fill their holds in the coastal waters. Modern shrimpers and Louisiana Sea Grant field agents estimate that, under these conditions, unrefrigerated shrimp cargoes had a transportation shelf life of only two to five hours, depending on seasonal temperatures. Shrimping was thus at best extremely perilous, and local commercial fishermen consequently concentrated their efforts on oyster harvesting until mid- to late nineteenth-century technological innovations greatly reduced the risk of shrimp spoilage.

To improve connectivity between Lake Pontchartrain and the French Quarter, Governor Francisco Luís Héctor de Carondelet authorized construction of a waterway from the back edge of the Mississippi River's natural levee to Bayou St. John in 1794. Following the Louisiana Purchase (1803), New Orleans mayor James Pitot, who was also president of the Orleans Navigation Company, secured governmental authorization to operate a toll canal from Bayou St. John to a "turning basin" (at the present location of Basin Street), necessary to permit sailing vessels to retrace their route. By the 1820s, seventy to eighty boats daily plied the Bayou St. John–Carondelet Canal–turning basin route. Despite eventual competition from railways and commercial canals, the waterway existed until 1936, when a new state constitutional amendment mandated closure of the original freight gateway to the heart of New Orleans.

Boats berthed in the Old Basin Canal, also called Carondelet Canal. (Photo from the Louisiana Digital Library, University of New Orleans, Frank B. Moore Collection, accession number 145–351.)

Isleños—Canary Island immigrants—were the initial colonial setters of St. Bernard Parish's Terre-aux-Boeuf area and the first Old World–immigrant group to exploit Lake Borgne's abundant aquatic resources. (Photo from the authors' collections, 2004.)

Steam-powered transportation provided the catalyst for the Louisiana commercial shrimp industry's geographic expansion. In the late 1840s, Crescent City area entrepreneurs funded construction of the Mexican Gulf Railroad, a branch of which, completed in 1847, extended from downtown New Orleans to Proctor's Shell Bank (also then known as Proctorville, now Shell Beach) along the shores of Lake Borgne specifically to transport seafood expeditiously to the city. A British travel guide, published in the year of the spur track's completion, noted that transportation of cargo from Proctor's Shell Bank to the main New Orleans terminal required "three to four hours." Sheltered from direct sunlight while aboard freight cars, Lake Borgne shrimp for the first time reached New Orleans in edible condition.

The Crescent City restauranteurs also quickly availed themselves of new opportunities to market maritime resources. In 1849, for example, the Pelican Restaurant, at the corner of Gravier and Union Streets, posted frequent local newspaper advertisements promoting its "shrimp pie." Additional restaurants and seafood merchants soon followed suit.

A. D. GRIEFF & CO.,

Wholesale Grocers

AND DEALERS IN

BUTTER,

LARD,

FISH, CHEESE, SOAP,

AND

WESTERN PRODUCE,

38, 40 & 42

OLD LEVEE.

Fish wholesalers such as A. D. Grieff & Co. played a pivotal role in the early success of New Orleans's burgeoning antebellum seafood distribution network. (Advertisement from A. Mygatt and Company.)

The synergy between the new fishery, the nascent regional transportation infrastructure, and urban consumers gained momentum as the Crescent City's burgeoning shrimp marketplace extended its geographic reach exponentially in the 1850s. In 1857, a second railway, the New Orleans, Opelousas and Great Western Railroad (NOO&GW), was completed between Algiers, across the Mississippi from the metropolis, and Brashear City (now Morgan City). Using the present Southern Pacific rail bed traversing some of the state's most forbidding wetlands, the NOO&GW afforded former backwater communities unprecedented communications and transportation services as well as economic opportunities. Entrepreneurs in whistle-stop communities were quick to recognize and seize the chance to provide seafood to consumers in communities, such as Thibodaux, too far inland to permit waterborne shipment of fresh shrimp. On September 15, 1855, J. J. Lamoureux posted an advertisement in the *Thibodaux Minerva* alerting local epicures that he had "made arrangements with Jone's [Jones's] Express, on the Opelousas Railroad, to keep up a regular supply of oysters, clams, croakers, red fish, red snappers, pompano, trout, sheep-head, flounders, crabs (soft and hard shell,) [and] shrimps, from the New Orleans market, during the entire season."

Recognizing the burgeoning growth of the regional marketplace, enterprising St. Bernard Parish residents—overwhelmingly Isleños, descendants of late eighteenth-century Canary Island immigrants—at the source of the shrimp supply chain moved quickly to establish territorial and commercial hegemony over the prime fishing grounds in the Lake Borgne–area estuaries. The native population's primacy was quickly challenged by Asian immigrants—reportedly Chinese and "Lascar" (Filipino)—lured to the area by the siren call of economic opportunity. The inevitable result was a slowly intensifying conflict, which reached a flash point on the eve of the Civil War.

The competition between the Isleños and Chinese was particularly acrimonious. An ostensibly local neutral observer ("an intelligent French Creole") reported to regional newspapers that the conflict stemmed from the Chinese refusal to allow their Spanish-speaking neighbors to dictate market prices for Lake Borgne seafood exports. The social friction resulting from the commercial rivalry was exacerbated by the strict residential segregation of the two communities. According to the *New Orleans Daily Crescent,*

> The Spaniards [Isleños] have Proctorville, the Chinamen live and fish at different places within five miles of Proctorville; the Chinamen have to come to Proctorville to send their fish up to the city; the Spaniards at Proctorville also fish and send their fish up to the city. . . .

On July 7, 1860, a confrontation in a Proctorville coffeehouse (a Victorian euphemism for bar) between the feuding parties, evidently precipitated by "inexcusable insults of some of the Spaniards," resulted in violence, leading to "some awful murders" and the narrow escape of Chinese fishermen pursued by an Isleño mob. In the wake of the riot, "some of the more cool and sensible" Proctorville Spaniards organized themselves into a vigilante force to prevent additional violence and to afford both belligerent parties equal access to the Lake Borgne railroad spur.

The internecine war within St. Bernard Parish's multiracial fishing community was soon overshadowed by the rapidly gathering national political storm that would shortly rip the nation apart. On January 26, 1861, Louisiana seceded from the Union, and on March 21, it joined the new Confederate States of America. After armed hostilities between the Confederacy and the United States began on April 12, New Orleans, the South's largest city and financial center, almost immediately became a focal point of the North's military strategy to defeat the Confederacy and reunify the country.

On April 23, 1862, a powerful Union flotilla under the command of Flag Officer David Farragut sailed past the Confederate fortifications near the mouth of the Mississippi River and hove to before New Orleans two days later. On April 29, a military contingent raised the Stars and Stripes at the United States Mint on Esplanade Avenue, and the Union occupation of New Orleans began.

New Orleans's capitulation constituted the opening gambit of a protracted military campaign for control of the Pelican State. This contest proved only marginally successful for Northern forces,

St. Bernard Parish's emerging shrimp industry engendered an economic ripple effect, as the Crescent City's maritime hardware stores—particularly J. Waterman and Brothers—rushed to satisfy the growing demand for shrimping-related equipment, especially seines.

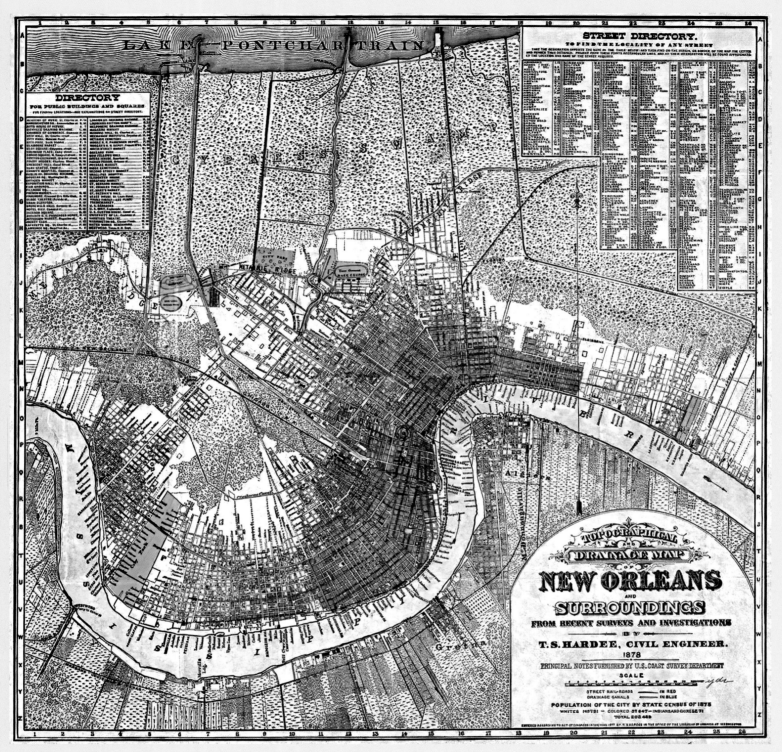

This famous map by civil engineer T. S. Hardee provides perhaps the best cartographic view of the complex of natural and artificial waterways that provided fishermen with direct access to downtown New Orleans. (T. S. Hardee, *Topographical and Drainage Map of New Orleans and Surroundings* [1878]. Courtesy of the Beinecke Rare Book and Manuscript Library, Yale University, New Haven, CT.)

despite their overwhelming numerical, logistical, and technological advantages. By the end of the contest, the Union military consistently controlled only the areas immediately along the Mississippi River and many of the coastal "Sugar Bowl" parishes.

The disruption caused by sporadic military operations was compounded by economic embargoes placed by both belligerent parties on commerce across military lines. The result was the temporary collapse of the region's embryonic shrimp fishery, despite the Crescent City's loss of access to its traditional sources of fresh meat in southwestern Louisiana and southeastern Texas. As early as June 19, 1862, the New Orleans *Daily Picayune* reported that New Orleanians, faced with the availability of a few "forlorn specimens of beef . . . in our markets," were compelled to find new dietary sources of protein. Among the most dependable of the available options was the freshwater prawn, which, despite the growing issue of water pollution resulting from the discharge of human waste from the rapidly expanding city and the daily dumping of offal from huge local slaughterhouses, was still reportedly available in "great abundance." The *Picayune* article also points to the ready availability of crabs and fish drawn from fresh and brackish waters in the immediate vicinity of New Orleans, but conspicuous by its absence is any mention of saltwater shrimp. The *Daily Picayune* would not mention shrimp again until March 5, 1865, three months before the formal cessation of hostilities in the regional military theater.

After a period of involuntary dormancy, however, the Louisiana saltwater shrimp industry would reemerge in the postbellum era. The reincarnated fishery would assume new and different characteristics that would define its evolutionary trajectory to the present.

FISH MARKET.

After passing through the Vegetable Market, the Fish Market is reached. This building, a structure of iron and glass, is one of the most interesting on account of the great variety of fish offered for sale. On the white marble tables, are seen brilliant red-snappers with large coral fins, the red fish, much liked in "courtbouillon," the much appreciated sheephead, the famous Spanish Mackerel, and, last but not least, the pompano, considered by gourmets to be the finest and most delicate fish that swims in any waters, and which strangers should not fail to taste at some good restaurant. Crabs, hard and soft, and shrimp from the lake and river, the former being the largest, but not esteemed as much as the latter, are sold in quantities. Crayfish, a small lobster-like fish, are sold from large baskets and used to make the famous "bisque" soup. These little fish are caught principally in the river, where they do great damage to the levees, by boring holes in them. Sea-trout, mullet, catfish, croakers and many other varieties are always on sale. The fish business is carried on by a class of Spaniards and Italians who are usually called "Dagoes." They own their own boats, small sailing-vessels, called luggers, having one mast on which they hoist a lateen sail. These boats go through the various canals to the fishing grounds on the Gulf, and lay in their stock, pack it away in ice boxes, and hasten to the city. Some of the fish are brought from greater distances, for instance the pompano, which is only found in certain spots on the Florida coast. Green turtle comes also from Florida, and is always to be had in the market. The proximity of New Orleans to the sea and fresh water streams makes it the best fish and oyster market in the United States after that of Mobile; while in winter the bayous and woods are filled with game of all kinds. Fish is cheap here in comparison to other large cities. A fine red-snapper or red fish, enough for ten persons, can be bought for 50 cents; sheephead are little higher, and small pompano sell as low as 50 cents each and as high as $5. Shrimp, 10 cents a plate, and hard crabs 15 cents a dozen. Near the end of the Fish Market is the Game Market, which in winter is stocked with wild ducks, geese, turkeys, rabbits, woodcocks, and all varieties of game. Wild ducks are sometimes very abundant, and sell lower than 50 cents a pair.

James Zacharie's observations constitute the best extant description of a nineteenth-century New Orleans fish market. (From Zacharie 104.)

The Louisiana coastal plain that emerged from the ashes of the war years was a pale reflection of its antebellum counterpart. In 1860, the Pelican State led the nation in per capita wealth; ten years later, it ranked among the poorest states in the Union. Louisiana's precipitous economic meltdown is seen perhaps most clearly in the collapse of property values, which declined as much as 90 percent in some coastal plain parishes, according to the 1860 and 1870 federal census reports. The economic Armageddon was compounded by social and political turmoil born of slavery's demise, the continuing postwar military occupation of Louisiana, and the intense, violent, protracted struggle for political domination and white supremacy.

It was into this dark world of turbulence and violence that the Louisiana shrimp industry was reborn. Persistent chaos allowed the fishery to take a different evolutionary path than the antebellum evidence circumstantially predicted. In 1860, the Louisiana seine-shrimp industry was concentrated in the Lake Borgne area, with a geographic reach limited to the Crescent City and the few towns and villages linked by rail to the metropolitan area. And, because of the unchallenged primacy of agriculture in Louisiana and the fishery's doubtful ability to attract venture capital for acquisition of emerging preservation technologies, the industry's developmental prospects seemed illusory at best. Yet three decades later, the industry was a national and international maritime fishery dynamo and an economic juggernaut.

This remarkably rapid metamorphosis was a product of four postbellum catalysts: an extraordinary, albeit short-lived, surge in Chinese immigration; the Dunbar family's establishment of the nation's critically important pioneer seafood cannery in New Orleans; construction of the nation's first ice plant in the Crescent City; and New Orleans's integration into a nationwide rail transportation grid by the early 1880s. Of these developments, the surge in Chinese immigration is certainly the most curious.

According to the population schedules of the 1850 federal decennial census, the first to indicate nativity, Louisiana was home to only thirty-three Chinese immigrants. That modest number fell

CHAPTER 2

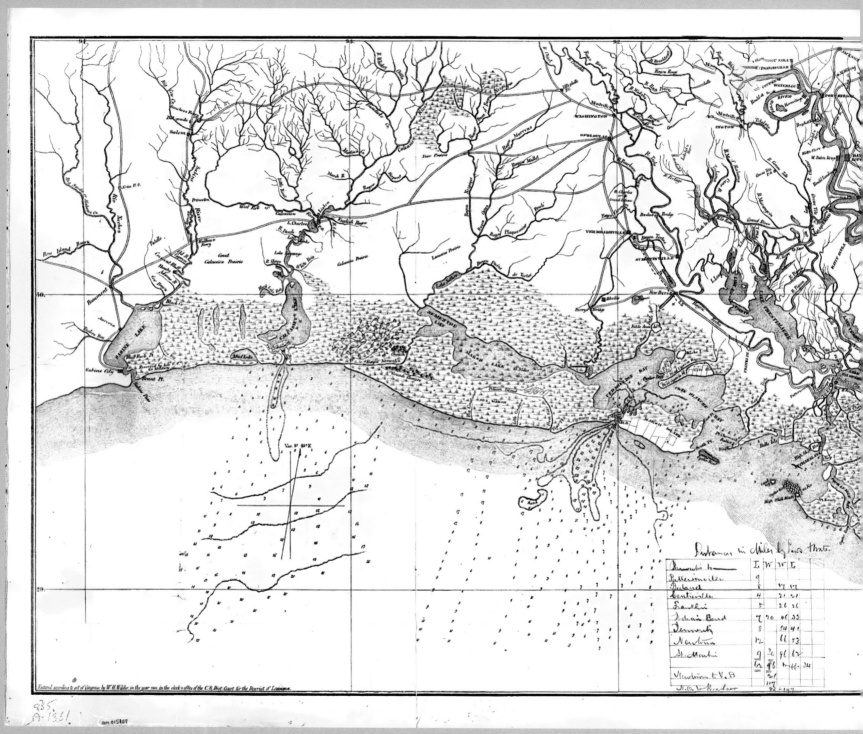

The Louisiana Coastal Plain, home to some of America's most productive fisheries. (From the American Geographical Society Library, University of Wisconsin–Milwaukee Libraries, 1861.)

April 22, 1907
Gift from Edwin W. West, Brooklyn, N.Y.

NOTA." The Longitude Calculated from Fort Morgan.

HYDROGRAPHICAL
&
TOPOGRAPHICAL
MAP
of Parts of the States of
LOUISIANA, MISSISSIPPI & ALABAMA
Compiled from the U. S. Coast Surveys,
The Topography from Plats on file in the General Land Office.
PUBLISHED BY
Messrs. HOLLE & Co.
Exchange Alley, N.Orleans.

NOTE.
The Soundings for simplicity are made in Feet instead of Fathoms.

Scale.
Statute Miles.
Nautical Miles.

Lith: by Pessou & Simon, No 116 Exchange Alley N.Orl.

AMERICAN GEOGRAPHICAL SOCIETY

"On fortunate trips each man belonging to the association will make $20 to $25. There are times, however, when contrary winds destroy all the profits and leave the fishermen losers both in pocket and labor" (New Orleans *Daily Picayune*, November 25, 1900).

Rare picture of a shrimp lugger transporting a seine crew. (Photo from Louisiana State University Libraries Special Collections, Hill Memorial Library, Ta4963057.)

"Hauling seine" was a backbreaking and dangerous occupation. Crews spent hours at a time in waist- to shoulder-deep waters, in which rip currents and aquatic predators were constant threats. (Photo from Louisiana State University Libraries Special Collections, Hill Memorial Library, Tate Album, Mss. 4963, LLMVC photo number 4963059.)

THE COMING MAN.—SCENE ON THE PIER OF THE PACIFIC MAIL STEAMSHIP COMPANY, SAN FRANCISCO—PASSENGERS DISEMBARKING AND BEING RECEIVED BY THEIR FRIENDS.—From a Sketch by our Special Artist.—See Page 121.

Chinese immigrants disembarking at San Francisco, circa 1870. (Lithograph from *Frank Leslie's Illustrated Newspaper*, May 7, 1870, 113.)

to zero ten years later, as the Asian newcomers migrated, evidently en masse, to the remote Lake Borgne fishing grounds generally ignored by the period's notoriously indolent census takers. However, by the early 1870s, the Pelican State's Chinese population rebounded to between 700 and 1,200 persons, according to conflicting governmental and journalistic reports; even at the lowest contemporary estimate, this elusive and transient community easily constituted the nation's largest Asian population east of the Rocky Mountains.

The Chinese influx into Louisiana ultimately resulted from civil warfare half a world away. Between 1850 and 1864, China was torn by military strife, as rival armed forces led respectively by a millennialist Christian-convert (the self-styled younger brother of Jesus Christ) and the Qing dynasty emperor, waged what in modern parlance would be labeled "total war" for control of the Celestial Empire. This conflict, arguably the most brutal military struggle of the nineteenth century, laid waste to huge swaths of the countryside and extracted a staggering toll in human misery. Historians currently estimate the death toll at twenty to seventy (possibly one hundred) million persons; additional millions were displaced, particularly in southeastern China's "maritime districts" around Canton (Guangzhou), where the centuries-old art of shrimp drying originated.

Most of the refugees fled to the neighboring ports of Macao and Hong Kong, where, because of the sudden glut in the labor market, they could not find gainful employment. Individuals "able to pay their own passage"—a distinct minority of the refugees—typically sailed from the British colony of Hong Kong to seek their fortunes in the

A "tea-server" tending to Chinese work crews in Louisiana's postbellum sugar fields. (Lithograph from *Every Saturday*, July 29, 1871, 116.)

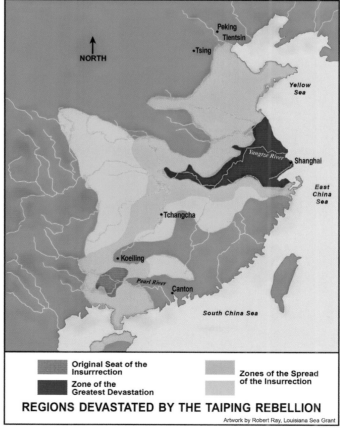

The Taiping Rebellion was a fourteen-year revolt (1850–1864) against the Qing dynasty.

Few vestiges of New Orleans's once vibrant Chinatown remain. Initially located along Tulane Avenue, between South Rampart Street and Elk Place, the original Chinese district was cleared by federal Works Progress Administration (WPA) reconstruction projects in the late 1930s. Some surviving Chinese businesses then moved to Bourbon Street and other French Quarter properties. (Photo from the authors' collections, 2015.)

In East Asian and Southeast Asian cuisine, dried shrimp are valued for their unique, savory taste (umami), perhaps the most important of the five doctrinal flavors of wok cooking: sweet, sour, salty, bitter, and spicy. Ingredients linked to these five culinary elements, along with traditional cooking techniques, diffused throughout North America through the efforts of Chinese immigrants.

promising and concurrently unfolding California and Australia gold rushes. Destitute migrants, driven by desperation, often signed personally disadvantageous labor agreements with *hongs* (Chinese trading houses) that parceled them off to Cuba and South America as indentured workers—then commonly identified as "coolies"—burdened with five- to eight-year bonded labor contracts and ultimately subjected to living and working conditions comparable to those of New World slaves. By the 1870s, Cuba, home to at least 125,000 "coolies," had perhaps the largest Chinese immigrant population in the western hemisphere. The success of Asian labor in the Cuban sugar industry proved crucial to Louisiana's postbellum effort to transplant the Chinese "coolie" labor model in the coastal sugar parishes.

The Louisiana sugar industry's interest in Chinese laborers resulted directly from slavery's demise during the Civil War. Despite the fact that the Emancipation Proclamation specifically excluded most Louisiana sugar parishes, the Union military occupation of parts of lower Louisiana effectively undermined the ability of plantation slave owners to force their bondsmen to remain subservient, productive, and tied to their plantation domiciles. Thousands of slaves fled captivity whenever Union forces invaded the sugar region west of New Orleans in the spring and again in the fall of 1863. The industry's resulting labor crisis persisted for the duration of the Civil War—indeed, until the end of Reconstruction in 1877.

Because the success of the region's extremely labor-intensive plantation crop regimes, principally cotton and sugarcane, was predicated on a dependable supply of cheap, docile, and obedient workers, Louisiana's planter class faced potential financial ruin. The least risk-averse among them, consequently, frantically cast about for alternative sources of laborers. For many financially beleaguered planters, nearby Cuba's Chinese labor model appeared to afford the most logical and plausible potential solution. In early 1867, Natchitoches-area native Jules H. Normand, who had resided in Cuba for a dozen years, returned to Louisiana with twelve Chinese laborers, all sugar industry veterans, in tow. In March, after announcing his willingness to serve as a de facto labor broker for Pelican State planters willing to experiment with Asian farmhands, Normand and his new partner, Natchitoches planter Benjamin W. Bullitt, transported more than fifty Chinese indentured laborers from Havana to New Orleans. These workers found immediate employment—most on a plantation bordering the Mississippi River.

Before the 1849 gold rush, only fifty-four Chinese nationals—often identified by contemporaries as "Celestials"—resided in California, but by 1870 the state's "Celestial" population exceeded forty-nine thousand. Though "gold fever" was typically the catalyst for the influx, a minority of the immigrants actually became involved in field prospecting. Instead, more than ten thousand Chinese laborers eventually found employment as railroad laborers on the nation's first transcontinental railroad. Legions of their countrymen toiled in local fisheries, building trades, and various low- and unskilled-labor industries. Still others became entrepreneurs, most conspicuously as restaurant and laundry owners.

The Chinese experiment was a crucial part of the Louisiana sugar industry's failed attempt to replace its African American labor force with immigrant workers. (Lithograph from *Every Saturday*, July 29, 1871, 113.)

"CHINESE CHEAP LABOR" IN LOUISIANA, — CHINAMEN AT WORK ON THE MILLOUDON SUGAR PLANTATION. SKETCHED BY OUR SPECIAL ARTIST.

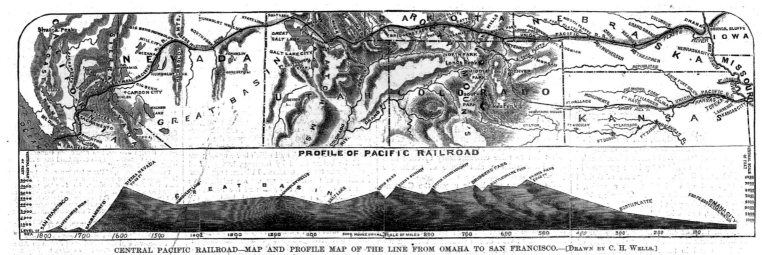

CENTRAL PACIFIC RAILROAD—MAP AND PROFILE MAP OF THE LINE FROM OMAHA TO SAN FRANCISCO.—[Drawn by C. H. Wells.]

This widely circulated map shows the route of the transcontinental railroad, built largely by Chinese and European immigrant laborers. (Map from *Harper's Weekly*, December 7, 1867, 772.)

Because of the initial venture's success, Normand and Bullitt opened an office in New Orleans and prepared to recruit for plantation owners the "thousands" of available Chinese purportedly eager to ply their new agricultural skills in Louisiana.

The Normand-Bullitt firm almost immediately found itself in competition with a rival labor brokerage established by Edward T. Wyches, another Louisianan transplanted to Cuba. Wyche's first importees reached New Orleans on May 18, 1867, and within a month, they had been placed on Bayou Lafourche–area plantations.

Despite the positive publicity generated by the industrious Asian newcomers and the resultant surge in planter interest, the importation of Chinese laborers came to a screeching halt by summer's end. The venture was ultimately a victim of its own success, for it attracted bureaucratic attention to human trafficking activities that had been banned by federal law for five years. This legislation resulted from pressure from United States diplomats in China, who, in the late 1850s, correctly identified the exportation of Chinese laborers to New World plantations and industries as a form of involuntary servitude closely akin to slavery. Acknowledging the claim's legitimacy, Congress adopted "An Act to Prohibit the 'Coolie Trade' by American Citizens in American Vessels" on February 19, 1862, which criminalized the transportation of "the inhabitants or subjects of China, known as 'coolies,' . . . [to] any place whatever, to be disposed of, or sold, or transferred, for any term of years or for any time whatever, as servants or apprentices, or to be held to service or labor." Violators were subject to severe penalties, including confiscation of their transport vessels.

THE BEST LINE WEST

Be Sure You Are Routed Right

Whether on Pleasure or Business

THE DIRECT ROUTE

WILL BE VIA

Southern Pacific

THROUGH LOUISIANA AND TEXAS

ELECTRIC BLOCK SIGNALS, OIL BURNING
LOCOMOTIVES—ALL STEEL EQUIPMENT

BEST DINING CAR IN AMERICA

For illustrated literature and full information,
ask any Southern Pacific Agent, or write

W. H. STAKELUM,
Division Passenger Agent,
Lake Charles, La.

J. H. R. PARSONS,
General Passenger Agent,
New Orleans, La.

The Southern Pacific and Illinois Central railroads connected Louisiana shrimp-drying operations with San Francisco's Chinese exporters and New Orleans–area seafood processors with lucrative consumer markets in the Midwest and Northeast. (Advertisement from A. Mygatt and Company 74.)

GREAT CENTRAL ROUTE

ILLINOIS CENTRAL

RAILROAD.

Important to Travelers. Time & Money Saved.

THE ILLINOIS CENTRAL

RAILROAD

FROM CAIRO,

AND ITS CONNECTIONS, FORMS

The most Expeditious, Cheap & Pleasant Route to

ST. LOUIS,

GALENA, DUBUQUE, ST. PAUL, CHICAGO, NIAGARA
FALLS, SARATOGA SPRINGS, NEW YORK, BOS-
TON, QUEBEC, PHILADELPHIA, BALTI-
MORE, WASHINGTON, MONTREAL,
PORTLAND, AND ALL

IMPORTANT POINTS NORTH & EAST.

(Advertisement from *Lumber Trade Journal*, January 1, 1916, 51.)

The 1862 act constituted the basis for federal intervention in the Louisiana-Cuba "coolie trade" after United States diplomatic authorities in Havana received intelligence reports that Wyches was essentially purchasing not only workers' labor contracts but also some laborers as human chattel. In effect, he was allegedly engaged in the black-market slave trade. On August 7, 1867, as Wyches arrived at New Orleans with twenty-three Chinese laborers, federal customs authorities arrested him for violation of the 1862 Anti-Coolie Act and confiscated the brig on which they had sailed from Cuba. Although the charges were dropped a month later, in large part because of pressure from Louisiana planters, and the importation of Chinese laborers resumed, the federal intervention gave both labor brokers and planters pause, and the fleeting promise of the early 1867 immigration ventures never reached their full potential. Indeed, the anticipated "coolie" torrent shrank to an intermittent trickle.

Now wary of the Cuban connection, Louisiana labor recruiters and their clients turned their attention to the Chinese mainland and San Francisco as potential sources of immigrant laborers. After 1867, these clients were often industrialists who sought to profit from the postwar South's increasingly frantic efforts to join the transformative technological revolution then sweeping the nation. America's first transcontinental railroad was completed on May 10, 1869, and regional economic prosperity thereafter hinged

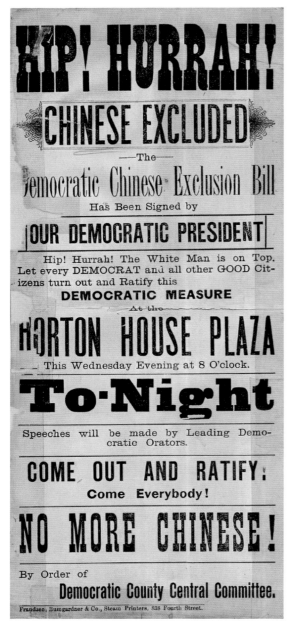

The Chinese Exclusion Act of 1882, sustained by continuing legislation, remained in force until 1943. (Photo courtesy of the Royal BC Museum, accession number PDP03732.)

increasingly on rail access to established and emerging eastern and western markets. The decades following the Civil War's conclusion were consequently a golden age for railroad construction in the former Confederate states of America.

Before the Civil War, railroads had relied on European immigrants—primarily Irishmen—to build rail beds, trestles, and bridges. After the conflict's conclusion, however, Europeans were increasingly unwilling to endure the backbreaking labor, deplorable and often dangerous living and working conditions, and subsistence wages. In the postbellum West and South, Chinese immigrants increasingly filled the void. In the former Confederacy, the Houston and Texas Central and the Alabama and Chattanooga railroads took the lead in recruiting Chinese manual laborers. In 1869–70, railway representatives successfully negotiated with California labor brokers for hundreds of Chinese workers—some with railroad construction experience in the Golden State, others new, unskilled immigrants—to report to southern construction sites by way of the new transcontinental railroad and subsequent waterborne and overland transportation from St. Louis. By late August 1870, nearly 1,200 laborers had been deployed in the field.

These labor experiments reportedly elicited great interest and, in retrospect, unrealistically high expectations. By late September 1870, the Houston and Texas Central's entire Chinese workforce had walked off the job and collectively initiated legal proceedings against their employer for breach of their labor contracts; within six months of their deployment, most of the Alabama and Chattanooga's Asian laborers had followed suit. Most, if not all, of the disgruntled immigrants subsequently made their way to southern Louisiana. Some initially found employment in textile mills operated by Samuel L. James of James, Buckner and Company on the Louisiana State Penitentiary grounds. Many others, working through Chinese labor agents, eventually entered the sugar plantation workforce. Their numbers were augmented by an undetermined—but evidently small—number of Chinese recruited in California specifically for plantation work in Louisiana.

In the sugar fields as in the railroad construction camps, employers blatantly ignored, or brazenly attempted to unilaterally modify, the terms of the employees' labor contracts—with predictable results. On the Millaudon Plantation near New Orleans, for example, Chinese laborers essentially kidnapped their agent to force him to hear their complaints. Tensions were further exacerbated by the ensuing confrontation between the Chinese and the local police and the subsequent shooting of a "sullen" worker by an intimidated foreman. It is thus hardly surprising that one year after their arrival, virtually all of the Chinese workers abruptly left the plantation. The Millaudon Plantation experience served as a template for the Chinese experience in the sugar bowl region as a whole.

By early 1872, most of Louisiana's erstwhile Chinese plantation workers had migrated either to New Orleans's emerging, but now long-forgotten, Chinatown or to the Louisiana coastal marshes south of the Crescent City, where the environment allowed the immigrants to avoid unbridled economic exploitation and practice the familiar economic pursuits of their distant homeland. Persistent economic and cultural connections between Louisiana's urban and rural Chinese communities created a synergy that allowed the immigrant enclaves to not only survive but also thrive in the period following congressional passage of the Chinese Exclusion Act of May 6, 1882. Thanks to completion of a southern transcontinental railroad between New Orleans and California, Chinatown residents were able to maintain vital contacts with their fellow expatriates on the West Coast and their countrymen in China. These connections, in turn, provided a dependable outlet for the goods

The San Francisco press gave full-throated support to the Chinese exclusion effort. ("Chinese Exclusion Convention Opens Fight in Defense of American Labor." San Francisco *Morning Call*, November 22, 1901, 1.)

"The great bulk of the shrimp caught in Louisiana are sold to the Chinese driers in the Barataria section, to the canners in New Orleans, and to the retail trade in New Orleans, only a small proportion being consumed in the fishing settlements. In the Barataria section there are three Chinese camps devoted to drying shrimp, principally for export to the Orient. This industry was begun in 1873 and although badly affected by the storm of 1893, and by serious competition with a similar business in Mexico, yet it is still in a prosperous condition. In 1897, these camps received 1,331,730 pounds of fresh shrimps, costing $10,304, which yielded 142,510 pounds of dried, worth $21,185. They also prepared. They did 61,147 pounds of dried fish, using 142,510 pounds of miscellaneous fresh fish, but most of the fish drying at temporary camps on Timbalier Island" (Townsend, *Statistics* 159).

CHINESE SHRIMPERS IN LOUISIANA.

They Buy the Fish for Export to Their Own Country.

Louisiana Shrimp in High Esteem in the Orient.

Shells Are Used to Fertilize the Worn Out Soil of China.

How the Fish Are Prepared for Shipment—Danger to Other Fish Involved in the Business.

The remote shrimp drying platforms were a continuing source of fascination to New Orleans's journalists, who marveled at the installations' exotic work force, product, and export connections. (From the New Orleans *Daily Picayune*, January 1, 1909.)

harvested, processed, and exported by the marsh residents, who were, as part of their cultural baggage, actively transplanting the Cantonese fishing industry—primarily shrimp and fish drying—in southeastern Louisiana's highly productive estuaries. By 1873, the Chinese-based industry, anchored in Louisiana's wetlands, handled 12 percent of the total shrimp caught in the Gulf.

The initial activities of these newly minted Chinese fisherfolk in the coastal marshes is lost to the mists of historical obscurity, their presence recorded only in rare and rapidly deteriorating photographs. Having deliberately sought out the insularity afforded by geographic isolation, socioeconomic semi-autonomy, and effective

The Chinese Exclusion Act marked the culmination of a xenophobic backlash against California's Asian influx. During the California gold rush, white Americans' view of the Chinese "invasion" changed from grudging acceptance, based on economic necessity, to open hostility as the surface placer mines were exhausted and competition for the remaining veins became exponentially more intense. Celestial immigrants, formerly tolerated by American citizens as a beneficial source of cheap labor, quickly morphed into economic pariahs who threatened the economic security of unskilled white laborers, who demanded higher wages than their Asian counterparts. Under the guise of protecting American institutions and values, politicians sympathetic to the white work force's concerns began to adopt legislation designed to neutralize any real or perceived economic advantage enjoyed by the Chinese "menace." A year after the start of the gold rush, the California legislature passed the Foreign Miners' Tax Act, which imposed a twenty-dollar-a-month duty on all Chinese miners. Repealed in 1851, this labor tax was replaced a year later by a still-onerous four-dollar-a-month fee. The government effort to shackle the Chinese immigrant workforce would continue unabated for decades in the California legislature, and this political vendetta generated nationwide was actively and sympathetically tracked by the nation's newspapers, which regularly sounded a toxin regarding the "Yellow Peril"—even in portions of the country without any Chinese immigrants.

This anti-Asian immigration crusade reached its zenith in 1882 with congressional passage of the Chinese Exclusion Act, which prohibited immigration of all Chinese nationals for ten years—with the exception of merchants, students, diplomats, and travelers. This statute, sustained by continuing legislation, remained in force until 1943.

In an August 27, 1844 article on the Barataria Bay–Grand Terre area, a New Orleans *Daily Picayune* correspondent penned the first mention of shrimp drying in coastal Louisiana, noting that "shrimps are caught and dried by the fishermen, and sent in barrels to market, where they sell at five and six dollars a barrel." The unnamed journalist fails to identify either the fishermen's ethnicity or the market's location, and it would appear that this operation was short-lived, for there is no further mention of shrimp drying in the region's newspapers until the postbellum era.

Levee Scene, New Orleans, La.

For nearly two thousand years, barrels were the containers of choice for shipment of bulk cargo. In New Orleans, the barrel manufacturing business, distributed throughout the city, met the needs of the regional shipping industry. (Postcard from the authors' collections, ca. 1900.)

invisibility to openly hostile authority figures, these Asian pioneers unsurprisingly left no reliable paper trail, and while modern researchers have ascribed the origins of the modern Louisiana shrimp-drying industry to various individuals—most prominently Lee Yeun, Chen Kee, Lee Yim, and Yee Fo, who patented the centuries-old process in 1885, the progenitor's identity and the location of the original drying platform both remain objects of dispute. All of these industry pioneers, however, were reportedly overshadowed by a remarkable woman, whose gender, tenacity, and business acumen made her a short-lived celebrity two and a half decades later. Her biography, which was syndicated nationally in 1896, provides the best available insight into the Louisiana dried shrimp industry's origins.

Quong Wo (possibly Wu), "an enterprising woman" with "feminine pluck," was the widow of a postbellum immigrant, who, according to posthumous news reports, evidently established a laundry in New Orleans' Chinatown before seeking his fortune along the coastal estuaries. Investing his savings in a "small boat," Quong occupied a "sand island . . . that nobody wanted, dried his shrimp in the sun, and when he had as much as twenty barrels ready he shipped them to China by an old tramp sailing vessel, going from New Orleans round the Horn." When his first shipment was favorably received in Canton, Quong sent a letter to his wife, urging her to secure the proceeds of his initial dried shrimp sale and then join him in Louisiana. This she did, traveling first to California and then on to New Orleans, reportedly by transcontinental railroad.

Following her arrival in Louisiana, Wo and her husband toiled industriously, and over the course of two and a half years, the couple slowly expanded their operation by hiring at least two employees. After her husband drowned when their lugger capsized during a tropical storm (probably in August 1879), Wo led an expedition to recover the boat and successfully resumed shrimp-drying operations. Working alongside her male employees, she typically spent five hours a day operating a purse net in chest-deep water. After an arduous workday, she tackled the business's administrative chores, which involved not only bookkeeping and other mundane tasks but also correspondence with Cantonese buyers. In her letters, Wo reportedly carefully avoided all mention of her husband's demise to thwart anticipated manifestations of gender bias, particularly male merchants' perceived penchant for "deceiv[ing] a poor lone[ly] . . . widow."

After three years of her oversight, Quong Wo's operation boasted twenty employees and two "long shanties," which evidently functioned as dormitories. By the mid-1890s, the business had fifty workmen, large permanent drying facilities, and an export business annually shipping "hundreds of barrels . . . to her native land."*

Other operators also achieved success in the remote marshlands. In the fall of 1882, nationally syndicated news articles noted some drying facilities boasted two-acre wooden platforms and insinuated they had onsite cooperages producing the Chinese-labeled barrels in which the shrimp were transported to Asian markets. These exports helped open the Louisiana shrimp industry's first international market. By 1899, Bayou State shrimpers had established a notable commercial presence in Europe and Brazil.

The rapid expansion of Louisiana's shrimp-drying operations in the twilight years of the nineteenth century raises several perplexing questions, the most puzzling of which is the issue of capital improvements financing, which required far more capitalization than the operators' modest annual profits. Most of the pioneering operations

Mrs. Quong Receiving a Proposal.

An artist's rendering of Mrs. Quong Wo. (From the *Washington Morning Times*, February 2, 1896.)

---

* The syndicated biography concludes with the following statement: "She is a rich woman. She practically rules the island where her home is. Many wooers have come to her, but she has sent them all away without offering them a share in the shrimp business. She might go back to China and live with all the pomp of a mandarin, but she could not be the power there that she is on her little Gulf island. So there she stays." *Sacramento Daily Union-Record*, April 19, 1896.

This early post–World War II era map shows
the extent of Louisiana's coastal wetlands.
(From O'Neil.)

The harvesting, curing, packaging, and exporting of shrimp in these industrial communities was extremely labor-intensive, and at the peak of the warm-weather drying season, a platform's resident crew could include five hundred to seven hundred men, women, and children. During the summer months, these facilities operated on a twenty-four-hour basis. The most robust laborers typically participated in the harvesting operations. In the estuaries, male laborers pulled seines and operated wind-dependent shuttle boats used to transport the harvest to the platforms. In the early twentieth century, following the introduction of gasoline-powered engines, forty to fifty vessels typically operated out of the larger platform communities.

Most of the remaining workforce labored in the various component phases of the drying operation. Shuttle boat crews offloaded the seine crew catches onto the platform docks. Other workers then transferred the "green" shrimp to nearby covered iron cauldrons, where batches of the newly caught crustaceans were boiled in super-saline brine for approximately ten minutes. Upon completion of the brining procedure, boiling station laborers transferred the shrimp to wooden wheelbarrows by means of large dip nets. Wheelbarrow crews then moved their cargoes to unused portions of the drying platform. Platform workers first spread the shrimp, then turned them repeatedly to ensure rapid and uniform sun-drying.

During the drying phase, which usually required twenty-four to seventy-two hours, moisture posed an ever-present danger because it leached the saline preservative from the shrimp. Coastal Louisiana parishes generally receive about seventy inches of rain a year, much of it during the prime shrimp-harvesting months. To mitigate this ever-present threat, platform crews devised specialized platform architectural styles. Louisiana platforms featured distinctive, gently undulating platform surfaces, with ridges typically cresting about three feet above the "valleys" at thirty-foot intervals. On the ridge crests stood A-frame wooden structures supporting massive tarpaulins that could be deployed as protective "tents" whenever rain showers threatened. (Runoff drained into the "valleys," whence it drained into the estuaries or evaporated.) These "tents" were open at each end to permit cross ventilation to prevent spoilage. Workers also deployed the tarpaulins each night to prevent dew from impregnating—and thus spoiling—the drying shrimp.

Once the desiccating crustaceans were thoroughly dry, the platform crew spread them uniformly over a section of platform, then began to "dance the shrimp" by shuffling their booted feet over the shellfish to separate the meat from the armor-like shells. During this operation, laborers relied on sea breezes to winnow the chaff. Additional winnowing occurred during the second depuration phase, when the entire batch was dumped into a "fanning" machine, which separates the meat from the shell. This piece of equipment was built by the Chinese on the same principle as the apparatus used to winnow grains. If necessary, the platform crew employed a third cleansing by placing the shrimp meat in bags and beating them to remove any remaining shell particles.

Once the shrimp were sufficiently clean for consumption, workers placed 220 to 230 pounds of dried meat (representing 1,540 to 1,610 pounds of uncured meat) into individual barrels for rail transportation to San Francisco commission merchant S. L. Jones. In 1883, Jones received the first known transcontinental shipments of Louisiana dried shrimp—forty tons over an eight-month period.

Total output of Louisiana's late nineteenth- and early twentieth-century shrimp platforms is difficult to determine because of fragmentary documentary evidence; however, circumstantial evidence suggests that, conservatively, individual platforms produced on average four hundred to five hundred barrels per season or from 620,000 to 775,000 pounds.

When rain threatened, labors hurried to move the crustaceans underneath the A-frame structure, then covered the framework with tarpaulins. (Photo from the authors collections, 1980.)

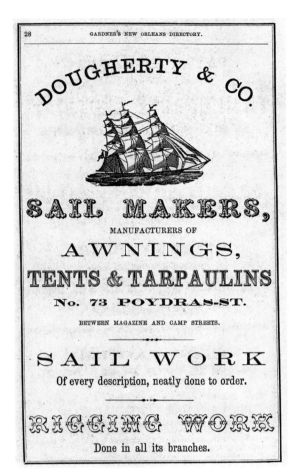

Until the Civil War, New Orleans was one of the nation's leading ports. During this period, before steam power completely supplanted sail power, sailmakers were critical service providers in the Crescent City's massive import-export industry. (Advertisement from *Gardner's New Orleans Directory*, 1858.)

For decades before World War II, Louisiana's commercial fishermen secured their equipment from specialized hardware stores in New Orleans's French Quarter. (Advertisement from *Gardner's New Orleans Directory*, 1871.)

For much of the past 150 years, specialists have provided shrimpers net maintenance and repair services. Today, net services consist primarily of "tarring" and repairing shrimpers' nets and furnishing unfinished shrimp net material. (Lithograph from *Harper's Supplement*, September 1, 1888, 78.)

were established just before the full onset of the Panic of 1873, an economic depression on the scale of the twentieth-century's Great Depression. Credit from traditional sources—New Orleans banks, which would have been virtually unobtainable because of racial bias before the panic—became unquestionably inaccessible after 1873, when the already fragile financial institutions were compelled to call in thousands of bad loans from overextended Louisiana planters. In addition, dried shrimp operations faced the absence of a local market as well as the vagaries of volatile weather and constantly changing environmental factors. In 1883, for example, a New Orleans *Daily Picayune* correspondent lamented that "the run of shrimp is sometimes small and the business dull for weeks at a time," meaning that cash flow was as unpredictable as the shrimp runs. Yet funding for the shrimp-drying businesses mysteriously materialized from somewhere, for, by the late 1880s, these physically remote operations typically consisted of gently undulating wooden elevated drying platforms—some of which encompassed an area comparable to three modern football fields—company stores, and dozens of individual residences that, collectively, constituted a fully functional village. In addition to the cost of platform-village construction, these operations had to acquire and maintain luggers and miscellaneous other boats, nets (both seines and cast nets), shrimp boilers, cordage used as boiler fuel, barrels, boxes, bags, tarpaulins, consumables and supplies for workers, as well as a host of miscellaneous other associated items.

The early expansion of Louisiana's dried shrimp industry roughly coincided with that of San Francisco Bay, which was also founded by Cantonese refugees. The latter operations were unquestionably funded by benevolent organizations commonly known as the Chinese Six Companies. Upon their arrival at San Francisco in the late 1840s and early 1850s, Chinese immigrants participating in the California gold rush quickly discovered that the interests of the territory's business and political leaders were antithetical to their own. Like other nineteenth-century immigrant groups, the Chinese initially banded together to create benevolent societies to provide mutual assistance in times of financial crisis—particularly burial, medical, and personal loans; over time, these mutual societies assumed aspects of both modern chambers of commerce and private banks, in keeping with the Cantonese tradition of *huiguan* (business support groups) The original benevolent society eventually split into six independent organizations, each representing a different Cantonese area. Branches of these organizations were established in other United States cities after 1882, but extant documentary and circumstantial evidence strongly suggests that external funding for Louisiana's first Chinese-owned dried shrimp operations originated in California. In mid-April 1879, the *New Orleans Daily Democrat* reported that Louisiana business interests were in "daily" contact with the Six Companies. While most of these transcontinental communications consisted of inquiries by Louisiana and Mississippi businessmen regarding the availability of Chinese day laborers, there is little doubt that enterprising immigrants themselves also sought out their fellow countrymen on the West Coast to explore financial underwriting possibilities.

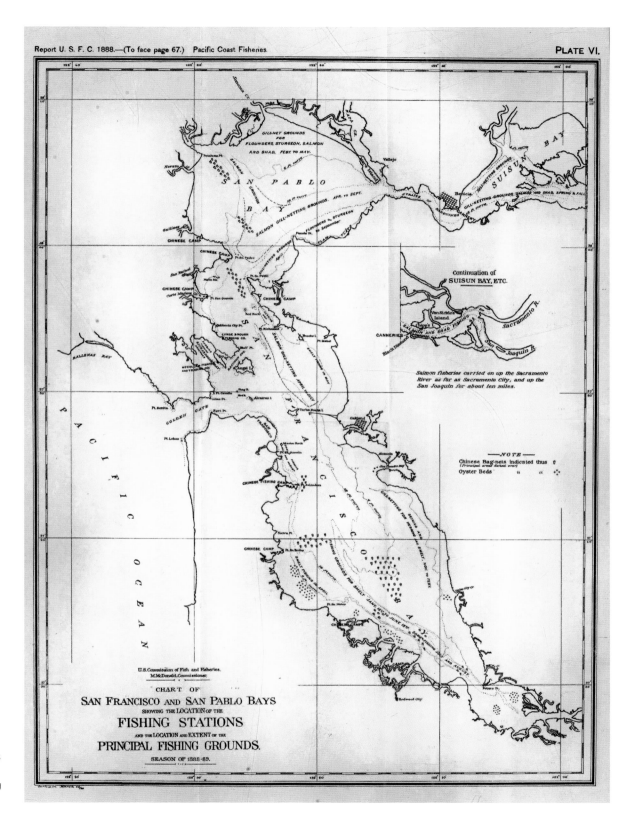

Report U. S. F. C. 1888.—(To face page 67.) Pacific Coast Fisheries.

PLATE VI.

This remarkable map clearly shows the Chinese dominance of the San Francisco Bay Area fisheries. Operating out of many fishing camps scattered throughout the region, these Asian immigrants intensively harvested shrimp and finfish, resulting in catastrophic depletion of commercial stocks by the early twentieth century. (Map from Bulletin of the United States Fish Commission, Volume XVI, 1888 [Washington, DC: Government Printing Office, 1892], 67.)

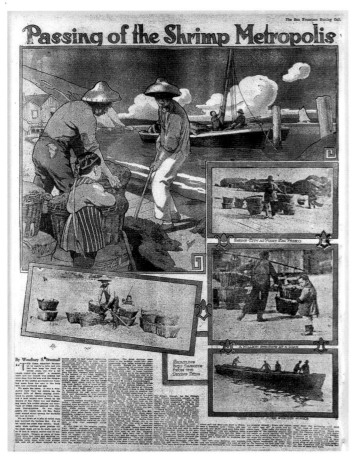

A full-page San Francisco newspaper report lamenting the implosion of the San Francisco Bay shrimp industry due to chronic overfishing. ("Passing of the Shrimp Metropolis," *San Francisco Call*, May 17, 1908.)

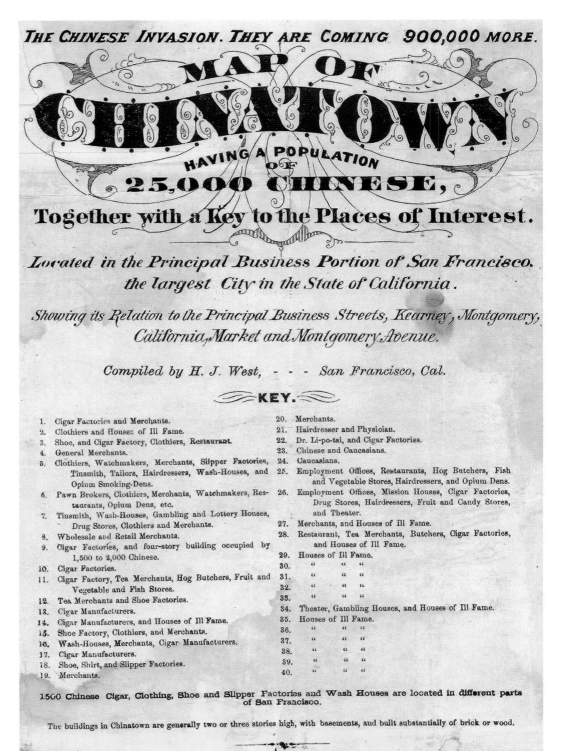

"The Chinese Invasion. They Are Coming." (Map of Chinatown © 1872; California Map Collection, Map 889; California Historical Society, San Francisco.)

The Chinese shrimp-drying "camps" in the San Francisco Bay region were remarkably similar to their counterparts in Louisiana's coastal marshlands. Despite the obvious concessions to different environmental factors, the camps were largely self-sufficient villages in which life centered on massive shrimp-drying operations. (Photo from the San Francisco Maritime National Historical Park, National Archives, Fish and Wildlife Photo Collection, photo number B11,16,014.)

The St. Malo shrimp-drying camp, located in southeastern Louisiana marshlands, is an example of a community supported by the state's aquatic resources. (Woodcut from *Harper's Weekly*, March 31, 1883, 196.)

Unlike the more substantial shrimp-drying operations, small operators maintained short-lived "camps." These palmetto shelters are representative of the ephemeral buildings typically found at these sites. (Photo from NOAA Photo Library, photographer Stefan Claisson, 1889. Courtesy of Gulf of Maine Cod Project, NOAA National Marine Sanctuaries, San Francisco Maritime National Historical Park, National Archives, Photo Number 25167.)

This image provides perhaps the best extant view of an elevated drying platform. All the construction material was delivered to the site by sailboat, which was itself an exceptional achievement. Notice the large woodpile used to fuel the vat boilers. Firewood was delivered by boats outfitted to carry stove-length logs. Crews boiled shrimp in brine before placing the crustaceans on drying platforms. This process used copious quantities of fuel. (Photo from NOAA Photo Library, photographer Stefan Claisson, 1889. Courtesy of Gulf of Maine Cod Project, NOAA National Marine Sanctuaries, San Francisco Maritime National Historical Park, National Archives, Photo Number 25170.)

A shrimping lugger moored at Ping Wing's Manila Village docks. Manila Village, the most famous of Louisiana's shrimp-drying platform communities, was a major landmark in southeastern Louisiana's coastal estuaries. (Photo from the authors' collections. Courtesy of Louisiana Department of Wildlife and Fisheries, Baton Rouge, LA, photographer and date unknown.)

Elevated boardwalks were ubiquitous architectural features at raised drying platforms, providing connectivity to other residences, the company store, and, of course, the gently undulating drying surface. (Photo from NOAA Photo Library, photographer Stefan Claisson, 1889. Courtesy of Gulf of Maine Cod Project, NOAA National Marine Sanctuaries, San Francisco Maritime National Historical Park, National Archives, Photo Number 25166.)

Relatively small shrimp-drying platforms were often located on shell reefs. (Photo from the authors' collections. Courtesy of Morgan City Archives, Morgan City, LA, photographer Jesse Grice, date unknown.)

Louisiana's largest shrimp-drying platforms were traditionally isolated industrial communities, complete with employee housing and company stores. Economic life in these villages centered on elevated drying platforms, typically raised on cypress pilings four to eight feet above the marsh surface. The elevated surface safeguarded against tidal action and facilitated the air flow crucial to the curing process. Along the platform's perimeter stood small wooden or palmetto-thatched cabins connected by a network of rickety raised catwalks. Walkways also provided access to wharves servicing the villages' fleets of shrimping luggers.

Luggers discharge their cargoes at a Terrebonne Parish shrimp-drying platform. Shrimpers offloaded their shrimp in "chinee" baskets, providing processors and fishermen with an accurate measurement of the catch. (Photo from the R. Bazet Collection, Nicholls State University Archives, Thibodaux, LA, ca. 1920.)

268   FRANK LESLIE'S ILLUSTRATED NEWSPAPER.   [DECEMBER 17, 1881.

CALIFORNIA.— AN EARLY MORNING SCENE IN A SAN FRANCISCO FISH-MARKET.— FROM A SKETCH BY A STAFF ARTIST.— SEE PAGE 267.

Like New Orleans's French Quarter food stalls, San Francisco's seafood market in 1881 was bustling with activity. (Lithograph from *Frank Leslie's Illustrated Newspaper*, December 17, 1881, 268.)

BOILING THE SHRIMPS FOR MARKET.

Whether at sites along San Francisco Bay or in Louisiana's wetlands, shrimp were dried in remarkably similar boilers, part of the material cultural baggage the Chinese brought to the Bayou State's fishery. (Artist rendering from the San Francisco *Call*, November 7, 1897, 18.)

In keeping with traditional practices, Chinese shrimp driers in Louisiana and California boiled fresh shrimp in brine before spreading them on drying platforms. The boiling vats consisted of brick vaults heated by wood-fired ovens. (Photo from the authors' collections. Courtesy of Louisiana Department of Wildlife and Fisheries, Baton Rouge, LA, photographer and date unknown.)

Wood-fired brick ovens used to heat the boiling vats at an unidentified drying platform. These boilers were essential visual components of all drying communities. (Photo courtesy of Louisiana Department of Wildlife and Fisheries, New Iberia Office, photographer and date unknown.)

Chinee baskets, for decades the standard measurement of weight in the Louisiana shrimp fishery. (Photo from the authors' collections. Courtesy of Louisiana Department of Wildlife and Fisheries, Baton Rouge, LA, photographer and date unknown.)

As in Louisiana, Chinese shrimpers in the San Francisco Bay Area used sturdy baskets to measure their catch. (Image from Carlsson, private collector at OpenSFHistory, accessed July 25, 2020.)

Two men transferring dried shrimp to chinee baskets on a Louisiana drying platform. (Photo from the authors' collections. Courtesy of Louisiana Department of Wildlife and Fisheries, Baton Rouge, LA, photographer and date unknown.)

Over time, metal baskets replaced their natural-fiber counterparts. (Photo from the authors' collections. Courtesy of the Maritime and Seafood Industry Museum, Biloxi, MS, 2019.)

Shrimp driers in Louisiana and California used the same traditional dehydration techniques, which required frequent rotation of the drying crustaceans to ensure rapid and even evaporation of remaining moisture. (Image from Carlsson, private collector at OpenSFHistory, ca. 1910, accessed July 25, 2020.)

Raking shrimp at a late twentieth-century Louisiana drying platform. (Photo from the authors' collections, 1980.)

CRUSHING THE SHELLS FROM THE DRIED SHRIMP

"Dancing the shrimp" in Louisiana (above) and California (below). Shuffling footsteps helped remove the shrimp shells from the flesh. The ammonia in the crustaceans' carapace and the sharp edges of their shells took a frightful toll on "dancers'" heavy leather footwear. (Artist rendering from Schoonover 1911:87.)

As in Louisiana, the rake was an omnipresent and indispensable tool on shrimp-drying platforms located around San Francisco Bay. (Woodcut from *Illustrated London News*, February 21, 1880, 180.)

An early twentieth-century Chinese shrimping junk in California waters. (Photo from NOAA Photo Library, photographer Stefan Claisson, 1889, courtesy Gulf of Maine Cod Project, NOAA National Marine Sanctuaries, San Francisco Maritime National Historical Park, National Archives, Photo Number 25955.)

This village was composed of Chinese shrimp fishers at Point San Bruno, San Francisco Bay, circa 1889. At least twenty-five of these rustic sites were visual reminders of the Chinese commercial shrimp-drying trade. (Photo courtesy of the San Francisco Maritime National Historical Park, National Archives, Fish and Wildlife Photo Collection, photo number B11.16,013.)

A Chinese shrimp-drying "camp" along the banks of San Francisco Bay. Note the drying shrimp on the foothill's slope (foreground and background). In California, at such sloping sites, Chinese fishermen sometimes utilized a mechanical roller—similar to a contemporary heavy-duty lawn roller—in lieu of the traditional "shrimp dance." (From Schulz and Lortie 89.)

This 1953 aerial photograph shows seven major drying platforms along Oyster Bayou, near the eastern end of Point au Fer, in coastal Terrebonne Parish. The documentary record is fragmentary, but it appears that at least eighty platforms were once scattered across south-central Louisiana's coastal wetlands. (Photo courtesy of John M. Anderson, Map Librarian, Louisiana State University, Department of Geography and Anthropology, Louisiana State University. Source: Aero Exploration Co. Aerial Photography, April 21, 1953, Photo CQC-1K-141. Scale 1:20,000. Washington, DC: Production and Marketing Administration, US Department of Agriculture, 1953.)

A repurposed sugar kettle functioned as a brine-boiling vat, along with a brick boiler in the background, at this unidentified early twentieth-century Louisiana drying platform. (Photo from the authors' collections. Courtesy of Louisiana Department of Wildlife and Fisheries, Baton Rouge, LA, photographer and date unknown.)

Boiling shrimp in brine in a California shrimp-drying village was the first stage in the drying process. (Image from Carlsson, private collector at OpenSFHistory, accessed July 25, 2020.)

Donald and Karen Davis at the Chinese Consolidated Benevolent Association of America headquarters, better known as the Six Companies, in San Francisco. Founded in 1882, the Six Companies continue to support Chinese communities throughout the United States. (Photo from the authors' collections, 2019.)

Wang (Wong), Li (Lee), and Zhang are the three most common surnames in mainland China, where these family members collectively number nearly three hundred million strong. Needless to say, these families are easily the world's largest. The San Francisco–based Wong Family Benevolent Association is an essential element in keeping family relationships and interrelated financial support in place. (Photo from the authors' collections, 2019.)

This Chinese Benevolent Society office in Halawa, Hawaii, is an example of one element in Chinese culture that can be found in Chinese communities around the world. (Photo from the authors' collections, 2018.)

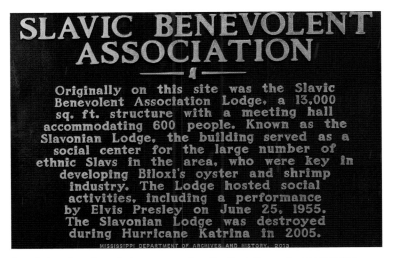

Associations for other ethnic groups, such as the Slavic Benevolent Association in Mississippi, the Croatian Benevolent Association in New Orleans, and the Progressive Benevolent Association of Convent, are part of the region's cultural landscape. (Photo from the authors collections, 2019.)

The Chinese Consolidated Benevolent Association, commonly known as the Chinese Six Companies, was created by San Francisco businessmen in the gold rush era as a safety net for Chinese immigrants from specific Chinese provinces. Like their counterparts in other nineteenth-century ethnic communities, this benevolent association was a defensive response to the overtly hostile nativist American government's failure to acknowledge and address the immigrants' cultural, social, and economic interests. In 1849, emigrants from China's Guangdong region (Canton) established San Francisco's Kong Chow Temple. Renamed and rededicated five years later by the Kong Chow Clan Association, the former temple became a multipurpose facility functioning primarily as a religious and community center. Embodying the Chinese tradition of *huiguan*, the center afforded homesick Cantonese-speaking immigrants' familiar food, shelter, and financial assistance. The facility also provided Cantonese immigrants with crucial translation services in their dealings with state and federal governmental agencies. This was particularly important for individuals seeking naturalization.

The Kong Chow Clan Association, which eventually split into two organizations because of internal strife, served as a model for all of the local community groups that followed in its wake. In the 1850s, four additional organizations—collectively known as the Four Great Houses—sprang into existence. In 1882, the six Chinese associations merged to form the Six Companies. Following consolidation, the united organizations functioned as a savings and loan association, a labor brokerage, a healthcare provider, a mentoring society, and a community defense league, battling racial stereotyping and prejudice.

It is highly probably these benevolent organizations, individually or collectively, funded the construction of Louisiana's first shrimp-drying communities and the associated ancillary equipment necessary to guarantee the success of these speculative ventures. Further, societies helped facilitate the movement of barrels of dried product from Louisiana's wetlands through the Port of San Francisco to foreign markets.

External financial assistance fueled explosive growth in the Pelican State's dried shrimp industry in the late nineteenth and early twentieth centuries. In 1880, there were perhaps less than a half dozen active drying platforms, but by the start of World War I, an estimated seventy-five shrimp platforms—the vast majority under Chinese ownership—stood above the marshes along the southeastern Louisiana coast. In addition, there were major Filipino drying operations at Cabanage (Cabinash) and Bassa Bassa—stilt villages and their attendant drying platforms—on Barataria Bay very similar to those of their Chinese neighbors, with whom they were often allied economically.

The confluence of myriad legal and economic factors, however, soon caused a gradual decline in the number and size of Louisiana's shrimp-drying operations. Platform operators—particularly those managed by Chinese immigrants—faced increasingly onerous challenges in maintaining their shrimp-drying workforce. The Chinese Exclusion Act, signed into law on May 6, 1882, officially banned all Chinese immigration into the United States until its repeal in 1943. While it did not effectively end Chinese immigration, the legislation made it increasingly difficult to introduce young laborers, particularly after the Coast Guard began intercepting Louisiana fishing boats believed to be involved in the introduction of undocumented individuals from mainland China. In fact, the drama and tragedy associated with these smuggling operations were once leitmotifs in the Pelican State's shrimp fishery lore.

The labor-recruitment challenges posed by the Chinese Exclusion Act quickly forced platform operators to employ whatever laborers were available—sometimes by unscrupulous means. Concrete evidence of these nefarious practices first surfaced in 1911, when federal authorities formally charged Louisiana residents Lee Yat, Ah Hee, and Joe Fung Lee with multiple counts of involuntary servitude in violation of the Peonage Abolition Act of 1867. Evidentiary affidavits presented at the trial contained eyewitness accounts of the systematic recruitment and brutal exploitation of vulnerable underemployed laborers residing in New Orleans's French Quarter tenements. An independent source maintains that

THE DAMAGE ALONG THE GULF COAST.

A Picayune Man Makes a Trip from the Rigolets to Biloxi.

Over a Hundred Lives Lost in the Louisiana Marshes.

Further Reports of the Wreckage of Small Craft.

Thirty Bodies Found on Cat Island— Passengers Arrive in the City from the Coast.

Major hurricanes repeatedly decimated shrimp-drying platforms. The unnamed storms of 1893 and 1915 were among the most lethal. (From the New Orleans *Daily Picayune*, October 6, 1893.)

Manila Village, located on the "margins of Grand Lake [upper Barataria Bay]," was early twentieth-century Louisiana's largest and most economically significant shrimp-drying facility. Local oral tradition maintains that the complex consisted of residences, ramshackle sheds, equally rickety ancillary outbuildings, a general store, a post office that operated from 1926 to 1949 under the byname Cabinash, and a massive forty-thousand-square-foot drying platform, roughly the size of a small modern Walmart discount store. The platform constituted the nexus of a substantial harvesting and processing operation, serviced, at its zenith, by approximately five hundred resident workers and perhaps as many as fifty shrimp boats. Despite its regional importance, the remote industrial settlement typically attracted wide public notice only when it was devastated by catastrophic hurricanes, or when the occasional newspaper reporter ventured into the wetlands describing the uncharted landscape's now forgotten communities. Hurricane Betsy's massive storm surge destroyed most of Manila Village's derelict remains in September 1965.

Manila Village, operated at the time of this photograph by Ping Wing, met all the criteria for a company town. Note the metal tracks installed on the wooden walkway to facilitate the offloading of cargoes by means of wheeled metal carts. (Photo courtesy of Louisiana Department of Wildlife and Fisheries, New Iberia Office, photographer and date unknown.)

Shrimp-drying platforms featured gently rippling decks to facilitate the drainage of moisture from the dehydrating shrimp. (Photo from the Blum and Bergeron Collection, Nicholls State University Archives, Thibodaux, LA, photographer and date unknown.)

A contemporary example of the wheelbarrows used on platforms. (From the authors' collections, 1976.)

Chin Bow Wing at a Chinese-owned Louisiana drying platform. (Photo from the authors' collections, 1964, provided by Chin Bow Wing.)

This photo shows how Manila Village—whether owned by Ping Wing or Jules Fisher—served as the epicenter of the shrimp-drying industry and the protype of an industry-based company town. (Photo courtesy of State Library of Louisiana, photographer Fonville Winans, 1938.)

In Marin County, the California Department of Parks and Recreation considerable assistance from the Friends of China Camp preserved North Americas last example of a shrimp-drying village. Located in San Rafael, along San Pablo Bay, the village boasted a population of nearly five hundred in the late 1800s. Like its Louisiana counterpart, it was an isolated company town providing dehydrated shrimp for the Asian market. Though separated by nearly two thousand miles, vestiges of the cultural diffusion of the shrimp drying industry from the Bay to the bayou country are still in the cultural landscapes of California and Louisiana.

recruiters promised potential hirelings "from four to ten dollars a day," a "share in the company," and free passage to the work site. Reticent potential recruits were offered whiskey and cash advances as additional enticements to secure their commitments.

The promised inducements quickly proved illusory when the laborer reached the workplace. One alleged victim maintained that, once transported to a remote shrimp-drying platform in Barataria Bay, his new employers presented him with a bill for his transportation to the site as well as a lengthy laundry list of charges for necessities—including mosquito netting, a mattress, and unspecified work "utensils"—that would be deducted against his meager earnings. As a result, the new recruit "found himself greatly in debt before he had been given an opportunity to work." Once trapped in a cycle of perpetual indebtedness, workers were reduced to the status of virtual slaves, physically bound to the platform until they had paid their bills and forced to work extraordinarily long shifts—sometimes thirty hours, according to one affidavit. Ever-present threats of violence by Chinese managers—which sometimes escalated into unreported shooting deaths of laborers—and the willful collusion of local mailboat captains, whose vessels constituted the only means of egress, effectively imprisoned distraught platform workers in a virtual prison without walls.

The federal effort to quash peonage in the shrimp-drying platforms apparently had little lasting effect, and anecdotal information suggests that the platform recruiters continued to prey on the unsuspecting poor—particularly immigrants—from Crescent City slums. The inevitable result was the rapid and thorough transformation of the platform villages from single-ethnicity enclaves to perhaps the South's most polyglot communities. Contemporary travelers visiting the platforms consistently marvel that their workforces represented every continent on the planet, except Antarctica.

Labor challenges were eventually eclipsed by the catastrophic weather events that could literally obliterate all trace of a platform community over the course of a few hours. For example, the powerful hurricane of September 1915 that pushed a twelve-foot storm surge into Barataria Bay was particularly destructive to all of

"When laws were passed early in this century to bar the immigration of Orientals into this country, Louisiana's tangled coastline once again became the home to smugglers of human cargo. This time it was not slaves brought against their will, but rather free men and women who had paid dearly for the opportunity.

The conditions of their voyage were worse if anything. Fishing boats would go out into international waters to meet schooners coming from Panama or Havanna [sic—Havana]. The would be immigrints [sic] would climb down the long rope ladders to the small fishing luggers, only to find out their new Captain's quandary.

He could not afford to be seen with them, yet there was no room for them below decks. The solution was to have them climb into barrels, which were then capped. For the next several hours they were curled up and cramped, sniffing for fresh air at the bung hole, on the deck of a vessel never intended for the open water through which it traveled.

Brought safely to the railhead at Lockport, where they were smuggled onto freight cars, it is said the Captain received $1500 a head for his passangers [sic]. A lot of money for a Captain and his small crew, but if caught they lost the boat and years of liberty in a Federal penitentiary.

There is a story of one captain who, spotting a Coast Guard cutter approaching him in the distance, rolled the barrels off his deck, Chinamen and all. Their screams were only silenced when the barrels finally sunk. As the cutter got closer the Captain congratulated himself for his quick thinking. But wait. Not possible! But it was [p. 380] true. The vessel he had sighted was a pleasure craft, out of Grand Isle on an outing, not the Coast Guard at all. The Captain had drowned several people and lost a fortune for nothing.

It is said he did not want to talk about that trip again, except to sometimes mutter to himself. He started to play with a piece of string, some said a piece one of the victims had dropped. It was just a nervous habit. As weeks then months passed, he spoke less and less to others, muttered more to himself. He had to sell his boat because no one would go out with him. He played with the string, making cat's cradles, tying and untying knots, until he was in a world of his own, with the string, and his mutterings, and the ghosts of the people he had murdered." (Hamilton and Associates, "The Cajuns" 378–80. See also Kane, *Deep Delta Country* 186.)

Elderly veterans of the shrimp-drying industry recall that, in the early twentieth century, some platform operators "shanghaied" unsuspecting laborers. This practice continued for decades, as labor recruiters shifted their focus from immigrants to homeless alcoholics from New Orleans's French Quarter. In an interview with Louisiana Sea Grant researchers, Freddie Matherne, whose family was involved in the Pelican State's shrimp industry for decades, stated that "my father used to go to New Orleans in a big paneled truck. And he used to go and pick up the men that worked on these platforms. Mostly, alcoholics, you know, down on their luck and what have you. . . . He used to go there and he would have a couple of cases—or a case—of wine and he used to tell them [that] if they [got] in the truck, he'd give 'em . . . one of them bottles of wine. So they used to get in the truck. He told some of them that hadn't . . . [gone] before that he's taking them to the Chinese platform. And then he would go to Harvey, where he had his boat parked. . . . And anyway, from there, he would give them another bottle of wine if they . . . [got] on the boat. Once they got on the boat, that's it, they was going onto that platform. So, in a way, he sort of Shanghaied them, but it did them good cuz they used to eat real good. . . . But when they got out there, they couldn't get no wine, no nothing."

the region's flourishing shrimp-drying businesses. Massive waves washed away the new Quong Sang (Sun) platform on Barataria Bay and drowned its entire workforce (variously reported as twenty-six to more than sixty persons), as well as its owner, whose gold-laden money belt dragged him inexorably to his doom beneath the rising tide. Manila Village was "wiped out . . . before the full fury of the storm broke," but its occupants successfully fled by lugger to higher ground. Three "camps" (platforms) operated by the Barataria Company were "demolished," while facilities at Bayou Rigeau [Rigaud], and the Rojas platform were "wrecked." The region's surviving shrimp-drying structures all reportedly "suffered greatly." The cumulative economic toll was massive—Manila Village's damages alone were estimated at $80,000 (approximately $2 million in 2020 currency), and some operations consequently did not recover. As a result, Louisiana's entire shrimp-drying industry began a slow, protracted decline that has persisted to the present.

Although, at first glance, canning and artificial refrigeration appear to be mutually incompatible, the convergence of these competing preservation technologies was essential to the Gulf Coast shrimp industry's remarkable late nineteenth-century success. Introduction of industrially produced ice gave impetus to the emergence of the then technologically advanced field harvesting operations necessary to sustain Louisiana's emerging world-class canning operations that, in turn, permitted the Gulf Coast shrimp industry to reach distant, formerly inaccessible markets by 1900.

Ice manufacturing in coastal plain municipalities after 1867 enabled shrimp boats to exploit inland and near-coastal waters at far greater distances from urban markets and processors and, thanks to the assistance of specialized boats designed to resupply the luggers with ice and transport their shellfish cargoes to canneries, to remain in continuous operation for exponentially longer periods. On November 25, 1900, the New Orleans *Daily Picayune* published a rare eyewitness description of the importance of ice in the harvesting fleet: "A lugger from 6 to 10 tons capacity is loaded with ice in New Orleans and proceeds with as much speed as possible to the fishing grounds, often as far as Grand Isle. There the seine skiff is waiting, and, in two or three days, the lugger is loaded with

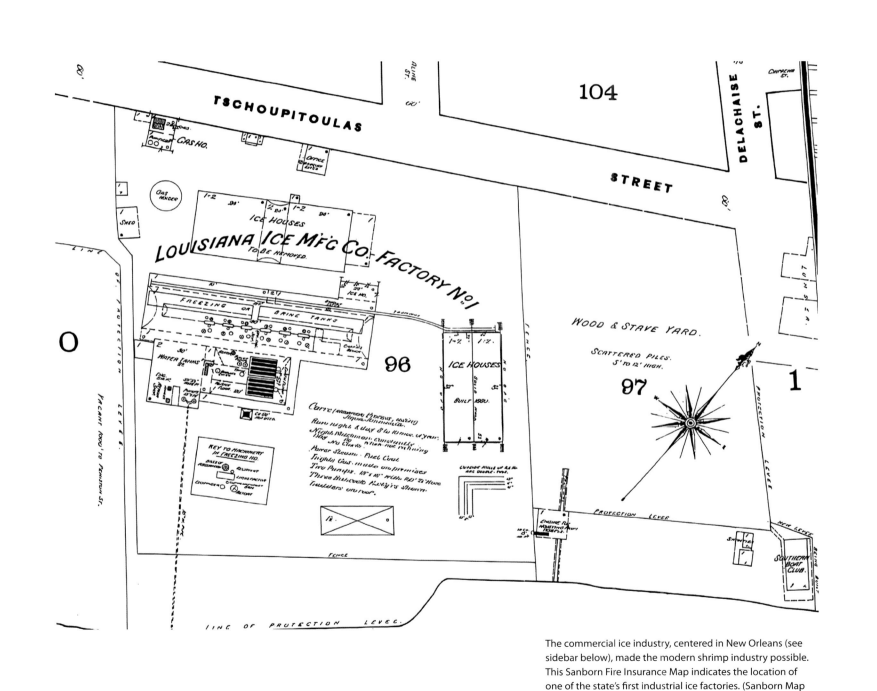

The commercial ice industry, centered in New Orleans (see sidebar below), made the modern shrimp industry possible. This Sanborn Fire Insurance Map indicates the location of one of the state's first industrial ice factories. (Sanborn Map Company, vol. 2, 1895.)

In 1859, Frenchman Ferdinand Carré invented the first practical modern refrigeration system. The device was patented the following year. Carré's invention proved a godsend for New Orleans, which had been dependent on block ice cut from frozen lakes in northern states—particularly the Northeast—throughout the antebellum era for its refrigeration needs. Trade disruptions during the Civil War and lingering regional animosities following the conflict dictated that the Crescent City seek another source of supply. By the end of 1865, New Orleans boasted three of Ferdinand Carré's commercial ice machines.

Nicolas Appert, inventor of the canning process, became known as the "father of canning." (From the authors' collections.)

The modern canning process was invented by Nicolas François Appert. Born in France in 1750, Appert, a self-taught inventor with extensive experience in the culinary arts, was enticed by the French government's offer of a twelve-thousand-franc prize to seek improved canning technology to sustain armies and ships deployed on active duty. In 1809, he claimed the prize for his method of preserving food in sealed bottles or jars that were heated after sealing and then kept sealed until use. One year later, Englishman Peter Durand patented the use of tin-coated iron cans as substitutes for jars.

shrimp and fish, which are carefully packed in crushed ice. When a load is secured the lugger known as the iceboat returns to New Orleans, where the cargo is sold and the trip repeated."

The exponential increase in late nineteenth-century New Orleans's shrimp recipes fueled the rise of the Crescent City's embryonic seafood canning industry. Industrial-scale commercial canning was introduced to the upper Gulf Coast by G. W. Dunbar & Sons, which established its first shrimp cannery at New Orleans in 1867. The canning operation initially offered its potential customer base a broad array of seafood, sea turtle, fruit, and vegetable products—all processed on a seasonal basis—but canned shellfish, particularly oysters and shrimp, afforded Dunbar & Sons the greatest potential profitability. Shrimp canning, however, presented unique technological challenges because of the chemical properties of the crustacean itself. A US government report noted that

> the quality of the product during the first year of the business was unsatisfactory, as the direct contact of the shrimp with the tin caused, during the process of cooking and thereafter, a precipitation of black or dark matter which discolored the shrimp and detracted from their flavor and richness, and the liquid in the shrimp constituted a medium for diffusing the coloring matter throughout the can, so that all the portions of the contents were equally affected and discolored.

The manifestly unappetizing results and the resulting public relations disaster forced the Dunbar firm to find a solution posthaste. Expedited research revealed that caustic chemicals residing in shrimp flesh—particularly sulfur—reacted to the cans' inner lining on direct contact. The Dunbars solved this issue by first interposing a cotton sack between the metal lining and the shellfish, amply filling the bag with crustaceans to prevent internal shifting, and then sealing the can without inserting a liquid filler. Upon achieving satisfactory results, the Dunbars applied for—and on June 20, 1876, received—Patent 178,916 for the processing innovation. (The patent was reissued on December 6, 1881).

Because of its unique design, the Dunbar can, which made possible the shipment of nondehydrated shrimp to distant markets,

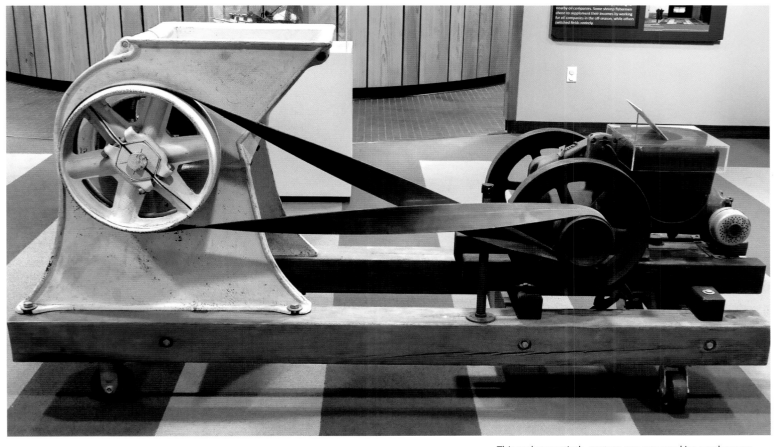

This early twentieth-century gas-powered ice crusher was used by the shrimping community along lower Bayou Teche. (From the collection of F. C. Felterman Jr., Patterson, LA.)

Because of the toll on footwear taken by ammonia and shrimp shells during "shrimp dances" aboard drying platforms, workers required a steady supply of heavy leather brogans. G. W. Dunbar, before he patented the seafood canning process, sold such shoes to many individuals in the shrimp and oyster industry. (Advertisement from A. Mygatt and Company 42.)

The steam kettle and retort were critically important to the canning process. (Photo from the authors' collections. Courtesy of the Maritime and Seafood Industry Museum, Biloxi, MS, 2019.)

STEAM KETTLE

These devices were used for steaming cans of shrimp. Baskets filled with packed cans were lowered into the approximately eight foot deep cooker which had been sunken into the floor. The lid was then secured, and steam under pressure was injected into the unit. Following the cooking process, the cans were taken to a labeling machine where the brand name was applied. The steaming process may be viewed in the images accompanying the exhibit.

Museum placard explaining the function of the steam kettle and retort. (Photo from the authors' collections. Courtesy of the Maritime and Seafood Industry Museum, Biloxi, MS, 2019.)

The Story of Shrimp

by Leonora Decuers
National Shrimp Canners and Packers Ass'n.

THE heart of shrimp land is in the South where shrimp abound in the coastal waters of the Gulf and up into the lakes and bays off the coast. For, from the waters in and around Louisiana, as well as from the waters of other Gulf and the South Atlantic states, come most of the shrimp now marketed throughout the entire world. California and Alaska contribute some shrimp to our total national production, but only locally consumed quantities are produced by other states.

There are several varieties of shrimp found in waters of all of the coastal states from Maine to Texas and from California to Alaska.

Those species which occur in sufficient quantities and of sufficient size to be commercially important in the South Atlantic and Gulf States are the common shrimp, the grooved shrimp and the sea-bob. Of the above, the common shrimp, scientifically known as a "Panaeus setiferus," constitutes about 90% of the total catch. All of the canned shrimp is of this species.

Ranking as the third largest fishing industry, the shrimp fishery has become so valuable to the Southern States, it was deemed necessary to have as much scientific information about shrimp as possible, in order to be able to know how to make the fullest use of this fishery without endangering the supply for future years. Therefore, the United States Bureau of Fisheries in cooperation with the states of Texas, Louisiana and Georgia conducted scientific investigations of shrimp and find that the shrimp lays its eggs during April, May and June in the waters of the Gulf or Ocean.

Estimates indicate that a shrimp may lay half a million eggs during the season. Instead of caring for the eggs as the crab and crayfish do, the parent shrimp deposit the eggs directly into the water where they drift with the tides and currents. The eggs hatch in a few days into tiny creatures that do not look at all like the parent shrimp, but have the appearance of tiny ticks. In a few days these tiny creatures have grown to a size of about a

quarter-inch and begin to move into the shallow waters of the bays and bayous. The inshore waters are the nursing grounds for the shrimp. They grow rapidly, and as they grow tend to seek larger bodies of water, eventually reaching the waters of the Gulf and my mid-summer attain sufficient size (about four inches) to appear in the commercial catch. By the end of September the young shrimp dominate the catch of the entire fishery. Because of this, there is a constant differentiation in the (Please turn to page 44)

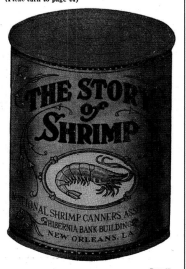

Editorial note: To the practical shrimp man this story of course is elementary; but to inland retailers, restaurant men and even some wholesalers, the information should be enlightening and of practical value in selling shrimp—because it gives something of the background of this most popular of all seafoods.

August 1949

Page 17

This article showcases the pivotal importance of canning to the shrimp industry. (Decuers, *Story of Shrimp*.)

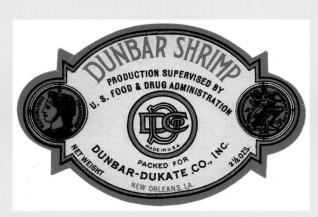

Rare glass container label. (From the authors' collections, date unknown.)

Public demand for canned seafood quickly transformed the marketing strategy of the shrimp industry. (Photo from the authors' collections, date unknown.)

Founded in 1872, Walle & Company's original headquarters building was repurposed after the firm's operations were moved to Roswell, Georgia. In 2019, the Chicago-based Fort Dearborn company acquired the company and closed the Harahan factory, ending the firm's 147-year history in Louisiana. (Photo from the authors' collections, 2015.)

Pioneering canners were quick to realize the value of attractive and distinctive label designs, which helped distinguish their products from those of competitors in an increasingly crowded and competitive market. Upper Gulf Coast canners typically turned to Walle & Company of New Orleans for labels with panache—attractive designs featuring bold colors and striking artwork capable of drawing consumers' eyes to otherwise unremarkable uniform cans crammed onto cluttered grocery store shelves. Over the course of its long existence (1872–2019), the Walle corporation produced some of the nation's best commercial artwork, particularly during the golden age of shrimp canning (ca. 1870–ca. 1930).

Distinctive and appealing commercial artwork, typography, coloring, and messaging is crucial to establishment of any brand's identity, and in the canning industry, a label's overall design functions as a manufacturer's de facto public face. Brand loyalist is most important to corporate survival, for conventional wisdom dictates it is far easier to retain an existing customer base than it is to recruit new customers. Advertisers have long recognized that Walle seafood labels—like most of their contemporary counterparts—consisted of several tightly integrated components: a graphical corporate logo, supplementary promotional language, and trademarked slogans, such as "packed in fresh artesian well water," "fresh from the Gulf," and "packed expressly for fine trade." Finally, early labels identified the cannery's handling process (i.e., wet or dry pack). Before 1918, coastal Louisiana canneries paired these standard design elements with a prominent reference to Barataria, the generic brand contemporary American consumers perceived as the de facto national gold standard, whether or not the manufacturers had a legitimate legal claim to the geographical term.

The Dunbars, who established and popularized the Barataria geographical brand, responded to the attempted co-optation of their famous trademark by vigorously prosecuting copycat product lines and by recruiting the federal government to uphold their exclusive claim to the Barataria name. In a landmark decision, the United States Department of Agriculture ruled in 1918 that under the terms of regulation 19 of the federal Pure Food and Drugs Act of 1906, the term "Barataria" could be applied exclusively to processed shellfish actually caught in the bay. In addition, the Department of Agriculture issued an advisory to American canners, directing them to cease and desist from mislabeling their product lines. The geographic guidelines established by such landmark rulings continue to resonate not only in the American seafood industry but also throughout the modern industrialized world.

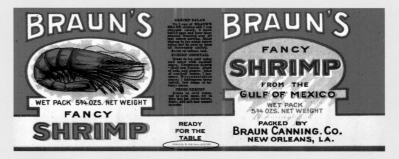

In very small print, note the Walle & Company name below "Ready for the Table." (Label from the Louisiana Historical Center, Louisiana State Museum, date unknown.)

A rare surviving Sancho Panza brand label, targeting the Latin American market. (Label courtesy of Chris Cenac, Houma, LA, date unknown.)

L. C. May, along with Southern Shell Fish and others, packed for the Spanish-speaking market, and their label's design has cultural overtones. (Label from the Chris Cenac collection, Houma, LA.)

Boldly colored images and clear, concise yet informative slogans were universal characteristics of the seafood canning industry labels. (Label from the Louisiana Historical Center, Louisiana State Museum, date unknown.)

ILLINOIS CENTRAL RAILROAD

THE GREAT THROUGH LINE

From the Lakes to the Gulf

IT IS THE SHORTEST ROUTE,
IT IS THE QUICKEST ROUTE,
IT IS THE BEST ROUTE,

AND IN FACT IT IS

THE ONLY DIRECT ROUTE

—— BETWEEN ——

CHICAGO and NEW ORLEANS,

PASSING THROUGH THE VERY HEART OF THE

Long Leaf Pine District of Mississippi

—— AND ——

THE GREAT SOUTHERN LUMBER BELT

OF TENNESSEE, MISSISSIPPI AND LOUISIANA.

Solid Vestibuled Trains of Baggage Cars, Elegant Day Coaches, and Pullman Buffet Sleepers run through between Chicago and New Orleans, without change, in 20 hours.

☞ For information regarding LUMBER MILLS AND DEALERS located on the line of the ILLINOIS CENTRAL RAILROAD, and for Freight and Passenger Rates, apply to the undersigned

T. K. EDWARDS,
Lumber Agent I. C. R. R.,
194 Clark St., Chicago.

F. B. BOWES,
Gen. N. Pass. Agt. I. C. R. R.,
194 Clark St., Chicago.

J. T. HARAHAN, 2d Vice-President.
HORACE TUCKER, Gen. Frt. Agent Northern and Western Lines, CHICAGO, ILL.

T. J. HUDSON, Traffic Manager.
D. D. MOREY, Gen. Frt. Agent Southern Lines, NEW ORLEANS, LA.

M. C. MARKHAM, Asst. Traffic Mgr.
A. H. HANSON, Gen. Pass. Agent, CHICAGO, ILL.

10

The nation's great rail trunk lines—such as the Illinois Central Railroad—permitted the fast and efficient distribution of Louisiana canned shrimp to inland consumer markets. (Advertisement from the authors' collection, ca. 1910.)

required multiple pre- and postproduction processes: workers first deheaded and peeled freshly caught shrimp, a tedious, time-consuming, and painful process, before moving the flesh to brining vats, where the tails sat for approximately an hour. Laborers then transferred the flesh to boiling kettles, from whence the shrimp moved to "drippers," in which they were thoroughly purged in cool water before moving to the cannery's production line. Once the cans' sacks were filled, workers closed and secured the bags, hand soldered the metal lids in place, and then moved the containers to finishing kettles, where the cans sat in boiling water for two hours. When the sanitation process was finished, cannery employees attached labels, the company's principal marketing tool, by hand and packed the finished cans in wooden boxes that were manufactured on site—forty-eight cans to the box. By the early 1900s, the state's shrimp canners shipped five hundred thousand boxes of canned produced by rail to a national network of jobbers and wholesalers who maintained contact with their suppliers through the then ubiquitous Western Union telegraph system. These procedures, which remained hallmarks of the manufacturing process, gradually evolved over time as new mechanical refinements and technological innovations were incorporated into the manufacturing process.

This newly patented preservation process virtually assured the Dunbar company of economic success, with a near monopoly on the shrimp canning business. The New Orleans–based operation quickly emerged as a national canning powerhouse, becoming, by 1888, the "largest establishment of the kind south of Baltimore," according to a leading national observer of the industrializing "New South." The Dunbar company's signature product—canned Barataria brand shrimp—was a runaway international success, primarily because the processed crustaceans were "the one tinned fish, whose flavor [was] little affected by the tinning process." By 1890, the brand appeared prominently in newspaper advertisements in Dallas, Texas; Honolulu, Hawaii; Lancaster, Pennsylvania; Memphis, Tennessee; Missoula, Montana; Mower County, Minnesota; San Francisco, California; and scores of other American municipalities. A decade later, Barataria shrimp cans were ubiquitous grocery shelf staples coast to coast.

MINE OYSTER—THE BATH.

A laborer sanitizing cans for processing. (Lithograph from *Harper's Weekly*, March 16, 1872.)

Soldering was the standard initial means of sealing cans, and lead poisoning was an ever-present danger to consumers. (Lithograph from *Harper's Weekly*, March 16, 1872.)

Newspaper Advertisements for Barataria Shrimp

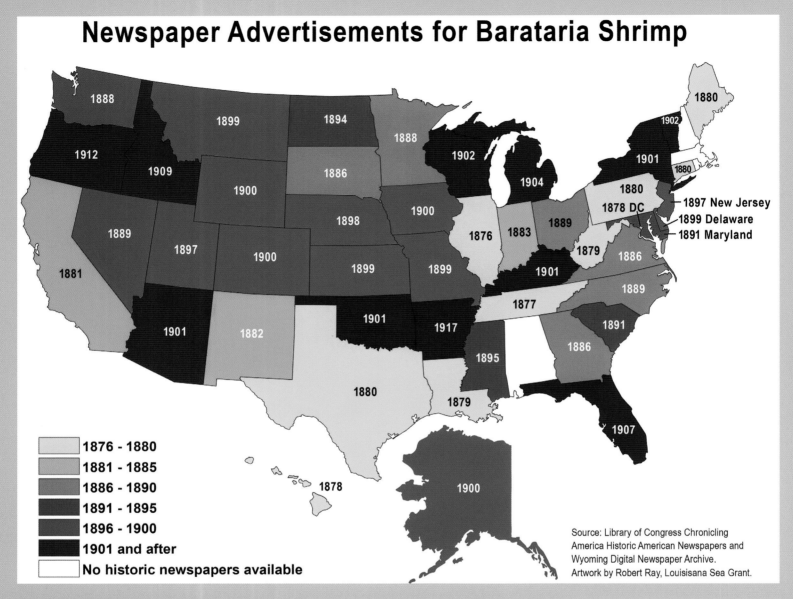

Legend:
- 1876 - 1880
- 1881 - 1885
- 1886 - 1890
- 1891 - 1895
- 1896 - 1900
- 1901 and after
- No historic newspapers available

Source: Library of Congress Chronicling America Historic American Newspapers and Wyoming Digital Newspaper Archive.
Artwork by Robert Ray, Louisisana Sea Grant.

This map illustrates the dates when Louisiana shrimp products first appeared in newspaper advertising. Note that the seafood industry successfully marketed its products nationally well before W. K. Kellogg began his aggressive "Toasted Corn Flakes" advertising campaign in 1907.

Barataria Shrimp Advertisement.
Rio de Janeiro Rio News, April 11, 1899

VICTORIA STORE

ESTABLISHED 1882

BERNARDINO TEIXEIRA & Co.

(SUCCESSORS TO ALVES NOGUEIRA & CO.)

Refrigerator goods, as fish, game, fresh butter, and cheese, fresh supplies every fortnight.

Sole-Agents for the celebrated Mineral Tablewater "Crystal."

Importers of finest Danish butter from T. & S. Plum and Heyman, Copenhagen.

Fresh Barataria shrimp, lobsters and salmon, Hungarian flour, oatmeal, bluepeas, evaporated apples and apricots and dried herbs, just arrived.

RUA DO OUVIDOR 46 and 48

Wine and Provision Merchants, Grocers and General Dealers.

(Label from the Louisiana Historical Center, Louisiana State Museum, date unknown.)

(Label from the Louisiana Historical Center, Louisiana State Museum, date unknown.)

(Label from the Louisiana Historical Center, Louisiana State Museum, date unknown.)

(Label from the Louisiana Historical Center, Louisiana State Museum, date unknown.)

(Label from the Louisiana Historical Center, Louisiana State Museum, date unknown.)

Dunbar's Pride label. (Label from the authors' collections, date unknown.)

Red Bird label. (Photo from the authors' collections. Can courtesy of Chris Cenac Collection, 2018.)

SHRIMPS

50 cases Barataria Fresh Shrimps,
100 tierces Magnolia Hams, best at 8½c,
25 boxes thin Breakfast Bacon,
50 half-barrels New Roe Herring,
5 tubs New Creamery Butter.

Oliver. Finnie & Co.

Throughout the late nineteenth century, America's leading grocers consistently and prominently featured promotional listings for Dunbar or Barataria shrimp. (Advertisement from *Memphis Public Ledger*, December 22, 1877.)

G. W. DUNBAR'S SONS,
NEW ORLEANS, La., U. S. A.,
The Original Packers of Fresh
BARATARIA SHRIMP,
IN LINED CANS,
—Have Obtained a—
SILVER MEDAL,
The only Award for Shrimp granted by the
INTERNATIONAL FISHERIES EXHIBITION,
At London, England.

(Advertisement in the San Francisco, CA *Call*, May 25, 1896.)

Dunbars, Lopez & Dukate
Company.
New Orleans La.
Largest Packers in the world of
High-Grade Canned Goods, Oysters
Shrimp, Okra and Figs.
Our Goods Sold by Wholesale Grocers the World Over.
1-27-16

(Advertisement in the New Orleans, LA *Herald*, December 16, 1915.)

THE MOHICAN COMPANY

WEDNESDAY and THURSDAY

POT ROAST All Lean - lb. 10c	SMALL FAMILY HAMS - - - lb. 16c	
1 lb. LIVER / ½ lb. BACON } - 15c	S. RLOIN STEAK - - lb. 16c	SHOULDER STEAK lb. 11c / ROUND STEAK - lb. 15c

FINE TABLE BUTTER - lb. 25c

Bermuda Onions qt. 6c	Fancy Lemons doz. 20c	Good Pineapples each 9c
New Cabbage - lb. 3c	Firm, Clean Dates lb. 8c	Sweet Oranges doz. 30c

Two Hour Sale Wednesday, 4 to 6 o'clock	Libby's Potted Meats - - can 5c, 8c
	Veal Loaf - - - - - - can 9c
Best Lamb Chops lb. 16c	Corned Beef - - - - can 14c-24c
Potatoes - - 4 qts. 15c	Roast Beef - - - - can 14c-24c
¼ lb. COCOANUT - - - - - - } - 9c 1 lb. CONFECTIONERY SUGAR }	Lunch Tongue - - - - can 25c
	Barataria Shrimp - - - can 11c

(Advertisement in Norwich, CT *Bulletin*, June 30, 1909.)

FOR SALE !
—BY—
E. P. Adams
QUEEN STREET,
FRESH GROCERIES
Received by every Steamer.

WHITTAKER'S STAR HAMS AND BACON.
Roast Beef, Roast Mutton,
Compressed Corned Beef,

Spiced Pigs' Feet !
IN TINS,

Baked Pork and Beans, in tins,
Green Peas,

YARMOUTH GREEN CORN,
Baltimore Succotash,
Fresh Salmon, 1 and 2 lb tins,
McMurray's Oysters, 1 and 2 lb tins,
Fresh Lobsters, Fresh Clams,
Fresh Barataria Shrimps,

GOLDEN GATE TABLE FRUIT,

(Advertisement in Honolulu, HI *Pacific Commercial Advertiser*, 1878.)

(Advertisement in the Portland, ME *Portland Daily Press*, July 9, 1880.)

(Advertisement in the Barre, VT *Daily Times*, November 30, 1904.)

(Advertisement in the Grangeville, ID Territory *Idaho County Free Press*, February 24, 1909.)

(Advertisement in Vinita, Indian Territory OK *Daily Chieftain*, March 8, 1901.)

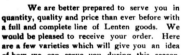

Freight forwarding services were critically important to the shrimp distribution process. (Card advertisement from the Blum and Bergeron Collection, Nicholls State University Archives, Thibodaux, LA, date unknown.)

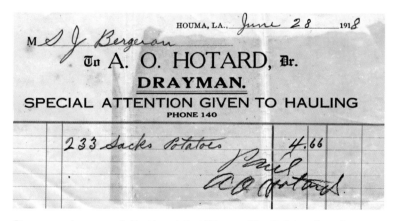

Drayage services were vital but largely invisible amenities. Bulk transfers of products from processing plants to overland shipping facilities, particularly rail terminals, required trained ground freight crews and sturdy vehicles. The shrimp industry initially relied on wagons, which were quickly supplanted by trucks in the early twentieth century. (Document provided by Thomas "Tommy" Chauvin, president of Chauvin Brothers Inc., Chauvin, LA, 1918.)

Luggers were flexible vessels, used on a seasonal basis as operators transitioned from shrimp to oyster harvesting and back again. This photo shows a lugger flotilla gathered in a canal, awaiting an opportunity to discharge their cargoes at a small canning factory at Murphy, near Jeanerette. (From Tulane University's Howard Tilton Memorial Library, photographer and date unknown.)

Queen of the South label. (From the authors' collections.)

The Dunbar company also enjoyed significant, albeit less spectacular, success in Europe. To penetrate this lucrative Old World market, the Dunbars entered their flagship product in international trade expositions and culinary competitions. "Their specialty is fresh Barataria shrimp, from the Mexican Gulf, sufficiently cooked for salads, mayonaise [*sic*], and all cold dishes, and ready for the table. This preparation was awarded the silver medal of merit at the Paris Exposition of 1878, and also at the International Fisheries Exhibition London 1883. Encouraged by their successes abroad, the house is making a grand display of its prime goods at the present [New Orleans] World's Fair, and will compete for the honors of award for general superiority" (Morrison, *Industries of New Orleans* 89). By 1890, the Dunbar cannery shipped "large quantities" of Barataria shrimp to "England and France," most of the existing American states, and many of the nation's territories. By the turn of the twentieth century, the Dunbar company had become the poster child of mass-marketing success in the American seafood industry.

The Dunbar cannery's international accolades and its attendant marketing success engendered a host of imitators. In 1879, the Pecor Brothers Company established a small, short-lived Galveston cannery in which processed shrimp were isolated from can walls by layers of paper and paraffin wax. The following year, W. M. Gorenflo and Company established a cannery at Biloxi. In 1884, Mississippi entrepreneurs established three additional major seafood processing and canning facilities. Within a decade, the Mississippi coastal community became New Orleans's principal competitor in the shrimp canning industry. In fact, the Biloxi canneries became such a strategic threat that the Dunbars felt compelled to become major investors in the Mississippi coastal community's burgeoning industrial infrastructure by 1885. These corporate marriages of convenience created an unparalleled pool of talent, experience, and capital in the American shrimp industry that quickly propelled the New Orleans–Biloxi partnerships into the limelight as the country's leading sources of canned seafood, particularly shrimp.

The exponential growth of the regional shrimp cannery industry's processing capacity fueled a corresponding expansion in

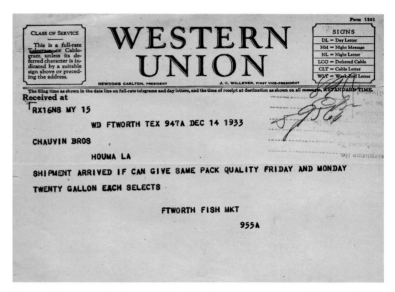

Telegraphic communications permitted Louisiana processors to cultivate, monitor, and sustain business contacts with wholesalers and retailers in major inland consumer markets. (Telegram provided by Thomas "Tommy" Chauvin, president of Chauvin Brothers Inc., Chauvin, LA, 1933.)

In 1918, the United States Department of Agriculture issued a circular banning usage of the term *Barataria shrimp* on can labels unless the enclosed crustaceans were actually caught in Barataria Bay. (Label from the Louisiana Historical Center, Louisiana State Museum, date unknown.)

C. ROYAL,
SAILMAKER, TENTS, AWNINGS, TARPAULINS, FLAGS.
Fall and Purchase Ropes fitted, furnished, and repaired.
Blocks of all sizes ready stropped. Sail and Rigging Work in all its branches.
NO. 3 POYDRAS ST., NEW ORLEANS.

Tarpaulins were essential to the dried shrimp industry, for dehydrating decapods had to be covered with these waterproof canvases whenever rain threatened to drench a platform. (Advertisement from A. Mygatt and Company 56.)

WILLIAM SMITH,
RIGGER,
Office and Loft, No. 4 Marigny Building,
THIRD DISTRICT, NEW ORLEANS.
Sail Bending, Rigging, &c. promptly attended to on reasonable terms.

The shrimp industry's demand for sailmakers declined precipitously following the widespread adoption of gasoline-powered engines after World War I. (Advertisement from A. Mygatt and Company 40.)

commercial output. In 1880, the Dunbar facility produced 351,000 pounds of processed Barataria shrimp; seven years later, canneries in the New Orleans–Biloxi industrial nexus shipped 1,395,168 pounds of seine-caught shrimp, delivered to the factories by sailing luggers, a few feluccas, ice boats, and perhaps a couple crude steam-powered vessels. The number of shrimp canneries continued to rise over the following decades as new technological developments made the Dunbar canning patent irrelevant. In the late 1880s, for example, A. Booth & Company of Chicago established a short-lived shrimp cannery at Morgan City, Louisiana—the first Louisiana processing facility outside New Orleans that was not barge-mounted. By the late 1920s, the Pelican State boasted twenty-eight shrimp canneries scattered across the southeastern coastal parishes.

As the canning industry grew and matured, its technological capabilities became increasingly sophisticated. According to G. B. Goode's 1887 report on the American fisheries for the federal government, "the entire business [was] conducted under a single roof, even to the making of the tin boxes [cans] and the solder." The manual production of individual cans was not only extremely time- and labor-intensive, but it was also unhygienic and environmentally hazardous. The lead solder used in can manufacturing was particularly problematic, for it exposed both cannery workers and consumers to the real threat of lead poisoning.

The resulting health concerns gave impetus to a revolution in can manufacturing that immediately impacted fresh shrimp canners.

In the late nineteenth century, European inventors developed the open-top can still widely used in commercial canning. In 1888, Max Ams of New York devised the double seam can, which featured a reinforced seam on the can cylinder, which not only prevented ruptures resulting from a build-up of internal pressure, but also did away with the need for lead solder. In 1896, Ams patented a process for sealing cans with double-crimp lids made completely airtight by gum and rubber gaskets. The following year, the Ams Machine Company introduced machinery capable of mass-producing cans featuring the inventor's innovations.

Advances in basic tin can design coincided with a dramatic increase in canneries' abilities to manufacture cans onsite. Between 1870 and 1900, the number of American canneries increased by 1,800 percent as entrepreneurs scrambled to satiate the skyrocketing popular demand for canned goods. However, even the most successful Gilded Age (ca. 1870–ca. 1900) cannery operations could not keep pace with the surging demand for canned products, for, using existing hand-assembly and hand-soldering methods, a skilled craftsman typically produced only ten cans per day. In 1887, Dunbar's entire workforce manufactured approximately 234,000 1.5-pound cans per season. Therefore, even a small army of seasoned artisans could not meet the challenge of processing Louisiana's annual shrimp harvest, which had ballooned to 12,565,415 pounds by 1902 through the deployment of numerous seine crews in shallow coastal waters.

As a result, United States inventors scrambled to resolve the canning industry's dilemma. Edwin O. Norton of Chicago, perhaps the most successful of these innovators, secured a patent on a side-soldering machinery capable of manufacturing and sealing 2,500 cans per hour. In 1901, the Norton Tin Can and Plate Company merged with sixty smaller competitors to form the American Can Company (ACC) under the direction of Daniel Reid and William Leeds. At its zenith, the American Can Company, part of the so-called Tin-Can Trust, systematically acquired can-making companies and controlled roughly 90 percent of the nation's tin-can manufacturing capacity, but its intimidating monopolistic policies and practices quickly proved to be its undoing. In creating the American Can Company,

In the early twentieth century, various journalists created and perpetuated a long-enduring myth about the origins of Louisiana's Filipino community centering around the establishment of Manila Village, the most widely known of the coastal plain's historic shrimp-drying operations. An unidentified contributor to *Bataan Magazine*, for example, asserted in 1943 that Filipinos came to America in 1710 and established a settlement "not far from New Orleans . . . known as Manila Village." Other writers have conflated the establishment of a short-lived, late-1770's Isleño (i.e., Canary Islander) settlement in the Barataria region with the founding of the drying platform a century later. This misconception has endured to the present; twenty-first century authors, in book-length publications released in 2006 and 2015, falsely asserted that Manila Village was established respectively in 1763 and 1750. These oft-repeated claims fly in the face of extensive colonial and antebellum documentation clearly indicating that Manila Village was not a vestigial remnant of an isolated eighteenth-century community founded by errant Filipino seamen.

Six years after the Dunbar family launched their New Orleans–based canning operation, Lazaro Lopez, William Elmer, W. K. M. Dukate, William Gorenflo, and James Maycock founded the first seafood cannery on the Mississippi Gulf Coast. This factory, which employed nearly ninety individuals and operated fifteen boats, existed until 1884. In 1882, the Dunbars established the Barataria Canning Company, and following dissolution of Lopez, Elmer and Company, the New Orleans entrepreneurs partnered with Lopez to create a new corporation entitled Lopez, Dunbar's Sons and Company. This firm served as the crucial organizational link between the Dunbars' New Orleans operation and Biloxi's emerging seafood processing infrastructure.

The Wonderful Story of the Tin Can

IF the tin can has been to you a common thing of commonplace service, think that way of it no longer. Think of the tin can for what it *really* is—a wonder of the times. Think of it as a monument to patient achievement in our personal interests.

What a tale it could tell! A tale to compel our respect and whet our appetites.

Once this tin can lay inert in the Earth in its original elements—had lain there since Time began—awaiting the hand of man that should bring it forth, make the metal, give it shape and crown it with great usefulness.

And while it thus lay, awaiting its destiny there likewise lay those other ingredients, from which Nature herself should bring forth the products of garden, orchard and field, so wonderfully nourishing and delicious.

You Get Choice Foods Because of It

What a stimulus to imagination! What a tribute could be written to what Earth holds in trust for her people! How she holds in one hand the secret of the peach, the pineapple, the succulent vegetable! How she holds in the other the no less wonderful secret of the means that shall carry her bounty to any table—anywhere—any time of the year.

Today, all these ingredients lie dormant together. Tomorrow, rising from the earth they meet again, each to triumph in "the miracle on your table."

The Needs of Your Own Table Developed It

But Nature's triumph means man's triumph also. The tin can of commerce was not born in a day nor without great industrial travail.

The can making industry in America parallels that of food-canning itself. In the beginning, each canner made his own cans, and a workman in those days could make by hand 150 per day.

Today, production of more than Six Billion cans annually for the canned food output of America is significant of the development of the tin can industry, and of the canned food industry, as well, which makes all these millions upon millions of cans necessary. The imagination is staggered by it. Expressed in terms of tables supplied, and of individuals served, it is almost beyond belief.

Science Stands Back of It

The "tin" can is a steel can, coated with tin. It is a product of science, of scientific research by hundreds of specialists who have studied every step of evolution beginning with analysis of the steel itself.

Extraordinary Care Has Surrounded It

For example, over a period of years, picked men from the laboratories of four great organizations united in the common effort of developing the tin container. These were the laboratories of steel manufacturers, tin plate manufacturers, can manufacturers, and the National Canners Association. Special "heats" of steel were experimented with, foods packed in the cans produced from the steel, and the results recorded with scientific accuracy. The thickness of the tin coating became a matter of scientific determination. Methods of sealing and imperviousness of joints are subjects of closest scientific scrutiny.

Respect the Tin Can

As the tin can stands on your grocer's shelves or on the shelves of your own pantry, this highly specialized little object claims your respect. The tin can unquestionably is the safest, most practicable and scientific food container that human skill and ingenuity have been able to devise for the benefit of mankind.

National Canners Association
WASHINGTON, D.C.

A nation-wide organization formed in 1907, consisting of producers of all varieties of hermetically sealed canned foods which have been sterilized by heat. It neither produces, buys, nor sells. Its purpose is to assure, for the mutual benefit of the industry and the public, the best canned foods that scientific knowledge and human skill can produce.

The Miracle on Your Table

By the second decade of the twentieth century, the National Canners Association was investing in full-page print media advertisements extolling the virtues of food packaged in tin cans. (Advertisement from *Evening Public Ledger*, January 10, 1920, 5.)

The American Can Company's New Orleans factory, near the banks of Bayou St. John, brought revolutionary canning technology to the Crescent City in 1905. At this time, the local oyster industry alone was annually shipping thirty million processed cans to consumers. (Photo from the authors' collections, 2011.)

(Lithograph from Antique Advertising Auctions, 2020.)

Reid and Leeds attempted to impose an anticompetitive agreement on the junior partners. Norton balked and, in 1904, he and his sons launched the Continental Can Company (CCC) in direct competition with the canning behemoth. Using patented manufacturing processes from the United Machinery Company, CCC established a New Orleans cannery in 1905, shortly after ACC's new, four-story Crescent City facility opened its doors along Bayou St. John.

These new-line companies brought an entirely new business model to the Gulf Coast seafood canning industry. In addition to operating their own major canneries, which produced approximately two-thirds of the ten million cans manufactured annually

"Shrimp are put up in what are known as dry and wet packs. In the dry pack no liquor is added, while in the wet pack brine is used. The process for dry shrimp is 1 hour at 240° F. or 4 hours at 212° F. for No. 1 cans, and 75 minutes at 240° F. and 4 hours at 212° F. for No. 1½ cans. The process for wet shrimp is 11 minutes for No. 1 and 12 minutes at 240° F. for No. 1½ cans.

The fill of 4½ and 9 ounces in the No. 1 and No. 1½ cans has the appearance of being light weight or slack filled. Experience has shown, however, that close filling causes matting of the shrimp and an unsightly appearance. The wet-packed shrimp are preferred by those who are familiar with the fresh article. They have better texture, odor, and taste than the dry packed. A barrel of good shrimp will pack 190 No. 1 cans or 100 cans of No. 1½.

Formerly shrimp were put up in bulk with a preservative. These were headless (only the head and thorax removed, the shell left on), and since that method of preservation is no longer approved, very few shrimp are obtained upon the market other than canned. Some pickled headless shrimp are put up in 1 to 5 gallon cans for hotels. These are boiled in strong brine for several minutes and put up in a saturated salt solution. They keep, but are very salty, and as it takes a long time to freshen them they are not available for immediate use" (Bitting, *Canning of Foods*).

Crushed ice being loaded into a trawler with the cabin aft. This class of vessel is identified as a Biloxi-type boat, known regionally as a *Biloxien*. (Photo from Standard Oil (NJ) Collection, Photographic Archives, Archives and Special Collections, University of Louisville, photographer Russell Lee, 1950, negative no. 67353.)

The New Orleans Cold Storage and Warehouse Company, established in 1886, provided ice for railcars, sailing ships, and refrigerated containers. Still in operation, this Crescent City firm is the oldest cold storage company in North America. (From the New Orleans Chamber of Commerce, retrieved March 11, 2021.)

Two trawlers docked at an unidentified picking shed. (Photo from the Standard Oil Collection, University of Louisville, photographer Russell Lee, 1950, negative number 67491.)

Between 1935 and 1950, the stereotypical shrimp boat evolved into its current design. (Photo courtesy of the National Archives and Records Administration, Prints & Photographs Division, College Park, MD, photographer Ben Shahn, 1935, call number LC-USF33–002053-M5, a0713OU.)

Shrimpers preparing to transfer large blocks of ice to their vessels. These transfers were arduous and dangerous, for the massive blocks, weighing up to five hundred pounds, could easily puncture wooden hulls if mishandled. (Photo courtesy of the National Archives and Records Administration, Prints & Photographs Division, College Park, MD, photographer Russell Lee, 1938, call number LC-USF33–011853-M1, LC-DIG-fsa-8a24625a.)

Louisiana Canning Plants Through Time

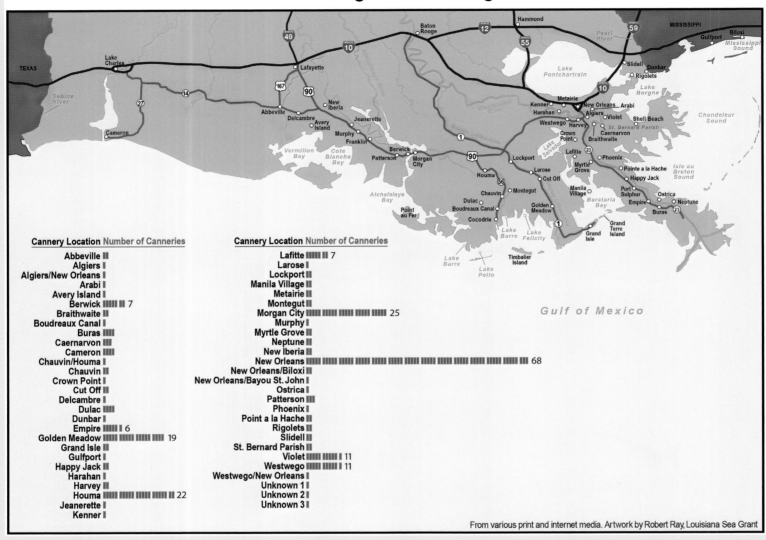

Cannery Location	Number of Canneries
Abbeville	▮▮▮
Algiers	▮
Algiers/New Orleans	▮
Arabi	▮
Avery Island	▮
Berwick	▮▮▮▮▮ 7
Braithwaite	▮▮
Boudreaux Canal	▮
Buras	▮
Caernarvon	▮▮▮
Cameron	▮▮▮▮
Chauvin/Houma	▮
Chauvin	▮▮
Crown Point	▮
Cut Off	▮
Delcambre	▮
Dulac	▮▮▮▮
Dunbar	▮
Empire	▮▮▮▮▮ 6
Golden Meadow	▮▮▮▮▮ ▮▮▮▮▮ ▮▮▮▮ 19
Grand Isle	▮▮
Gulfport	▮
Happy Jack	▮▮
Harahan	▮
Harvey	▮
Houma	▮▮▮▮▮ ▮▮▮▮▮ ▮▮▮▮▮ ▮▮ 22
Jeanerette	▮
Kenner	▮

Cannery Location	Number of Canneries
Lafitte	▮▮▮▮▮ 7
Larose	▮
Lockport	▮▮
Manila Village	▮▮
Metairie	▮
Montegut	▮
Morgan City	▮▮▮▮▮ ▮▮▮▮▮ ▮▮▮▮▮ ▮▮▮▮▮ ▮▮▮▮▮ 25
Murphy	▮
Myrtle Grove	▮
Neptune	▮
New Iberia	▮
New Orleans	▮▮▮▮▮ ▮▮▮▮▮ ▮▮▮▮▮ ▮▮▮▮▮ ▮▮▮▮▮ ▮▮▮▮▮ ▮▮▮ 68
New Orleans/Biloxi	▮
New Orleans/Bayou St. John	▮
Ostrica	▮
Patterson	▮▮▮
Phoenix	▮
Point a la Hache	▮▮
Rigolets	▮
Slidell	▮▮
St. Bernard Parish	▮▮
Violet	▮▮▮▮▮ ▮▮▮▮▮ 11
Westwego	▮▮▮▮▮ ▮▮▮▮▮ 11
Westwego/New Orleans	▮
Unknown 1	▮
Unknown 2	▮
Unknown 3	▮

Gulf of Mexico

From various print and internet media. Artwork by Robert Ray, Louisiana Sea Grant

Two hundred and fifty-eight Louisiana seafood canneries have been documented. The state's last surviving shrimp canner, Bumble Bee, closed after Hurricane Katrina (2005).

(Label from the Louisiana Historical Center, Louisiana State Museum, date unknown.)

(Label from the Louisiana Historical Center, Louisiana State Museum, date unknown.)

(Label from the Louisiana Historical Center, Louisiana State Museum, date unknown.)

(Label from the Louisiana Historical Center, Louisiana State Museum, date unknown.)

(Label from the Louisiana Historical Center, Louisiana State Museum, date unknown.)

(Label from the Louisiana Historical Center, Louisiana State Museum, date unknown.)

(Label from the Louisiana Historical Center, Louisiana State Museum, date unknown.)

(Label from the Louisiana Historical Center, Louisiana State Museum, date unknown.)

(Label from the authors' collections, date unknown.)

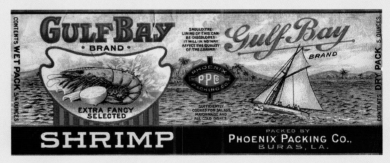

(Label from the Louisiana Historical Center, Louisiana State Museum, date unknown.)

(Label from the Louisiana Historical Center, Louisiana State Museum, date unknown.)

(Label from the Louisiana Historical Center, Louisiana State Museum, date unknown.)

The Dunbar line dominated the American canned shrimp industry for decades. (Image from the Smithsonian National Museum of American History, L. D. Leininger, accession number 1979.044.)

The former Dunbar cannery at 333 Chartres has been repurposed as the headquarters for Turn Services. (Photo from the authors' collections, 2014.)

in the United States during the early 1930s, the Continental and American Can Companies leased solderless canning equipment to small rural seafood processors lacking the financial wherewithal to underwrite even modest capital projects. This led directly to the proliferation of shrimp canneries in Louisiana's coastal parishes.

By the early 1930s, Louisiana had twenty-eight canneries that shipped "a little more than 400,000 cases." A comparison with other states suggests Louisiana packed nearly four times as much as any other seafood producing state. By 1932, the state's canning industry canned about 50,000,000 pounds of shrimp annually. Six years later, the catch had expanded to 76,368,000 pounds, due in part to the advent of deepwater shrimping at Morgan City. The unrelenting increase in fishery productivity placed ever-greater demands on the regional shrimp processing infrastructure.

Improved onsite can manufacturing technologies constituted the first wave of increased mechanization in the shrimp canneries. The introduction of Link-Belt conveyors in the factories would follow, as would municipal electrification and other innovations after the Second World War. Many coastal communities did not enjoy

WOOD USED IN THE CASES OF CANNED SHRIMP SHIPPED IN THE 1920S

Each wooden case used in the distribution of canned shrimp required 92 linear inches of an 8-inch-wide board. Between 1921 and 1930, 7,555,221 cases were shipped to consumers. The total wood required equaled 695,080,332 linear inches, or 10,970 miles of an 8-inch-wide board. This is about half the distance around the world at the Tropic of Cancer. The cases of canned oysters would add significantly to this ten-year total. American and Continental Can Companies added locations in Louisiana to meet the demand for cans.

RIGHT OFF THE OCEAN FLOOR

You are always glad to know of a delicious new food—something that you can serve economically in many different ways—something that will put a new zest in your daily bill-of-fare. Here it is—CANNED SHRIMP. This dainty, nutritious sea-food comes from the Gulf of Mexico and the Atlantic Ocean.

You know how delicious lobster is; you'll find the same rich flavor in canned shrimp, only more delicate. Shrimp are really like small lobster. The meat is firm and fine-flavored as a nut kernel; the delicate pink color is caused by boiling the shrimp just before they are packed in the cans.

Caught in nets on the clean ocean floor, the shrimp are shelled and the shrimp meats packed in sanitary cans in the big, clean packing houses right on the water's edge. Each can contains nothing but the selected meats.

CANNED Shrimp

For years shrimp have been the celebrated delicacy of Southern tables; the world-renowned French restaurants of New Orleans serve them as one of their choicest sea-foods.

Now you can have this famous delicacy right in your own home. Canned shrimp come to you boiled and practically ready for the table. They can be served in fifty different ways, for luncheon or dinner, or in the chafing dish for Sunday supper. Every first class grocer sells them.

Send a postal today for your free copy of "Fifty Southern Recipes for Serving Canned Shrimp." This unusual book contains the most famous Southern and French-Creole recipes for preparing shrimp. It is beautifully illustrated in color.

U. H. DUDLEY & CO., Distributors, Duane and Hudson Streets, *New York City*

Buy a can of shrimp today at your grocer's and try one of the recipes given below. There's no waste in a can of shrimp — an ideal food for the "meatless day."

BAKED SHRIMP

1 can shrimp   ¼ tablespoonful butter   3 tomatoes
¼ cup grated bread crumbs or crackers

Butter a dish well and place within it a layer of grated bread crumbs or powdered crackers. Stew the tomatoes in the butter, and sprinkle with pepper and salt. Place a layer of tomatoes in the dish and spread over it the grated crackers or bread. Wash the shrimp, season well; put a layer of shrimp in the dish. Repeat layers of tomatoes, crumbs and shrimp, ending with a layer of crumbs. Place small dabs of butter over the top. Bake till well browned.

SHRIMP AND SPAGHETTI

1 large can shrimp   1 pound spaghetti
1 finely chopped onion

Add spaghetti to a pan of boiling water containing salt; boil until cooked, but not soft, which will take about half an hour. Fry the shrimp in hot lard with the chopped onion; season lightly with salt and pepper. Spread the shrimp over the spaghetti, and decorate with long strings of spaghetti wound around.

JELLIED SHRIMP SALAD

1 large can shrimp
½ envelope gelatine
1½ cups clarified broth
1 tablespoonful lemon juice
1 tablespoonful capers
½ pint cooked peas   2 truffles

Pour the gelatine into ¼ cup cold water; let it soak for five minutes; dissolve it in hot broth (clam, chicken, fish or vegetable) and let it cool. Stand a mold in ice water; chop the truffles; pour into the mold the shrimp, truffles, lemon juice, peas and capers into the broth, and with this fill the mold. Garnish with lettuce, quartered lemons, and slices of hard boiled egg; or with lettuce and peas dressed with French dressing, omitting the peas from the mold.

A representative example of early twentieth-century print media advertisements that helped expand the canned shrimp market across the country. (From the *Saturday Evening Post* 190, no. 13 [September 29, 1917]: 43.)

TIN REQUIRED FOR THE CANS OF SHRIMP SHIPPED IN THE 1920S

The tin required per can is 8.5 inches. There were forty-eight cans in a case, or 408 linear inches of tin per case. In the period between 1921 and 1930, 7,555,221 cases were shipped to customers. The total tin required equated to 308,130,168 linear inches, or 4,863 miles of an 8-inch roll of tin. The top and bottom add about 1,000 miles to equal 5,863 miles. Canned oysters would add considerably to this ten-year total. American and Continental Can Companies added locations in Louisiana to meet the demand for cans.

Table 2.1
Cases of canned shrimp shipped in the United States between 1921 and 1930

1921	655,364
1922	579,797
1923	700,429
1924	718,517
1925	735,714
1926	732,365
1927	852,764
1928	851,831
1929	909,949
1930	818,491
Total cases with 48 cans/ case	7,555,221

An example of the various size cans used in the shrimp industry. (Photo compliments of Laitram Machinery, Kenner, LA, date unknown.)

CHILD-LABOR STANDARDS FOR THE NATION'S CHILDREN

No Child Under 16 Years of Age Should Leave School for Gainful Employment

To School

TO FULL-TIME WORK IN INDUSTRIALIZED AGRICULTURE

TO FULL-TIME WORK IN INDUSTRY AND COMMERCE

School Is Their Full-Time Job

A basic 16-year minimum age, applying to industrial work at any time and to agricultural work during periods of required school attendance, is the standard set by the child-labor provisions of the Fair Labor Standards Act, administered by the Children's Bureau, which apply to producers of goods for shipment in interstate commerce.

Children working for their parents in agriculture or other occupations except manufacturing and mining are exempt from these provisions.

U. S. DEPARTMENT OF LABOR
CHILDREN'S BUREAU

The horrific working conditions in northern Gulf Coast seafood processing factories gave impetus to the successful movement for child labor laws in the early twentieth century. (National Archives, Records of the Children's Bureau, US Department of Labor, Children's Bureau, 1941.)

Child labor protesters. (Photo from Ostrander, "Child Labor.")

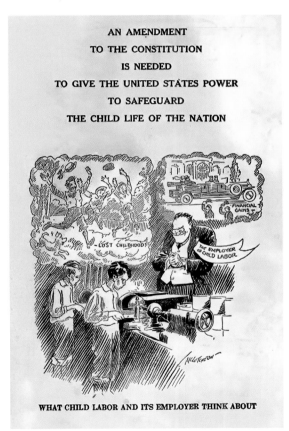

AN AMENDMENT TO THE CONSTITUTION IS NEEDED TO GIVE THE UNITED STATES POWER TO SAFEGUARD THE CHILD LIFE OF THE NATION

WHAT CHILD LABOR AND ITS EMPLOYER THINK ABOUT

Anti–child labor literature. (Poster courtesy of VCU Libraries Gallery, "An Amendment to the Constitution Is Needed to Give the United States Power to Safeguard the Child Life of the Nation," accessed September 12, 2020, https://gallery.library.vcu.edu/items/show/82555.)

electrical service until the late 1940s, and plants south of Houma, along lower Bayou Lafourche, in Cameron, and along the Mississippi River south of New Orleans consequently relied on steam power.

Like the canneries' power source, the vital process of cleaning, culling, and sorting raw shrimp—a grueling, labor-intensive process—remained fundamentally unchanged until the post–World War II era because the laborers' skills could not then be replicated by machines. Gulf Coast canneries relied exclusively on female and child laborers to process shrimp by hand. Barataria brand shrimp,

Two child laborers at a Gulf Coast seafood cannery. (Photo courtesy of the National Archives and Records Administration, Prints & Photographs Division, College Park, MD, photographer Lewis Hine, 1911, reproduction number LC-DIG-nclc-00907.)

This image by Lewis Hine, perhaps the most famous photo of child laborers in the seafood processing industry, helped thrust the child labor issue into America's public consciousness. (Photo courtesy of the National Archives and Records Administration, Prints & Photographs Division, College Park, MD, photographer Lewis Hine, 1911, reproduction number LC-USZ6–1306.)

A shrimp "picker's" bucket, used by Lou Anna Guidry in the mid-twentieth century. Pickers were paid according to the number of heaping buckets they produced over the course of a work shift. (Photo from the authors' collections, bucket courtesy of Roland and Lou Anna Guidry, 2019.)

Beginning in 1937, state and federal public health officials became increasingly involved in monitoring and policing the activities of Louisiana's shrimp processors. (From the collection of F. C. Felterman Jr., Patterson, LA.)

for example, was initially processed entirely in-house at Dunbar's New Orleans facility. During the early 1880s, the Dunbar cannery's shrimp production line reportedly employed approximately 165 individuals—25 men and 140 women and girls—during its five-month production cycle. Tasks were assigned by gender. Males made "cans and superintend[ed] the packing, while the [females] prepare[d] the meats by removing the shells and appendages after the shrimp [had] been boiled" (Goode, *Shrimp and Prawn Fisheries* 806). In the first decade of its operation, Dunbar employees were overwhelmingly local residents. This work regime was replicated in Biloxi canneries and ultimately in all factories associated with shrimp processing.

The promise of industrial employment initially proved attractive to the urban poor whose limited skills and circumscribed opportunities condemned them to a variety of unpalatable work options. This is particularly true of women, for whom prostitution was often the only gainful employment opportunity in Gilded Age New Orleans. Along the Mississippi coast, canneries evidently served as magnets for individuals fleeing the oppressiveness of rural tenantry.

Cannery wages were initially attractive. In 1889, the *New Orleans Item* reported that local Dunbar employees earned "a high wage": women, $2.50 a day; young women, $2.00–$2.50 a day; girls twelve to fifteen years of age, $1.50 a day. The factory manager informed the *Item* reporter that "vacancies seldom occur; when they do there are plenty of reserves to fall back upon." But attitudes quickly changed on both sides of the employment equation. The uncertainty of employment resulting from irregular shrimp boat dockings, the low wages offered by the canneries, and the grueling working conditions in the workplace quickly alienated the native New Orleans workforce. Similar circumstances existed in the Biloxi area, where, in 1890, canners complained to journalists that "the only trouble was they could not get labor enough," despite the rapid growth of the Mississippi community's population, which rose from 1,540 in 1880 to 3,234 in 1890. As a result, the canners resorted to brutal exploitation of transient seasonal contract workers in one of the most shameful chapters of America's labor history.

In 1881, William K. M. Dukate, a pioneer in the Biloxi canning industry, traveled to Baltimore to examine the operations of the city's then flourishing oyster canning companies. Although the focus of his fact-finding mission was production-line technology, his attention was quickly diverted to the Maryland facilities' exploitation of cheap, controllable, and obedient seasonal laborers—overwhelmingly Polish and Eastern European immigrants collectively known as "Bohemians." News of Dukate's discovery quickly diffused among upper Gulf Coast cannery operators faced with static, "expensive" local labor pools. Most factories soon began experimenting with Bohemian laborers, first on a small experimental basis, and, by the 1890s, on a surprisingly large scale. In September 1905, owners of the seafood canneries of the upper Gulf Coast—primarily those

Children working in a picking shed. (Photo courtesy of the National Archives and Records Administration, Prints & Photographs Division, College Park, MD, photographer Lewis Hine, 1911, reproduction number LC-DIG-nclc-00900.)

A rare view of the interior of a Bohemian laborer's quarters. (Photo courtesy of the National Archives and Records Administration, Prints & Photographs Division, College Park, MD, photographer Lewis Hine, 1911, reproduction number LC-DIG-nclc-00921.)

According to New Orleans *Daily Picayune* reports, the transient seasonal employees were "guaranteed their transportation to the packing house, food and lodging during the term of their engagement, and return trip tickets, and are paid variously—some weekly wages, but a large majority of piece work."

THE LOOKOUT CANNERY

Opens With Full Force of Bohemian Oyster Workers.

[Special to the Picayune.]

Bay St. Louis, Miss., Oct. 23.—About 100 Bohemian oyster shuckers from Baltimore reached Bay St. Louis and Lookout, La., last evening to work for George W. Dunbar's canneries, located at both of these places. Several hundred more are expected to arrive some time next week, and will be divided between the two plants.

The factory at the Bay has been in active operation since a few days after the 15th of September, and gave employment to a number of our people.

The plant at Lookout, La., started several days ago and is in full blast.

The factory town identified on early maps as Lookout was eventually dubbed Dunbar. Though isolated, this community had an active post office from 1903 to 1916. (From the New Orleans *Daily Picayune*, October 24, 1903.)

in the New Orleans and Biloxi areas—announced their intention to import "four thousand or more Bohemians and Poles from Baltimore." The availability of a large number of additional seasonal laborers was made possible by the rapid decline of the Baltimore oyster canning industry as a result of overharvesting, habitat loss, and environmental degradation.

New Orleans–area canneries alone annually accounted for approximately 1,500 Bohemians, who traveled to the Gulf Coast aboard chartered boxcars. Once the transient workers reached their destinations, cannery managers routinely assigned the men to miscellaneous support operations—typically as manual laborers on the cannery docks, as hands aboard mother ships transferring ice to coastal fishing boats and raw seafood to the canneries, or, in plants processing both oysters and shrimp, as oyster shuckers—and the women and children to the shrimp-peeling sheds. Despite cannery companies' contemporary public pronouncements about their "not laborious" and "healthy" workplaces, cannery jobs were grueling, hazardous, tedious, labor intensive, and unremunerative. Seafood canneries were, in fact, dehumanizing workplaces in which laborers were reduced to industrial peonage.

Female cannery workers were paid on the basis of piecework, typically one to three cents a pound for peeled shrimp. (One pound of unpeeled shrimp produces a half pound of peeled shrimp.) Most women in the production lines made less than five dollars per week—less than a living wage in the cannery factory "towns." As a result, mothers were compelled to press their children as young as four years of age into service as peelers.

Even with the financial assistance of their children, mothers routinely failed to make enough to improve their families' wretched economic lot; indeed, they endured a hand-to-mouth existence in

Starting a shift before sunrise was problematic for sleep-deprived workers because of scant natural and artificial light in the picking sheds. Because of the diminished sense of touch resulting from chronic ammonia exposure, crews frequently had to rely on their experience to peel enough shrimp to earn their daily bread.

which economic disaster was an ever-present specter. Work in the canneries was irregular, being entirely dependent on the arrival of raw product from the coastal fishery. When shrimp were plentiful and deliveries virtually continuous, women and children worked exceptionally long hours, even by the lax standards of the early twentieth century. According to the United States Department of Labor's child labor researcher Viola I. Paradise, "Since the work depended on the catch, it was very irregular, beginning any time between 3 and 7 o'clock in the morning, and lasting a few hours, a whole day, or occasionally on into the evening" (Paradise, *Child Labor* 5–6).

Gulf Coast canneries typically entrusted management of the predominately female workforce to the *padrones*. Padrones (*bosses* in Italian) were labor brokers who recruited Eastern European families in Baltimore for employment as temporary workers. They migrated seasonally between agricultural fields in Mid-Atlantic states and the Gulf Coast's seafood factories. Cannery companies reportedly paid padrones one dollar per head for recruited families, whom the padrones transported to canneries by rail and supervised on-site. A preponderance of anecdotal information indicates that padrones controlled their charges through incessant intimidation. Women and children, the most vulnerable members of the factory workforces, were the usual targets. According to child labor activists who infiltrated the Bohemian workforce in the early twentieth century to report abuses, padrones employed threats of instant termination, immediate settlement of existing bills at the company commissary, and loss of return transportation to Baltimore. This approach was particularly effective with widows and victims of spousal abandonment—typically about 25 percent of a cannery's female workers—who lacked both the relative financial security of a husband's income and literacy in the language of their contract.

An excerpt from congressional hearings on labor abuses at Louisiana canneries: "Families have to buy from the company store. One day the owner of [the] cannery saw a woman coming out of another store, [and] said, 'You can not work in my cannery if you don't buy in my store.' The woman said, 'you charge too much. You charge 10 cents a loaf for bread. I buy it for 6 cents at other stores.' He said, 'I don't care, if you work in my cannery you buy from my store.' In the . . . cannery the people are paid in checks, which they can only cash every 30 days. They won't give them care for fear they will leave." (Statement of Miss Elizabeth Watson, of the International Child Welfare League, *A Bill to Prevent Interstate Commerce in the Products of Child Labor, Hearings on H.R. 8234* 303).

"Women and children pick up the shrimp [in the processing troughs], break off the head with one hand, and squeeze the flesh from the shell with the other. This process is called picking in some communities and peeling in others. . . . [W]hen the shrimp cup is full, the worker takes it to be weighed. The peeled shrimp are then washed, boiled, cooled, and cleaned; that is, picked over, to remove any bits of shell or any 'whiskers' which may have adhered. Then they are packed in cans, and the cans are sealed and processed. . . . " (Paradise, *Child Labor* 13–14).

In addition to what would now be classified as a hostile workplace, female cannery workers and their children faced numerous health hazards at the job sites. Laborers typically peeled and "picked" shrimp in conditions barely imaginable by twenty-first-century Americans. Workers toiled without breaks, aside from a few minutes for lunch, standing on wooden crates and leaning over elevated troughs filled with iced shrimp. An investigative report by the United States Children's Bureau (published in 1922) provides perhaps the best extant description of the canneries' picker sheds:

Most of the cannery work is wet and is in cold, damp, drafty sheds, the oyster shuckers or shrimp pickers standing among the empty oyster shells or shrimp hulls. Besides the discomforts of standing at their work and the exposure to cold and dampness, the workers are subjected to certain hazards in the processes themselves. . . . An acid [actually, ammonia] in the head of the shrimp—according to the statements of employers as well as employees—eats into the hands, making the flesh raw and sore. Many workers can work on shrimp only two days at a time and must then take a few days off to let their hands heal. A shrimp "thorn" [rostrum] which protrudes from the head of the shrimp, may run into the hand and break off. This sometimes results in serious infection. More than three-fifths of the [picker] families reported some injury, including cuts, burns, infections, soreness, and rawness, caused by the acid in the shrimp, and occasionally serious accidents.

The pervasive ammonia exposure mentioned above sharply limited pickers' wages, for workers—adults and children alike—were obliged to curtail their work schedules at precisely the times when the income potential was greatest. Turn-of-the-twentieth-century shrimpers typically iced down their catch to prevent spoilage from Louisiana's relentless heat and humidity. Prolonged exposure to ice hardened the shrimp shells, making the crustaceans not only harder to peel but also much more likely to pierce the pickers' skin. Canneries attempted to mitigate ammonia exposure by providing workers alum water tubs in the picking sheds, but abundant anecdotal information from pickers and the canneries' on-site physicians makes it abundantly clear that these modest mitigation efforts were ineffective. Because women and "older girls" were frequently reassigned from the picking sheds to the packing assembly lines during the canning phase of production, children, who remained at the picking stations, bore the full brunt of the chemical exposure.

Myriad investigators concurred that shrimp factory work posed a major health hazard to laborers with the greatest ammonia exposure—the children. Secretions from the shrimp heads were so potent and toxic that they reportedly ate "through the leather of your shoes." Workers consequently eschewed any type of protective gear because, as one worker reported, "you can't wear nothing to protect [yourself] because the acid [ammonia] eats through everything." Ammonia exposure alone resulted in inflammation and bleeding lesions. One worker reported that "shrimp makes your hands bleed so badly you can hardly rest when night comes." Some laborers insisted that no one could endure more than two or three consecutive days' exposure on the "picking" line, after which "you have to stay home a day and do a washing and rest your hands." More serious were the wounds inflicted by the shrimp "thorns." One girl informed child labor investigators that thorns typically pierced pickers' hands "four or five times a day." The resulting festering wounds often developed into serious bacterial infections.

The health issues stemming directly from handling raw shrimp were compounded by the ancillary environmental issues. Ice in the picking troughs not only kept the sheds uncomfortably cool but also made the pickers' digits achy and stiff. Melting ice quickly permeated pickers' clothing and covered the shed floor, making all movement hazardous. In addition, picking sheds were perpetually filled with decomposing discarded shells, the stench of which was reportedly overpowering.

The dreadful cannery workplace conditions, appalling even by deplorable Gilded Age standards, were brought to the attention of the American reading public by contemporary muckrakers, whose sensational stories of workplace abuses seared on the national

"It is in the oyster and shrimp sheds of the Gulf Coast states . . . that canning reaches the acme of child labor horror" (Lindsey and Creel, "Children in Bondage" 20).

Congress would not enact national child labor standards until 1938, thirty-two years after Louisiana's child labor legislation. During the interim, the NCLC's greatest achievement was establishment of the United States Children's Bureau within the Department of Labor.

consciousness the need for economic, political, and social reform. Child labor reform was in the vanguard of this progressive crusade, and the exploitation of children by factories—particularly canneries, bag and box manufacturers, and cotton mills—occupied the spotlight in the unfolding campaign.

On the national level, the National Child Labor Committee (NCLC), founded in 1904, lobbied for change with disappointing results. Three years later, Senator Albert Beveridge of Indiana introduced the first national legislation regulating the use of children in the workplace. With its defeat, child labor opponents shifted their focus to state legislatures.

In Louisiana, sisters Jean and Kate Gordon of New Orleans, two of the nation's leading feminists, were perhaps the most outspoken child labor critics. Thanks largely to their efforts, the state legislature adopted its first child labor legislation in 1906. Passage of this regulatory bill appeared to put the Pelican State in the national mainstream regarding labor reform. Northern Gulf Coast shrimp canneries, which notoriously allowed child laborers as young as four years of age, could no longer allow boys under the age of twelve and girls younger than fourteen. Illiterate children below fourteen were universally banned in an ultimately unsuccessful effort to force canneries and local governments to educate transient child laborers. Finally, the maximum workweek for children under eighteen was limited to sixty hours.

On paper, Louisiana's initial child labor legislation appeared to be an important first step toward eradication of a workplace evil, but in reality, it was so severely crippled by budgetary limitations written into the bill by industry-friendly legislators that little actually changed in the picking sheds. From the outset, the Pelican State's enforcement mechanism was inadequately staffed, consisting of a commissioner and two field agents, who were required to "cover the whole State outside of New Orleans." Although charged by the enabling legislation with responsibility for all potential child labor venues, these administrators, commonly known as inspectors, were actually able to visit only a small fraction of targeted venues because of their paltry $100 monthly travel budget. Frequent visits were imperative to effective enforcement because of the irregularity of the shrimp cannery schedule. To put the child labor bureau's financial dilemma into perspective, its $8,500 initial annual budget was dwarfed by the Louisiana Department of Wildlife and Fisheries' $175,000 appropriation. This discrepancy was not lost on contemporaries, who wryly noted the state valued "critters" far more than its human resources.

Governmental enforcement of child labor regulations was further hamstrung by the complicity of impoverished parents and their children with the cannery managers. A landmark federal early twentieth-century investigation into child labor in shrimp and oyster canneries noted:

> Parents were often afraid to admit that their children worked. One family had heard rumors that the wages of all working children under 14 were to be taken from them, and that they would not be allowed to work. In another locality an impression was current that parents would be fined if they allowed children to work; and, as the agents were sometimes taken for inspectors, this influenced the parents to deny or minimize the work of their children. Some concrete examples will illustrate. One woman said: "I never let my children work. You can if you want to, but there's a $25 fine [$388 in 2020 currency] if you're caught, and you'd be paying more than they can make. Lots of children do work, and when the inspector comes[,] they run and hide. They're on to him, and run whenever they see a stranger. They can get away into places where you'd never think of looking." Still another mother said: "I hope soon to get working papers for Jane [aged 12] and John [aged 10]. They are working now, but if the inspector catches you, you get fined $50 [$776 in 2020 currency]. The kids watch for him, and they holler if they see him coming and hide till he gets out. (Paradise, *Child Labor* 11–12.)

The resulting ineffectiveness of enforcement efforts meant that child labor would be "taken for granted" in cannery communities until World War II, despite radical changes in the composition of the factory workforce during the second decade of the twentieth century.

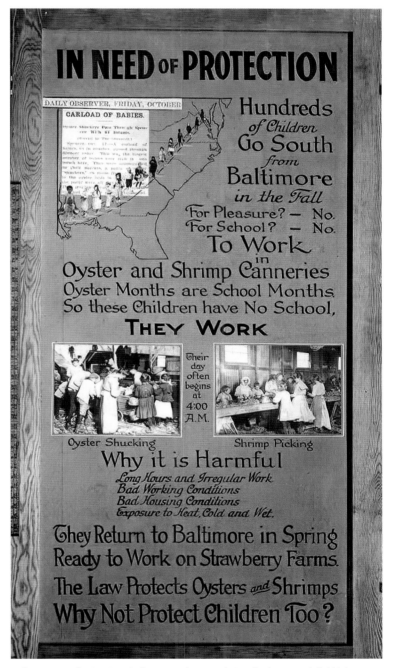

Reformers used Lewis Hine's dramatic photos to bring the horrors of child labor to the general American public. (Poster courtesy of the National Archives and Records Administration, Prints & Photographs Division, College Park, MD, photographer Lewis Hine, 1913, reproduction number LC-DIG-nclc-04877.)

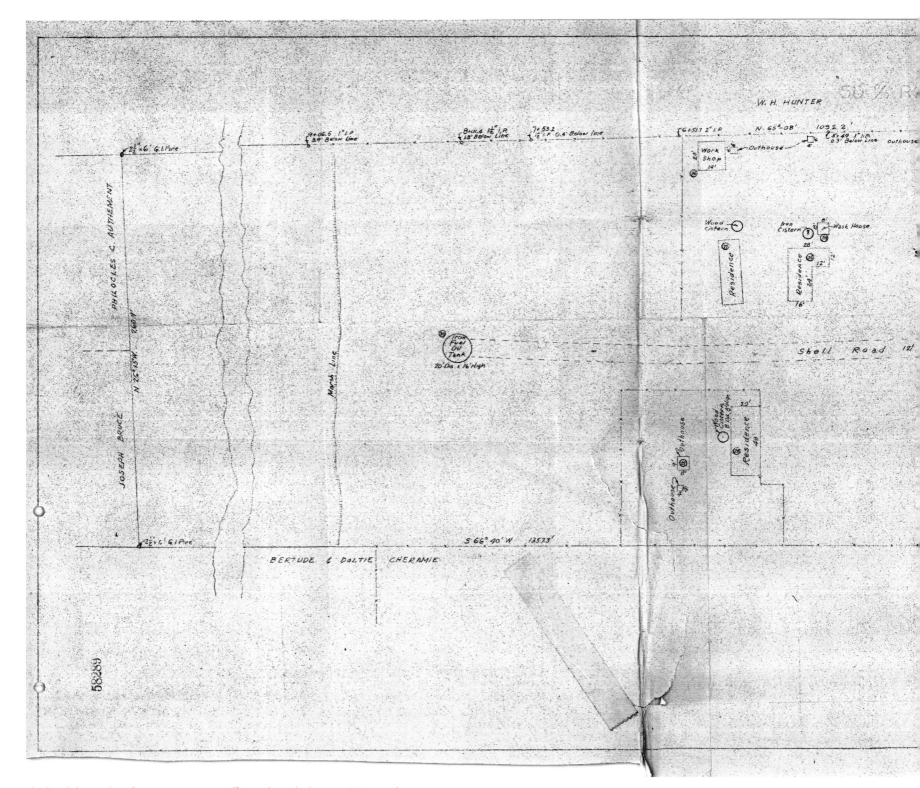

This hand-drawn plan of a Louisiana cannery offers perhaps the best surviving visual documentation of the physical layout of an early twentieth-century processing plant. (Cannery drawing from the authors' collections, Lafourche Parish Clerk of Court records, 1942.)

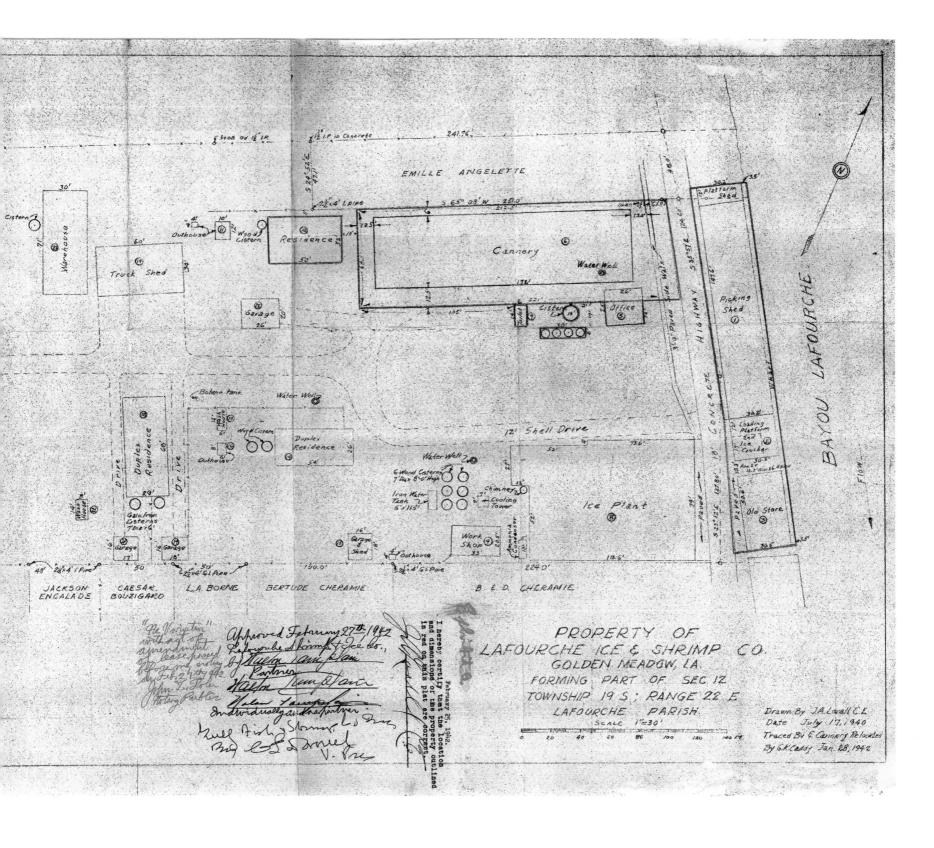

PROPERTY OF
LAFOURCHE ICE & SHRIMP CO.
GOLDEN MEADOW, LA.
FORMING PART OF SEC. 12
TOWNSHIP 19 S; RANGE 22 E
LAFOURCHE PARISH.

SCALE 1"=30'

Drawn By J.A. Lovell C.E.
Date July 17, 1940
Traced By & Cannery Relocated
By G.K.Caddy Jan 28, 1942

The United States' entry into World War I created an unprecedented labor crisis in the shrimp canning industry. Many, perhaps most, of the Polish cannery workers were technically German citizens, while the Bohemians, Eastern European natives, were unnaturalized immigrants who technically remained citizens of the Austro-Hungarian empire, technically resident enemies of the United States. The American government consequently classified these potential fifth columnists as enemy noncombatants following America's declaration of war against Germany on April 6, 1917, and Germany's ally, Austria-Hungary, on December 7, 1917. Using their new war powers, American civilian officials imposed travel restrictions on the transient cannery workforce, mandating that they "should not approach within 10 yards of water fronts and harbors." The net result was an immediate shift from immigrant to native workers, as locals—primarily Cajuns—supplanted Bohemians and Poles in the factories outside New Orleans.

The abrupt transformation of the cannery workforce, coupled with the virtual destruction of the dried shrimp fishery's infrastructure, signaled the end of an era in Louisiana's shrimp industry. During the decades immediately prior to America's involvement in World War I, the fishery had been controlled and manned primarily by "outlanders"—persons who were immigrants to the coastal plain; following the war, the composition of the factories' administration and labor forces would more accurately reflect the local population's extended family mentality. This dramatic demographic shift coincided with the retooling of the industry's harvesting operations. Before World War I, Louisiana's shrimp fishery was concentrated almost entirely in the Pelican State's brackish coastal estuaries; however, with technological advancements resulting in large part from the war effort, the industry's geographic focus would shift to the offshore waters, with consequences that would forever change the coastal economy and the lives of the families dependent on it.

America's entry into World War I (April 6, 1917) constituted a major watershed in the development of Louisiana's coastal seafood industry. The onset of war not only effectively terminated the ruthlessly exploitative temporary worker program, but it also added renewed impetus to the ongoing technological metamorphosis of the shrimp fishery's harvesting and processing operations. Changes wrought by the late nineteenth century's Industrial Revolution had been inexorable but narrowly focused and unevenly paced, as the introduction of pioneering technologies engendered sudden bursts of change followed by fluctuating periods of stagnation and slow progress. National mobilization for the war effort in 1917, however, unleashed social, economic, and technological forces that—when coupled with local and regional innovations—would thrust the industry into the vanguard of industrial change and integrate it even further into national and international market systems.

This World War I poster urges consumers to eat fish rather than meat. Louisiana's shrimp fleet benefited economically from such conservation programs. (From the Library of Congress, produced by the Canada Food Board, artist E. Henderson, ca. 1917.)

CHAPTER 3

SCENE IN THE ISLAND OF CHENIER CAMINADA, IN THE GULF OF MEXICO—MR. L. COLLINS, THE MAYOR, SCHOOLMASTER, AND "OLDEST INHABITANT," AND A GROUP OF HIS PUPILS AND PROTEGES.—FROM A SKETCH BY JAS. E. TAYLOR.

Myriad cultural groups have long made a home in south Louisiana's isolated wetlands. Four years before the Great October Storm of 1893, Chênière Caminada was a thriving fishing community of "nearly 1,600." The village was one of many industrial settlement nodes scattered across south Louisiana's coastal plain. At a time when seines were used in shrimp harvesting, fisherfolk had to live as close as possible to the highly perishable resource. (Lithography from *Frank Leslie's Illustrated Newspaper*, August 1, 1868, 309.)

THE FLOODED LOUISIANA DISTRICT.

Several tropical systems battered the United States in 1893, making that year one of the deadliest in the country's hurricane history. Along the northern Gulf Coast, the October storm flooded Louisiana's sea-level parishes between the Atchafalaya Delta and the eastern margins of Lake Borgne. (Map from *New York World*, October 9, 1893.)

SOUTH'S OLDEST COLONY.

COMPOSED OF CHINESE AND OTHER ORIENTAL SHRIMP FISHERMEN.

Hidden Away in the Labrynthine Bayous of Louisiana — Their Habits Are Incredibly Simple and Semi-Savage — Interesting Story of a Chinese Prince.

Hidden away in the labyrinthine bayous of lower Jefferson parish, Louisiana, and scattered about the margins of Grand lake. Little lake and the musically named Cheniere Caminada is a strange colony, the bare existence of which is practically unknown. It numbers, all told, at least 2000 people, three-fourths of whom are Chinese and the rest Manila men and unclassifiable mongrels. They live in brushwood camps near the edge of the water, their habits are incredibly simple and semi-savage, and their business is the catching and drying of shrimp.

This singular settlement recently came to the surface in some litigation on the calendar of the New Orleans courts over the ownership of a piece of adjacent property, but the industry has been quietly pursued, from time out of mind, in almost unbroken isolation. Its product is never seen in the New Orleans market, but is shipped direct to San Francisco and New York and consumed entirely by the Chinese. At certain seasons the shrimp are caught by the million in rude hand nets and spread in layers on platforms, built over the surface of the water. The hot sun soon shrivels them up and they become desiccated. When thoroughly dry they are brown and brittle and have a sweet, nutty flavor that is far from disagreeable. In this condition they are packed loosely in barrels holding about 250 pounds each and sent to native merchants on Mott and Doyers streets in New York and to the famous Chinatown of 'Frisco. At both places they are in lively demand and are eaten either as condiments, without further preparation, or with a curry of rice. Even American barbarians find them very good.

America's journalists and their readers maintained a long-lived fascination with south Louisiana's multiethnic fishing communities. ("South's Oldest Colony Composed of Chinese and Other Oriental Shrimp Fishermen," *Winnsboro (SC) News and Herald*, January 14, 1899.)

ANGUISH WRUNG
DISTRACTED HEARTS

For Two Thousand Loved Ones Dead.

THE STORM'S FEARFUL WORK.

Whole Families Wiped Out of Existence by the Waves.

Sad Scenes Everywhere in the Desolated Districts---Noble Work of a Catholic Priest---A Lugger Captain's Anguish---Money Damage Five Million Dollars.

(Fort Worth, TX *Gazette*, October 5, 1893.)

The most conspicuous initial result of war mobilization was the canneries' immediate transition to local labor pools. Within days of America's declaration of war, the northern Gulf Coast factories' use of transient Eastern European immigrants ended abruptly. These laborers were the mainstay of not only the factory production lines but also some of the harvesting operations. The immigrants were immediately supplanted by locals, primarily Cajuns outside greater New Orleans. Their emergence as the new face of industry's blue-collar workforce was not mere happenstance. By 1900, according to a detailed New Orleans *Daily Picayune* report on the Louisiana shrimp industry, Cajuns, particularly survivors of the terrible 1893 Chênière Caminada hurricane that claimed approximately two

(Benton, LA *Bossier Banner*, October 7, 1915.)

THE GREAT HURRICANE.

New Orleans passed through the worst storm in its history Wednesday of last week, September 29th. The city was near the center of the tropical hurricane, which reached a sustained velocity of 86 miles an hour for ten minutes, and 120 miles for a period of twenty seconds. The center of the storm passed New Orleans about twenty miles to the westward at 5:50 p. m.

All railroad traffic into New Orleans was completely blocked as a result of the hurricane and telegraph and telephone communication cut off.

After passing New Orleans the hurricane swerved toward the northeast and passed between that city and Jackson, Miss. Not a single town, hamlet or fishing camp east of New Orleans to Mobile escaped damage from the wind and high tides. Almost every point along the Louisiana and Mississippi coasts reported damage to property more severe than in the great storm of 1909.

The lower Mississippi coast was turned into an inland sea by the breaking of the levees, especially on the west bank, and live stock was generally destroyed.

Houses were totally wrecked and a great many damaged; several ferryboats were wrecked and others dismantled on the river front, and vehicles and pedestrians were blown about freely by the storm in Canal Street. Practically not a single church escaped damage, and several must be rebuilt.

The tide water along the gulf coast ranged from two and a half feet in the streets along the Bay of Mobile to about sixteen feet at Rigolets, where the greatest loss of life was recorded.

The property loss at Biloxi, Miss., will amount to $1,000,000.

Twenty-two tugs and boats were sunk in the Mississippi River between Natchez and New Orleans.

It is estimated that $1,000,000 will be required to rebuild the broken levees along the river front.

The death toll of the storm is placed at 375, and perhaps much more.

An appeal for help says: "Plaquemines Parish is ruined—set back twenty years. Water swept half, probably more, of its area. This year's crops are a total loss. Most of the cattle and poultry were drowned. Half, possibly more, of the buildings in the parish are wrecked; in many cases washed away. The damage to the levee system will be $100,000. The roads are washed out. All the school houses are down. Many hundreds, possibly several thousand, people are homeless, destitute and hungry. The lower half of the parish is practically wiped out; the balance suffered much."

The semi-truck was first manufactured in 1899, but the modern commercial trailer, originally designed to be towed behind a Ford Model T, was not invented until 1918. The trucking industry lived in the shadow of the nation's mature railroad system until the 1930s, when the emergence of nationwide networks of paved roadways allowed a new generation of freight carriers to gain prominence. By the early 1950s, refrigerated trucks had become the preferred means of transporting fresh Louisiana shrimp to northern markets. (From the Blum and Bergeron Collection, Nicholls State University Archives, Thibodaux, LA.)

The Dunbar company's remarkably effective product promotional campaign produced rapid dividends, and, within two years, grocery stores in many parts of the country began advertising the Dunbar and Barataria shrimp brands. This promotional success hinged on the efforts of packers and jobbers, who effectively utilized Western Union's extensive telegraph network. (From the Blum and Bergeron Collection, Nicholls State University Archives, Thibodaux, LA.)

thousand lives, had quietly established themselves as the dominant force in the coastal fishery west of the Mississippi River. Indeed, a *Daily Picayune* reporter maintained that "the fresh shrimp business is altogether in the hands of the Creoles [the regional late nineteenth-century euphemism for Cajuns]." Cajuns would continue to dominate the Louisiana shrimping industry for four generations. The keys to their success were adaptability, pragmatism, and their willingness to embrace advantageous technology.

CANNERIES

Before introduction of refrigerated railcars and tractor-trailer trucks, the fortunes of the coastal shrimp harvesting infrastructure were tied directly to the health of the regional canning industry. In the first two decades of the twentieth century, Gulf Coast seafood canneries faced several major problems. Two were inextricably intertwined. The Biloxi canneries, many of which were owned in part or in full by Louisiana business interests, obtained almost all their seafood from offshore waters claimed by Louisiana. The diversion of the Pelican State's most valuable aquatic resources across state lines quickly generated economic and political repercussions that resonated throughout the regional fishery and beyond. The interstate dispute, which threatened to devolve into violence when Louisiana deployed machine gun–equipped patrol boats to enforce

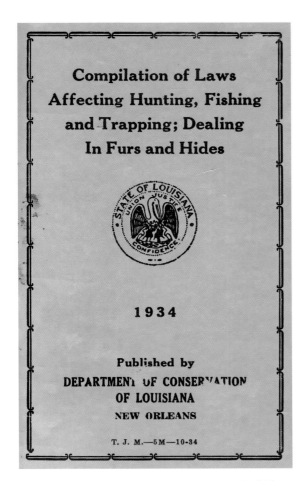

In 1934, Louisiana enacted legislation making it unlawful for nonresidents to catch shrimp for processing or consumption in other states. This statute forced Mississippi canneries to either open facilities in Louisiana or form partnerships with a Louisiana-based processor. (From the Louisiana Department of Wildlife and Fisheries, Baton Rouge Office Archives, Baton Rouge, LA.)

Although most of the Dunbar canneries' output was consumed domestically, some of their products were exported to foreign markets. This label suggests it was printed for application to a shipment bound for British India, where curries were an integral part of the regional cuisine. (Label from the Louisiana Historical Center, Louisiana State Museum, New Orleans, LA, date unknown.)

Patrol boats were outfitted with military-grade weapons to patrol for "oyster pirates" and other interlopers who openly defied Louisiana's 1934 shrimp harvesting law. (Photo from *Report of the Conservation Commission of Louisiana*, September 1, 1912–April 1, 1914.)

its maritime boundary claims, was ultimately settled peacefully by the United States Supreme Court, which, in 1906, formally established the offshore territorial limits of the rival neighboring claimants to the northern Gulf Coast's seafood bounty. Although interstate oyster harvesting received the lion's share of contemporary journalistic attention during the boundary dispute, the diversion of shrimp also created a firestorm that was exacerbated by labor issues that transcended political boundaries.

In the years immediately preceding the Great War, upper Gulf Coast canneries confronted sporadic threats of unionization by

In the landmark 1906 *Louisiana v. Mississippi* case, the United States Supreme Court ruled that the offshore boundary between the Bayou State and the Magnolia State extended from "the most eastern mouth of Pearl River into Lake Borgne and extending through the northeast corner of Lake Borgne, north of Half Moon or Grand Island, thence east and south through Mississippi Sound, through South Pass between Cat Island and Isle à Pitre to the Gulf of Mexico."

Shrimp, often called the most popular shellfish in the United States, became common during the golden age of canning, when the cannery industry learned that colorful labels, publications, and free cookbooks were essential to enticing consumers to sample their wares, particularly in previously untapped markets. (Photo from the Louisiana Historical Center, Louisiana State Museum, New Orleans, LA, date unknown.)

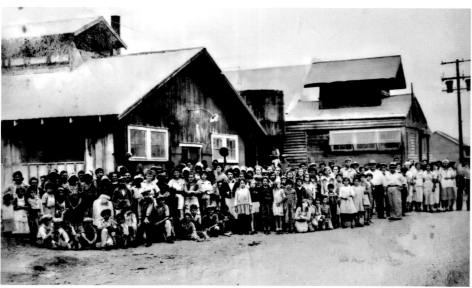

As the canning business expanded in Louisiana and Mississippi, each new processing facility became a settlement node. Before machinery largely replaced hand labor, a cannery required a labor force that could be mobilized by the sound of a steam whistle. Cannery employees needed to live within "ear-shot" of the factory to respond to this piercing summons. In remote settlements, where the existing labor force was insufficient, cannery operators recruited laborers, often though advertisements in local and regional media. (Photo from Chenier Hurricane Centennial 128.)

In the mid-nineteenth century, the United States developed industries that required skilled labor. Canning "towns" provided work and wages, but pay was low and working conditions were horrendous. Shocking abuse of women and children was commonplace. Yet any job was preferable to unemployment. Indian Ridge canning plant was one of the "down-the-bayou" company towns located on Bayou Petit Caillou and Robinson Canal. (From the authors' collections, used with permission from the Theriot family, per Jason Theriot, Houston, TX, 1935.)

Like all canneries outside the New Orleans metropolitan area, the Indian Ridge Canning Company's address was meaningless to most consumers, who valued only the packaging label and the canned product: Barataria Shrimp. (Label from the Louisiana Historical Center, Louisiana State Museum, New Orleans, LA, date unknown.)

disgruntled workers disaffected by unacceptable wage standards and hazardous working conditions. The growing discord first came to a head in July 1915, when labor activists forced the Dunbar, Lopez and Dukate Company to temporarily shutter its large Pass Christian, Mississippi plant, after four of the corporation's shrimp schooners were intercepted, boarded, and temporarily detained at Biloxi Bayou, Louisiana, by approximately forty armed longshoremen aboard the powerboat *Chads*. While aboard the cannery boats, the labor organizers seized the "seines, skiffs and nets" intended for use in the shrimp fishery. Longshoremen also intercepted and boarded two

Ice boats were a linchpin component of the shrimp industry's supply chain, as the vessels guarantee the shrimp fleet could "fish shrimp" for longer periods and the cannery had a reliable, uninterrupted supply of raw product. (Photo from *Jefferson Parish Yearly Review*, [1944]: 39A.)

J. C. Julian cannery vessels later the same day in Louisiana waters. In its detailed coverage of the incidents, the New Orleans *Daily Picayune* reported that "on departing from each boat the crew was solemnly warned not to be caught out shrimping until the strike is off." Cannery owners throughout the Mississippi coast refused the labor union's demands and instead tried to destroy the unionization effort by closing their plants. Dunbar, Lopez and Dukate announced it would sell surplus canned stock that year and move the operation—including 104 nonunion workers—temporarily to New Orleans.

The 1915 confrontation set the tone for following decades. Whenever unionization became a viable threat to their bottom line, cannery owners moved their operations to new, increasingly remote locations, where the specter of labor unrest had not yet taken root. By the start of World War II, shrimp canneries had sprung up in Morgan City, Pointe à la Hache, Golden Meadow, Indian Ridge/ Boudreaux Canal, and numerous other isolated coastal communities.

Interwar canneries also had to adapt to the ever-expanding annual shrimp harvest. Cannery operators continued to rely on a resource-acquisitions system established in the late nineteenth century. However, because of the growing size of the catch, the traditional "ice boats," formerly small luggers, were replaced by large, motorized "freight boats" (that also eventually came to be known as "ice boats")—essentially schooners with nearly twice the cargo capacity of their predecessors.

The largest of the second-generation ice boats had a cargo capacity of 10.5 tons. During the state-regulated seasons, these inland freighters shuttled continuously between cannery docks and common estuarine shrimping sites, where they cruised in search of shrimpers affiliated with their processing plants. Like the ice boats themselves, the trawlers flew distinctive corporate pennants, which served as ocular beacons, allowing the freighter captains to rendezvous with shrimpers who, because of monetary advances, were under legal obligation to sell their catch to the ice boats' owner(s).

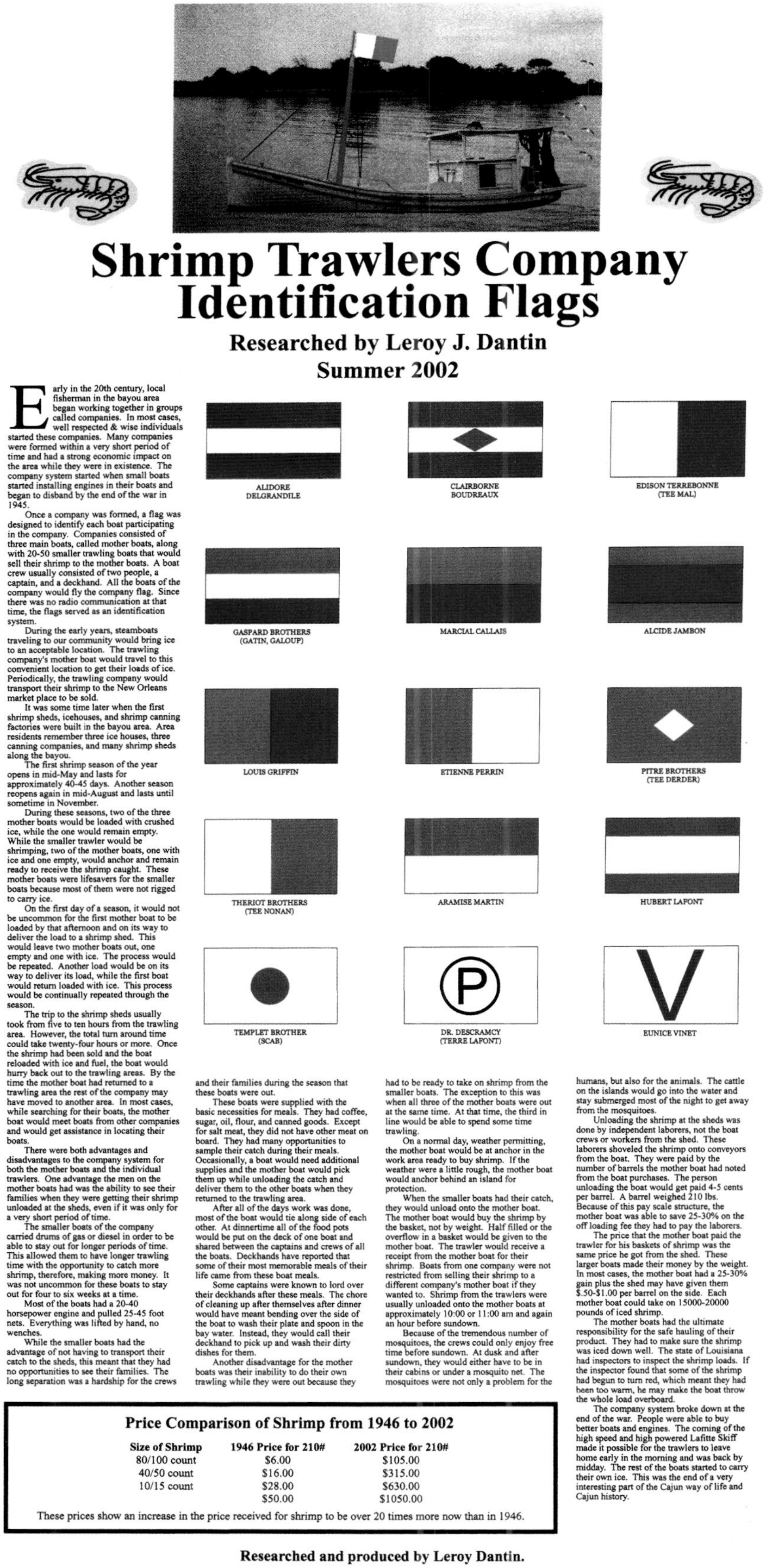

Shrimp Trawlers Company Identification Flags

Researched by Leroy J. Dantin
Summer 2002

ALIDORE DELGRANDILE
CLAIRBORNE BOUDREAUX
EDISON TERREBONNE (TEE MAL)
GASPARD BROTHERS (GATIN, GALOUP)
MARCIAL CALLAIS
ALCIDE JAMBON
LOUIS GRIFFIN
ETIENNE PERRIN
PITRE BROTHERS (TEE DERDER)
THERIOT BROTHERS (TEE NONAN)
ARAMISE MARTIN
HUBERT LAFONT
TEMPLET BROTHER (SCAB)
DR. DESCRAMCY (TERRE LAFONT)
EUNICE VINET

Early in the 20th century, local fisherman in the bayou area began working together in groups called companies. In most cases, well respected & wise individuals started these companies. Many companies were formed within a very short period of time and had a strong economic impact on the area while they were in existence. The company system started when small boats started installing engines in their boats and began to disband by the end of the war in 1945.

Once a company was formed, a flag was designed to identify each boat participating in the company. Companies consisted of three main boats, called mother boats, along with 20-50 smaller trawling boats that would sell their shrimp to the mother boats. A boat crew usually consisted of two people, a captain, and a deckhand. All the boats of the company would fly the company flag. Since there was no radio communication at that time, the flags served as an identification system.

During the early years, steamboats traveling to our community would bring ice to an acceptable location. The trawling company's mother boat would travel to this convenient location to get their loads of ice. Periodically, the trawling company would transport their shrimp to the New Orleans market place to be sold.

It was some time later when the first shrimp sheds, icehouses, and shrimp canning factories were built in the bayou area. Area residents remember three ice houses, three canning companies, and many shrimp sheds along the bayou.

The first shrimp season of the year opens in mid-May and lasts for approximately 40-45 days. Another season reopens again in mid-August and lasts until sometime in November.

During these seasons, two of the three mother boats would be loaded with crushed ice, while the one would remain empty. While the smaller trawler would be shrimping, two of the mother boats, one with ice and one empty, would anchor and remain ready to receive the shrimp caught. These mother boats were lifesavers for the smaller boats because most of them were not rigged to carry ice.

On the first day of a season, it would not be uncommon for the first mother boat to be loaded by that afternoon and on its way to deliver the load to a shrimp shed. This would leave two mother boats out, one empty and one with ice. The process would be repeated. Another load would be on its way to deliver its load, while the first boat would return loaded with ice. This process would be continually repeated through the season.

The trip to the shrimp sheds usually took from five to ten hours from the trawling area. However, the total turn around time could take twenty-four hours or more. Once the shrimp had been sold and the boat reloaded with ice and fuel, the boat would hurry back out to the trawling areas. By the time the mother boat had returned to a trawling area the rest of the company may have moved to another area. In most cases, while searching for their boats, the mother boat would meet boats from other companies and would get assistance in locating their boats.

There were both advantages and disadvantages to the company system for both the mother boats and the individual trawlers. One advantage the men on the mother boats had was the ability to see their families when they were getting their shrimp unloaded at the sheds, even if it was only for a very short period of time.

The smaller boats of the company carried drums of gas or diesel in order to be able to stay out for longer periods of time. This allowed them to have longer trawling time with the opportunity to catch more shrimp, therefore, making more money. It was not uncommon for these boats to stay out for four to six weeks at a time.

Most of the boats had a 20-40 horsepower engine and pulled 25-45 foot nets. Everything was lifted by hand, no wenches.

While the smaller boats had the advantage of not having to transport their catch to the sheds, this meant that they had no opportunities to see their families. The long separation was a hardship for the crews and their families during the season that these boats were out.

These boats were supplied with the basic necessities for meals. They had coffee, sugar, oil, flour, and canned goods. Except for salt meat, they did not have other meat on board. They had many opportunities to sample their catch during their meals. Occasionally, a boat would need additional supplies and the mother boat would pick them up while unloading the catch and deliver them to the other boats when they returned to the trawling area.

After all of the days work was done, most of the boat would tie along side of each other. At dinnertime all of the food pots would be put on the deck of one boat and shared between the captains and crews of all the boats. Deckhands have reported that some of their most memorable meals of their life came from these boat meals.

Some captains were known to lord over their deckhands after these meals. The chore of cleaning up after themselves after dinner would have meant bending over the side of the boat to wash their plate and spoon in the bay water. Instead, they would call their deckhand to pick up and wash their dirty dishes for them.

Another disadvantage for the mother boats was their inability to do their own trawling while they were out because they had to be ready to take on shrimp from the smaller boats. The exception to this was when all three of the mother boats were out at the same time. At that time, the third in line would be able to spend some time trawling.

On a normal day, weather permitting, the mother boat would be at anchor in the work area ready to buy shrimp. If the weather were a little rough, the mother boat would anchor behind an island for protection.

When the smaller boats had their catch, they would unload onto the mother boat. The mother boat would buy the shrimp by the basket, not by weight. Half filled or the overflow in a basket would be given to the mother boat. The trawler would receive a receipt from the mother boat for their shrimp. Boats from one company were not restricted from selling their shrimp to a different company's mother boat if they wanted to. Shrimp from the trawlers were usually unloaded onto the mother boats at approximately 10:00 or 11:00 am and again an hour before sundown.

Because of the tremendous number of mosquitoes, the crews could only enjoy free time before sundown. At dusk and after sundown, they would either have to be in their cabins or under a mosquito net. The mosquitoes were not only a problem for the humans, but also for the animals. The cattle on the islands would go into the water and stay submerged most of the night to get away from the mosquitoes.

Unloading the shrimp at the sheds was done by independent laborers, not the boat crews or workers from the shed. These laborers shoveled the shrimp onto conveyors from the boat. They were paid by the number of barrels the mother boat had noted from the boat purchases. The person unloading the boat would get paid 4-5 cents per barrel. A barrel weighed 210 lbs. Because of this pay scale structure, the mother boat was able to save 25-30% on the off loading fee they had to pay the laborers.

The price that the mother boat paid the trawler for his baskets of shrimp was the same price he got from the shed. These larger boats made their money by the weight. In most cases, the mother boat had a 25-30% gain plus the shed may have given them $.50-$1.00 per barrel on the side. Each mother boat could take on 15000-20000 pounds of iced shrimp.

The mother boats had the ultimate responsibility for the safe hauling of their product. They had to make sure the shrimp was iced down well. The state of Louisiana had inspectors to inspect the shrimp loads. If the inspector found that some of the shrimp had begun to turn red, which meant they had been too warm, he may make the boat throw the whole load overboard.

The company system broke down at the end of the war. People were able to buy better boats and engines. The coming of the high speed and high powered Lafitte Skiff made it possible for the trawlers to leave home early in the morning and was back by midday. The rest of the boats started to carry their own ice. This was the end of a very interesting part of the Cajun way of life and Cajun history.

Price Comparison of Shrimp from 1946 to 2002

Size of Shrimp	1946 Price for 210#	2002 Price for 210#
80/100 count	$6.00	$105.00
40/50 count	$16.00	$315.00
10/15 count	$28.00	$630.00
	$50.00	$1050.00

These prices show an increase in the price received for shrimp to be over 20 times more now than in 1946.

Researched and produced by Leroy Dantin.

Cannery flags are a forgotten part of this industry. This rare poster identifies some of the flags used and the companies involved in the industry. (Poster from the authors' collections. Produced by Leroy Dantin, Golden Meadow, LA, 2002.)

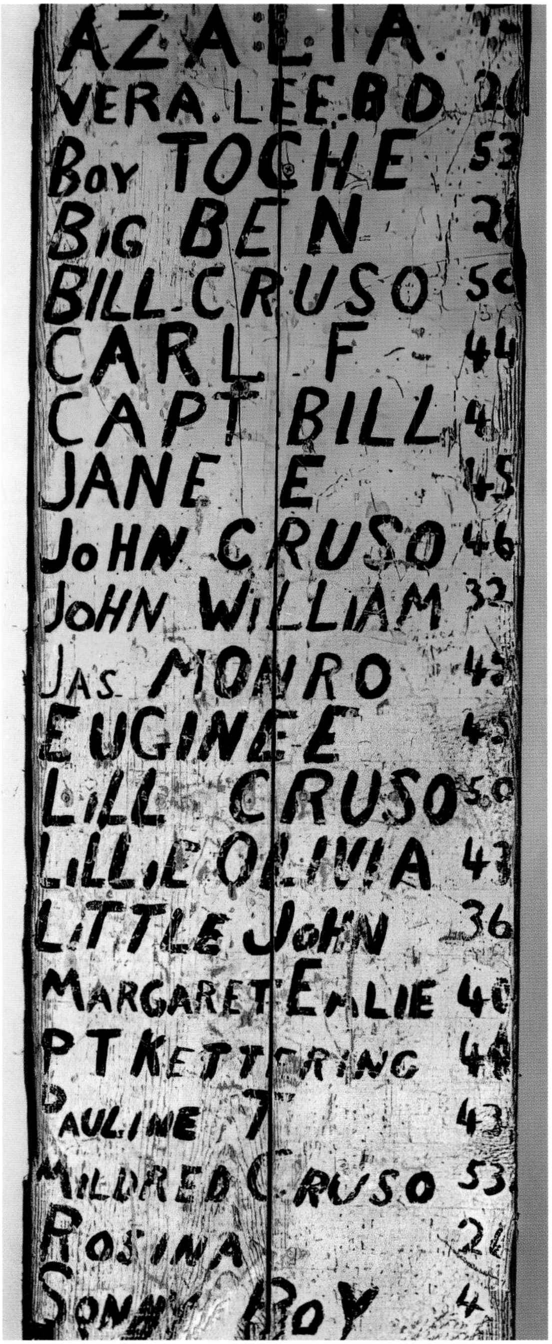
AZALIA
VERA LEE BD
BOY TOCHE 53
BIG BEN
BILL CRUSO
CARL F 44
CAPT BILL
JANE E 45
JOHN CRUSO 46
JOHN WILLIAM 32
JAS MONRO
EUGINE E
LILL CRUSO
LILLIE OLIVIA 43
LITTLE JOHN 36
MARGARET EMLIE 40
PT KETTERING
PAULINE T 43
MILDRED CRUSO 53
ROSINA
SONNY BOY

As in Louisiana, Mississippi's trawler fleet used cannery flags to identify the boats that would offload and be resupplied by the cannery's ice boat(s). This list identifies the boats affiliated with one Mississippi seafood cannery. (Photo from the authors' collections. Courtesy of the Maritime and Seafood Industry Museum, Biloxi, MS, 2019.)

Cannery flags on a shrimp boat's mast indicate who buys the captain's catch. (Left photo from the authors' collections. Used with permission from the Theriot family, per Jason Theriot, Houston, TX, 1935.)

Before the Federal Aid Highway Act was passed in 1921, Louisiana's inland labyrinth of natural and engineered waterways were the principal corridors of commerce. Barge-loads of fuel drums moved along the waterways, offloading at docks to supply the needs of Louisiana's watermen. (From the authors' collections, used with permission from the Theriot family, per Jason Theriot, Houston, TX, 1935.)

In some communities, shrimp canneries relied exclusively on local laborers, usually women, to process the ice boat deliveries. In others, the factories used a combination of local and imported laborers. The Indian Ridge cannery at Boudreaux Canal in lower Terrebonne Parish, for example, reportedly supplemented its local Cajun workforce with African American workers trucked from the Smith Ridge community on upper Bayou Little Caillou.

Composition of a cannery's workforce depended largely on the frequency of ice boat landings and the volume of the catch. Because the work schedule revolved around the unscheduled lugger arrivals, smaller canneries were compelled to rely on local laborers who, once summoned by steam whistle, could provide their own transportation to the factories on short notice at all hours. On the other hand, larger canneries, where work timetables were based on the scheduled arrivals of large company-owned ice-boat schooners or motorized luggers, could more accurately gauge when larger labor pools were needed.

Louisiana cannery workers endured the same working conditions and earned the same wages regardless of the corporate employer's size because cannery work was universally piecework. Managers issued each "picker" a tally card and a bucket on arrival. Heaping buckets of peeled shrimp, logged by managers on the tally cards, constituted the basis of daily reimbursement, which was customarily rendered in cash. The best pickers could expect to earn two dollars per day—a princely sum in Great Depression–era coastal Louisiana; however, most earned far less.

Anecdotal evidence indicates that shrimp processed by hand in interwar canneries was entirely free of governmental scrutiny or regulation until approximately 1935, when federal inspectors first began to visit the small-town factories. Prior to that date, hundreds of can samples were seized and condemned because of spoilage. Jarvis (*Principles and Methods*, 271) reported the "industry placed itself under a voluntary inspection system administered by the Seafood Inspection Service of the U. S. Food and Drug Administration. To obtain this service the individual packer desiring inspection must apply for it. For his request to be granted, his equipment must

In the cannery business, work was seasonal, and workloads depended on highly variable daily harvests. Cannery workers often started well before sunrise, and the workday could last a few hours, a whole day, or occasionally well into the night. These photos are of a cannery where women worked with their male counterparts, and young children were often part of the scene. (From the authors' collections. Used with permission from the Theriot family, per Jason Theriot, Houston, TX, 1935.)

Southern Shell Fish also marketed to Spanish-speaking countries. Note that even when the product was destined for a foreign country, the term "Barataria" dominates the label. (Label from the Louisiana Historical Center, Louisiana State Museum, New Orleans, LA, date unknown.)

Successful canning business Southern Shell Fish of Harvey, Louisiana, often described as the largest shrimp packing plant in the country, was the ultimate prototype of the northern Gulf Coast company town. The photo shows, left to right, the screened unloading wharf, behind it the shelling room, the packing house, the receiving station, the ice manufacturing plant, and, behind it, the warehouse. (Photo from NOAA Photo Library, NOAA Central Library Historical Fisheries Collection, The Southern Fisherman, ca. 1939, photographer unknown, photo number 24764.)

From its inception, the Walle Company's graphic artist's attention to detail, color, and design were critical to all seafood processors' marketing efforts. (Label from the Louisiana Historical Center, Louisiana State Museum, New Orleans, LA, date unknown.)

Women weighing cans. (Photo from the authors' collections, photographer unknown, ca. 1935.)

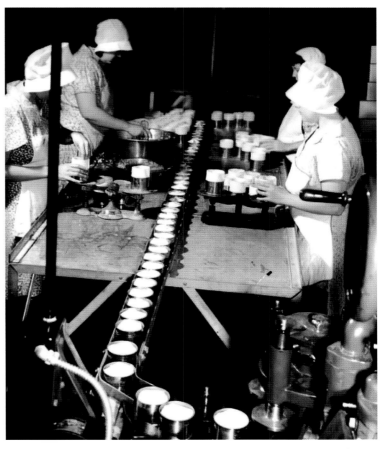

Women working the line in a St. Mary Parish seafood canning factory. (Photo from the State Library of Louisiana Historical Photographs Collection, photographer unknown, 1940.)

Steam whistles, such as this brass unit from a now defunct Patterson seafood processing plant, summoned local "pickers" whenever shrimp boats arrived fully laden at the docks. (From the collection of F. C. Felterman Jr., Patterson, LA.)

By the late 1930s, canneries were voluntary participants in the Food and Drug Administration's inspection program and noted their involvement through their labels. (Label from the Louisiana Historical Center, Louisiana State Museum, New Orleans, LA, date unknown.)

The Food and Drug Administration (FDA) inspectors were consistently Anglophone "Yankees," who had trouble communicating with the overwhelmingly Francophone shrimpers. Locals with limited English vocabularies were pressed into service as makeshift translators. A translator's child recalled, "No, we could make them understand. My daddy's English was not the best, but he could make them understand. We made out with the men from the FDA and at that time three-fourths of the fishermen didn't speak English, [they] only spoke French. The conversation was mostly in French but two of the men understood enough English. My daddy would explain to the fishermen what they had to do, and they understood and followed the regulations. He made them understand that they could not buy shrimp and lose them [i.e., allow them to spoil]. We were not that big in those days and the fishermen understood what they had to do to have good shrimp to be able to sell them to the factories" (Theriot interview.)

comply with certain standards and the operation of the plant must conform to certain regulations drawn up by the Administration." Originally, the industry paid for health inspections, but in 1935, Congress subsidized the process through establishment of the Seafood Inspection Service. In the 1936–1937 season, federal agents examined nearly forty canneries in Georgia, Alabama, Mississippi, Louisiana, and Texas.

Such inspections were of critical importance to the industry's continued viability, for former cannery employees recalled that cannery "ice boats" often bought tainted shrimp from independent lugger captains who lacked the means or inclination to purchase ice. The indiscriminate use of tainted shrimp posed a persistent insidious threat to public health, and the inspectors accordingly ordered the wholesale destruction of the canneries' inventories of unsold tins. The federal government subsequently installed resident inspectors and transient supervisors to monitor the factories' canning processes. At Boudreaux Canal, the Indian Ridge Canning Company provided inspectors with food and lodging to assist in educating local fishermen and ice boat captains about the unacceptability of unrefrigerated shrimp.

DRIED SHRIMP

Until the 1920s, the technology-driven dynamism transforming the Pelican State's shrimp fishery and its attendant canneries seems to have largely bypassed its oldest component industry.

The Quong Sun Company was the epicenter of the state's Chinese shrimp industry. When incorporated by Lee Yat and Chin D. Hoy in 1923, the company maintained its corporate offices at 400 Dauphine Street in New Orleans and at Grand Lake, Louisiana. Yat's father may have been the first Chinese to dry Louisiana shrimp. Born in San Francisco in 1860, Lee Yat reputedly came to Louisiana with his father as some of the Bayou State's first Chinese immigrants. When his father died, Lee Yat inherited the family's enterprise, which eventually became the Quong Sun Company. Quong Sun's crown jewel—a thousand-acre site located along Bayou Dufon (sometimes spelled Defond, D Fon, or Dufond)—was already a mature facility in the 1920s. The fledgling corporation also owned four commercial seines and seven gasoline-powered fishing boats: *U.S.A.*, *Bayou Dufon*, *American Boy*, *Chinese Girl*, *Shanghai*, *New Orleans*, and *Quong Sun*. These vessels originally moved seine crews to shrimp harvest sites and carried the dried product to New Orleans for transshipment to California. Seine crews were eventually replaced by trawl boats operated by a captain and one or two crew members. (Advertisement from the authors' collections, from *Jefferson Parish Yearly Review* [1936]: 42.)

Indeed, except for the personnel changes wrought among the workforce by the Chinese Exclusion Act, the dried shrimp industry's field operations appear to have been caught in a time warp. Chinese entrepreneurs remained firmly in control, and the day-to-day operation of the isolated drying platforms remained largely unchanged from the 1880s, with one notable exception: the platform owners no longer provided the harvesting operations' essential equipment. As late as April 1922, the New Orleans *Times-Picayune* reported that East Asians, "without exception, constitute the proprietary class. They own the platforms and the buildings, they manufacture the . . . shrimp. . . . [O]ther nationalities furnish the fishermen, who are furnished board and lodging by the Chinese owners, and who are paid by the catch." These fishermen were typically organized into work gangs consisting of a "seine-skiff or small lugger" owner, a seine owner, and a sixteen-man seine crew.

ONE CHINAMAN HELD, TWO STILL ON TRIAL,

For Holding White Men in Peonage at Shrimp Camps.

One Witness Hints at Murder Never Made Public.

Referee Bell Reports Against Prof. B. V. B. Dixon's Discharge,

Deciding There Was False Swearing and Concealment of Assets in Bankruptcy Matter.

Because governmental control over platforms was illusory at best, accusations of peonage were newsworthy and sensational. (Newspaper article from the New Orleans *Daily Picayune*, September 7, 1911, 5.)

The Quong Sun incorporation papers indicate that the company's production facility was located at Bayou Dufon and Grand Lake. A search of the US Board on Geographic Names database lists Bayou Dufon as a geographical feature in the Barataria Bay area, but not Grand Lake. However, several members of the Barataria Terrebonne National Estuary Program (BTNEP) recall that Grand Lake was a regional colloquial idiom for the northern portion of Barataria Bay.

No extant information suggests Quong Sun was in the canning business. However, the firm had its own private label, packaged by another regional cannery. (Label from the Louisiana Historical Center, Louisiana State Museum, New Orleans, LA, date unknown.)

Unlike the canning industry that marketed products under an assortment of brands, Quong Sun's trademark was "Green Dragon," which symbolizes prosperity, health, and wisdom but also represented the emperor. (Barrel label from the authors' collections. Courtesy of J. L. Risenden Jr., no date.)

In Louisiana, the Chinese are a forgotten minority because so many members of this community lived in isolation and were never part of the cultural mainstream. (Photo from the *Jefferson Parish Yearly Review* [1940]: 46.)

However, postwar changes were afoot in the industry's still-maturing distribution infrastructure. As many small drying operations succumbed to catastrophic hurricane-related losses in the first two decades of the twentieth century, a few New Orleans–based distributors marshalled their financial resources to consolidate and resuscitate the surviving platform enterprises. Vertical integration of the production and distribution segments of these newly consolidated operations, however, proved a formidable challenge beyond the capability of many entrepreneurs. Only Quong Sun, which was officially dissolved in July 1984, achieved lasting success. Businessmen Lee Yat and Chin D. Hoy formally established the Quong Sun Company in 1923, but according to news reports filed during Yat's notorious 1911 peonage trial, the enterprise had existed informally for some time under Yat family management before the articles of incorporation were registered. In fact, Lee Yat's obituary claims that his father "established the first [shrimp] pickery of that nature in Louisiana" sometime before 1880.

Quong Sun survived in large part because of the impressive corporate resources that permitted it to weather financial and

Jules Gabriel Fisher was a Louisiana state senator from 1924 to 1943, and for many years he lived part-time at Manila Village. Ownership of the hamlet remains a matter of controversy, for some accounts identified the senator as the island's owner. For example, pre-1910 records suggest Fisher was the owner of the "Fisher Shrimp Company" at Manila Village. Yet actual ownership of the famous facility remains a mystery, for the Chinese former operators may have entered a handshake arrangement with Fisher to maintain their anonymity. (Label from the Louisiana Historical Center, Louisiana State Museum, New Orleans, LA, date unknown.)

66   JEFFERSON PARISH YEARLY REVIEW

Fisher Shrimp Co., Inc.

Plants

CABINASH, LA.

GRAND ISLE, LA.

PACKERS OF SUN-DRIED SHRIMP

Postoffice: Cabinash, La.

New Orleans Office: 822 Perdido St.

This advertisement is the only documentation indicating Jules Fisher operated two "plants"—a euphuism for the drying operation—at Cabinash, the post office address for Manila Village, and at Grand Isle. (Advertisement from the authors' collections, ca. 1940.)

On June 2, 1911, for example, the New Orleans *Daily Picayune* published the following: "If there is anywhere in America a survival of feudalism as it existed in the middle ages, it is on Lee Yat's so-called island or marshland in Barataria Bay. Lee Yat is indeed lord of all he surveys. He owns the Island of Bayou Du Fon, body and soul, water and all, and no hand is ever raised against his authority. . . . Lee Yat owns about 700 acres. Besides the big drying platform, he has a warehouse, a commissary and twenty-odd dwellings for his fishermen. During the first season, which is the one current in April and May, there are in the neighborhood of fifty fishermen employed. During the second season, which extends from about August 1 to October 31, an additional seventy-five or eighty are recruited from the surrounding islands and fishing camps on the coast" (New Orleans *Daily Picayune*, June 2, 1911).

environmental crises that claimed less well capitalized rivals. Under the astute leadership of Chin D. Hoy, who succeeded Lee Yat as president of Quong Sun following Yat's death in May 1925, the company diversified its holdings.

The continuing production and market volatility created by the consolidation and restructuring of the Chinese-owned drying operations during the post–World War I era afforded "outsiders" an unprecedented opportunity to gain a foothold in the shrimp-drying industry. The Fisher brothers of Lafitte, Louisiana, were perhaps the first Caucasian entrepreneurs to establish a meaningful presence in the Louisiana dried shrimp industry. According to contemporary news reports, the Fisher operation did "a bigger business than any single [Chinese] firm" as early as 1911, and by 1920, the family business had expanded from its Barataria Bay base in Jefferson Parish by constructing installations in Dog Lake and Lake Felicity in Terrebonne Parish.

The Fisher brothers soon found themselves in competition not only with established Chinese rivals but also with a variety of native Louisianan interlopers. Before 1920, Pelican Lake Packing Company, Blum and Bergeron, the Chauvin Brothers, and the St. Martin Company operated numerous platforms in Terrebonne Parish estuaries. These pioneering operations were joined by small, independent, generally family-owned Cajun operations lacking the financial wherewithal to construct and maintain traditional platform facilities. In a remarkably informative oral interview recorded by Louisiana filmmaker Glen Pitre, Joseph D. Theriot, a Terrebonne Parish resident who spent more than fifty years in the local shrimp industry, recalled that, before the start of World War II,

> The Cajuns [i.e., independent shrimpers] would buy some wood and would go where there was a high spot on the coast, a little island or something, and boil and dry their shrimp. My father-in-law and my uncles would go to a shell reef. There were good little islands of shells [middens]. . . . People use to put the dried shrimp into sacks, and they would beat the shrimp to get the hulls off before they would sell them.

P. O. BOX
441
—
CABLES:
UNGE
TOPEKA
—
CODES:
MILLER'S
BENTLEY'S
—
TELEPHONE
3-2349
—
ALL OFFERS
SUBJECT
CONFIRMATION
IF NOT OTHER-
WISE STATED
—

B. W. UNGE : 820 KANSAS AVENUE : TOPEKA : KANSAS, U. S. A.

Topeka, Kansas, August 18, 1933.

Messrs. Chauvin Brothers, Inc.,
P. O. Box No. 425,
Houma, Louisiana.

Gentlemen:-

This will confirm our telegram dated August 15th, and
your reply 16th, confirming sale of four large barrels, eight small
barrels and five jute bales Sun-Dried Shrimp.   The details of this
order are as follows:-

4	Large Barrels, (210#), 840 Lbs. Medium Size Sun-Dried Shrimp - @ 20¢ per pound	$168.00
8	Small Barrels, (100#) 800 Lbs. Medium Size Sun-Dried Shrimp - @ 20½¢ per pound	182.00
5	Jute Bales (10/10 Craft Paper) 500 Lbs. Small Size, Sun-Dried Shrimp @ 18¢ per pound	90.00
		$ 440.00

DISCOUNT:

Our Commission 5% 22.00

You may draw on us at sight through $ 418.00
The National Bank of Topeka, Topeka, Kansas, with your invoice
Certificate of Quality, (Enclosed herewith), and R.R. B/L. or Dock
Delivery Receipt attached.

((In this connection we understand the weights in large
barrels are subject to variation; however as our buyer has specified
"210# Barrels", we have so indicated herein. If they run more than
this, you will, of course, revise the figures quoted above. And for
our information, will you please state the general practice in handling these Large Barrel orders; i.e., Do you fill orders according to
specific weights given, between 210# and 240#, or is it the general
practice to simply order so many Large barrels, and you fill in the
actual weights, when loaded out. Please advise us on this point.))

SHIPMENT:-

Please consign this shipment to order/notify A. E. Hegewisch,
701 Queen & Crescent Bldg., New Orleans, La., making shipment promptly
on or before August 26th.

PACKING:-

Please pack in your Standard new wooden barrels and Bales,
for export, as indicated above.

---- 1 ----

Prior to World War II, telegrams and letters were the primary means of ordering shrimp products. In this instance, barrels and "craft paper boxes" of dried shrimp were to be shipped to Topeka, Kansas, where the sun-dried product was repackaged. (Letter provided by Thomas "Tommy" Chauvin, President of Chauvin Brothers Inc., Chauvin, LA, 1933.)

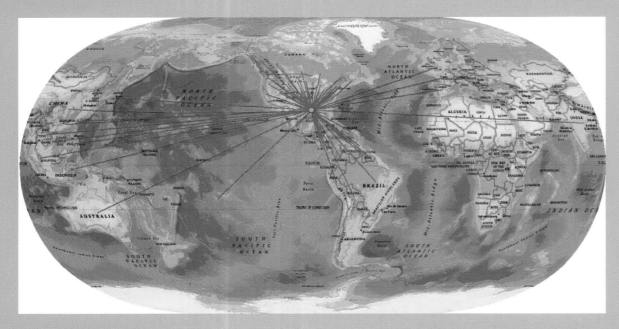

The spatial distribution of Blum and Bergeron's product line from Houma to consumers around the world is a testimony to the business owners' acumen. (Cartography by DeWitt Braud, Louisiana State University, Coastal Studies Institute. Base map: National Geographic, Esri, DeLorme, HERE, UNEP-WCMC, USGS, NASA, ESA, METI, NRCAN, GEBCO, NOAA, increment P Corp.)

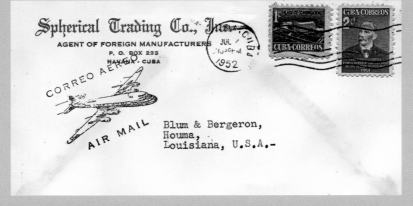

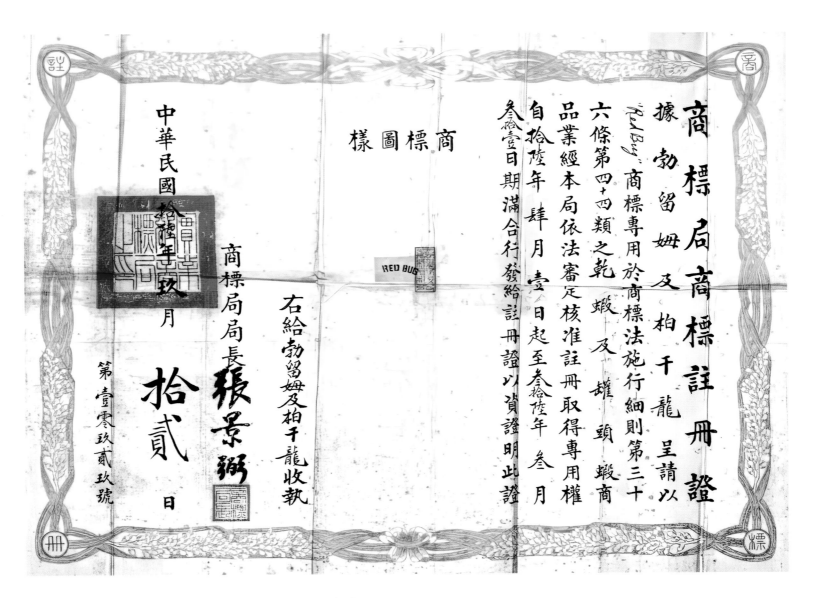

商標局商標註冊證

據勃留姆及柏千龍呈請以"Red Bug"商標專用於商標法施行細則第三十六條第四十四類之乾蝦及罐頭蝦商品業經本局依法審定核准註冊取得專用權自拾陸年肆月壹日起至參拾陸年參月參拾壹日期滿合行發給註冊證明此證

樣圖標商

RED BUG

中華民國拾陸年玖月

商標局局長張景

右給勃留姆及柏千龍收執

第壹零玖貳玖號

拾貳日

Journalist J. B. Dauenhauer Jr. reported thirty-seven platforms in coastal Louisiana four years before the start of World War II.

By World War II, Louisiana natives had thus mastered the fundamentals of shrimp drying from the micro to the macro scale, and while the most visible entrepreneurs possessed formidable financial resources and political clout—Jules Fisher was a state senator and key future ally of legendary populist Governor Huey P. Long, while Dr. Leon Jastremski of Pelican Lake Packing was head of the state board of health—they lacked their Asian competitors' long-established distribution network with mainland China, the world's largest consumer of dried shrimp. The Houma-based firm of Blum and Bergeron soon filled the void.

In this 1883 article in the New Orleans *Daily Picayune*, Daniel Dennett reported that, over an eight-month period, Chinese settlements along Barataria Bay shipped approximately 40 tons of dried shrimp in 350 tierces—casks or barrels individually weighing 220 to 230 pounds—to S. L. Jones in San Francisco for transshipment to China. The China connection—via the San Francisco Bay Area—remained critically important after Caucasian-owned dried shrimp enterprises began to supplant their Chinese predecessors. Blum and Bergeron, for example, received trademark protection for their "Red Bug" brand from the Chinese government before World War II. (Official Chinese Trademark Document from the Blum and Bergeron Collection, Nicholls State University Archives, Thibodaux, LA.)

In its heyday, the Blum and Bergeron Company distributed more than two million pounds of dried shrimp annually (about ten thousand barrels). Because of modest local demand, the product required a market beyond New Orleans and south Louisiana. Exploitation of external markets required the services of wholesale grocery brokers and distributors. In the second decade of the twentieth century, Lazare Levy's New Orleans wholesale grocery company became one of the first wholesale grocers to distribute Blum and Bergeron's shrimp. Later, Blum and Bergeron secured the services of Henry Loose, a former agent of the Trans-Pacific Company who served as the Houma firm's export manager for more than fifty years. Thanks to Loose's efforts, Blum and Bergeron shipped thousands of barrels to San Francisco for transshipment to Chinese markets in the twentieth century. (Photo from the Blum and Bergeron Collection, Nicholls State University Archives, Thibodaux, LA.)

(Barrel stencil courtesy of Blum and Bergeron Inc., Houma, LA.)

(Barrel stencil courtesy of Blum and Bergeron Inc., Houma, LA.)

(Barrel stencil courtesy of Blum and Bergeron Inc., Houma, LA.)

(Barrel stencil courtesy of Blum and Bergeron Inc., Houma, LA.)

(Barrel stencil courtesy of Blum and Bergeron Inc., Houma, LA.)

Blum and Bergeron's office and warehouse on Bayou Terrebonne, at the corner of West Main and Barrow Streets, was the mainstay of the family business for more than a century. In 2018, the firm moved to a more modern facility in Houma. (Photo from the Blum and Bergeron Collection, Nicholls State University Archives, Thibodaux, LA.)

Leopold Blum and Shelly Bergeron, the original partners, came from highly disparate backgrounds. Blum, a Jewish wholesale grocery salesman, first visited Terrebonne Parish around 1900. Because the region's agrarian economy, like that of the nation, was still reeling from the effects of the Panic of 1893, many residents of lower Terrebonne Parish engaged in a barter economy. Compelled to accept agricultural produce as payment from his rural customers, Blum quickly realized an opportunity to establish himself as an independent commission broker. However, as an outlander and a Jew in a conservative Catholic community, he opted to form a partnership with local Cajun tavern-keeper Shelly Bergeron in 1906 to secure a reliable entrée with insular local fishermen. (Blum and Bergeron would not legally formalize the partnership until 1912.) According to family lore, a Bayou Little Caillou resident (Blum descendants now recall only the person's surname—Authement) approached Leopold soon afterward and asked him to find a buyer for a "barn full of unshelled dried shrimps in sacks." Blum subsequently contacted a California dried shrimp broker, who had recently returned from China with "the exclusive patent to sell dried shrimp in that country." Blum and Bergeron eventually forged a lasting professional bond with Trans-Pacific Company affiliate Henry Loose. For more than half a century, Loose was instrumental in marketing the Houma firm's product to Asian markets. At its zenith, the company exported two million pounds (one thousand tons) of dried shrimp per year, primarily to China and Far Eastern markets.

This fortuitous contact provided the Houma company with a springboard for global distribution of Louisiana dried shrimp, but access to the Chinese market alone did not ensure success. As

Like their Quong Sun competitors, Blum and Bergeron also had a private canned shrimp label, but the firm never actively operated a cannery. (Label courtesy of Blum and Bergeron Inc., Houma, LA.)

Twelve years after its modest launch, Blum and Bergeron warehoused products in Houma and San Francisco. The firm's corporate archive indicates that it purchased $43,020 worth of dried product in 1921. Within three years, their annual purchases exceeded $154,000 before rising to $201,000 in 1930. In 1930, the first full year of the Great Depression, $152,000 of the Blum and Bergeron output was sold for distribution to California and Asian markets. Over the following decade, the company averaged $150,000 in annual acquisitions, approximately 15 percent of which was sold throughout San Francisco. Blum and Bergeron is now evidently the world's oldest family-owned dried shrimp wholesaler.

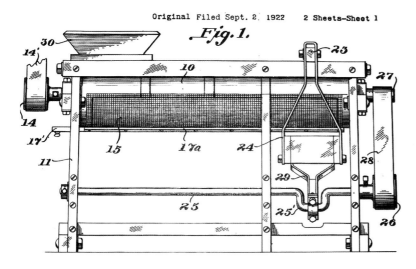

Original Filed Sept. 2, 1922   2 Sheets—Sheet 1

Fig.1.

The diagram used in Blum and Bergeron's original patent application for a mechanical peeling and shelling machine, filed on September 2, 1922, and approved May 6, 1924. (Patent diagram from the authors collections. Courtesy of Blum and Bergeron Inc., Houma, LA.)

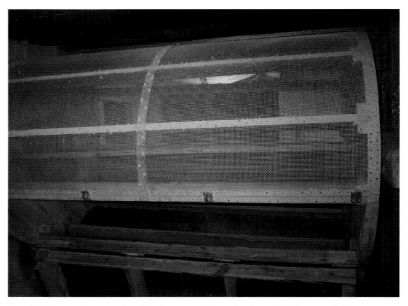

The shelling machine, outlined in the patent, brought about the demise of shrimp dance. (Photo from the authors' collections, 2009.)

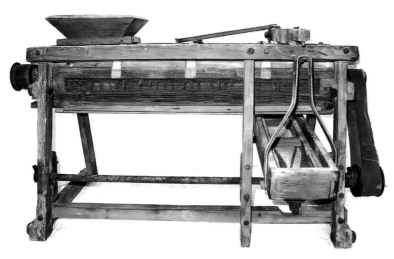

Shelly Bergeron and Fred Chauvin applied for a patent on their shrimp-shelling machine on September 2, 1922, and the US Patent and Trademark Office issued the patent on May 6, 1924. The original scale model of the patented shrimp-shelling machine (patent US1493425A). (From the authors' collections. Courtesy of Blum and Bergeron Inc., Houma, LA.)

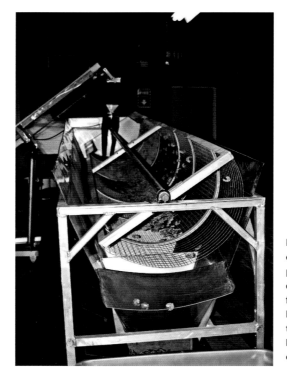

In the company's warehouse, employees clean, grade, and package in cardboard boxes dried shrimp purchased from a coterie of companies. Filled boxes are now shipped to clients primarily by FedEx. (From the authors' collections, 2009.)

Part of the weighing and grading equipment used in the firm's packaging operation. (From the authors' collections, 2009.)

When shrimp-drying activities were outdoors, the final step in separating meat from shells involved "dancing the shrimp" to pulverize and remove the hulls. The shell refuse resembled a fine sawdust, commonly called *bran* or *dust* in Louisiana. This product was once considered useless. However, Blum and Bergeron found markets for bran in Mexican condiment manufacturing, the aquarium fish food industry, and zoos, which use it to fortify flamingo feed. (From the authors' collections, 2009.)

The shelling machine removes the shells in the form of "dust" fragments. The product is put in recycled coffee sacks and delivered to Blum and Bergeron's warehouse. (Photo from the authors' collections, 1976.)

in the nineteenth century, political turmoil in mainland China created economic ripples that lapped onto Louisiana's Gulf shore. Beginning with the Boxer Rebellion in May 1900 and continuing until July 1926, the Chinese mainland was wracked by intermittent fighting between monarchists and nationalists seeking to unify the badly fragmented nation under a viable central government. In 1926, just as the nationalists claimed victory, the right- and left-wing contingents of the new coalition government turned on each other, plunging the war-torn nation, once again, into a brutal civil war that continued until Japanese forces invaded the mainland in 1937. The resulting instability in Chinese currency and the continually fluctuating demand for Louisiana dried shrimp forced brokers like Blum and Bergeron to diversify their client portfolio. By the beginning of American involvement in World War II (1941), Blum and Bergeron and, to a much lesser extent, the Quong Sun company had successfully infiltrated the Philippine, Hawaiian, Cuban, Panamanian, Guiana, Peruvian, and Bolivian markets.

Blum and Bergeron's continued success—and, by extension, that of coastal Louisiana's dried shrimp industry—hinged not only on the owners' business expertise but also on a critical technological innovation patented by Shelly Bergeron and Fred Chauvin in the early 1920s. Bergeron's device consisted of a cylindrical revolving drum covered with chicken wire attached to a wooden frame. Dried shrimp placed in this cage were rotated continuously until centrifugal force removed shells from the crustaceans' desiccated flesh. This device

"Shipment of Louisiana sun-dried shrimp to markets in the Philippine Islands, is being planned by citizens of Bayou Dufon and Bayou Barataria. This new market is sought by Louisiana companies to offset the effect of the recent decline in the Chinese market, caused by the depreciation of Chinese currency" ("Shipment of Louisiana Sun-Dried Shrimp," *Assumption Pioneer*).

Over the ensuing decades, the Blum and Bergeron company along with Louisiana Dried Shrimp, Price Seafood, and Hi Seas of Dulac would survive into the twenty-first century. By 1964, Quong Sun was involved in the dried shrimp industry exclusively as a distributor. The venerable Chinese enterprise ceased to exist in 1984.

The United Fruit Company was one of Blum and Bergeron's first clients. The Houma firm used United Fruit's Central American operations as an additional springboard for global expansion of its distribution network. Blum and Bergeron utilized a large assortment of freight forwarders to meet their needs in the southern Gulf of Mexico region and the Caribbean rim nations. (Card advertisements from the Blum and Bergeron Collection, Nicholls State University Archives, Thibodaux, LA.)

Blum and Bergeron utilized the Fern Line for dried shrimp shipments to the Orient. (Card advertisements from the Blum and Bergeron Collection, Nicholls State University Archives, Thibodaux, LA.)

proved far more efficient than either the bag-beating technique of independent Cajun fishermen or the labor-intensive "shrimp dance" employed by generations of Chinese platform operators. In fact, the Asians' major American competitors, who almost universally embraced the Bergeron-Chauvin invention, enjoyed an exponential economic advantage, for one machine operator replaced dozens of day laborers. In addition, the mechanical sheller allowed operators to process dried shrimp in interior spaces, where the crustaceans were safe from both voracious aquatic birds and the volatile elements, particularly sudden thunderstorms that could destroy acres of drying shrimp in mere minutes. The Bergeron-Chauvin shelling machine's impact was virtually instantaneous, and by the end of 1921, nationally syndicated news articles predicted that the "shrimp dance" would shortly go "into the lumber-room of memories" ("'Shrimp Dance' Passes Away," *Grand Forks Herald*).

The shrimp-shelling machine also made it easier for shrimp driers to collect and market internationally an important industry byproduct. Meal or bran—the undecomposed waste (shells and carapaces) of dried shrimp processing—has been the industry's most important secondary product since the Chinese created a shrimp-drying beachhead along the banks of San Francisco Bay. Shrimp meal has several significant industrial and agricultural applications, including fertilizer, pigmentation, and livestock and aquarium fish feed production. Outside interest in Louisiana shrimp meal—long locally considered a nuisance waste product—evidently first emerged in 1921, following Louisiana commissioner of conservation M. L. Alexander's address to a joint assembly of the

The efficacy of the shelling machine prompted a rash of counterfeit imitations at drying platforms throughout Terrebonne Parish, forcing Blum and Bergeron to issue cease and desist letters to the owners and managers operating in violation of the inventors' proprietary rights. In a sharply worded letter dated April 23, 1926, the Houma firm formally alerted the transgressors that they were in violation of the nation's patent laws and advised them that, unless royalties were forthcoming, they would "bring suit to enjoy the further use of [the shelling] Machine and to recover damages and profits by reason of infringement." The absence of further official correspondence in the matter suggests immediate compliance, with one notable exception. The Fisher Shrimp Company owned by state senator Jules G. Fisher and his family—directed their New Orleans attorney to respond with a sharp rebuttal, alleging that the Fisher operations had designed, built, and operated a cylindrical shelling device long before issuance of the Blum and Bergeron patent and, furthermore, that "if all of the facts were known," it would have been "impossible" for the initially aggrieved party "to have had your patent issued." The seemingly inevitable litigation between the emerging titans of Louisiana's dried shrimp industry was averted when Blum and Bergeron solicited the opinion of Mason, Fenwick and Lawrence, a Washington, DC firm, in May 1924. Patent attorney D. W. C. Lawrence responded approximately two months later, positing that, in his view, there was no "doubt as to whether or not the [Fisher] machine in question is an infringement" the patent-holders' rights, despite some superficial similarities. The absence of additional relevant material in the Blum and Bergeron corporate archive suggests that the controversy died at this point.

The patent dispute is significant because of the light it sheds on the dried shrimp industry in coastal Terrebonne Parish in the post–World War I era. First, the cease and desist letters provide the physical addresses—set out below—of the shrimp-drying platforms allegedly infringing on the Blum and Bergeron patent. It is notable that *all* of these platforms were operated by local, non-Asian entrepreneurs. Most of these operators had Cajun surnames—Authement, Bourg, LeBlanc, Chiasson, Foret, Boudreaux, Chauvin, Lapeyrouse, Robichaux, and Pellegrin. Second, the absence of any mention of the rapidly declining number of Asian operators suggests that they continued to use traditional cleaning and winnowing methods (i.e., the "shrimp dance"), which were less efficient and far more labor intensive. These platforms were therefore increasingly less competitive. Finally, the emerging dominance of Cajun owner-operators suggests linkage in with the now Cajun-dominated local shrimp-harvesting infrastructure.

Blum and Bergeron bulk-shipped their product to resale businesses that repackaged Louisiana dried shrimp in small cellophane bags as salty treats. (Photos from the authors' collections, 2020.)

Table 3.1

LOCATION OF TERREBONNE PARISH DRYING PLATFORMS Based on the documentary record and local lore.		
Bayou Tortue	3	10%
Grand Pass d'Azile	4	13%
Coon Road, Little Caillou	2	6%
Red Fish Bayou	3	42%
Chanomy(?)	1	3%
Grand Caillou, Below Sister Lake	1	3%
Cocodrie, Little Caillou	3	10%
Little Caillou	1	3%
Unknown	1	3%
Bayou DuLarge	2	6%

American Fisheries Society and the National Association of Game and Fish Commissioners at Allentown, Pennsylvania. Alexander subsequently received a letter from Pennsylvania commissioner of fisheries N. R. Buller inquiring about the availability of shrimp meal from Louisiana shrimp driers, because the regional Chinese distributors, who allegedly held a stranglehold on the product, charged exorbitant prices. This inquiry seems to have provided the catalyst for national distribution of Louisiana shrimp meal. The international marketing of this product began in earnest following the Nazi takeover of the German government in 1933. Just before the First World War, Germany chemists devised a method of producing nitrogen from alternate sources when natural nitrates were not available. Nitrates are essential to gunpowder production. Because of treaty-imposed postwar restrictions on the German military, the Nazi government cast about for additional sources of nitrogen for its aggressive rearmament program. Because shrimp meal boasts exceptionally high nitrogen concentrations (11 percent, calculated as ammonia), the Louisiana platform byproduct proved invaluable to the German military-industrial complex.

The dynamism and resilience that characterized and sustained the traditional shrimp preservation industries also distinguished the fresh shrimp fishery. The initial postwar surge in technological innovation and adaptation coincided with the ready availability of internal combustion engines and petroleum-derived fuel in the Pelican State's coastal fishing villages. Before boats in Louisiana's large commercial fleet became highly specialized after the Great War, fishing vessels were designed for maximum operational flexibility. For example, luggers, easily the Pelican State's most common fishing boat type, served alternately as oyster and shrimping vessels on a staggered, seasonal basis to permit owner-operators a steady, year-round income. Between 1904 and 1908, the Louisiana Oyster Commission registered 1,800 coastal craft of various sizes and designs, although luggers were unquestionably the most common. Of these myriad fishing vessels, nearly 97 percent of the fleet relied entirely on sail power; only 58 boats were propelled by internal combustion engines. By 1920, sailing vessels were virtually a memory.

Contemporary observers concurred that 1917 was the pivotal year for the Louisiana fishing fleet's adoption of the internal combustion engine. On August 10, 1917, five months after the country entered World War I, Congress empowered the new United States Food Administration to manage national food production, distribution, and consumption. This agency, whose slogan was "Food Will Win the War," actively promoted food rationing through "Meatless Tuesdays," "Wheatless Wednesdays," and myriad complementary campaigns as a means of ensuring adequate provisions for the military. By early 1918, some patriotic Americans even called for establishment of a "fish week ... to conserve the meat supply." The nation's rapid shift to maritime protein sources was pronounced and sustained throughout the conflict. Writing in 1921, journalist Robert Morgan recalled that "when the European war came on, ... it ... imposed a greater demand than ever for the products of ... fisheries, in the Government's search for abundant food supplies to take the place of the meats which went to sustain the American Expeditionary Force and to feed our allies in the great conflict." (Morgan, "Motor Boats" 27.)

Nationwide meat rationing afforded Louisiana shrimpers an unprecedented economic growth opportunity. In 1917, *Leslie's Weekly*, a nationally circulating newspaper in print from 1855 to 1922, reported that the United States' coastal population annually consumed, on average, twenty pounds of fish (the paper's euphemism for oysters, shrimp, and mussels), but in communities at least two hundred miles from any seacoast, the consumption rate fell to less than a half-pound. Louisiana's shrimp processors thus enjoyed for the first time a captive inland market.

However, the war effort also presented the industry with unprecedented challenges. In 1918, the Louisiana shrimp industry employed approximately 5,200 men working aboard "some 1,100 boats." Approximately half of these shrimpers were reportedly conscripted into various branches of the military by the war's conclusion, and undrafted fishermen scrambled to offset the loss of manpower by means of new and far more efficient propulsion and harvesting technologies. The first of these was the internal combustion engine.

TODAY IS "MEATLESS" TUESDAY

You will find an extensive variety of choice dishes available

NO BEEF, PORK, VEAL OR LAMB SERVED TODAY

(Posters from the Mayor La Guardia Collection, New York City Department of Records and Information Service, ca. 1917.)

MEMBER OF U.S. FOOD ADMINISTRATION

Food will win the war

We observe Meatless days Wheatless days - Porkless days

and carry out all conservation rules of the U.S. Food Administration.

Originally established in World War I, Meatless Tuesdays were part of the government's efforts to conserve all forms of meat. (Poster from the Chicago Public Library, ca. 1917.)

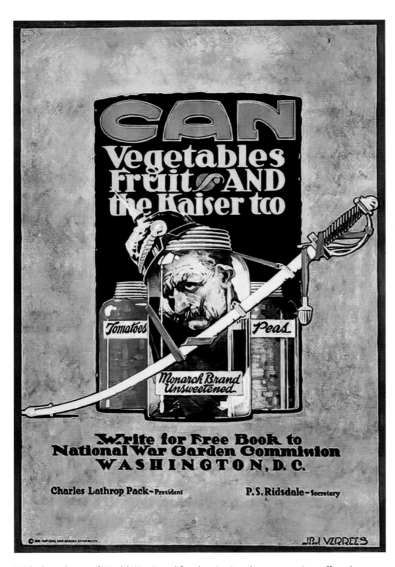

With the advent of World War II and food rationing, home canning offered families a way to supplement their food supplies. Commercially produced canned shrimp also benefitted consumers' need for protein. (Poster from the Chicago Public Library, ca. 1917.)

Many now elderly informants recall that, when the state's shrimp fleet transitioned from sail to engines, many boat owners installed Fairbanks-Morse power plants. One of these engines is still in use (2020) and geared to pull boats up the shipways in a bayou-side shipyard along Lower Bayou Lafourche. (Advertisement from *Soards' New Orleans City Directory for 1935*.)

In Louisiana's coastal plain, the paradigm shift occurred in stages. Commercial interests led the way forward, as freight companies enthusiastically embraced gasoline-powered propulsion technologies in the second decade of the twentieth century. In late 1916, *Power Boating* magazine rhapsodized about the rapidly unfolding transformation: "New Orleans is a city which practically lives off its power boats [i.e., small, motorized cargo vessels]. More than any other town of its size in the new world, is the Crescent City dependent on trade boats, driven by gas engines for its daily bill of fare."

Louisiana canneries, which closely monitored the transition, had also experimented with petroleum-powered motors since the turn of the twentieth century. Acquisitions managers turned first to naphtha engines, which boatmen had successfully used in small, East Coast boats in the late 1880s and early 1890s. These propulsion systems, however, were dangerous to operate and difficult to maintain, and Louisiana fishermen consequently soon abandoned them in favor of more stable emerging propulsion technologies. Kerosene motors quickly gave way to single-cylinder and, later, multicylinder gasoline engines. Single-cylinder motors—typically engines manufactured by Lockwood-Ash (Jackson, Michigan) and Nadler (Plaquemine, Louisiana)—were first employed in small folk boats—pirogues, chalands, esquifs, and bateaux—but they were

'ARTHUR DUVIC'S SONS
Marine Supplies and Gasoline Engines
ALL SIZES IN STOCK

120-122 Chartres Street
Phones Main 0988-0989-1717

1304 St. Charles Ave.
Phone Raymond 2872

NEW ORLEANS, LA.

Arthur Duvic's now forgotten supply firm provided gasoline engines to Louisiana's marine fleet in the years immediately before World War II. (Advertisement from *Soards' New Orleans City Directory for 1935*.)

incapable of propelling larger, heavily laden commercial fishing vessels. (Locals dubbed these motors "putt-putts" because of their distinctive exhaust signature.) Canneries, which were dependent on the uninterrupted operation of their shrimping fleets, turned first to the Fairbanks-Morse Corporation, which had a new marine engine product line that had sold nearly 168,000 engines; then to the Atlas Company, an Oakland, California manufacturer that sold its machines through the Arthur Duvic Company of New Orleans; Lathrop Marine Engines; and, finally, Gray Marine, an up-and-coming maker of small marine engines. As early as 1916, according to journalists, the largest canneries in the New Orleans area "could not exist without the aid of boats driven wholly or in part by gasoline engines." The Barataria Canning Company alone used five sixty-foot "power freighters" to transport shrimp from coastal luggers to inland factories. Two of these freighters used thirty-six-horsepower, heavy-duty Fairbanks-Morse engines, while the remainder of the fleet used a variety of marine engines. The shrimp industry's adoption of gas-propulsion was accelerated in the following months by wartime food shortages, which resulted in explosive growth in public demand for domestic seafood. By 1918, upper Gulf Coast canneries operated "more than 350" power craft.

During the canneries' protracted initial flirtation with gas pro-pulsion, small, independent boat operators—including oystermen and shrimpers—were reportedly "slower here [the Louisiana Gulf

In the coastal vernacular, *motor* was a generic term for gasoline engines. Regional commercial fishermen and trade journalists used the terms *motor* and *engine* interchangeably until the advent of large electrical motors.

Repurposed automobile engines provided many trawler captains with engines that could be converted easily to marine use. (Photo courtesy of the National Archives and Records Administration, Prints & Photographs Division, College Park, MD, photographer Russel Lee, 1938, reproduction number LC-DIG-fsa-8a24196.)

Coast] than elsewhere in adding power craft to their utilities." Their cautious approach ultimately paid hefty dividends, for by America's entry into World War I, the Ford Corporation had inadvertently emerged as the preeminent source of small maritime engines. During the Ford Model T's heyday—1908 to 1927, a pivotal epoch when approximately fifteen million cars were produced—large numbers of preassembled engines were shipped to dealerships in wooden crates. Although these motors were intended exclusively for automotive use, Louisiana's ever-resourceful independent fishermen quickly discovered that Ford's four-cylinder engines were readily adaptable to nautical use. Automotive motors were relatively cheap, dependable, and easily repairable. More importantly, the twenty-horsepower Model T engine and its successor, the forty-horsepower Model A motor, were sufficiently powerful to propel a lugger from four to ten miles per hour, depending on winds, tides, and cargo displacement. For the first time, Louisiana shrimpers were no longer slaves to the vagaries of the winds.

By freeing shrimpers from their dependency on sails, gas-powered boats made harvesting operations more efficient, dependable, and remunerative, for crews were able to transport to market multiple cargoes in the time formerly required by a single trip. In fact, following the American entry into World War I, the newly motorized shrimp fleet supplied enough product to the Crescent City to offset local beef shortages and stabilize commodity prices. In September 1917, *Power Boating* magazine observed:

> One of the most important classes of work boats, not only in New
> Orleans but all along the gulf coast[,] is that which carries the fish,
> oysters, shrimp, and other sea foods to the market. Their impor-
> tance has increased enormously since the beginning of the war,
> because, by the aid of the gasoline engine, they were able to add
> largely to the food supply of all the gulf states, while they make
> so much faster and more frequent trips from the fishing grounds
> under power than they did in the old days under sail that prices
> of this class of food have risen very little in proportion to those of
> other necessities of life [R. Jurado, "With the Bread Winners" 31–32].

Small inshore trawlers did not have large holds, so the catch was deheaded on deck and put in seventy-pound barrels for the trip to the ice boat or home port. (Photo from the Louisiana Department of Wildlife and Fisheries, New Iberia Office, photographer and date unknown.)

Small and efficient inshore Lafitte skiffs, outfitted with skimmer nets, can still be seen throughout the Louisiana coastal plain. (Photo from the authors' collections, 2018.)

This timely technological paradigm shift was wrought not by newly constructed vessels but by "rebuilt luggers with an engine installed." (Powered luggers and their smaller marine cousins later morphed into Lafitte skiffs.) Lugger power plant installations were performed either by the boat owner, who typically functioned as captain, navigator, engineer, mechanic, and sometimes shipwright, or shipyard owners operating out of their own bayou-side front yards. Second-generation former shrimpers born between the world wars recall that their fathers used a variety of gasoline and, later, diesel engines in their boats, including Fairbanks-Morse nautical motors, Ford automotive power plants, and a variety of other engines readily available from dealers, shipyards, and even the Sears, Roebuck mail-order catalog.

In addition, by extending a vessel's range exponentially, gas engines effectively cut the industry's fetters to coastal waters. In 1912, A. W. Bitting, author of a government report on the state

Less common engines in Louisiana's *entre-deux-guerres* shrimping fleet included representatives of the Regal Gasoline, Michigan Marine Motors, Frisco Standard, Clinton, Hercules, Atlas, Cushman, Palmer, Globe, Clay, Weber, Moto Go, Pivert, and Sears, Roebuck brands. Pivert's factory was in New Orleans.

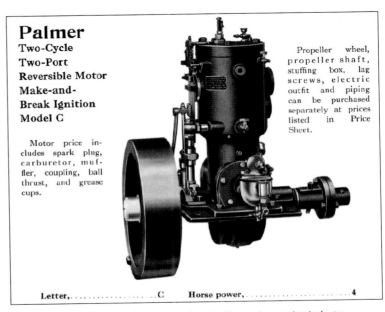

Palmer
Two-Cycle
Two-Port
Reversible Motor
Make-and-
Break Ignition
Model C

Motor price includes spark plug, carburetor, muffler, coupling, ball thrust, and grease cups.

Propeller wheel, propeller shaft, stuffing box, lag screws, electric outfit and piping can be purchased separately at prices listed in Price Sheet.

Letter,....................C   Horse power,.........................4

Introduced in 1899, Palmer became a stalwart in the marine engine industry as many Gulf Coast oystermen became converts. (Advertisement from the Old Marine Engine Discussion Board, http://www.oldmarineengine.com/discus/messages/3430/827.html, retrieved March 7, 2020.)

Prior to 1917, state license records show 300 commercial shrimp seines operations were active in Louisiana's coastal waters. By 1949, only 4 active shrimp seines operations reportedly remained, while 3,310 mechanized trawls were in use. With the availability of gasoline engines, rated at more than one hundred horsepower, the industry was able to exploit new fishing grounds. Using new and refined gear, trawlers began to expand into deep waters. As the power of marine engines increased, so did the size of the boats' nets. Larger nets required new rigging methods to maximize the harvest. (Photo from the authors' collections. Courtesy of the Maritime and Seafood Industry Museum, Biloxi, MS, 2019.)

Staff Photographer J. Baylor Roberts

A Shovelful Would Make a Lot of Salad
From the hold of an incoming boat the iced shrimp is unloaded quickly into tubs and rushed to the cannery. Delay may mean spoilage (page 510).

For decades, a shovel and a strong back were required to transfer a lugger's catch from a hold to a seventy-pound basket. Since none of the boats had scales, the catch was measured by a careful tally of baskets. The total was then converted to barrels, the industry standard by which captains were paid. This practice persists to the present. (Photo from the authors' collections, 1944.)

The traditional means of transferring shrimp from a hold to a picking shed. (From the authors' collections. Used with permission from the Theriot family, per Jason Theriot, Houston, TX, 1935.)

of the United States canning industry, observed that "shrimp are caught only in shallow water along the shore. Before this year (1911), all catches had to be made in less than 6 feet." Within three decades, the focus of the Louisiana shrimp industry had shifted to far offshore waters, where "jumbo" shrimp would be "discovered" before the Japanese attack on Pearl Harbor (December 7, 1941). This discovery would fundamentally transform the Louisiana shrimp industry, making both the canning and the dried shrimp industries largely irrelevant, triggering their protracted decline throughout the remainder of the twentieth century.

Louisiana shrimpers were initially lured offshore not by the often-illusory promise of more productive fishing grounds but rather by the firm prospect of lucrative income from illicit activities. Success in these illegal endeavors, however, was contingent on adoption and mastery of the emerging propulsion technologies. Hence, shrimpers' use and gradual enhancement of the internal combustion engine continued unabated following the Great War's conclusion in November 1918 and the ensuing, precipitous postwar decline in popular demand for Gulf shrimp.

Manuel Molero was actively engaged in the rum-running business. (Photo from the authors' collections. Courtesy of Dot and Michael Benge, 2016.)

The Louisiana coast was the site of America's most notorious rum-running episode—the *I'm Alone* incident. On March 22, 1929, the United States Coast Guard cutter *Wolcott* intercepted the *I'm Alone*, a Canadian-flagged schooner laden with liquor from Belize, in international waters off the Louisiana coast. When the rumrunner's captain refused orders to surrender his ship, the *Wolcott* gave chase—eventually with the assistance of the cutter *Dexter*. The pursuit continued into the central Gulf of Mexico and culminated when the *Dexter* fired on, and sank, its prey, in the process killing one of the nine crewmen. The Coast Guard transferred the survivors to New Orleans, where they were incarcerated.

Destruction of the *I'm Alone*, the crew member's death, and the incarceration of the survivors created a serious international incident that strained Canadian-American relations and resulted in litigation against the American government, which was ultimately forced to pay compensation to the aggrieved owners and crew. As an interesting sidenote, shortly after the *I'm Alone* sank, federal authorities seized a large cache of liquor aboard Chicago-bound freight cars in Vermilion Parish.

This now largely forgotten phase of the fishery's evolution was driven directly by political developments unrelated to the shrimp fishery. On January 16, 1919, the Eighteenth Amendment became part the United States Constitution, establishing a nationwide prohibition on the manufacture, transportation, and sale of alcohol. The amendment, which went into effect on January 17, 1920, was, unsurprisingly, hugely unpopular in laissez-faire, predominately Catholic southern Louisiana. Because of its porous coastline and its virulently "wet" (i.e., anti-temperance) population, Prohibition enforcement in the Pelican State's coastal plain was a fool's errand. From 1920 until 1933, when Prohibition was repealed, large numbers of foreign-flagged freighters laden with Canadian, Bahamian, and Cuban liquor anchored in international waters off the Louisiana coast and awaited contact with Louisiana boatmen—primarily shrimpers according to local oral traditions—who would offload cases of contraband and smuggle them into coastal marsh communities after eluding Coast Guard patrols unfamiliar with coastal Louisiana's labyrinth of uncharted waterways.

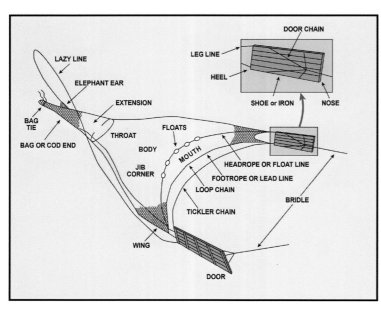

The components of a shrimp trawl that keep its mouth open as the shrimp are "herded" into the bag or cod end. (Artwork by Robert Ray from a variety of sources.)

This trawl board shop closed in August 2019. (Photo from the authors' collections, 2019.)

C. H. Townsend, author of *Statistics of the Fisheries of the Gulf States* (1899), provides the most comprehensive extant snapshot of the Barataria Bay seine fishery in the twilight years of the nineteenth century. According to Townsend, there were forty active seines, employing 412 men and seventy-nine boats. The nets that they deployed had a cumulative length of 37,620 feet (an average of 940.5 feet per net). These operations reported an annual catch of 4,286,626 pounds of shrimp, valued at $76,223.

Eluding federal authorities became exponentially more difficult in April 1924, when Congress extended America's offshore territorial limit from three to twelve miles. Because Louisiana shrimping vessels were shallow-draft boats designed for inland waters, they had difficulty negotiating the far-offshore swells. In addition, they were drastically underpowered compared to contemporary, increasingly fleet Coast Guard vessels. The disadvantages resulted in the arrest and imprisonment of some local rumrunners, but the lure of easy, ill-gotten wealth was too great for fishermen to ignore. To mitigate their speed disadvantage, Louisiana shrimpers began to operate in near offshore waters, where they were much closer to liquor-laden freighters and where, they quickly discovered, larger, adult shrimp flourished.

Harvesting offshore shrimp required new technologies, particularly trawl nets. From the colonial era, Louisiana fishermen had primarily used seines pulled through shallow water by laborers. Use of seines entailed deployment of work crews by sailboat; the slow, tedious, and laborious dragging of nets; loading the catch into a boat's hold; then waiting for favorable winds to transport the shrimp to New Orleans markets or canneries. This time-honored process held sway until 1917, when the "shrimp trawl" was introduced into the Pelican State's coastal wetlands. Just prior to World War I, Louisiana shrimpers deployed three hundred state-licensed commercial seines, but by 1949, only three were still in operation.

The transition was initially necessitated by manpower shortages resulting from the wartime draft. According to the Louisiana

Department of Conservation, "the trawl enabled one man to do the work of ten men pulling the traditional seines." The use of trawl nets aboard vessels newly converted to motor power revolutionized the industry. In 1890, 3,276 (80.5 percent) of the 4,068 Louisiana residents gainfully employed in the fishing industry were involved in "shore or boat fisheries," operating 168 commercial seines. Commercial seines, which typically stretched 900 to 1,350 feet in length (although the New Orleans *Times-Picayune* reported a 2,700-foot-long [.52-mile-long] net in use in Barataria Bay in 1914), remained the "principal form of [harvesting] apparatus" until World War I, but its ascendancy was eclipsed by the rise of the otter trawl, introduced into the Pelican State in 1917. State reports indicate that only four trawls were deployed in 1917, 250 in 1919, and 983 in 1921. "Meanwhile, the number of seines in use by Louisiana shrimpers declined by fifty percent during the same period." By 1922, only 106 large seines remained in use, while shrimpers employed 1,221 licensed trawls pulled by 1,021 gas-powered vessels.

Because of the greater operating range and harvesting efficiency of the gas-powered shrimp luggers, the regional fishery's postwar output increased so rapidly that, in the fall of 1921, Louisiana and Mississippi canneries and the Barataria area drying platforms were compelled to temporarily suspend operations because the unexpected glut had "so clogged" their facilities. This startling development, which the Louisiana Department of Conservation attributed "to the abandonment by fishermen of the seine in favor of the trawl," raised several red flags in the seafood industry and in the state government.

Aware that overfishing had virtually destroyed Chesapeake Bay's once seemingly inexhaustible oyster fishery as well as the West Coast's premier shrimp fishery in San Francisco Bay, Louisiana politicians and businessmen surely experienced a disturbing sense of déjà vu as the otter trawl's success raised the specter of irreparable marine resource depletion. Overfishing in the Pelican State's estuaries had been a perennial issue since the rise of the dried shrimp industry had given rise to widespread use of small-mesh seines. These seines were optimized for the capture of small

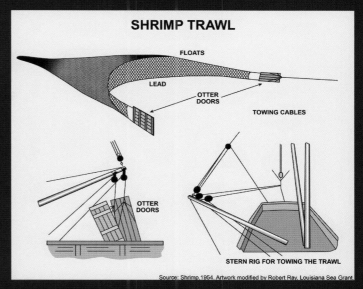

The otter trawl is enshrined as a crucial technological milestone in this country's fishing history. (Bullis, *Gulf of Mexico Shrimp Trawl Designs*.)

The otter trawl's origins extend to Victorian England. Patented in 1894, the trawl was used by approximately three thousand British fishing vessels by the turn of the twentieth century. New Englanders soon successfully adapted the net to the demands of local fisheries, but the innovative harvesting technology was not employed in the southern United States until the United States Bureau of Fisheries research station at Beaufort, North Carolina, used an otter trawl for marine fish and invertebrate surveys. The research staff soon discovered the net was admirably suited to the needs of the shrimp industry, and shrimpers along the southern Atlantic Coast quickly embraced the technology. In 1917, the trawl first appeared in Louisiana waters introduced from the Atlantic fisheries by an unknown fisherman.

Shrimpers' continued postwar reliance on trawls resulted from the new pull nets' inherent economic advantages. Seines could only be operated in shallow water, while trawl nets permitted shrimpers to range widely over geographically scattered and ecologically diverse offshore and near-shore shrimping grounds. Early twentieth-century seines typically required an operating crew of fifteen to twenty men, while luggers generally used a two-man crew. Shrimpers, who had traditionally deployed seines only during the summer and very early fall, could significantly extend the season through trawl use. Finally, trawls were substantially more efficient, allowing shrimpers to harvest their catch in much less time than their shallow-water counterparts.

This photo shows the final preparatory deployment of trawl nets and boards to "fish shrimp." (Photo courtesy of Louisiana Wildlife and Fisheries, New Iberia Office, photographer and date unknown.)

(Photo from the authors' collections. Courtesy of Morgan City Archives, Morgan City, LA, photographer Melvin Hardee, date unknown.)

(Photo from the Standard Oil (NJ) Collection, Photographic Archives, Archives and Special Collections, University of Louisville, photographer Martha Roberts, 1946, negative no. 43641.)

In 1923, E. A. Tulian, an administrator in the United States Fish Commission, penned the following succinct description of the rationale behind Louisiana's closed seasons, which, he believed, would allow significant expansion of the annual shrimp harvest without endangering this critical renewable marine resource: "during the colder months when the large shrimp take to deeper waters, there is a closed season on inside waters where the smaller ones congregate, this season extending from December 1st to February 15th inclusive. The destruction of young shrimp, thus prevented, combined with the fact that the adult shrimp spawn in the open gulf where they are not as readily available during the breeding season, are, in my opinion, the factors which will permit still further expansion of the shrimp industry without reaching the critical point [irreparable resource depletion]."

The size of this small vessel's trawl boards is impressive. (Photo courtesy of Louisiana Wildlife and Fisheries, New Iberia Office, photographer and date unknown.)

brown shrimp and seabobs—the mainstays of the dried shrimp industry—but they also produced a staggering amount of finfish bycatch. This inadvertent environmental toll was compounded when Louisiana and Mississippi seafood canneries also deployed dozens of large seining crews using equipment virtually identical to that of the drying platform employees. By 1899, according to federal researcher C. H. Townsend, the shrimp bycatch in the Barataria Bay area alone consisted of 494,965 pounds of trout, redfish, channel bass, mullet, and croakers.

Louisiana's maritime fisheries conservation effort began on July 14, 1910, with passage of Act 245, mandating a closed season on saltwater shrimp extending annually from June 1 to July 14. Supplementary legislation—Acts 59 of 1912 and 193 of 1916—established a second closed season between December 1 and February 15 and mandated net licensing as a means of regulating minimum net mesh sizes. By the start of World War I, it was illegal to use nets with a net mesh "less than three-quarters of an inch square or one and one-half inches stretched for taking saltwater shrimp." These mesh limits allowed juvenile shrimp to elude capture until they reached maturity.

Recognizing that conservation was necessary for the industry's long-term viability, Louisiana shrimpers generally, albeit initially grudgingly, complied with the net regulations, with one notable exception: fishermen attached to the surviving shrimp-drying platforms continued to use small-mesh nets to harvest the small brown shrimp and seabobs favored by consumers. Only the Louisiana Department of Conservation's persistent threats of net confiscation and destruction eventually compelled the drying platform operations to comply.

Through compliance with the new conservation laws, Louisiana shrimpers realized an almost immediate, unprecedented bonanza. Federal fishery reports indicate the Louisiana shrimp catch grew from 8,581,000 pounds in 1908, to 23,160,586 pounds in 1916, and 28,950,732 pounds in 1918. (Accounting techniques varied by agency; hence the totals vary within the documentary record.) The 337 percent increase in production becomes even more remarkable because "there were less vessels and men employed in this industry in 1916 than in 1908" (Alexander, *Biennial Report* 1918).

Use of trawl nets necessitated structural changes to a boat's rigging. The *Commercial Fisheries Review* ("Development of the [Shrimp] Industry" 4–5) provides perhaps the best succinct description of the initial innovations: "These early luggers were adapted for trawling by the simple expedient of adding a set of towlines and a trawl. Sometimes, a platform was extended off the stern to provide room for pulling in the net. Up until the late 1930's, few of these vessels carried power-driven machinery for putting out or taking in trawls."

Widespread, sustained deployment of trawls gave impetus to a variety of emerging support-services industries. Among the first of these were the local net manufacturing and maintenance companies. For much of the twentieth century, thriving family-owned custom net-making and dipping shops operated—often in backyards—along Bayou Lafourche between Raceland and Port Fourchon, in shrimping communities to the west of Bayou Lafourche, and in

Shannon Hardware of Morgan City (1873) and Houma, Chauvin Brothers of Chauvin (1875), Davidson (1885) of Houma, and J. H. Menge (1900) of New Orleans were among the most notable hardware stores in the coastal parishes during the interwar era.

New Orleans East. Oral accounts indicate that there were from three to five net-dipping facilities along lower Bayou Lafourche by the mid-twentieth century. Trawling was far more hazardous to netting than seine-pulling, for entire nets were often lost by snagging submerged objects. Nets that survived underwater hazards required regular tar-dipping because "the high temperature of the [coastal] water . . . exerts a destructive influence on twine, which becomes rotten much more rapidly than in Northern Waters" (Collins and Smith, 95).

Regional hardware stores—complemented by a wide assortment of ancillary facilities and services—also profited from the rapid mechanization of southern Louisiana's shrimp fleet. Oral history indicates that coastal community hardware stores also sometimes became engine distributors as well as providers of generic and specialized hardware for newly mechanized boats—everything from bolts, winches, and propellers to spark plugs. Journalist Harry H. Dunn reported in 1921 that these stores typically stood "on the banks of navigable streams, where engine parts, equipment, or tools for making even minor repairs are sold." Hardware stores also functioned as critical hardware suppliers to local boatyards tasked with building and maintaining the shrimp fleet.

Finally, the industry's postwar transformation was contingent on the rapid deployment of new fuel delivery and boat-to-market systems. Fuel availability was the most critical factor in the fishery's modernization. Contemporary observers consistently lamented the absence of dockside fuel depots outside New Orleans. In 1921, for example, *Power Boating* magazine noted that "there is not an oil-filling [dockside] station from Galveston to Tampa." Instead, commercial fishermen initially had to secure fuel at hardware stores or, in some cases, local pharmacies. Petroleum distribution companies, however, quickly built out the necessary infrastructure, evidently beginning with the cannery sites and later extending to dockside facilities in coastal communities. The rollout of the

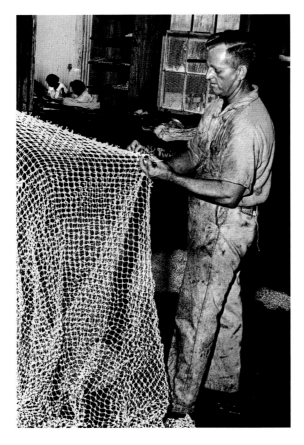

One of coastal Louisiana's last remaining net shops. (From the authors' collections, 2018.)

An example of the tedious process of mending and repairing nets. (Photo from the authors' collections. Courtesy of Morgan City Archives, Morgan City, LA, photographer Cross Studio, date unknown.)

Man attending to a damaged fishing net. (Photo from the Standard Oil (NJ) Collection, Photographic Archives, Archives and Special Collections, University of Louisville, photographer Martha Roberts, 1946, negative no. 43660.)

Lawrence "Chine" Terrebonne mending a net in his Golden Meadow net shop. (Photo from the authors' collections, 2018.)

Tarring is a fundamental part of continual net maintenance routines. (Photo from the authors' collections, 2015.)

Numerous shops across the coastal plain "tar" nets to protect webbing and prolong a net's life. "Dipping" or "tarring" a net is but one part of an open-ended maintenance process. Bottom debris is an ever-present hazard. In fact, oil-field rubble is so prevalent in Louisiana's waters that a Fishermen's Gear Compensation Fund was created by Act 673 in 1979 "to compensate commercial fishermen whose fishing gear, equipment, or vessels are damaged by underwater obstructions in the Louisiana Coastal Zone." (Photo from the authors' collections, 1997.)

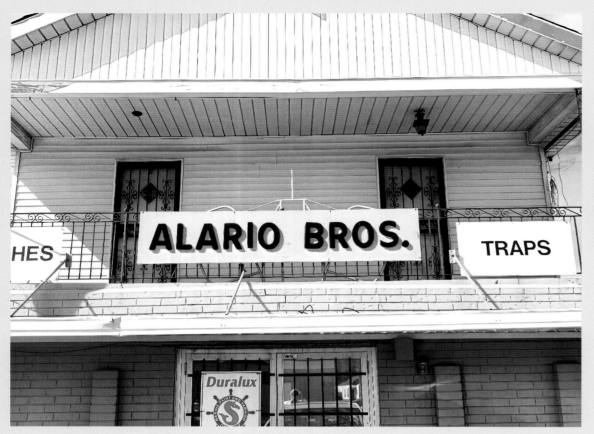

A marine hardware store, like its automotive counterpart, offers a wide assortment of goods to meet every maintenance or repair need. Items are typically crammed into every nook and cranny. (Photo from the authors' collections, 2018.)

Crawfish webbing. (Photo from the authors' collections, 2018.)

This webbing, manufactured in the Philippines, can be used to create nets of nearly any size. (Photo from the authors' collections, 2018.)

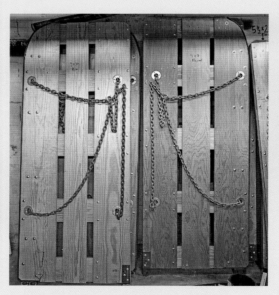

Test trawl boards. (From the authors' collections, 2018.)

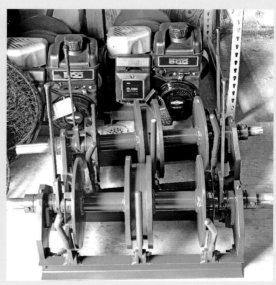

A twelve-inch double-drum winch. (Photo from the authors' collections, 2018.)

Part of Alario's broad selection of steel and galvanized blocks. (Photo from the authors' collections, 2018.)

Swivels. (Photo from the authors' collections, 2020.)

Shovels. (Photo from the authors' collections, 2018.)

Water-resistant galvanized blocks with shackles. (Photo from the authors' collections, 2018.)

Fishing boots are a necessity, as they are designed to survive exposure to a range of chemicals, as well as maritime wear and tear. On the northern Gulf Coast, white is the preferred color. (Photo from the authors' collections, 2018.)

Seventy-pound plastic baskets. (Photo from the authors' collections, 2020.)

Wooden blocks. (Photo from the authors' collections, 2018.)

Boxes of oakum are used in caulking wooded boats. This time-consuming practice is a dying skill. (Photo from the authors' collections, 2018.)

The modern self-service grocery is a business concept established by Clarence Saunders, who founded the Piggly Wiggly store chain in 1916. Previously, grocery store clerks handled goods removed from shelves at customers' request. In end-of-the-road shrimping villages, grocery stores gradually followed national trends, but until they were connected to inland communities by roadways, grocery deliveries were made by steamers. (From the Blum and Bergeron Collection, Nicholls State University Archives, Thibodaux, LA.)

A shrimp boat—with the characteristic red bow insignia—on the ways of a Lockport shipyard in 1967. (Photo from the State Library of Louisiana, Historical Photographs Collection, photographer Art Kleiner, 1967.)

maritime fuel infrastructure—spearheaded by the Texas Oil Company (later Texaco, now Chevron)—coincided with the development of a credit system tailored to the needs of the shrimp fishery's powerboat owners, who paid for their pre-voyage fuel purchases only after their catch was sold.

The ready accessibility of fuel permitted shrimpers to extend the length of their voyages, resulting in a corresponding increase in the size of their catch. Informants who came of age before World War II recall that their fathers' outings quickly stretched from two to fifteen days to twenty days in length. The result was,

Highway Map and Guide of LOUISIANA

This map, published in the 1930s, clearly indicates that "filling stations" were not part of coastal shrimping communities. In addition, there were no fuel retailers noted along the bayous south of Houma and Thibodaux. (Map from the authors' collections, ca. 1930.)

"The boats from Bayou Little Caillou and Boudreaux Canal work in Lake Barre, Lake Pelto and go sometimes 30 miles out into the Gulf. There are only two men to the crew of each boat, the captain and the deck hand. They stay out 15 days at a time, eating mostly canned food, but transfer every evening their day's catch to ice boats which draw alongside for their cargo and rush it to the plants. When asked what hours the men work, Desire T. Theriot, manager of the Indian Ridge Canning Company, laughed and said: 'All hours. They work from can't to can't.' He said, 'They work from daybreak to dark.'"

"All work is on shares. The captain receives one and one-fourth shares for his work; the deck hand, one share, and the company, one and one-fourth shares. This is when the boat is company owned. If the captain owns the boat, he receives two and one-fourth shares for his work. Almost all of the shrimpers now are organized into the Gulf Coast Fishermen and Trappers' Association" (New Orleans *Times-Picayune*, August 7, 1936).

initially, a corresponding increase in the size of the annual harvest and, eventually, the establishment of a permanent far-offshore presence that resulting in exploitation of the fishery's ultimate prize—"jumbo" shrimp.

JUMBO SHRIMP

Contrary to coastal Louisiana lore, "jumbo shrimp" were not "discovered" by transient Florida fishermen at Ship Shoal, near Morgan City, circa 1937. Native Lafourche Parish shrimpers had been commercially harvesting small quantities of the large white shrimp—later universally dubbed "jumbos"—for nearly two decades before their purported discovery. As early as 1918, Louisiana fishermen, using powered vessels, had begun trawling the near-shore and offshore waters up to eighteen miles from the coast, where they found "a bounteous supply of adult shrimp," including "jumbos." On October 30, 1920, for example, the *Abbeville Progress* reported that "fishermen are taking in large quantities of deep-water shrimp by the trawls and are selling them for $8 [$27.63 in 2020 currency] a box to canning factories and platforms for drying. The size of the shrimps average [*sic*] five to a pound." Oral sources also affirm that Terrebonne Parish shrimpers regularly trawled for large white shrimp in the waters near Timbalier Island and Grand Isle before the 1930s. Finally, by 1934, Louisiana's shrimp processors formally applied the following size gradients for sorting crustaceans destined for canning: small, medium, large, and jumbo. Louisiana's commercial fishermen and processors were thus quite familiar with "jumbo" shrimp long before they were officially "discovered."

The highly publicized discovery of jumbo shrimp off Ship Shoal near Morgan City around 1937 was nevertheless a pivotal moment in the industry's history because the unprecedented media blitz that accompanied it engendered a national culinary sensation, which "created new outlets for the . . . [Louisiana] catch." Despite this historical event's undisputed significance, the circumstances surrounding it remain clouded in mystery and lingering controversy.

Contemporary regional newspapers are strangely silent about this momentous event and the person or persons responsible for it—a fact that Morgan City jumbo shrimp publicists once openly acknowledged—and modern print and online media consistently disagree about the year in which the discovery took place. Nevertheless, since the mid-1950s, Morgan City journalists and antiquarians, citing "waterfront legend," have credited Captain Theodore "Ted" Anderson with finding the aquatic haunts of the nation's most famous animate oxymoron sometime in the 1930s. This contention was first given credence by Lela Lehmann in the 1955 annual seafoods and marine industries issue of the *Morgan City (LA) Daily Review*. In her report, *Review* editor Lehmann spun a detailed "new 'Anderson' fairy tale" in which the "rugged Scandinavian" skipper and his two-person crew sailed to Morgan City's wharfs with forty to fifty barrels of gargantuan (six count) white shrimp. Anderson would have been compelled to toss this shrimp overboard because of local packers' refusal to process such behemoths had it not been for the timely intervention of Paul Messick, a shrimp buyer representing the John R. Hardee Company, a Fernandina, Florida seafood packing and distribution firm accustomed to marketing large white shrimp (jumbos) harvested in South Atlantic waters to East Coast markets. At the corporation's behest, Messick had the shrimp deheaded, packed, and trucked out of state. The Hardee experiment laid the foundation for a lucrative new fishery that reinvigorated the then flagging Morgan City economy. Once in print, the tale became gospel, a permanent, prominent feature of local lore.

This tale, however, has a rather curious denouement. Industry boosters founded the Morgan City Shrimp Festival (later known as the Shrimp and Petroleum Festival) in 1942 to promote the community's best-known commercial product and to honor community figures who contributed significantly to shrimping's harvesting and processing enterprises. The selection of festival royalty began in 1942, and while local shrimp industry icons Bertoul Cheramie (1945) and John Santos Carinhas (1946) rightfully reigned over the first few festivities, Anderson (1964)—attributed with putting Morgan City on the map as the 'Shrimp Capital of the World'—was ignored for two full decades.

The shrimp taken by the Morgan City fleet from the deep waters of the Gulf of Mexico are the biggest anyone has ever seen. Some run to 14 inches in length

Extant early twentieth-century literature indicates some jumbo shrimp were fourteen inches long. (Photo from *Collier's Magazine*, March 16, 1946. Courtesy of Morgan City Archives, Morgan City, LA.)

Giant Shrimp Schools Found Off Coast May Change Industry

(The Times-Picayune Washington Bureau)

Washington, April 20th—A school of shrimp covering an area 25 miles square has been discovered by the bureau of fisheries in deep water off the Louisiana coast, the bureau of fisheries reports today. This discovery is expected by bureau officials to revolutionize shrimp fishing.

With the beginning of winter shrimp leave coastal waters on their spawning migration. Mature shrimp never return to the coastal waters. Eggs and young shrimp are carried into coastal waters in the spring and summer by currents. This has meant in the past that the catch has been comprised largely of immature shrimp.

Until the bureau of fisheries sent its specially equipped steamship Pelican on an exploratory trawling expedition, there was no proof that the shrimp kept closely enough together in deep water to make commercial fishing possible. The winter's work, however, has demonstrated that shrimp in deep water move in highly concentrated schools.

Once a school is located, commercial fishing can be carried on successfully, the bureau finds. By tapping these off-shore reservers larger shrimp are caught. This makes available a new source of supply as the shrimp caught never would have returned to coastal waters. It will also make possible some conservation of supplies of immature shrimp.

Further surveys will be made next winter to ascertain the location of shrimp schools.

Plans also are being made to attempt to follow the migration when it starts so that schools may be located in deep water without expensive trawling operations.

(From the New Orleans *Times-Picayune*, April 21, 1938, 1.)

(left) The European fishermen who migrated to Florida brought, as part of their cultural baggage, blueprints of boats used in the Mediterranean. In the 1920s and 1930s, these Old World designs were incorporated into the Sunshine State's shrimping fleet as shrimpers transitioned from repurposed boats to vessels with a cabin-forward architecture built by local shipyards. Examples of these innovative vessels are pictured here in the St. Augustine harbor. (From the Library of Congress, photographer Frances B. Johnston, 1936–1937, https://www.loc.gov/item/2017886152/.)

(right) Some repurposed boats initially used by Florida shrimpers resemble Louisiana's Biloxi-class vessels, which also featured aft cabins. (From the Library of Congress, photographer Frances B. Johnston, 1936–1937, https://www.loc.gov/item/2017886151/.)

Sollecito (Mike) Salvador, a Sicilian who followed many of his countrymen to the New World, arrived in Fernandina, Florida, in 1898. Salvador quickly recognized the commercial value of shrimp, which had been viewed locally as an inconsequential bycatch product. After cultivating contacts with northeastern distributors, Sollecito—with the cooperation of his relatives Antonio Poli and Salvatore Versaggi, who operated a small fleet of shrimp boats—began shipping boxcar-loads of Florida shrimp by railway express (for decades the country's two largest rail express services were Railway Express and Wells Fargo & Company Express) to major northeastern metropolitan centers. (Photo from the authors' collections, 2020.)

Wooden boats were the norm in Fernandina, Florida, as this early example of a local shrimp boat's keel and ribs testifies. The temporary "ribband" along the side helps form the exterior of the hull's shape before the external planking is added. (Photo courtesy of Nick Deonas, a boatbuilder who represents the Deonas and Tiliakos boat builders of Amelia Island, FL, date unknown.)

Tiliakos Boat Building Co.

BOAT BUILDER AND REPAIRER
FOR OVER 45 YEARS

P. O. BOX 474
FERNANDINA BEACH, FLORIDA   32034

PHONES: OFFICE 261-3262
          NIGHT 261-3438   AREA CODE 305

Long and Burke (25) report that "northwest Florida was inhabited by men born into a tradition of boatbuilding who were adept at using adzes, drawknives, planes and chisels and, by World War I, the Tiliakos family of Fernandina, FL, among others, had begun launching boats built specifically for shrimping." (Photo courtesy of Nick Deonas, a boatbuilder who represents the Deonas and Tiliakos boat builders of Amelia Island, FL, date unknown.)

A second, less widely publicized local creation myth contends that Bertoul Cheramie—Louisiana's self-styled "Shrimp King"—is instead responsible for forging the Florida connection that provided the catalyst for development of Louisiana's jumbo shrimp industry. Adherents of the Cheramie rendition credit Bertoul with forging the Fernandina link and introducing the Florida-class, or *Floridien*, shrimp boat into Louisiana. Before World War II, the self-made seafood mogul owned processing plants in Morgan City, Golden Meadow, Chauvin, Buras, Algiers, Pass Christian, Franklin, Cameron, Lockport, Myrtle Grove, and Galveston. In fact, at the time of the jumbo shrimp discovery, Cheramie's company was the largest seafood producer in the United States, employing more than five thousand people and operating sixty vessels in the Gulf of Mexico. Cheramie's advocates also credit him with a second contribution of equal importance to the Fernandina connection—the introduction of ready-to-cook frozen breaded shrimp, which he distributed to American consumers primarily in more affluent East Coast markets by means of refrigerated trucks. By the Korean War era, Cheramie consolidated his entire product line under the Ho-Ma label.

In light of extant circumstantial evidence, it would appear that the truth lies outside the two "traditional" versions of the creation myth. According to the living descendants of the Florida expats, the formerly thriving deepwater shrimpers operating along the Sunshine State's upper Atlantic Coast faced steadily declining Depression era harvest yields when word reached them of the availability of "jumbo shrimp" in Louisiana's Gulf waters. Felice Golino, owner of the St. John's Shrimp Company of St. Augustine, Florida, with a satellite office in Patterson, was the first of the interested Floridians to explore the profitably of exploiting the Bayou State's largely untapped offshore resource. His interest was reciprocated by Patterson, Louisiana's civic leaders, who established a new shrimp processing facility to entice Golino to move his operation—including "4 or 5 [Floridien] boats"—permanently to the banks of lower Bayou Teche. John Santos Carinhas followed suit in 1938, and the Versaggi Shrimp Company transferred six boats from St. Augustine

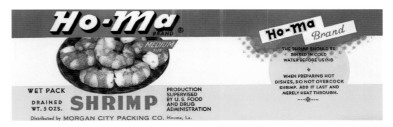

Bertoul Cheramie's Ho-Ma brand shrimp was marketed nationally. (Label from the Chris Cenac collection, Houma, LA.)

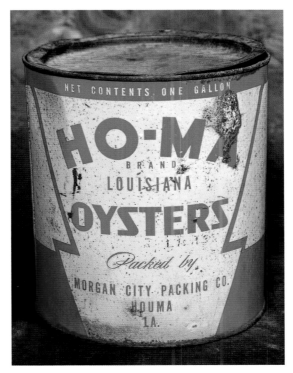

For at least a half century, oysters and shrimp were packaged in large cans, such as this one-gallon tin. (Photo from the authors' collection.)

Before President Dwight D. Eisenhower signed the Federal Aid Highway Act of 1956, establishing the Interstate Highway System, Louisiana's packing plants filled orders by means of refrigerated trucks navigating a network of two-lane state and national highways. Bertoul Cheramie's seven company-owned refrigerated trailers distributed frozen seafood to markets not easily accessible by rail. This was possible because, in 1949, the Interstate Commerce Commission authorized unlicensed trucks to carry shrimp from packers to distributors, but only if the word *fish* appeared on the vehicle. (Photo from the authors' collections. Courtesy of Morgan City Archives, Morgan City, LA, photographer and date unknown.)

Once a boat was "on shrimp," the work began when the nets' contents were dumped on deck. The bycatch had to be sorted and the shrimp deheaded before the boat hands moved them to the hold. Introduction of the saltbox improved a crew's efficiency, as the super-saline solution simplified separating out the nontarget species. All the catch was put in the saltbox. The bycatch floated to the top and thereby separated the shrimp from other aquatic species. (Photo from the authors' collections. Courtesy of Morgan City Archives, Morgan City, LA, photographer Melvin Hardee, ca. 1950.)

After every drag was dumped on deck, crew members used gloved hands to remove the bycatch. (Photo from the Standard Oil (NJ) Collection, Photographic Archives, Archives and Special Collections, University of Louisville, photographer Martha Roberts, 1946, negative no. 43647.)

Like drums of fuel aboard fishing boats in the early twentieth century, fifty-pound poly bags of salt are now a commonplace deck fixture. (Photo from the authors' collections. Courtesy of Morgan City Archives, Morgan City, LA, photographer Melvin Hardee, ca. 1950.)

ST. JOHNS SHRIMP COMPANY

FELICE GOLINO, Owner

WHOLESALE PRODUCERS AND DISTRIBUTORS OF

LARGE OCEAN PRAWN, SHRIMP AND FISH

ST. AUGUSTINE, FLA.

Nº 232

Week Ending *August 6* 193*8*

Boat *Mussolini*   Owner *John Ballestri*

Date		Lbs. Shrimp	Lbs. Fish	Price Per Lb.	Total		Supplies	Memorandum
8	6	9 Bbl	75 #	5. 62½	54	00		Headed
8	6	25 Bbl	75 #	5. 62½	144	00		Heads on
		654 Bbl for heading			6.24			
					204	24		
					14.00		28 00	Ice ✓
					190	24		

OTAL

Amount of Check. $ 190.24

Born in Italy in 1896, Felice Golino became, on arriving in Louisiana, an active member of the state's large Italian community. Before relocating, he was a businessman who, through his St. John's Shrimp Company, based in St. Augustine, Florida, delivered shrimp to New York's famous Fulton Market. When he became involved in the jumbo shrimp fishery in the late 1930s, he brought these crucial business connections to Louisiana. (From the collection of F. C. Felterman Jr., Patterson, LA.)

In the 1930s, Golino's boat, the *Benito Mussolini*, was considered one of the largest shrimp trawlers in Louisiana. This vessel was part of a fleet of fourteen trawlers in the St. John's Shrimp Company's fleet that offloaded their cargoes at the company's new Patterson fish house. Eight other privately owned vessels also unloaded at this dock. After Pearl Harbor, the *Benito Mussolini* and a sister trawler, the *General Badoglio*, were renamed the *Enterprise* and *Gulf Clipper*. (From the collection of F. C. Felterman Jr., Patterson, LA.)

One of the original Florida boats used in the Morgan City/Patterson jumbo shrimp fishery. (From the Collection of F. C. Felterman Jr., Patterson, LA.)

Similarly, shrimp fisherman John Santos Carinhas brought his family and nine shrimp boats to Patterson in 1938. A native of Portugal, Carinhas immigrated to New York, where his two older brothers lived, at the age of seventeen. His work in the shrimp and fishing industries led him to Fernandina, Florida, where he, like Golino, operated a successful shrimping business. Carinhas was so successful in Morgan City that he expanded his fleet almost every year. To meet this need, Carinhas established his own boat-building facility, the Patterson Shipyard, in the early 1940s.

Three pioneering, Florida-connected entrepreneurs—Felice Golino, John Santos Carinhas, and Sal Versaggi—founded the jumbo shrimp industry along the banks of lower Bayou Teche, transforming Patterson, a former cypress logging center, into a shrimp processing and distribution hub. (From the collection of F. C. Felterman Jr., Patterson, LA.)

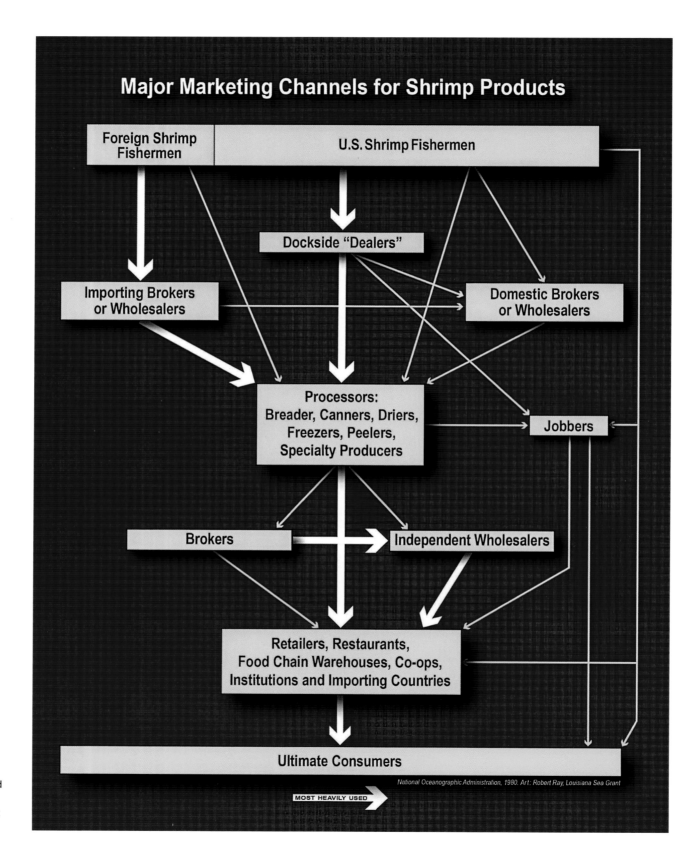

The complexity of the supply chain web was—and is—underappreciated by the public. (National Oceanic and Atmospheric Administration, 1980.)

The improved national highway system meant that out-of-sate wholesalers could use their trucks to transport shrimp directly from Louisiana's processors, saving time and money and thereby increasing their profit margins. (Photo from the authors' collections. Courtesy of Morgan City Archives, Morgan City, LA, photographer unknown, ca. 1950.)

E. J. Hartley owned a Patterson trucking service that transported fresh shrimp to northern markets in wood boxes containing one hundred pounds of headless shrimp mixed with crushed ice. (From the collection of F. C. Felterman Jr., Patterson, LA.)

One of the tractor-trailers used by Dean Blanchard Seafood Company, based on Grand Isle. (Photo from the authors' collections, 2018.)

Before moisture resistant corrugated packaging, inexpensive wooden crates, often reinforced with metal wire to improve their stability, were commonplace throughout the industry. Like the first rail cars of shrimp transported from Brunswick, Georgia, or Fernandina, Florida, to New York City, laborers packed shrimp barrels with alternating layers of shrimp and ice. Often the barrels or boxes were re-iced during the journey. These open boxes of layered shrimp and ice made re-icing easier as they were trucked to their destination. Over time, the barrel slowly disappeared from the shrimp distribution chain. (From the collection of F. C. Felterman Jr., Patterson, LA.)

Trucking lines connected the Louisiana shrimp docks with New York, Boston, Philadelphia, Atlanta, and other burgeoning consumer markets. The wooden one-hundred-pound shrimp box was the typical shipping container. (From the Collection of F. C. Felterman Jr., Patterson, LA.)

Louisiana shrimpers welcomed the appearance of coastal Louisiana fuel pumps, which allowed them to abandon the forty-two-gallon fuel barrels for large internal fuel tanks. (Photo from the Standard Oil (NJ) Collection, Photographic Archives, Archives and Special Collections, University of Louisville, photographer Edwin Rosskam, 1945, negative no. 25953.)

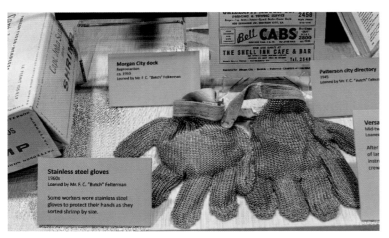

When the canning industry relied on female and child laborers on the shrimp processing line, ammonia in the shrimp's head ate into employees' hands, making the flesh raw and sore. Under these conditions, a picker could only work a few days before they had to leave the line and let their hands heal. Emerging more than a half century later, stainless-steel gloves became available to protect the hands of processing-plant workers picking and sorting shrimp and crew members sorting bycatch. (From the collection of F. C. Felterman Jr., Patterson, LA.)

to Patterson sometime later. The Versaggi contribution to the initial development of the jumbo shrimp industry in the Patterson area cannot be overstated. Within five years of establishing a foothold along the Louisiana coast, the Florida transplants added thirteen additional trawlers to their burgeoning fleet and constructed a major local shrimp-packing plant.

These enterprising transplants brought with them longstanding contacts with upper East Coast distributors and retailers, which they fully exploited in cooperation with the Patterson shrimp processing facility's administrators. The Versaggi connection with New York City's famous Fulton Fish Market, where a family-owned stall in the market dated from the 1930s, was particularly significant, but Patterson shrimpers and processors also soon established a significant presence in Chicago and Philadelphia, where their products were transported to markets in ice-packed trucks. The result was a fundamental reinvention of the Louisiana shrimp industry and the marketing and distribution apparatus that molded and sustained it. In a word, it created the business paradigm that persists to the present. Therein lies the real significance of the jumbo shrimp discovery.

Versaggi Shrimp Co.

Owners: John, Virgil, Joe, Manuel & Dominic Versaggi
Managers of Patterson Facility: John & Virgil Versaggi
Location: 1222 Main Street
Moved to Patterson in 1940
Book Keepers: Russel Governale & Mona Cardinale
Net Makers: Sebby Cardinale, Walker Lancaster, Billy Thompson
Mechanic: Austin Watson, Al Templet

The Versaggi Brothers
Manuel, John, Joe, Dominic, Virgil

The Fish House At 1222 Main Street
Built in 1940 & still stands today (2008) under different ownership.

Dominic Versaggi With Ace Captain, Domingo DaCruz
Some of the other captains were: Eph Bodenmueler, Roy Adams, Norman Adams, Walker Lancaster, Roy Blanchard, Blackie Lamaire, Earl Lamaire, Issac Trahan, Billy Thompson, Wilson Gooding

Book Keepers, Mona Cardinale & Russel Governale

Boats From Florida
FORTUNE, PIONEER, PROSPERITY, SPARTAN, SAN SALVADORE

Boats Added In Louisiana
LIBERATOR, TRAVELER, MONTERREY

Not Pictured: CHALLENGER, CHAMPION, COMMANDO, CONQUEST, CRUSADER, DEFENDER, INVINCIBLE, MAYFLOWER, MESSENGER, MIDSHIPMAN, MISS GINA, NAVIGATOR, SAL & ZINA, WARRIOR

Versaggi Shrimp Company's Patterson Connection

Young Salvatore Versaggi left Augusta, Sicily in the late 1800s, sailing as a merchant seaman on a tramp steamer. He settled in New Zealand for a time where he found work as a stevedore. Within five years he had saved enough money to head back to Sicily where the Versaggi and Litrico families had arranged a marriage between their children Salvatore and Vicenzina. Their first child, a son named John, was born there. Not long after, Salvatore sailed for New York where he hoped to find a better life for his family. Again, he found longshoreman work and sent for his family. In the course of his work on the docks, Salvatore fell and severely injured his back. The doctors told him he would have a better life with the back injury if he moved to a warmer climate. He settled in Cape Canaveral, Florida and began catching shrimp along the beach with a seine. It didn't take long to figure out that many more shrimp could be had through the use of a boat. Thus began the Versaggi Fleet, first powered by sail and later by tractor and other engines. Sadly, Salvatore's days were numbered, and he died at a young age leaving a wife and seven children behind. John and his mother took on the arduous task of managing the small fleet of boats. The younger sons became involved as they grew older and the family moved the operation to St. Augustine where a better harbor and facilities were available. However, the shrimp business was never one to lean toward stability, and the discovery of shrimp off the coast of Louisiana was cause for the Versaggis to head West. Led by brothers John and Virgil, they built a fish house in Patterson and began an aggressive program to increase the size of their fleet. They soon became a leading producer of shrimp from the Gulf of Mexico. Patterson held more than just a business interest for two of the Versaggi boys. John married a Patterson girl, Mary "Hon" Felterman, and their three children were born here. Dominic married Rosalie Guarisco of Morgan City, and they settled in Patterson, raising four children. There is much more to the story of the Versaggi Shrimp Co. and their expansion into other ports including one in South America, but since this story is about the shrimp industry in Patterson, the rest will be told on another day.

A short history of the Versaggi Shrimp Company, one of the long-forgotten pioneering companies to operate in the Gulf's deep waters from Patterson shrimp sheds. (From the collection of F. C. Felterman Jr., Patterson, LA.)

Like Bertoul Cheramie and others, Sal Versaggi expanded his business operations into Texas. Versaggi's brand was easily recognizable throughout the Gulf Coast. The family's first generation pioneered the offshore shrimp industry in Florida. The second generation developed a large fleet operating out of Patterson and elsewhere along the northern Gulf of Mexico. The third generation operates internationally from the company's headquarters in Tampa, Florida. The Versaggi Shrimp Company is presently (2021) considered one of the largest distributors of fresh and frozen shrimp in the United States. (From the collection of F. C. Felterman Jr., Patterson, LA.)

The quest for jumbo shrimp greatly expanded the Bayou State fishery's geographic footprint, which now encompasses three distinct shrimping areas: inshore, outside, and federal waters off coastal Louisiana. (Photo from the authors' collections. Courtesy of Louisiana Wildlife and Fisheries, New Iberia Office, photographer and date unknown.)

The "discovery" of jumbo shrimp (10 to 20 count) created a national culinary sensation. America's insatiable appetite for this oxymoronic crustacean attracted significant numbers of Florida mariners, largely descendants of Portuguese, Italian, and Greek immigrants, whose deepwater vessels and cutting-edge technologies revolutionized the Louisiana shrimp industry. (Photo from the authors' collections. Courtesy of the Morgan City Archives, Morgan City, LA, photographer and date unknown.)

When shrimpers purportedly discovered jumbo shrimp in the Gulf of Mexico, the Louisiana fishery's focus shifted from the shallows of Louisiana's estuaries, where juvenile shrimp flourished, to the ocean depths, where oversized adult decapods thrived. Because traditional shallow-draft vessels were unstable, cumbersome, and unfit for long-distance offshore trawling necessary to harvest mature "jumbo" adults, Louisiana shrimpers found themselves at a competitive disadvantage, for their opportunistic counterparts in nearby states possessed the deepwater technologies necessary to take immediate advantage of the promising new fishing grounds. In the mid- to late 1930s, large numbers of deep-hulled, stable, fifty- to seventy-foot Florida-type trawlers—dubbed *Floridiens* by Louisiana's native Francophone shrimpers—operated out of Morgan City. (The actual number of the Florida migrants is presently unknown, but the Sunshine State's shrimping fleet shrank from 764 vessels in 1930 to only 539 in 1940—a roughly 30 percent decline.)

The influx compelled native trawler captains to adapt posthaste. For generations, southeastern Louisiana bayous were lined with family-owned-and-operated shipyards that produced luggers and other small folk boats for local consumption. It was to these facilities that Cajun boatmen turned for locally adapted Florida-type trawlers. This is particularly true of shrimpers along lower Bayou Lafourche. Within three years, according to anecdotal evidence, south Louisiana fishermen were operating their own Floridiens in the coastal waters.

The Cajun-hybrid Floridien, outfitted with an assortment of important new architectural and mechanical improvements, allowed Louisiana's coastal fishermen communities to expand their range from inshore and near-shore to offshore waters. Unlike the flat-bottomed, shallow-draft luggers formerly used exclusively by Pelican State shrimpers, these larger vessels were round-bottomed and extremely seaworthy. The Floridien's distinctive cabin- and engine-forward configuration afforded helmsmen far greater visibility and more expansive storage and workspace in the hold than other contemporary trawler designs. This layout—the inverse of

Louisiana's original jumbo shrimp fleet was based in Patterson, Berwick, and Morgan City. Within five years of World War II's conclusion, these boats annually delivered to the tri-cities' shrimp sheds at least ten million pounds of deepwater decapods. Contemporary newspaper reports indicate that 1,200 local people were employed by the industry. (Newspaper photo from the authors' collections. Courtesy of the Morgan City Archives, Morgan City, LA, photographer Marvin Hardee, ca. 1950.)

the lugger's hold-forward configuration—was far better suited to offshore trawling. Finally, Floridiens boasted far more robust engines, which were necessary for deepwater operations.

The Floridien's rigging and nets were also superior to those used for a generation aboard the inshore lugger fleet. The new trawlers featured robust mechanized winches, massive outrigger booms, and much larger cone-shaped nets designed for dragging over soft mud bottoms in near-shore and offshore waters, where adult shrimp congregate.

Introduction of the Floridien transformed the Louisiana shrimp industry. Between 1935 and 1940, the average annual production equaled 81,900,000 pounds—about four times the weight of the Eiffel Tower. Despite suspension of new Floridien construction

Louisiana shrimp boats were customarily constructed in small, family-owned shipyards along navigable waterways. A typical boatbuilder laid out a keel, without blueprints, in his yard. Then, once the keel and ribs were in place, neighbors contributed their labor to the construction project until the job was completed. (From the authors' collections. Used with permission from the Theriot family, per Jason Theriot, Houston, TX, 1935.)

From the industry's inception to the late twentieth century, Louisiana shipwrights constructed thousands of wooden shrimp boats, usually made of cypress. The Bayou State was the national leader in cypress production for nearly fifty years, and local mills could easily produce the required planking for a seaworthy shrimping vessel. (Photo from the Standard Oil (NJ) Collection, Photographic Archives, Archives and Special Collections, University of Louisville, photographer Arnold Eagle, 1946, negative no. 44428.)

Over time, the shrimp fleet required out-of-the-water maintenance, and a new service industry emerged to fill the need. (Photo from the authors' collections, 2018.)

Coastal Louisiana's self-taught ship carpenters/shipwrights had easy access to the "wood eternal" (cypress) from a variety of local mills. (Photo from the authors' collections. Courtesy of the Rathborne family, New Orleans, LA, photographer unknown, ca. 1940.)

Throughout the Bayou Country, small family-owned repair yards fronted the bayous. These boatyard sites, which used "ways" to lift boats out of the water for repairs, were rarely more than two hundred feet wide. (Photo from the authors' collections, 2018.)

Aboard Florida-class trawlers, shrimpers deploy specialized otter trawl nets by lowering the booms near the water's surface. This configuration features boards at opposite sides of the net's mouth, as well as floats on the head rope and weights on the foot rope. At the end of a "drag" (i.e., trawl run), the crew elevates the booms and the retracting net mouth closes and seals the bag. Closure of the bag is facilitated by a "lazy line," which is loosely secured around the mouth of the bag while towing. When the crew is ready to retrieve the net, the lazy line is "hooked" and led through the snatch-block (a pulley) which is then hoisted to the end of the boom. As the winch retrieves the rope, the bag's mouth closes. On larger trawlers, winches draw the net over the boat's stern and the catch is dumped on the deck. The crew then either sorts the shrimp on the deck, while seated on a small, low bench, or, using a shrimp shovel, moves the decapods to a sorting table. On inland trawlers, crewmen transfer the catch from the net to a saltbox.

The *Euphemie* undergoing repairs. (From the authors' collections, 2018.)

Even in a state of advanced decay, a slipway's distinctive design is immediately recognizable. (Photo from the authors' collections, 2018.)

By the 1960s, Louisiana's shrimp boat builders began to replace wood with fiberglass in construction of small inland trawlers. Fiberglass is strong and does not rust, corrode, or rot, reducing reoccurring maintenance costs. The steel-hull and fiberglass boats in juxtaposition at the dock pictured here have the same general form and function despite their different construction materials. (Photo from the authors' collections, 2018.)

After World War II, wooden boats were slowly replaced by steel-hulled "fishing factories," designed to work in deeper water. (From the authors' collections, 2018.)

Side profile of the *Biloxien Ian Myles* looking for shrimp. (From the authors' collections, 2020.)

because of material and labor shortages during World War II, the fishery's output continued to grow throughout the early 1940s. From 1940 through 1946, the average annual harvest ballooned to 100,681,000 pounds (50,340.5 tons), reflecting a wartime increase as the nation struggled to fill the dietary void resulting from civilian meat and perishable food rationing.

The robust jumbo shrimp harvest proved a fleeting financial bonanza to the formerly struggling Louisiana shrimp industry. Commercial fishing has always been fraught with financial insecurity, and the decade preceding the discovery of jumbos, the Great Depression (1929–1941), and the end of Prohibition (1933) had economically battered Louisiana's shrimpers. Prohibition's end had deprived the fishermen of their lucrative smuggling income, while the national economic crisis had suppressed sales of such luxury items as canned seafood. The number of American packing plants engaged in seafood canning consequently declined by 23 percent between 1929 and 1938. Nevertheless, the jumbo shrimp revelation launched a national culinary sensation (1937–1941)—based largely on the popularity of the suddenly ubiquitous shrimp cocktail—that engendered a regional economic miracle. As a result, shrimp prices spiked temporarily. In 1939, for example, buyers paid shrimpers

For more than a century, the barrel has been the standard unit of measurement in the northern Gulf Coast shrimp fishery. For purposes of convenience in recent decades, shrimpers used a basket or a *panier de champagne* to transfer shrimp from their holds; these smaller baskets are designed to hold seventy pounds—three champagnes to the barrel. When off-loading at a dock, processors have traditionally required shrimpers to present heaping basketfuls of their catch; this practice has remained contentious because a captain's income is based on the weight and price of his shrimp, both of which are skewed by the gratuitous portions above the basket rims which are customarily excluded from the calculations.

The labor-intensive job of handling shrimp and ice with small metal baskets. (Photo from the authors' collections. Courtesy of the Morgan City Archives, Morgan City, LA, photographer Marvin Hardee, ca. 1965.)

At the National Canners Association's 1931 annual meeting in Louisville, Kentucky, southern cannery representatives sponsored a "shrimp dive," featuring "cocktails" made with canned shrimp. The dish was such a success that seafood marketers immediately began extolling the virtues of the shrimp cocktail throughout the land. Within months, the dish was a staple appetizer on most American restaurant menus. (Photo courtesy of Louisiana Wildlife and Fisheries, New Iberia Office, photographer unknown, ca. 1955.)

$8.50 per barrel for their catch, which collectively totaled 395,000 barrels (worth $61,425,695 in 2020 currency).

Relatively flush times continued into the World War II years, when imposition of rationing gave impetus to an exponential increase in national shrimp consumption. The cost of waging global warfare took an immediate toll on America's domestic economy. On January 30, 1942, one month after the Japanese attack on Pearl Harbor, the Emergency Price Control Act established the Office of Price Administration (OPA) and endowed it with the authority to establish price controls on and rationing of essential commodities. Within weeks of the program's establishment, more than 90 percent of the civilian population registered for ration books.

Compliance with the ration program registration requirement was essential because, over the next fourteen months, the OPA restricted civilian access to gas, sugar, meat, cheese, canned fish, condensed milk, and myriad other common consumer goods, establishing a points-based allotment system predicated on the use of government-issued food coupons and a points-based value system.

CREOLE GUMBO

CUT a chicken in pieces and fry in hot lard. Add an onion, sliced, 1 spoonful flour, 2 dozen oysters, and several pieces of ham, and fry till brown. Add 1½ quarts water and boil for an hour. Season with chopped parsley, salt and strong pepper. Add 1 large can shrimp and cook for fifteen minutes longer; then pour at once into a tureen, and add boiled rice.

CHICKEN AND SHRIMP GUMBO

BOIL 1 chicken in 1½ gallons water, till reduced to one half. Fry it in 1 tablespoonful lard, with 1 onion, 1 slice ham, and 1 can of okra. Add 8 tomatoes, and the water that the chicken was boiled in. Boil about 2 hours, then add 1 large can shrimp and cook about fifteen minutes longer. Serve with boiled rice. Season with garlic, pepper, 2 teaspoonfuls salt, 2 bay leaves and a sprig of thyme.

CREAMED SHRIMP

HEAT half a pint of thick cream with 1 cup milk; add 4 tablespoonfuls of tomato soup; pepper and salt to taste, then add 2 cans shrimp, and 1 can of peas. Heat thoroughly and serve on crisp crackers or toast.

FRICASSEE OF SHRIMP, POULETTE STYLE

TO one large can of shrimp add a sauce made as follows: ¼ cup butter, ¼ cup flour, ½ teaspoonful salt, and 1½ cups white stock; add one minced chalot, sliced mushrooms, a pinch of pepper, and a tablespoonful of anchovy essence. Heat without boiling, add the beaten yolks of two eggs and ½ cup cream, and finally a teaspoonful of lemon juice. Serve hot at the table on thin crisp slices of toast.

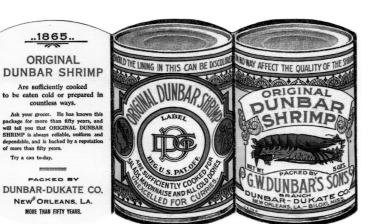

FRICASSEE OF SHRIMP POULETTE STYLE

STEWED SHRIMP

CHOP ½ a small onion fine and brown it in a half a teaspoonful of butter. Add 3 large juicy tomatoes, chopped fine, with their juice; stir well and brown slightly. Add a stalk of celery, thyme, a bay leaf, a dash of cayenne, and salt and garlic to taste, all chopped fine. Cook 10 minutes and add 1 large can shrimp; cook 10 minutes more and serve. Do not add any water.

SHRIMP BUSH

PACK the shrimp into a small, deep dish or tumbler, and press them down hard; when turned over they will cling together in a solid mass. Take dainty bits of celery tips and asparagus tips, or fried parsley for the decorations, and serve with quartered lemons, as an hors d'oeuvre.

SHRIMP BUSH

STUFFED CUCUMBERS WITH SHRIMP

BOIL 6 cucumbers with salt until half cooked. Scoop out the centers and mix them with 1 can shrimp, 2 tablespoonfuls tomato, ½ cup mushrooms, 1 cup fresh bread crumbs, 1 tablespoonful butter, 1 teaspoonful salt, ½ teaspoonful minced parsley, and ¼ teaspoonful minced onion; chop fine and fry in butter. Fill the cucumbers with this, sprinkle with bread crumbs, and put a piece of butter on each. Bake about ten minutes.

ESCALLOPED SHRIMP

PLACE in a baking dish a layer of shrimp; spread bread crumbs over them, sprinkle with salt and pepper and bits of butter. Repeat this operation until the dish is nearly full, with crumbs on top. Pour over them a sauce made of 1 cup milk, a tablespoonful of butter, and a tablespoonful of flour. Bake about fifteen minutes in a hot oven.

(Recipe booklet from the authors' collections.)

Many canning companies provided recipes on their labels as a means of promoting shrimp consumption. Although this practice is now commonplace, it was then an innovative marketing tool. (Recipe booklet from the authors' collections.)

(Label from the Chris Cenac collection, Houma, LA.)

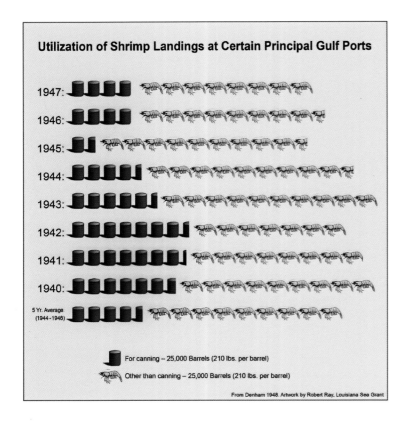

Utilization of Shrimp Landings at Certain Principal Gulf Ports

1947:

1946:

1945:

1944:

1943:

1942:

1941:

1940:

5 Yr. Average (1944-1946)

For canning – 25,000 Barrels (210 lbs. per barrel)

Other than canning – 25,000 Barrels (210 lbs. per barrel)

From Denham 1948. Artwork by Robert Ray, Louisiana Sea Grant

After World War II, shrimp production declined to approximately half the 1940 level.

PHONE 41

Biloxi, Miss. 1941

O. P. A.

SHRIMP CEILING PRICES

Delivered to Factory Wharf

Per Bbl.--210 Lbs.	Wharf Price	Frt. Boat Price
Under 9 Count per Pound	$32.00	$28.50
9-12 Count Inclusive per Pound	28.00	24.50
Over 12-15 Count Inclusive per Pound	24.00	20.50
Over 15-18 Count Inclusive per Pound	20.00	16.50
Over 18-25 Count Inclusive per Pound	17.00	13.50
Over 25-39 Count Inclusive per Pound	14.00	10.50
Over 39 Count per Pound	11.00	7.50

In World War II, President Roosevelt issued Executive Order 8875 creating the Office of Price Administration (OPA). The OPA's main responsibility was establishment of price ceilings on consumer products—including shrimp—to keep wartime inflation in check. (From the Blum and Bergeron Collection, Nicholls State University Archives, Thibodaux, LA, 1941.)

Over the course of the war, the OPA issued a series of civilian ration books replete with small red or blue stamps bearing preassigned values, commonly known as points. Meat, fish, and dairy purchases required red points; dried, canned, and bottled foods blue points. An individual's ration books typically contained a monthly allotment of sixty-four red points or forty-eight blue points. A consumable's point value was based on its availability and the popular demand for it, and meat became effectively inaccessible to most civilians after November 1943. For example, a typical contemporary grocery advertisement, published in the November 10, 1944 issue of the Wilmington, NC *Morning Star*, lists Grade A round steak for forty cents a pound *and* fifteen red points. Thus, a pound of moderately tough beef constituted nearly one-fourth of a person's monthly meat allotment. Protein-rich jumbo shrimp, on the other hand, were not only one cent a pound cheaper but, more importantly, they required no precious ration points whatsoever. Given the

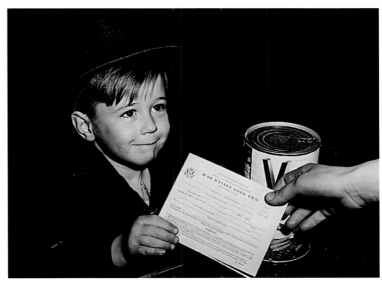

Rationing, introduced in stages over the course of World War II, impacted virtually every family in the country. The system was designed to conserve crucial supplies and prevent speculation on food, shoes, metal, paper, rubber, and other crucial materials. By the end of the war, approximately 5,600 local rationing boards, staffed by more than 100,000 citizen volunteers, monitored and administered the program. (Photo courtesy of the National Archives and Records Administration, Prints & Photographs Division, College Park, MD, photographer John Vachon 1943, reproduction number LC-USW3–022900 LC-DIG-fsa-8d28228.)

An "Eager School Boy Gets His First Experience in Using a Ration Book," World War II. (Office for Emergency Management, Office of War Information, Overseas Operations Branch, New York Office, News and Features Bureau, image number 535567, National Archives and Records Administration, Still Image Records Service, College Park, MD.)

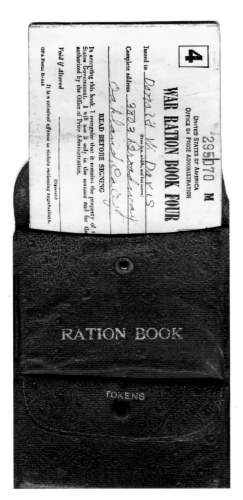

Rationing set limits on purchases of certain high-demand items. The federal government assigned "points" represented by small stamps, which had no cash value but were required to purchase food items. Throughout the war, the government issued stamps in ration books. (Ration book from the authors' collections, 1943.)

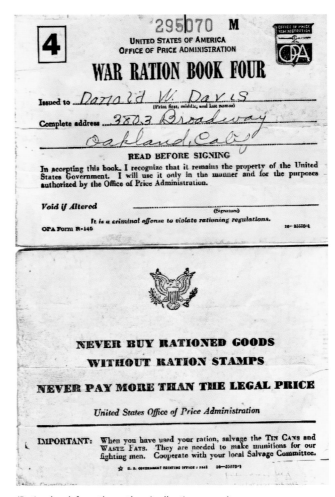

(Ration book from the authors' collections, 1943.)

In 1899, New Orleans and Biloxi boasted the only shrimp processing facilities in the United States. These factories relied on women and children as their primary labor force. In 1900, 18 percent of all American workers were under the age of sixteen. This shocking trend continued into the 1940s as corporate moguls bent on maximizing profits, during the war, blatantly ignored state and federal laws governing working conditions, hours worked, and age restrictions on employees. (From the New Orleans *Times-Picayune*, October 1, 1940.)

All store items had a posted price and a ration book stamp requirement, as this 1944 advertisement demonstrates. Jumbo shrimp were not rationed, saving a consumer valuable points thereby increasing the demand for Louisiana-harvested decapods. (From the Wilmington, NC *Morning Star*, November 10, 1944.)

alternatives, it is hardly surprising that America's homemakers, forced by circumstances to embrace flexibility and innovation, modified their daily meal menus whenever possible to include Louisiana's new signature seafood.

The resulting spike in consumption fueled corresponding growth in coastal Louisiana's shrimp harvesting activity. In May 1942 alone—just four months after the imposition of rationing, the federal fishery market news service reported 32,882 barrels (16.4 tons) harvested for non-cannery consumption. Because of the unprecedented demand, upper Gulf Coast shrimp sold for as much as sixty dollars a barrel (twenty-eight cents a pound)—a sevenfold increase since the jumbo shrimp craze of the late 1930s.

Less prominent, but equally important, was the role of the Pelican State's seafood canneries in the nation's "Fish for the War Effort" campaign to feed the nation's civilian and military populations. Wartime metal shortages, however, initially threatened the seafood canning industry's viability. Following the onset of rationing, the War Production Board ruled that, after December 31, 1942, tin cans would be diverted from the American oyster industry. This decision was successfully appealed by Louisiana's powerful congressional delegation, which secured an exemption until April

After the outbreak of World War II, tin was considered a strategic metal, and its civilian use was severely limited. However, the government granted the shrimp processing industry a rare exemption to prevent disruption of a critical food supply chain. (From the Blum and Bergeron Collection, Nicholls State University Archives, Thibodaux, LA, ca. 1942.)

In World War II, posters with vivid graphics, bold colors, and catchy slogans exhorted the public to ever-greater exertions to meet the needs of the war effort. (From the Library of Congress, artist Thomas A. Byrne, 1941–1943, https://www.loc.gov/item/98518289/.)

"Ride Together" poster. (From the Library of Congress, artist Harry Russell Ballinger, 1941–1943, https://www.loc.gov/resource/cph.3f05431/.)

"Americans! Share the Meat" poster. (From the Library of Congress, https://lccn.loc.gov/96507329/.)

Despite the emerging preference for fresh shrimp in the national marketplace, canned shrimp remained an important component of the American food supply. In 1940, the Louisiana shrimp industry reportedly shipped 1,116,249 cases (53,579,952 cans, based on the standard allotment of 48 cans per case) in 1940. If the cans (measuring 3.25 inches in diameter) were placed together in a single line, they would cover 2,749 miles—nearly the roundtrip distance between New Orleans and Salt Lake City.

Before the Second World War, United States canneries annually consumed approximately 62,200 tons of tinplate—roughly 41 percent of the world's output. The colloquial term *tin can* is a misnomer, as every can is formed from a steel sheet coated with a film of tin approximately 0.00008 inches thick. The tin coating resists corrosion, facilitates soldering of the joints, and enhances the can's appearance.

30, 1943. Louisiana's canneries consequently were largely exempt from metal resource diversions that closed or repurposed seafood canneries elsewhere in the United States. Because approximately two-thirds of the domestic shrimp supply was harvested in Louisiana's estuaries, Pelican State factories operated at capacity with governmental authorization and contracts until the war's conclusion.

Maintaining full production in wartime posed major labor and supply challenges. Because of manpower shortages resulting from the military draft, some of Louisiana's beleaguered seafood processors resorted to banned labor practices. During the first three years of the war, governmental investigators reported numerous child labor law violations as well as abuses in the notorious "shrimp nickel" payment system in which tokens were redeemable exclusively at a company store.

Manpower issues, however, constituted only half of the twin challenges facing Louisiana's seafood processors. To ensure an uninterrupted supply of raw product to the shrimp canneries, the federal government granted trawlers special fuel and conscription exemptions, particularly for seasoned captains. The underpinnings of these exemptions included the expanding national security role assumed by Louisiana shrimpers in 1942 and 1943, when German U-boats preyed virtually at will on oil tankers and freighters in the upper Gulf of Mexico. Cajun shrimpers collectively became a de facto civilian naval auxiliary force, forming a second line of maritime defense. Scanning Gulf waters for enemy submarines while they pursued jumbo shrimp, trawler crews provided the Coast Guard with an important, if informal, surveillance network.

Basic communications issues constituted the greatest impediment to this crude surveillance system. Before World War II, shrimp boat crews commonly used vernacular hand signals to communicate internally and externally. For example, aboard trawlers, a deckhand either brought his hands together above his head or motioned a hand like a pointer's tail toward the water to indicate the presence of shrimp in a try net. A captain would then typically point to an arm to notify nearby vessels of the discovery—the higher up the

In the post–World War II era, a new generation of Cajun mariners met the country's surging demand for wild-caught shrimp, just as their fathers and grandfathers did during the world wars. (Photo courtesy of Louisiana Wildlife and Fisheries, New Iberia Office, photographer, John Blanchard, 1965.)

arm, the larger the shrimp. The shrimpers' signaling system was simple and effective, but it was obviously inadequate in maritime war zones. Not surprisingly, anecdotal information from the surviving children of World War II–era shrimpers indicates that Cajun mariners began to acquire military surplus two-way radios as soon as they became available.

POST–WORLD WAR II ERA (1945–1965)

Harvesting

During the war, Louisiana's shrimpers were the principal beneficiaries of the surging demand for fresh and canned shrimp. During the early 1940s, a single shrimp boat could optimally generate $250 per day in gross income—offset by an estimated $8.25 per day in cumulative expenses. Yet environmental factors often made these industry-wide earnings standards unattainable. Unseasonable weather, sporadic freshwater flooding, and storms generating small-craft warnings routinely negatively impacted the industry. In down years, coastal Louisiana fishing families—suddenly reduced to near-subsistence status—supplemented their offseason income by trapping fur- and hide-bearing animals.

On December 1, 1942, the United States government imposed nationwide gasoline rationing to promote conservation of rubber, a critical military resource then in short supply. The Office of Civilian Requirements, Rural Industries Division, administered the civilian program, including fuel allocations to commercial fisheries until July 21, 1942, when Executive Order 9204 created the Office of Fishery Coordination. The latter agency coordinated "the Government's plans, programs, and policies relating to the fishery industry . . . and to assure the production of an adequate supply fishery products during the war." In addition to securing resources for American fishing fleets, the Office of Fishery Coordination "secured draft deferments for fishermen" and collected fisheries data.

Civilian residents of Louisiana's maritime parishes also organized coastal watch teams popularly known as "Swamp Angels." Some volunteers patrolled the beaches for submarine sightings and evidence of attempts by Nazi spies or saboteurs to infiltrate the Bayou State's porous coast. Others built and continuously manned Civil Air Patrol towers. Still others participated in the "trawler navy" or assisted the Houma-based US Navy blimp fleet to better patrol the northern Gulf of Mexico.

There has never been a universal standard for individual compensation in the Louisiana shrimp industry. Proceeds are often divided among the boat owner, captain, and crew on the basis of a 40/20/40 formula, but the distribution formula is not universal. In such an arrangement, 40 percent of the net proceeds are allotted to the boat owner, 20 percent to the captain, and 40 percent to the crew. This allotment system is intended to provide fair compensation to the owner, who is typically also responsible for the vessel's license, fuel, and at least half the ice.

A Biloxi-type trawler tied up at a Mississippi dock. (Postcard from the authors' collections.)

In Mississippi and Louisiana, Biloxiens are similar in design, but they use different rigging. (From the authors' collections, 2018.)

By engaging in such complementary seasonal activities, Louisiana's resilient shrimpers survived the inevitable periodic fluctuations in supply, demand, and pricing, particularly in the early post–World War II era when shrimp consumption slumped. Indeed, the Pelican State's shrimp industry not only survived, but actually expanded in a period of marketplace contraction due to the return of former servicemen to the coastal parishes after 1945. As a result, the number of licensed trawls increased from 1,736 in 1943 to 3,310 in 1949.

After World War II, Delcambre morphed into an important shrimp port serving the deepwater fleet's needs. In this photo, wooden Biloxi-type and Florida-class boats sit side by side. The difference in their rigging is clearly visible. (Photo from the State Library of Louisiana, Historical Photographs Collection, photographer unknown, 1943.)

Since discovery of marketable hydrocarbons in the Louisiana coastal zone, the shrimp and oyster industry and the oil and gas business have been intertwined. (Photo from the Standard Oil (NJ) Collection, Photographic Archives, Archives and Special Collections, University of Louisville, photographer Russell Lee, number 67537.)

OFFSHORE OIL
An Economic Path for Some Louisiana Shrimpers

The 1901 discovery of oil at southeast Texas's Spindletop dome ushered the Petroleum Age into the northern Gulf Coast region. The birth of Louisiana's oil industry took place nine months later at Evangeline, less than one hundred linear miles east of Spindletop. These two events collectively ignited a Southern "oil rush" focusing on salt domes, geological features particularly commonplace in the neighboring states' coastal plains and marshes. Marshlands were a wildcatter's nightmare because, according to J. Reilly, the indigenous *prairie tremblante* was "too thin to plow and too thick to drink."

The petroleum industry was initially unprepared to work in this protean alluvial environment, and drilling did not begin in earnest until technological innovations of the late 1920s and early '30s permitted exploration, production, and distribution of subsurface hydrocarbons. Once engineering and logistic challenges were resolved—and government regulations were modified to permit use of dynamite for seismic surveys in public waters—the wetlands became an oil and gas exploration and development hotspot. The industry's southward migration took a crucial step forward in 1947, when the Kerr-McGee Corporation completed a well in Gulf waters beyond sight of land, initiating a "black gold" rush onto Louisiana's continental shelf.

The now frequently overlooked contributions of local shrimpers were critical to the energy industry's successful transition from terra firma to terra paludis. In the coastal wetlands, oil company administrators quickly learned that any drilling operation's success hinged on logistical support from a flotilla of shallow-draft repurposed fishing vessels superbly adapted to local waterways and captained by experienced, highly skilled mariners intimately familiar with the region's poorly mapped and ever-changing coastal bayous, lakes, and estuaries.

These former fishermen, lured away from their near-subsistence existence by the promise of steady employment and ample wages, quickly discovered that their intimate association with nearshore and, later, offshore oil operations constituted a springboard to unforeseen professional and financial success. As oil exploration moved continually deeper into the Gulf of Mexico, energy companies required ever-larger and more sophisticated logistical vessels and ancillary support services. Enterprising first-generation shrimpers-turned-oil-entrepreneurs adapted quickly to satisfy their corporate employers' evolving maritime needs. Dick Guidry, Parker Conrad, Otto Candies, Ovide "Jock" Cenac and his brother Alphonse, Eldridge "Tot" Williams, Minor Cheramie, Sidney Savoie, Shane Guidry, Bobby Orgeron, Donald Bollinger, Norman McCall, Nolty Theriot, Butch Felterman, and Edison Chouest were among the most notable of these pioneers, who have collectively become known as the Cajun Mariners.

As they "struggled toward success," these innovators' hard work, risk tolerance, and business acumen—honed in the Louisiana seafood industry—eventually paid handsome dividends as they doggedly strove to design and build America's first oil-centric offshore logistical support fleet. Maritime service contractors initially converted shrimp and oyster boats for use in south Louisiana's offshore oil field. The operational limitations of these repurposed vessels quickly compelled Louisiana's fishermen and shrimp shipwrights to devise—by trial and error—more suitable new boat designs for the offshore petroleum business. In the 1960s, Edison Chouest, a former commercial shrimp fisherman, purchased a sixty-five-foot steel-hulled utility vessel contracted to the Humble Oil Company (now ExxonMobil). From this modest beginning, Edison Chouest Offshore metamorphosed into a global shipbuilding and offshore petroleum service company that coordinates the activities of a fleet of platform supply vessels, anchor handling tugs, oil spill–response boats, and highly specialized vessels designed for job-specific tasks in the offshore industry. Like Chouest Offshore, Cenac Towing sprang from humble beginnings. The firm's founders converted wooden oyster luggers into support vessels to assist the Texas Company's (later Texaco's) exploration efforts in lower Terrebonne Parish. Cenac Towing and Marine Services eventually grew into a leading national provider of specialized boats and barges moving petroleum-based products on the nation's inland waterways. Like his contemporaries, Morgan City native Butch Felterman bought a shrimp boat and became one of the youngest captains in the region. He acquired more watercraft and, in 1965, converted a steel shrimp boat into an oilfield service vessel. Felterman's Galaxie Marine then gradually expanded into a twenty-six-boat flotilla at the time of its sale in 1996.

Other oil service pioneers specialized in boatbuilding. Based in Lockport, Bollinger Shipyard's roots date back to 1946, when Donald Bollinger established a marine machine shop on eighty acres fronting Bayou Lafourche. After Kerr-McGee's offshore oil discovery, Bollinger began to provide barges, workboats, and modified fishing boats to energy industry giants participating in the black-gold rush. Bollinger subsequently expanded well beyond its original "bayou-side" facility, eventually operating thirteen shipyards and forty drydocks in Louisiana and Texas. In recent years, the Bollinger corporation became a primary shipbuilder for the United States Coast Guard; in 2019, the company delivered its 175th cutter.

Like Donald Bollinger, Parker Conrad started out "laying keels" for wooden shrimp trawlers in Morgan City. When oil companies began leasing, chartering, and renting available local boats, Conrad judiciously made the transition from wooden boats to steel-hulled crew boats designed specifically to transport support personnel, fuel, potable water, and cargo to offshore drilling rigs. After more than seven decades, the company continues to fabricate, convert, and repair a wide array of marine transportation vessels at its five facilities in Louisiana and Texas.

While Bollinger Shipyards and Conrad Industries and other shipyards were producing boats, master mariner Norman McCall, a former World War II submariner, operated an ex-Navy mine sweeper for Pure Oil Company (part of Chevron). From this experience, McCall learned offshore exploration companies' needs. He consequently purchased a small crew/utility boat that became the foundation for the McCall Crew Boat Rentals Company, whose fast, low-maintenance vessels featured aluminum hulls. McCall's business merged with SEACOR in 1996.

Other Cajun Mariners found their niches in offshore oil exploration provinces well beyond Louisiana's shores. Nolty Theriot, for example, helped pioneer oil exploration in the North Sea and successfully developed an anchor hauling tug/supply vessel.

These Louisiana entrepreneurial pioneers literally invented the offshore oilfield service industry—from building or refining double-hulled barges, offshore supply and support vessels, port facilities minimizing supply boat turnaround, anchor-hauling equipment, towboats, pipe-laying barges, lift boats, jackup barges, push boats, tractor tugs, and modular components for offshore drilling rigs to innovative diving helmets. Coastal Louisiana businessmen consistently met the challenges of improving and innovating all facets of the marine transportation business with a can-do attitude that was embedded in their DNA by their shrimp- and oyster-harvesting ancestors.

A wooden Floridien along Bayou Lafourche, circa 1950. (Photo from the Standard Oil (NJ) Collection, Photographic Archives, Archives and Special Collections, University of Louisville, photographer Russell Lee, negative no. 67536.)

Despite the economic vagaries of the Great Depression and World War II eras, Louisiana's seasonal shrimp harvest followed a predictable pattern of interrelated activities. Before departure, early twentieth-century boat captains and buyers entered into a nonbinding handshake agreement regarding purchase prices based on a weight-based tail count. Once underway, captain and crew sailed directly to established fishing grounds, with Biloxi-type luggers plying the inland waters and Floridiens trolling deepwater habitats. Once nets were deployed, the vessels typically allocated from thirty minutes to more than two hours per "drag."

Retrieval of the catch was different aboard inshore and offshore vessels. Upon completion of each drag, pre–Great Depression era lugger crews, working from a wooden platform along the gunwales, used dip nets to remove shrimp from the trawl's terminal "bag" or "cod end." The crew placed and iced half the net's contents in the hold before beginning the laborious process of deheading the remaining half. Once in port, crews transferred the field-processed catch to processors' cold storage units. In 1947, industry publications indicate that the Gulf Coast's thirteen cold storage warehouses—six of which were in Louisiana—had a collective capacity of 7,750,000 pounds (3,875 tons). After World War II and the installation of refrigeration units on small trawlers, shrimpers froze the shrimp while returning to port, and by the mid-1950s, the Floridiens boasted below-deck brine-freezing equipment.

Only small inshore and near-shore shrimping vessels continued to rely on ice boats or freight boats for field support. Around the end of World War II, the second-generation ice boats were replaced by larger factory vessels. Measuring up to 100 to 150 feet in length and engineered to meet the requirements of the frozen seafood market, these new vessels featured integral handling equipment, particularly processing tables and appurtenances, as well as industrial freezers. The growing demand for such technological enhancements kept upper Gulf Coast shipyards busy in the two decades following the end of World War II.

Louisiana shrimpers were initially more reticent in adopting other advanced technologies, particularly emerging communications

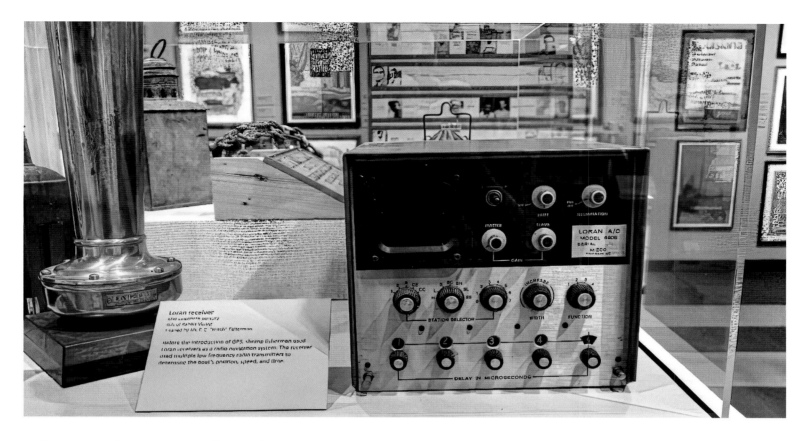

Loran receiver
after sixteenth century
Gift of Conni Vuong
Loaned by Mr. F. C. "Butch" Felterman

Before the introduction of GPS, shrimp fishermen used
Loran receivers as a radio navigation system. The receiver
used multiple low frequency radio transmitters to
determine the boat's position, speed, and time.

and navigational instruments. A few trawler captains invested in shortwave radios (initially known colloquially as "come back" radios and, later, as citizens band radios), advanced long-range navigation technology (RADAR and LORAN, both products of World War II research), motorized winches, and other "modern" equipment. By the 1970s, such equipment became essential workplace tools, and these technologies are now standard on the large boats.

In the postwar era, shrimp boat captains were far more amenable to low-tech upgrades to their vessels. During the 1950s, many Louisiana shrimpers drafted their wives as summer-season deckhands and cooks to reduce labor costs. However, improved profits came at a hidden cost, for their spouses demanded—and secured— immediate improvements to living conditions aboard the working boats. The universal first improvements were "bathroom" installations. According to one former captain, lavatories were followed in later years by more technologically advanced amenities, including "air-conditioning, radios, tape players, televisions, DVDs, computers, and cell to satellite phones."

Improvements requiring structural changes to shrimp boats often required the assistance of shipwrights operating out of

United States military developed the long-range navigation system (LORAN) during World War II. It was first used by aircraft and convoys crossing the Atlantic. The first generation of this equipment was expensive to operate, and it was eventually replaced by Loran-B, which offered improved accuracy. After the war, the United States Navy released surplus receivers—the original models—to the public. Commercial fishermen snapped up these units and pressed them into service as navigational tools. (From the collection of F. C. Felterman Jr., Patterson, LA.)

Yellowing image of a crowd of people and many boats.
(From the authors' collections. Used with permission from
the Theriot family, per Jason Theriot, Houston, TX, 1935.)

backyard facilities. In addition to retrofitting trawlers, postwar
coastal Louisiana shipyards were also active in new boat construction. As in the pre–World War II era, new construction focused on
divergent inshore and offshore designs. Along Bayou Lafourche,
for example, the Louisiana, Lafourche, and Allied shipyards were
equipped to build steel-hulled vessels sixty to eighty feet in length.
Featuring a bow-mounted pilothouse, an open deck aft, and an
average net displacement of 115 tons, these boats were built for long-
range, deep-sea trawling. Such vessels typically had a 7,000-gallon
fuel capacity, a 200-gallon oil reservoir, and at least a 1,200-gallon
potable water tank. Because of their massive size, these trawlers
used diesel engines and, beginning in the late 1970s, Kort nozzles
to increase propeller thrust.

As Louisiana's offshore trawler fleet moved from wooden to
steel hulls, Lafitte skiffs replaced most of the venerable Biloxi-type
luggers in inland waters. First introduced around 1953, the Lafitte
skiff, boasting a cargo capacity of less than five net tons, typically
extends twenty to fifty feet in length, while its beam usually measures
six to nine feet. Possessing smooth, flat hulls, these shallow-draft
shrimp vessels can operate in water only eighteen to twenty-four

Color image of a boat with two green nets. (Photo from the authors' collections, 2018.)

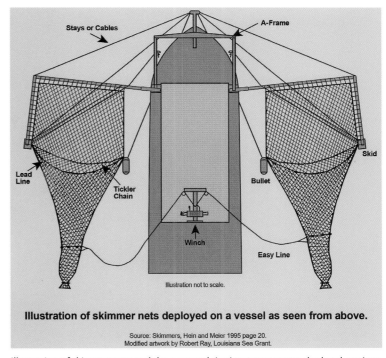

Illustration of skimmer nets and the gear and rigging necessary to deploy them into the water.

A Lafitte skiff with nets deployed. (Photo from the authors' collections, 2018.)

A Lafitte skiff unloading at the shrimp dock during the May and August seasons is a common sight throughout coastal Louisiana. (Photo courtesy of Louisiana Department of Wildlife and Fisheries, New Iberia Office, photographer unknown, 1964.)

In 1940, Louisiana boasted 2,400 active shrimp boats. After World War II, 3,030 shrimp boats were in operation, most powered by diesel engines made by Fairbanks-Morse, Cummins, Caterpillar, and others. Smaller, lighter modern diesel motors now power the shrimping fleet. (Photo courtesy of Louisiana Department of Wildlife and Fisheries, New Iberia Office, photographer, ca. 1945.)

By the mid-1950s, a marine diesel engine cost between $8,000 and $10,000 ($76,000 to $95,000 in 2019) and represented a substantial part of a boat owner's total fixed investment. Later, when blast-freezing units became part of a boat's standard equipment, trawlers' capital expenditures again increased significantly.

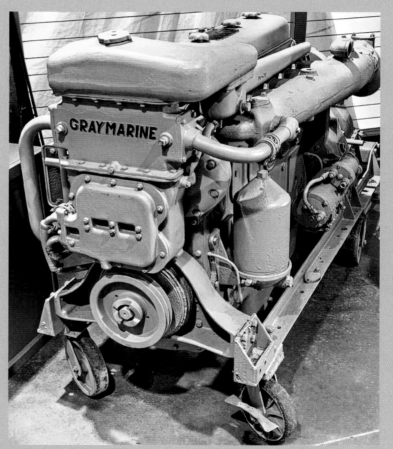

Post–World War II diesel engine. (Photo from the authors' collections.)

Rudolph Diesel's United States patent expired in 1912. Many companies, including Fairbanks-Morse, began building new versions of Diesel's engine. Diesel power plants were reliable and efficient. Yet it took time for Louisiana's fishing fleet to adopt diesel marine engines. After 1945, war-surplus Gray Marine and Detroit Diesel 671 engines—and, to a lesser extent, Caterpillar and Cummins marine engines—became the standard power plants aboard most shrimp boats. (Photo from the authors' collections. Courtesy of the Maritime and Seafood Industry Museum, Biloxi, MS, 2019.)

inches deep. Although the classic lines of a Lafitte skiff's hull are unmistakable, there is little consistency in certain above-deck features. For example, cabins are optional, though most Lafitte skiffs have a tarpaulin work-area cover or a half cabin. There is also little consistency in the craft's power plants, which initially ranged from 85- to 115-horsepower marine gasoline engines to recycled automotive engines.

Diesel engines, such as Cummins marine engines, quickly replaced the Biloxi-type gas power plants in the postwar era as shrimpers came to appreciate the diesel's inherent fuel efficiency and torque advantages. In short, a diesel engine can move a greater load with less engine strain and significantly less fuel consumption than its gasoline counterpart. Because of the correlation between a vessel's length and its tonnage, a diesel's advantages typically become more pronounced as a ship's length surpasses thirty-five feet, and by the 1960s, Louisiana's shipwrights were typically constructing inshore trawlers forty-five feet to sixty feet long. During the post–World War II era, Gray Marine (army surplus) and General Motors 671-horsepower diesels were the most common power trains in the Louisiana fishing fleet.

Like its diesel power plant, the Lafitte skiff featured maximum efficiency in design and performance. The multifunctional skiff's design supported crabbing and hand-line fishing and afforded a speedy means of moving to and from wetland-centric fishing and hunting camps. Built for operation within a thirty-mile radius of its home port, the skiff's postwar crew typically consisted of only one man, although when shrimp prices were exceptionally high, a vessel's operator often added an additional crewman. Because of the limited available onboard manpower, many skiffs were equipped with a power winch attached to mast or a "pulling rack" near the stern to recover trawl nets that usually measured thirty to forty feet. On more modestly equipped boats, operators pulled nets by hand into a rectangular box fitted across the skiff's bow.

Proliferation of the Lafitte skiff operators in the coastal parishes helped lift postwar production totals, which paradoxically benefited the industry but not necessarily the shrimpers. The growing number

The butterfly (*poupier*) or wing net first appeared in Louisiana waters in the 1950s. These nets, which are easy to use and require a small initial investment, are attached to a rigid frame supported by a floating or fixed platform. At nightfall, the fixed platform operators lower the net into the upper water column. Once in the water, the current and/or tides "push" shrimp into the net. This is an easy and efficient method to catch shrimp migrating through a waterway. A small hand winch is used to retrieve the net. (Photo from the authors' collections, 2014.)

A poupier on a floating platform. (Photo from the authors' collections, 2019.)

Twin City Fishermen's Co-op. Assn., Inc.

HOME OFFICE

MORGAN CITY. LA.

Phones 2681-2-3 --- P. O. Box 809

Producers and Shippers — Louisiana and Texas Brands

Fresh and Frozen Shrimp

MORGAN CITY, LA.
Packing Plant

Packing and Freezing Plant
PORT ISABEL, TEXAS

We are glad to have been the sponsors of a brochure, (the first page of which is reproduced above), which has attracted much interest and favorable comments and will, we are sure, reflect benefits on the entire port.

TWIN CITY FISHERMEN'S CO-OP. ASS'N., INC.

Louisiana's nascent jumbo shrimp fishery attracted significant numbers of Florida's Atlantic Coast fishermen looking for "greener pastures." Many migrated to the Patterson–Morgan City area to trawl for jumbos. (Newspaper photo from the authors' collections. Courtesy of the Morgan City Archives, Morgan City, LA, photographer unknown, ca.1945.)

With operations based in Port Isabel, Texas, and Morgan City, Louisiana, the Twin City Fishermen's Cooperative Association was the first major link between Texas and Louisiana fishing communities. The harvest by the co-op's members helped solidify Morgan City as the "Jumbo Shrimp Capital of the World." (Photo from the authors' collections. Courtesy of the Morgan City Archives, Morgan City, LA, date unknown.)

Before the advent of canning, barrels were the shrimp fishery's shipping containers of choice. Canners, however, required radically different transport packaging. In the first two decades of the twentieth century, the seafood canning business used wooden boxes to distribute shrimp products to markets throughout the United States. The subsequent invention of the corrugated cardboard box again revolutionized the shipping, packaging, and handling of shrimp. Fiber boxes are simple, efficient, cheap, and durable, and their low weight significantly reduces transportation costs. In addition, the boxes' uniform color provides an ideal background for corporate logos. (From the collection of F. C. Felterman Jr., Patterson, LA.)

of self-employed shrimpers meant greater competition for finite resources and potential income. It also meant that, unless shrimpers organized and presented a unified front to processors, they had no leverage regarding the prices they received for their catch. Processors knew full well that for every shrimper who balked at proffered terms, two would step forward to accept them. Nor would this situation improve in the decades immediately following World War II, for highly individualistic shrimpers refused to organize in their self-interest. In fact, one postwar observer lamented that "I could not organize them with a machine gun."

The Twin City Fishermen's Cooperative Association, organized in 1946 but formalized in 1947, was a notable exception. The co-op processed members' catch at plants in Morgan City and Port Isabel, Texas. Two other cooperatives—the Lafitte-based Barataria Fisherman's Cooperative and the St. Mary Fisherman's Cooperative—were chartered by the state by 1960. However, the combined membership of the three co-ops was only 106, a tiny percentage of the state's trawler captains.

Like their inshore counterparts, offshore shrimpers had little interest in unionization, but unlike the former, they had other options, thanks to the mobility and attendant commercial flexibility afforded by their Florida-class vessels. The result was divergent evolutionary paths taken by Louisiana's inshore and offshore trawler fleets, and the figurative gulf between these disparate tracks became ever more pronounced in the two decades following the conclusion of the Second World War. This divergence resulted in large part because of the relative lack of regulation in federal and international waters. Because of the long-running Tidelands litigation between Louisiana and the United States government over coastal territorial limits and offshore oil revenues, the legal boundary between state and federal waters remained a matter of dispute for decades, and enforcement of regulations remained fluid because of overlapping territorial claims. With few exceptions, deepwater trawlers could harvest decapods year-round by either circumventing state regulations in areas where boundaries were in dispute or by migrating to more productive but less well-regulated

The Louisiana shrimp industry's major output shifted from canned to frozen products during the post–World War II era, and five-pound cartons of frozen shrimp became commonplace in supermarkets. Like earlier canned products, frozen shrimp packaging labels featured bold colors, stunning graphics, and general consumer eye-appeal. (Photo from the authors' collections. Courtesy of the Morgan City Archives, Morgan City, LA, date unknown.)

The co-op developed markets in Texas, Louisiana, and other states. It followed a trend established by Morgan City entrepreneur John Santos Carinhas, who in 1940 built the first freezer plant in Morgan City, which helped preserve shrimp moving from the Bayou Country to either the Windy City or New York's Fulton Fish Market. (Photo from the authors' collections. Courtesy of the Morgan City Archives, Morgan City, LA, date unknown.)

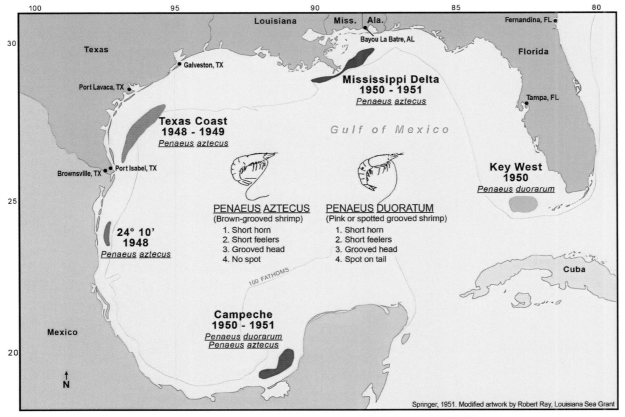

NEW GROUNDS FOR GROOVED SHRIMP

By 1950, new shrimping grounds were discovered beyond coastal Louisiana and Mississippi.

WESTWARD EXPANSION OF THE LOUISIANA SHRIMP INDUSTRY

Expansion of the commercial Louisiana shrimp fishery beyond Berwick Bay began during World War II, as Louisiana shrimpers sought to satisfy the insatiable national demand for jumbo shrimp. In 1944, four small "shrimp houses" operated in the village of Cameron, processing and shipping to eastern markets 12,230 barrels of locally harvested decapods. Two years later, 170 shrimp trawlers were permanently based at Cameron, and these vessels harvested 25,500 barrels of shrimp valued at $1,402,500 ($18,554,068 in 2020 currency). By 1950, Cameron also boasted a significant menhaden fishing and processing operation. The isolation and limited storage capacity of these nascent processors, which compelled some fishermen to transport their catch to Morgan City (approximately 125 miles linear distance to the east), provided the initial impetus for construction of the Louisiana Coastal Highway (now LA 82), which was not completed until the mid-1950s.

Significant shrimp harvesting operations in lower Vermilion Parish, the present nexus of the southwestern Louisiana shrimp industry, materialized after those in neighboring Cameron Parish. Local tradition maintains that Bayou Carlin, Delcambre's link to Vermilion Bay and the Gulf of Mexico, was too narrow and shallow to support a robust commercial fishery in the 1930s. During the Great Depression, the community reportedly had a short-lived oyster cannery and a "shrimp processing shop" serviced by a "few small boats." The Louisiana Department of Public Works reported in 1948 that "no shrimping boats are permanently based in Vermilion Parish, though there are transit operations in and out of Abbeville."

waters in the southwestern Gulf of Mexico. For example, in 1946, shrimpers discovered bountiful shrimping grounds in the Bay of Campeche off Mexico's western Yucatan coast. The mobility of the Florida-class trawlers permitted Louisiana shrimpers to not only seek and exploit aquatic resources throughout the western Gulf of Mexico but also to establish new bases of operation at venues where competition for decapods was less intense.

By the end of 1947, forty-eight American trawlers had obtained Mexican commercial fishing permits and vessel registries in order to harvest the Bay of Campeche's abundant pink shrimp. (After 1950, these nomadic shrimpers also began to harvest spotted-grooved shrimp in commercial quantities.) Other venturesome Louisiana shrimpers transferred their operations to Port Aransas, Texas, as well as Delcambre and Cameron, Louisiana. Following the lead of the state's Fernandina Beach and St. Augustine transplants, many Bayou Lafourche and Morgan City shrimp captains moved from these geographic nodes to Brownsville, Galveston, Port Aransas, and Port Lavaca. Anecdotal information indicates that most of the migrant fishermen were formerly based in Lafourche Parish.

As the Louisiana shrimp industry expanded its geographic footprint, the fishery maintained its productivity while adapting to new technological and economic realities. By the 1960s, deepwater trawlers were effectively mobile factories, with onboard refrigeration units that allowed them to stay at sea for protracted periods. In the 1950s, onboard freezers cost nearly $20,000—approximately $180,000 in 2020 currency. Deployment of these industrial freezers was essential because, by 1971, the American frozen seafood market was reported at $1.5 billion ($9,404,970,863 in 2020 currency), and shrimp accounted for about half of these frozen food sales.

Shrimp Processing

The frozen seafood food industry's success came at the expense of traditional canneries. Like the trawler fleet, Louisiana's shrimp processing industry was transformed by various technological innovations in the immediate aftermath of World War II. Rural

After receiving a patent for his peeling machine design in 1947, J. M. Lapeyre joined his father, Emile Lapeyre, and his uncle Fernand Lapeyre in establishing Peelers Inc. to lease the new technology. Today, Laitram Machinery, Inc., which operates a manufacturing plant in Harahan, Louisiana, leases and sells equipment featuring Lapeyre engineering to shrimp processors around the world. (Photo courtesy of Laitram Machinery, Kenner, LA, date unknown.)

Lapeyre's first prototype peeling machine is now in the Maritime and Seafood Industry Museum in Biloxi, Mississippi. Damaged during Hurricane Katrina (2005) and subsequently restored by the Laitram Company, the machine is back on permanent display. (Photo from the authors' collections. Courtesy of the Maritime and Seafood Industry Museum, Biloxi, MS, 2019.)

electrification programs brought dependable, continuous power to the most remote processors and canneries. Reliable electrical power, in turn, made possible widespread adoption of both industrial flash-freezing technology and the groundbreaking Lapeyre shrimp-peeling machine. Electrical and telephone lines began to appear in coastal communities in the late 1940s. Improved land-based communications and electrically powered refrigeration machinery allowed the Louisiana shrimp industry to extend its geographic reach and market share through frozen processed-food exports.

Of the myriad watershed changes transforming the postwar shrimp industry, the Lapeyre shrimp peeler had the most significant initial impact. On December 9, 1947, polymath J. M. Lapeyre, a Houma native who patented 191 inventions in his lifetime, filed a patent application for a machine designed to eliminate the high labor costs associated with manual shrimp peeling. Patented in January 1951 (#2,537,355), the Lapeyre device, one of only four Louisiana inventions designated a National Historic Mechanical Engineering Landmark, immediately revolutionized the shrimp industry, not only in the Pelican State, but throughout the world. The Lapeyre peeling machine made it possible for a cannery to process between forty

Laitram's corporate literature notes that "the shrimp peeler was the first of more than 100 pioneering inventions born in the mind of J. M. Lapeyre, leading his contemporaries to consider him the most complete engineer with whom they had ever associated." Lapeyre eventually secured 191 patents, making him one of his generation's most prolific inventors. (Photo from the authors' collections. Courtesy of the Maritime and Seafood Industry Museum, Biloxi, MS, 2019.)

"Light" poster. (From the Library of Congress, artist Lester Beall, ca. 1935, https://www.loc.gov/item/2010646236/.)

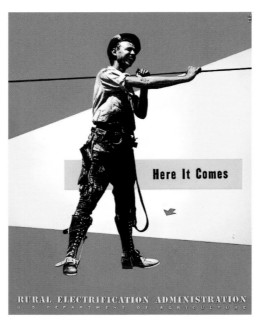

"Here It Comes" poster. (From the Library of Congress, artist Lester Beall, ca. 1935, https://www.loc.gov/item/2010650609/.)

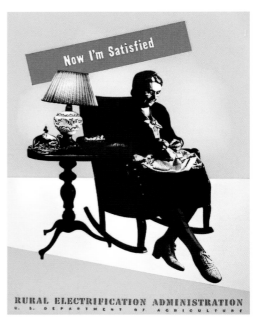

"Now I'm Satisfied" poster. (From the Library of Congress, artist Lester Beall, ca. 1935, https://www.loc.gov/item/2010650602/.)

thousand and sixty thousand pounds of raw heads-on shrimp in a ten-hour shift, eliminating the need for hand-peeling altogether. In addition, the peeler could sort processed shrimp by size, typically between a 10 and 200 count. Using the business model first introduced into the Louisiana seafood industry half a century earlier by the Continental and American Can companies, Lapeyre leased his peelers to processing businesses, thereby ensuring the inventor of a steady, stable revenue stream. (Lease fees were based on the number of revolutions registered on main drive motor—fifty-five cents per one hundred cycles of the machine's rollers.) By 1953, all of Louisiana's shrimp canneries used the invention, and by 1960, the Lapeyre mechanical peeler was a fixture in processing plants throughout the United States, Europe, South America, Australia, the Pacific Rim, northern Europe, and Iceland.

Processors' widespread adoption of Lapeyre's invention forever changed the economics of the American shrimp industry. First, the price of shrimp declined as processors passed the reduced manufacturing costs to distributors and consumers. Reduced retail prices in turn increased popular demand for fresh and fresh-frozen shrimp—at the expense of the canned seafood industry, which endured a rapid decline in active factories as market shares and profit margins shrank. As early as 1948, Louisiana journalist James

THE EARLY SHRIMP INDUSTRY'S FUEL SUPPLY CHAINS

Shrimp processing operations—whether located on wooden platforms elevated on cypress piers above the marsh, or in conventional factories situated inland along coastal waterways—have always been sustained by local and regional fuel providers, whose products and services, naturally, evolved over time as driers and canners embraced emerging technologies. Despite their critical importance, however, these historical fuel supply chains have been forgotten, largely because of the absence of relevant documentation lost to hurricanes and human negligence. For example, extant eyewitness accounts of late nineteenth- and early twentieth-century Asian wooden drying platforms note the ubiquitous presence of large vats or kettles suspended above brick-frame hearths. Platform crews boiled suitably small shrimp in brine in these vessels before scattering them across the platforms' gently undulating surfaces for sun-drying. Contemporary images of drying platforms show large racks of firewood used to fire the boiling operation; yet firewood was such a commonplace commodity that visiting writers routinely ignored this vital consumable. Even so, circumstantial evidence indicates woodyards delivered innumerable cords—128-cubic-foot allotments of firewood measuring 4 feet high, 8 feet wide, and 4 feet deep—for nearly fifty years. Yet nothing is known about the geographic source of the firewood (possibly Gibson or Chacahoula woodyards), the frequency of the deliveries (probably weekly), the method of transportation (presumably schooners), or the amount of fuel cumulatively consumed in the platform hearths over a half century (undoubtedly millions of cords).

Conventional factories were tethered to very different power sources. The Dunbar processing plant in New Orleans, the nation's shrimp canning pioneer, required steam and electricity to operate, and in a remarkable case of historical synchronicity, availability of this cutting-edge energy supply coincided with the development of the South's electric power industry, which was tied to the birth of the Crescent City's commercial ice manufacturing business. In 1868, the world's first documented commercial ice factory opened in New Orleans. Dunbar's shrimp factory, which became operational in 1875, immediately relied on this then exotic power source as well as the more conventional steam technology already successfully deployed in East Coast canneries. In most of coastal Louisiana, however, steam power remained predominant.

Steam technology remained an integral part of every Louisiana shrimp cannery's production line well into the twentieth century. Over the course of the twentieth century, shrimp cannery operations gradually migrated to such isolated sites as Dunbar, the Rigolets, Ostrica, Pointe à la Hache, Myrtle Grove, Phoenix, Happy Jack, Dulac, Golden Meadow, and numerous other remote coastal communities where electricity was then unavailable. Assembling the mobile steam "plants" took time—one relocation effort included "three large houses," a steam plant, and ancillary equipment—but the plants' mobility afforded canning companies the luxury of periodic relocations to dodge incipient labor movements.

In the post–World War II era, however, electricity gradually supplanted steam as canneries' primary power source. Electricity was available in much of New Orleans as early as 1882, and by the 1930s, electric service was virtually universal in south Louisiana's municipalities. But most of rural Louisiana lacked access to the region's slowly expanding electrical grid until creation of the federal Rural Electrification Administration (REA) in 1936. Communities and businesses situated along the natural levees bordering lower Bayou Lafourche generally before America's entry into World War II (1941), while lines to the more isolated coastal communities typically were not electrified until the 1950s.

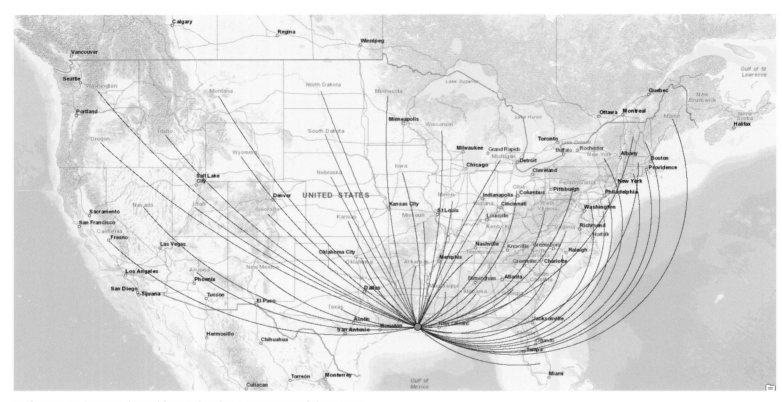

Gulf Crown products are shipped from Delcambre, a community of about 1,800 residents, to all the coterminous states. (Cartography by DeWitt Braud, Louisiana State University, Coastal Studies Institute. Base map: Esri, HERE, DeLorme, USGS, Intermap, INCREMENT P, NRCan, Esri Japan, METI, Esri China (Hong Kong), Esri Korea, Esri [Thailand], MapmyIndia, NGCC, © OpenStreetMap contributors, and the GIS User Community.)

The introduction of the Lapeyre Automatic Shrimp Peeling Machine in 1949 revolutionized the Louisiana shrimp industry. Each machine was capable of peeling approximately one thousand pounds of shrimp per hour—comparable to the collective output of approximately 150 experienced human peelers. (Photo from the authors' collections, 2015.)

A modern shrimp processing plant is fully equipped to transform raw shrimp from a receiving dock to a finished consumer product. (Photo from the authors' collections, 2015.)

On Bayou Grand Caillou, David Chauvin's Seafood Company's complex includes a fuel/ice dock, a supply house, a retail store, a "Bluewater" brand processing plant, and an IQF facility. This is one of many integrated shrimp processors in coastal Louisiana. (Photo from the authors' collections, 2019.)

Tidelands Seafood Company in Dulac, Louisiana, is a vertically integrated processor, whose stainless-steel equipment cleans and grades by "count" the shrimp offloaded at the facility. (Photo from the authors' collections, 2019.)

In 1977, Robert Samanie Jr. founded Samanie Packing Company, specializing in "Captain Bob's" frozen peeled shrimp. Samanie sold the firm in 1999, and by 2020, it had ceased to exist. (Photo from the authors' collections, 1982.)

Like Samanie Packing Company, Deep South Seafood has suspended operations. (Photo from the authors' collections, 1982.)

Faith Family Shrimp Company is a wholesale retail dealer in Chauvin. Operated by Chad and Angela Portier, the company owns five commercial fishing vessels that annually land approximately two million pounds of wild-caught Gulf shrimp. (Photo from the authors' collections, 2018.)

Located "down-the-bayou" from Al's Shrimp Company, this sign is the only reminder of the shuttered company's existence. Such artifacts are emotionally charged symbols of globalization's impact on Louisiana's shrimping communities. (Photo from the authors' collections, 2020.)

Captain Blair's has also closed. In its heyday, "Captain Bob's" products were staples in New York's Chinatown kitchens. (Photo from the authors' collections, 2018.)

This highly integrated business affords consumers a range of products from freshly caught decapods to shrimp baguette po'boys. (Photo from the authors' collections, 2018.)

INTERVIEWS WITH ROLAND AND LOU ANNA GUIDRY, LAFOURCHE PARISH*

LOU ANNA GUIDRY

Lou Anna and Roland Guidry. (Photo from the authors' collections, 2014.)

AUTHORS (AU): I would like to begin with a question for you [Lou Anna]. Could you describe for us a family in which the husband is on a boat in the middle of the Gulf and the wife remains at home with the kids? . . .

Lou Anna Guidry (LAG): It wasn't pretty. It was hard. Sometimes he was away for six weeks at a time. Sometimes four weeks. Occasionally three weeks. And when the first child arrived—a little girl . . . One day he cleaned himself up [and came home] and he had grown a beard. She cried; she didn't recognize him. Cried and wanted to have nothing at all to do with him until he shaved himself, and she recognized her father. But everything that involved running a household and caring for children—seeing about the car when it needed an oil change, running to the supermarket or a doctor's appointment, cooking, cleaning, everything you can think of that you have to do in life, you had to do it alone. Cutting the grass, because when he got home, he was tired. He had been gone a long time. He had things to do on his boat. So, he didn't have much time to help me. What he could do, he did, but it was not his fault. It was just the way it was. And I was not the only one. It was accepted. That simply was life. . . .

AU: So, when he [the husband] was on the boat, you were both the mother and the father?

LAG: That's right. He [Roland] can do a better job of describing his experiences.

ROLAND GUIDRY

Roland Guidry (RG): It was hard to be separated from the family. And the little children, you never see them. She [Lou Anna] is the one who raised them. If they turned out well, it wasn't my doing, it was all her achievement. When the husband returned with the boat, it was necessary to fix whatever was broken. It was necessary to sell the shrimp—or oysters—and prepare to leave again. You don't make money sitting at home. You ice down your hold and you leave. It was somewhat like bondage. But it made you a better man, I guess.

---

* This interview was conducted in Cajun French and translated by the authors.

Nelson Gowanloch observed that "the shift … from canned seafood products to fast frozen seafoods is apparent to everyone." The post-war spike in consumer demand for frozen shrimp coincided with the rise of television advertising and the American supermarket, which was emerging as the nation's principal outlet for frozen processed foods. In 1954, the Swanson corporation launched an unprecedented television media blitz to promote its frozen, pack-aged meals—subsequently dubbed "TV dinners." Within a year of the product line's launch, Swanson had sold twenty-five million TV dinners at a unit retail price of ninety-eight cents.

Although the frozen food pioneer initially focused on bland basic fare, such as turkey dinners, the corporation rapidly broadened its product line to include Gulf Coast shrimp. Frozen breaded shrimp dinners played a pivotal role in this diversification effort. Featuring six tails whose diminutive size and physical imperfections were effectively masked by breading, Swanson's frozen fried shrimp TV dinner promised a balanced meal (processed peas and crinkle-cut fries included) centered on fried shrimp that were "fried crispy on the outside, *juicy* and tender on the inside" and "tangy cocktail sauce" that made "the shrimp extra-good."

Popularized by the TV dinner craze, breaded shrimp soon became nearly ubiquitous, even appearing prominently on the burg-er-centric menus of new fast food restaurants catering to America's burgeoning car culture. Shrimp had moved from a sidebar culinary curiosity to the very heart of America's mainstream food culture, and the popular appetite for "America's favorite shellfish" grew with each passing year. By 1960, Americans annually consumed sixty-one million pounds of breaded shrimp.

Distribution

The Lapeyre peeler's then breathtaking processing and sorting capabilities magnified the need for improved communications capabilities between processors and consumers, particularly bulk consumers on whom the season's economic fortunes hinged. Because of the rapidly changing marketplace, in which business relationships

In recent decades, historians have attributed Swanson's remarkable success to a variety of factors. During World War II, working women lacked time for traditional meal preparation and consequently embraced culinary shortcuts whenever possible. Faced with the challenge of feeding their rapidly growing baby boom families, young mothers were thus more amenable to shortcuts when national postwar prosperity made it possible for them to indulge in what their Depression-era counterparts would have considered a shameful, self-indulgent luxury—a processed meal.

were quickly transcending political boundaries, reliable international telephonic communications were indispensable.

Postwar commercial shrimp distribution consisted of the following sequential transactions: First, processors acquired shrimp directly from trawlers by means of cash purchases—a tradition persisting into the twenty-first century. Then, processors negotiated directly with restaurant or supermarket chain owners—or their representatives—who typically arrived at a Louisiana processing facility as the season opened to discuss bulk shipments, often while the recently unloaded shrimp in question were machine-processed (peeled and sorted) to produce the desired count. In other cases, buyers prepaid for future bulk shipments. Purchases were consistently made in cash, and sales of one hundred thousand pounds were not unusual. Such massive transactions helped transform the Louisiana shrimp industry from a modest regional supplier of fresh shrimp in 1900 to a billion-dollar, international mega-business by the beginning of the twenty-first century.

A regional communications revolution helped make this economic transformation possible. Nearly seventy years after a talking telegraphy company opened its doors in New Orleans, telephone and electric power lines crossed the marshlands to the "end-of-the-road communities" that had emerged as the regional shrimp harvesting and processing hubs over the previous half century. In addition, by the 1960s, the Pelican State's highway system expanded to reach the most remote shrimping communities, linking them directly for the first time with crucial inland markets. Now able to ship processed food in bulk directly to customers by refrigerated trucks, cannery and processing plant owners retooled their shrimp "sheds" to streamline the production of customized bulk orders. Production facilities, which formerly consisted of several specialized buildings, were now centered in a single dockside structure housing mechanical peelers and industrial freezers. Shrimp offloaded at the processor's wharf were peeled, cooked, canned, or fresh-frozen and ready for shipment within a matter of hours.

Frozen raw shrimp constituted the bulk of the coastal processors' postwar shipments. Processing facilities typically packed fresh-frozen shrimp in eight-ounce, ten-ounce, twelve-ounce, one-pound, and five-pound cartons. Packages weighing one pound or less were geared to supermarket customers, while processors marketed five-pound cartons to restaurants and other large institutional consumers. Refrigerated trucks typically transported bulk orders directly to major institutional buyers, although processors used railroad cars on occasion.

POSTWAR TRANSITIONS

Processing

The frozen shrimp industry's rapid ascendancy came at the expense of seafood canners, whose slide into oblivion began before the beginning of the Korean War. In 1950, for example, only 13 percent of Louisiana's shrimp harvest was canned. Fully 65 percent reached consumers as frozen tails, and the erosion of canneries' market share accelerated as frozen seafood processors added in-house deveining, breading, and custom-packaging capabilities. This trend continued unabated into the Vietnam War era (ca. 1964–1975). America's per capita consumption of frozen processed shrimp doubled between 1950 and 1970. The canning industry's downward trajectory continued unabated into the early twenty-first century. Seafood canneries in Georgia and the Carolinas were the first to close, but declining market share slowly but surely claimed victims along the northern Gulf Coast as well. In the early 1950s, Louisiana boasted twenty-one seafood canneries. By the start of new millennium, only one remained—the Bumble Bee cannery at Violet—and its canning operation ceased because of devastation wrought by Hurricane Katrina in 2005.

As seafood products migrated from grocery shelves to supermarket freezers, so did research and development capitalization. By the late 1950s, Louisiana boasted a new research laboratory specializing in frozen fish products, and the following decade, groundbreaking quick-freezing inventions began to appear in shrimp trawlers.

As quick-freezing became the new standard, coastal processors developed a distribution network for frozen and, to a lesser extent, raw products that demanded a year-round supply. The changing

Relationships between parties to bulk transactions sometimes transcended the business realm, particularly in cases where close business ties extended over multiple generations. Anecdotal information indicates that clients' children often accompanied their parents to processors' Louisiana facilities, where they met—and established enduring friendships with—the host children. These intergenerational friendships persist in the twenty-first century. For example, members of the Authement family, fourth-generation Cajun owner-operators of Dulac's Hi-Seas company, have maintained a close relationship with Southern California–based Chinese American shrimp wholesalers for so long that the latter have literally become part of the Authement extended family.

marketplace engendered fundamental changes in the manner in which Gulf decapods reached distributors and consumers. For example, before the 1950s, Chicago, a crucial market for Louisiana's shrimp, received fresh shrimp by rail service. By the early 1950s, all decapods sent to the Windy City were frozen, and as early as 1954, 97 percent of the 17,347,000 pounds of the frozen shrimp shipped to Chicago arrived by refrigerated truck.

This new distribution model's dependence on rapid and convenient access to major highways linking coastal processors with inland markets, coupled with the heavy acquisition, operating, and maintenance costs of refrigeration and processing equipment, rapidly transformed the Louisiana shrimp industry. During the canning industry's early twentieth-century heyday, processing and distribution operations were situated as close as possible to the principal shrimp harvesting sites. As the canning industry waned in the post–World War II era, this model was replaced by a new paradigm in which processing and distribution operations were centralized in communities—principally Houma, Morgan City, Delcambre, Intracoastal City (a.k.a. "Icy"), and, to a lesser extent, New Orleans—with easy access to metropolitan markets via US Highway 90 and, later, the interstate highway system.

Conservation

As post–Korean War era experience makes abundantly clear, the sustained growth of the American shrimp industry was limited only by individual markets' road access, and with the advent of the interstate highway system in 1958, all major markets were within easy reach of the Bayou State's processors. To prevent overharvesting in the face of persistently strong national demand, Louisiana began adopting aquatic resources conservation laws in the wake of World War II to protect the shrimp fishery. Acts 78 and 210 of 1946, sponsored by the Louisiana Department of Wildlife and Fisheries, established a broad regulatory framework intended to control the size of the Bayou State's trawler fleet and prevent poaching by out-of-state shrimpers—with the notable exception of Mississippi

"Today, since the discovery of productive offshore shrimp grounds, a considerable amount of centralization has taken place. . . . However, few of the fishing communities have ceased to exist because of this centralization. They still retain their function as primary sites for the exploitation of the particular marine products that are locally abundant, but the processing and transshipment of the products is becoming . . . centralized. Refrigerated trucks and motor-driven vessels carry the raw product to the larger centers [i.e., Houma, Morgan City, and New Orleans] that process and prepare for further shipment" (Padgett, "Physical and Cultural Associations" 481–93).

Internet product reviews suggest many American shoppers are deeply concerned about the geographical origin of the shrimp they consume. Their concern is warranted in part because of chemical additives present in farm-raised shrimp, particularly imports from Indonesia and China. Canned Bumble Bee tiny shrimp is a product of Indonesia. (Photo from the authors' collections, 2019.)

trawlers because of a preexisting interstate reciprocity agreement. For example, Act 210 imposed strict trawler licensing requirements to regulate the number of active shrimpers in state waters. In addition, the legislation levied a tax on fishing boats, established inside and outside seasons, and regulated trawl nets' length. Finally, the legislation imposed a severance tax of fifty cents per barrel on shrimp shipped across state lines by any means other than common carrier to ensure that "no one except bona fide residents of Louisiana are permitted to fish for shrimp." These conservation measures were intended to preserve the Bayou State's position as America's dominant supplier of shrimp—70 percent of the national total, 90 percent of the Gulf harvest.

Louisiana's postwar conservation efforts met with considerable resistance from inshore trawlers who sought to capitalize on the "spectacularly high . . . prices" then offered by brokers, retailers, and French Market vendors for out-of-season contraband shrimp. The Department of Wildlife and Fisheries initially used "mild" enforcement efforts in an unsuccessful effort to breach this wall of popular opposition. When it became obvious that another approach was needed, new Wildlife and Fisheries Commissioner Luther S. Montgomery initiated a rigorous enforcement campaign. In April 1946, Wildlife and Fisheries agents intercepted fourteen shrimp boats operating in Louisiana's inshore waters during a closed season, arrested the crews, and confiscated 100 barrels of

Individual quick frozen (IQF) wild-caught Gulf shrimp would not exist without the contributions of Clarence Birdseye, the "father of frozen food" who, in 1927, applied for a freezing machine patent. The Birds Eye frozen food company's product line paved the way for American consumers to "eat out of their freezers." Louisiana shrimpers and processors were among the prime beneficiaries of this culinary trend because of the strong post–World War II public demand for frozen shrimp. (Photo from the authors' collections, 2020.)

In coastal Louisiana's linear bayou towns, shrimp docks and their associated business and governmental facilities became hubs of community life. The town's business infrastructure—water towers, post offices, stores, icehouses, picking sheds, packing plants, fuel docks, and so forth—were all clustered around the bustling waterfront. In addition, the processing plants' docks functioned not only as critical economic drivers but also as effective social hubs for the largely female workforce, which usually included many mariners' wives. (Painting courtesy of Andrew (Andy) Gibson, Tidelands Seafood Company, Dulac, LA, 2020.)

shrimp. In March 1948, Wildlife and Fisheries officers apprehended fifty-two trawlers for violations of shrimp laws and confiscated 155 barrels of undersized decapods (90 to 100 count). Meanwhile, the department's efforts expanded to include individuals employing seine crews in an effort to circumvent the state's enforcement efforts targeting trawlers on inland waters. As the foregoing arrest records and news reports attest, conservation laws alone provided little actual deterrence to "outlaw" shrimpers, particularly fishermen at the lower end of the fishery's industrial food chain, where postwar competition was becoming increasingly intense as the number of licensed trawlers exceeded three thousand and remained above that statistical plateau for most of the 1950s. The *Louisiana Game, Fur, and Fish* magazine, replaced by the popularly acclaimed and widely circulated *Louisiana Conservationist*, reported in June 1948 that the "imposition of good conservation practices is fought bitterly by the very fishermen who would benefit most by enactment and enforcement of such restrictions." This resistance flew in the face of the proven efficacy of conservation measures first put in place by the Louisiana government in the early twentieth century, measures that had ensured the fishery's sustainability for nearly a half century.

Escalating pressure on miscreants by Department of Wildlife and Fisheries agents and wardens eventually produced results. By the early 1950s, the department deployed teams of enforcement agents aboard small aircraft and speedboats. Working in tandem, the airborne and waterborne units reportedly "greatly reduced" the once "widespread disregard" for the state's postwar shrimp conservation regulations. By 1958, the percentage of Louisiana boats intercepted for close-season violations declined, while that of out-of-state vessels—with Texas and Mississippi registries—increased.

Louisiana shrimpers' erstwhile resistance to conservation measures and the ecological science underpinning them came at a particularly pivotal moment in the fishery's history when environmental changes threatened not only the industry but also the communities and way of life that sustained it. Louisiana's shrimp production is inextricably linked to the health of the coastal estuaries that function as vital decapod nurseries. These estuarine environments, in turn, were originally dependent on the original, labyrinthine system of interconnected waterways that allowed the transmission and diffusion of freshwater and nutrients from the Mississippi River and its distributaries to the coast. But unregulated water flow through this network always held the inherent risk of flooding in the diffusion zone. The flooding threat was particularly onerous to vulnerable agricultural interests, which mobilized considerable political clout to persuade the state government and local levee boards to sever the arterial connections between the Mississippi and two of its major distributaries—Bayous Plaquemine and Lafourche—around the turn of the twentieth century. The interrupted flow of sustaining nutrients was greatly magnified by construction of the massive current Mississippi River levee system to mitigate the threat of catastrophic riverine flooding in the wake of the disastrous 1927 "high water" event.

The impact of these massive hydrological changes was initially gradual and cumulative, and accordingly, the environmental consequences were not immediately ineluctable. Scientists first noted significant environmental changes in the 1950s, when a severe, prolonged drought exacerbated the lack of riverine freshwater diversion and resulted in a "cataclysmic drop in abundance of white shrimp which coincided with a sudden increase in abundance of . . . brown shrimp" (Condrey and Fuller). These changes, however, attracted little public attention because the decline of one commercially exploitable species was offset by the rise of the other. Even in the early 1970s, when Sherwood Gagliano and his research

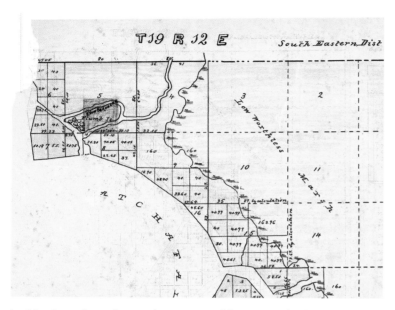

Louisiana's near featureless marshes are some of the youngest lands in America. The uninhabited coastal *marais* (wetland) was a surveyor's nightmare and often identified by cartographers as "worthless" and "unfit for human habitation." (Map courtesy of T. Baker Smith, LLC, Houma, LA.)

associates discovered that Louisiana was losing coastal land mass at the alarming rate of sixteen and a half square miles per year, coastal plain residents remained unconvinced. Although short of late Depression and World War II era totals, annual production levels were sufficiently robust to persuade Bayou State shrimpers that the initial reports of land loss and concomitant environmental degradation were either overblown or fallacious. However, by the 1980s, Gagliano's findings were inescapable, for large swaths of Louisiana's fragile coastline were rapidly morphing into open water. Only when it became clear that land loss threatened the estuaries on which the shrimp life cycle depended did grassroots attitudes change in the Louisiana fishery. A shrimper survey published in 1996 indicated that 70.3 percent of the respondents believed that "science is efficacious." (Margavio and Forsyth 117.)

Fisheries sustainability research also played a critical role in changing shrimpers' attitudes toward evidence-based science. In the post–World War II era, state conservation programs were supplemented by federal oceanography research intended to enhance fisheries' sustainability and avoid a recurrence of the food shortages brought on by wartime rationing. In the Gulf of Mexico, the federal research effort was spearheaded by the NOAA's *Oregon*, one of four research vessels commissioned by the United States government to find and study new exploitable fishing grounds. Stationed at Pascagoula, Mississippi, from 1950 to 1967, the *Oregon* ventured as far afield as French Guiana and the Caribbean rim, but most of its research centered on the northern Gulf of Mexico.

Production figures for the early post–World War II era nevertheless make it clear that augmented conservation efforts were necessary. Louisiana's annual production levels fell from an average of one hundred million pounds between 1940 and 1946 to only forty million pounds between 1957 and 1962 (excluding the anomalous 1960 harvest). After ten years of disappointing yields, Louisiana shrimp landings began to rise significantly in 1963. Between 1965 and 1975, Bayou State shrimpers reported an average annual harvest of seventy-one million pounds, and while this figure represented a significant increase over late 1950s figures, it still was approximately ten million pounds below the 1935–1940 average yield. To put this discrepancy into perspective, one must recognize that the Vietnam War era shrimping fleet was not only much larger but also significantly better equipped than its Depression era counterpart. By the mid-1970s, however, Louisiana's shrimp output had rebounded to near record levels—more than ninety million pounds annually.

The temporary dip in Louisiana's output created an opening for foreign imports. Although Bayou State shrimpers continued to dominate America's domestic shrimp production, they could not keep pace with the nation's surging consumer demand for cheap shrimp, which accelerated following the Vietnam War with introduction of all-you-can-eat buffet lines. To compensate, United States food brokers began to import sizable quantities of decapods, with imports rising eightfold—five million to forty million pounds—between 1945 and 1950. By the mid-1980s, shrimp had evolved from a gourmet entrée to a fast food product, described by critic Jeff Johnson as a "kind of tasteless frozen [product] used by most chain outlets and fast-food eateries, the batter at least gives the flaccid morsel some character."

As the demand for convenience foods escalated, consumer demand for fresh, unprocessed shrimp declined. Because they afforded brokers and retailers greater profit margins, frozen foods became the new norm, resulting in a changing pattern of consumption. This culinary metamorphosis was greatly facilitated by a rapid population shift from rural, agrarian-based settlements to metropolitan centers and an increase in disposable income in the post–World War II era. By 1971, the frozen seafood market reportedly generated $1.5 billion ($9,404,970,863 in 2020 currency) in revenue. Processed shrimp accounted for about half of these frozen food sales.

As Americans consumed ever-greater quantities of shrimp, the focus of the import trade shifted to Central America. The Mexican transplants are particularly significant, for they played a pivotal role in opening the door to foreign shrimp imports. Most of the northern Gulf Coast expats sailed from Carmen, along the Bay of Campeche, harvesting substantial quantities of pink or spotted-grooved shrimp.

Designed by naval architect H. C. Hanson, the *Oregon* was built by Grunderson Brothers of Portland, Oregon, and completed by Astoria Marine of Astoria, Oregon, in 1946. Measuring one hundred feet in length and twenty-six feet in beam, the vessel had a draft of fourteen feet and a displacement of 219 gross tons. The *Oregon* operated in the Pacific Ocean until its reassignment to Pascagoula, Mississippi, in late 1949. The research vessel reached its new port of call on January 5, 1950. Three months later, the *Oregon* began systematically searching the Gulf of Mexico for new, "commercially exploitable" sources of decapods and finfish.

This roadside sign attests to the ubiquitous popularity of "All-U-Can-Eat-Shrimp"—even in domestic shrimping communities threatened by the flood of imported shrimp used in buffets. (Photo from the authors' collections, 1999.)

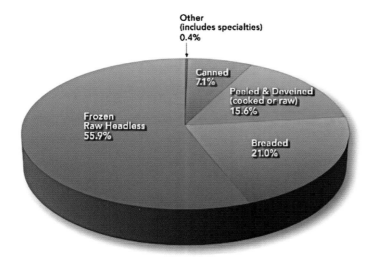

Value of Shrimp Products of the Gulf States, 1976

Other (includes specialties) 0.4%

Canned 7.1%

Peeled & Deveined (cooked or raw) 15.6%

Frozen Raw Headless 55.9%

Breaded 21.0%

Note: Some of the products have been processed from raw products imported from other states or from foreign countries.

Source: National Marine Fisheries Service, Processed Fishery Products, Annual Summary, 1976 (Washington D.C.: Department of Commerce).

Between 1945 and 1946, American consumers bought 800 million pounds of frozen food, including tons of Louisiana shrimp. Because of the public's demand for frozen shrimp, there was a seismic shift from canned products to frozen ones in supermarkets.

As shrimp moved from the back of the menu to the front page, the restaurant trade demanded a quality product. The Gulf of Mexico's fishing fleet delivered. (Photo from the authors' collections, 2015.)

Less than two years after the conclusion of World War II, the Carmen-based shrimp fishery was responsible for a massive increase—estimated by industry experts at 800 percent above 1941 levels—in the quantity of Mexican shrimp imported into the United States. This influx of foreign shrimp—targeted at the convenience food industry of the upper Midwest—so alarmed the Louisiana industry that Third District Congressman James "Jimmie" Domengeaux sponsored legislation (H.R. 2187) limiting Mexican imports to pre-1947 levels. "This situation," Domengeaux argued, "can and will wreck an American business that has taken long years of toil, courage and sacrifice to develop to its present importance." Despite support from prominent Gulf Coast canneries, Domengeaux's plea largely fell on deaf ears, and his bill was consigned to a footnote of history. Shrimp

Once a shrimp boat is "on shrimp," the captain and crew must work together seamlessly if the run is to be successful. (Photo from the authors' collections. Courtesy of the Morgan City Archives, Morgan City, LA, photographer Melvin Hardee, ca. 1965.)

A captain at the wheel of his boat. (Photo from the authors' collections. Courtesy of the Morgan City Archives, Morgan City, LA, photographer Melvin Hardee, ca. 1965.)

imports consequently continued to climb steadily throughout the late twentieth century in large part because of the imports' substantially lower price point. Meanwhile, domestic production remained steady, partly because of plateauing demand for "wild caught" shrimp, partly because of finite natural resources, and partly because of Americans' growing affinity for all-you-can-eat buffets.

Ever-increasing domestic consumption drove United States importers to seek out more productive foreign suppliers, whose substantially lower start-up and operating costs as well as freedom from costly environmental regulations gave their aquaculture operations an inherent competitive edge over wild fisheries. By the early 1970s, India emerged as the leading shrimp exporter, with Pakistan and the Persian Gulf countries following in descending order of importance.

During the Second World War, the United States government encouraged Mexican shrimp imports in an effort to alleviate the nation's protein deficiency. Tariffs on Mexican shrimp were lifted in 1943, and imports rose gradually throughout the war years. In 1947, however, American cannery officials predicted that Carmen-based exporters would mushroom to approximately 24,000,000 pounds—an eightfold increase over the 1941 total—during the calendar year. By 1950, Mexican imports, which accounted for 98.64 percent of all foreign shrimp consumed in the United States, had risen to 39,652,640 pounds—roughly 51 percent of the combined Louisiana-Mississippi harvest that year.

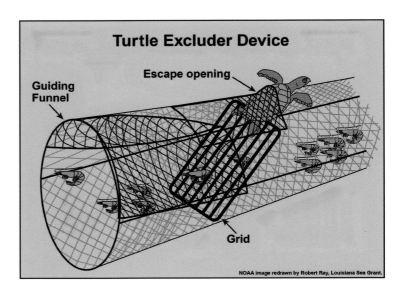

When caught in a fishermen's net, a sea turtle can escape, thanks to the design and configuration of a turtle excluder device. (From "NOAA Issues Final Rule to Require Turtle Excluder Device Use for all Skimmer Trawl Vessels 40 Feet and Greater in Length," https://www.fisheries.noaa.gov/bulletin/noaa-issues-final-rule-require-turtle-excluder-device-use-all-skimmer-trawl-vessels-40.)

By the early 1970s, imported decapods thoroughly dominated the American shrimp industry. For example, seafood industry analyst P. M. Roedel estimated the 1972 national consumption of shrimp at "420 million pounds heads off" and the United States' breaded shrimp consumption at between 100 and 105 million pounds. By comparison, Louisiana's 1973 shrimp harvest—the nation's largest—was approximately 58 million pounds (heads off) (Roedel).

In addition to foreign competition, Louisiana shrimpers faced an increasingly restrictive regulatory environment born of environmental concerns. Bycatch—nontargeted aquatic species unintentionally captured by seines and dragnets—has been a matter of increasing ecological concern since the introduction of the otter trawl in the early twentieth century. Before World War II, seine and small inshore boat crews typically ate or sold much of the bycatch, but with the introduction of the large, steel-hulled factory ships of the Vietnam War era, most of the bycatch was destroyed, raising concerns of species depletion and irreversible ecological damage. To address the bycatch problem, the federal government encouraged the voluntary use of turtle excluder devices (TEDs, or "Georgia Jumpers") on shrimp trawls. TEDs, which permit a captured sea turtle to escape drowning, became mandatory in 1987, eliciting pushback from Bayou State shrimpers, who believed the regulation put them at an even greater competitive disadvantage against their foreign competitors. Responding to pressure from their constituents, Louisiana legislators responded with a bill prohibiting Louisiana Department of Wildlife and Fisheries agents from enforcing federal turtle excluder device regulations. (This law remained in force until 2015, when it was repealed with the support of the Louisiana Shrimp Task Force.)

VIETNAMESE INFLUX

Louisiana shrimpers' longstanding opposition to TEDs reflects a deeply entrenched siege mentality that emerged in the coastal fishing communities during the Vietnam War era. During the Vietnam War and its aftermath, the shrimp fishery faced its most serious challenges since 1945. First, following the United States' entry into the Vietnam conflict (1964), shrimping families lost sons to the military draft, and the resulting labor issues posed a financial hardship. In addition, the 1973 oil embargo caused fuel prices to spike to unprecedented levels, again inflicting a serious financial blow. Finally, the strong surge in foreign shrimp imports during the late 1960s and 1970s threatened to submerge the domestic industry by suppressing prices.

By the early 1980s, Louisiana's predominately Cajun shrimpers also faced unexpected competition in their own backyards because of a new Asian influx. In April 1975, the People's Army of Vietnam (North Vietnamese) captured Saigon, the South Vietnamese capital, and the American armed forces withdrew from the country. Communist North Vietnam quickly consolidated the divided country into the Socialist Republic of Vietnam before launching a campaign of retribution against former South Vietnamese partisans.

As is the case with many of Louisiana's coastal communities, the oil and gas industry initially dominated Intracoastal City's (a.k.a. "Icy") visual landscape, but as its footprint faded in recent decades, seafood-related businesses have emerged from the shadows to become the primary economic engines. In Icy, Vietnamese captains operate steel-hulled refrigeration vessels that deliver their shrimp to land-based Vietnamese-owned processing businesses that, in turn, rely on Vietnamese distributors. The 2020 hurricane season significantly impacted these businesses, but Intracoastal City's resilient Vietnamese fishing community is determined to continue their fishing tradition. However, the immigrants find themselves at a crossroads. The fleet's component vessels and its most experienced captains are aging. Increasing numbers of these venerable seamen are opting to retire and sell their boats—sometimes to foreign buyers—because their white-collar children and grandchildren have no interest in following in their footsteps. In addition, the fishery's primary labor force is also rapidly changing as transient workers replace family members as deckhands. The resulting instability is exacerbated by shrinking profits in the era of COVID-19 and unbridled foreign competition. Time and fate will ultimately determine the destiny of this now beleaguered community.

France obtained control over northern Vietnam following its victory over China in the Sino-French War (1884–1885). French Indochina was formed in 1887. Until communist forces under the leadership of Ho Chi Minh defeated France in 1954, French culture was deeply ingrained in the fabric of Vietnam. Language, café culture, cuisine, religion, architecture, foodways, and infrastructure were imprinted on the population. Following the fall of Saigon in 1975, many Vietnamese refugees migrated to south Louisiana with the assistance of Catholic Social Services. South Louisiana was attractive to the Vietnamese because its climate, foodways, and dominant religion were similar to those of their Asian homeland. (From the authors' collections, 2007.)

Nguyễn Cao Kỳ was chief of the Republic of Vietnam's air force before leading the nation as South Vietnam's prime minister from 1965 to 1967, when the nation transitioned to an elected government. In exile, he lived for a time in the Grand Caillou community of Dulac before his shrimp fishing venture failed, and he relocated to Southern California, where he died in 2011. (From the authors' collections, date unknown.)

An estimated two million refugees fled the purge, many leaving Vietnam in small, overcrowded fishing vessels in search of asylum wherever sympathetic Pacific Rim governments provided housing. The exodus compelled the United States—South Vietnam's principal ally—to open its doors to more than a million refugees.

The United States government initially housed Vietnamese refugees at military bases at Camp Pendleton (California), Eglin Air Force Base (Florida), Fort Indiantown Gap (Pennsylvania), and Fort Chaffee (Arkansas). Most of the Fort Chaffee internees ultimately migrated to coastal Louisiana, where the fishing culture, temperate climate, predominate Catholic faith, and rice-based cooking tradition collectively provided a more familiar and congenial haven than most settlement options.

Most of Louisiana's new Vietnamese immigrants were natives of the Mekong Delta, whose environment and climate closely mirrored those of their adopted wetland home. Catholic Social Services took the lead in resettling the Bayou State's Vietnamese refugees in New Orleans East and throughout the Mississippi delta region. Because many refugees were experienced fishermen, Gulf Coast seafood processors recruited them to work as oyster shuckers and crab pickers.

Like their Chinese counterparts who came to this country in the 1850s looking for a new beginning, the Vietnamese found acculturation and assimilation initially difficult, in part because of their implementation of traditional tools and techniques that were often illegal in coastal Louisiana and in part because they posed a direct threat to the natives' long dominance of the shrimp fishery. Relations between the rival communities were acrimonious from the start, with the interlopers facing harassment, intimidation, litigation, and compulsory instruction by local mariners. Discord persisted even after Vietnamese watermen learned and applied American shrimp trawling and ground-fishing methods. Older Vietnamese mariners, accustomed to working collaboratively within their kinship groups, rankled at the prospect of retraining with less experienced Cajun shrimpers. Cajuns, on the other hand, were vexed by Vietnamese fishing practices that openly violated unwritten local

Vietnamese fishermen considered contact between fishing boats natural and inevitable. To the Vietnamese, a boat was a disposable tool. Maintenance was consequently inessential, and fit vessels devolved over time into jerry-rigged craft, lacking fire extinguishers, life preservers, safe-fuel containers, running lights, and properly marked nets—all notable violations of Coast Guard regulations. On the other hand, the established fishing communities, particularly south Louisiana's Cajun shrimpers, took pride in their boats to the extent that vessels became cherished extensions of their nuclear families.

About fourteen thousand Vietnamese immigrants live in New Orleans. Many, if not most, are devout Catholics. True to their religious roots, the community has built several Catholic churches. Our Lady of La Vang, located in New Orleans East, memorializes a reported Marian apparition at a time when Catholics were persecuted and killed in Vietnam. The original Our Lady of La Vang church, built in Vietnam in 1928, was destroyed in 1972. The New Orleans East church represents a religious and visual connection to the immigrants' Asian homeland. (From the authors' collections, 2013.)

maritime rules. For example, native shrimpers never made contact with other vessels, while Vietnamese trawlers frequently tapped or nudged competitors' boats. Native trawler owners abhorred rust, dents, and scratches, and in their view, the resulting hull damage was entirely unacceptable.

In addition, natives and immigrants clashed over harvesting techniques, rules of the sea, and fundamental conservation issues. Vietnamese shrimpers, who considered the seascape an open resource, believed that a maximized harvest was paramount, regardless of conservation restrictions or local maritime customs. The Asians, for example, did not respect traditional local fishing zone rules and invaded local trawlers' fishing space. In addition, American and Vietnamese fishing techniques were incompatible, and the resulting discordance created dangerous navigational situations on the high seas. Americans pulled trawls in circular patterns, while the Vietnamese used random trawling patterns. The Asians also flagrantly violated generations-old local maritime protocol by flocking to productive waters without first receiving the customary invitation from the captain who fortuitously "discovered" the shrimp run.

Tensions created by these early offshore encounters gradually escalated throughout the 1980s as the immigrants established an ever-larger presence in the fishery. The native response to the

The Vietnamese business model relied heavily on pooled financial resources to underwrite entry into the Louisiana shrimp industry. (From the authors' collections, 2007.)

perceived existential threat to their livelihood took many forms: Some disgruntled Louisiana shrimpers evidently circulated rumors about the supposed Vietnamese propensity for eating dogs and cats, while others maintained that the immigrants were cholera carriers and thus posed a serious health threat to their host communities. Other locals evicted Vietnamese boats from a publicly owned Louisiana wharf. A few coastal suppliers refused to sell fuel or ice to Vietnamese boats. Local officials claimed overcrowding and unsanitary conditions aboard Vietnamese vessels. Vietnamese fishermen received anonymous death threats through the mail. Verbal threats unfortunately eventually progressed beyond words. Guns were fired, boats were sideswiped, trawl nets were cut, and some boats and dwellings were burned.

Over time and through education provided by the Coast Guard and the Louisiana Sea Grant extension program, the Vietnamese were gradually integrated into the Louisiana shrimping community through the diffusion of information regarding the laws, regulations, and customs of the commercial fishing industry. Their exemplary drive, resilience, and adaptability have made the Vietnamese community one of America's great success stories. Like countless immigrant groups before them, their success was based on a collective community effort. Often their kinship groups morphed into vertically integrated enterprises, consisting of packinghouses, shrimp sheds, and fleets of boats. Perhaps the best example of this synergy is presently found at Intracoastal City, in lower Vermilion Parish. By the twenty-first century, Vietnamese refugees began to dominate the Gulf of Mexico's fishing industry. Anecdotal estimates suggest Vietnamese immigrants now own about 20 percent of Louisiana's trawler fleet but harvest about 60 percent of the annual catch.

With the Vietnamese community's rise to prominence, the Louisiana shrimp industry has come full circle. Asians introduced the commercial shrimp industry into the Bayou State in the late nineteenth century, and one hundred years later, the fishery began to recoup much of its lost Asian character. The Asian connection put Louisiana's shrimp industry on the global economic map by forging commercial ties to foreign markets, particularly in the Far East. It is thus ironic that, in this period of Asian resurgence in the Louisiana fishery, the Asian connection would facilitate a reversal of the flow of exported shrimp through established channels and, in so doing, sow the very seeds of the Louisiana industry's own potential demise.

Like the Cajuns before them, hardworking, tenacious Vietnamese have quietly made their mark on Louisiana's shrimping industry. Like their Catholic Francophone neighbors, the community's matriarchs have spearheaded intracommunity efforts to preserve many cultural traditions. (From the authors' collections, 2008.)

The Vietnamese fishing community has successfully acculturated into the regional mainstream. For example, Vietnamese fishermen have embraced the Cajun Blessing of the Fleet tradition, adding their own cultural elements to the ceremonies, such as the release of paper boats for luck. In addition, there is a notable ongoing regional fusion of Vietnamese and Cajun culinary traditions. Such cultural connections have been facilitated by local churches. (From the authors' collections, photographer Chuck Cook, 1987.)

FRIENDS DON'T LET FRIENDS EAT IMPORTED SHRIMP

In *American Catch*, a masterful historical overview of the American fishing industry, Paul Greenberg astutely observed that America's insatiable appetite for shrimp "opened up our markets to Asia. This occurrence has effectively decoupled the American consumer from the American coast and reattached us to ever more distant shores" (92). The nation's ever-increasing reliance on Asian producers has had catastrophic consequences for the domestic shrimp fishery, particularly that of coastal Louisiana—the United States' leading producer of decapods since the late nineteenth century. The inherent dietary and endocrinological benefits of Louisiana's wild-caught shrimp are now entirely lost on a generation of Americans whose principal exposure to the crustaceans has been in all-you-can-eat buffets.

The American consumers' indifference to the geographical origins of the aquatic foods they eat poses a direct threat to a unique way of life that has evolved in the Bayou State's coastal marshes over the past 150 years. Public apathy is a direct result of deep-seated, stereotypical images of the Louisiana coastal plain and its denizens. The earliest maps of the coastal wetlands, which clearly reflect this mentality, consistently identify the marshes and estuaries as "uninhabitable" and "useless" lands. As longtime Louisiana Wildlife and Fisheries administrator Allan Ensminger, who spent his entire career in the coastal wetlands, observed before his passing in January 2019, "these marshlands were by and large just considered as wastelands to [nineteenth- and early twentieth-century] developers. The only thing they were interested in was land that you could farm." By extension, persons doomed to live in these inhospitable wetlands merited equal popular disdain—except when their traditional ecological knowledge proved essential to exploitation of the area's mineral resources, which were essential to the nation's economic wellbeing.

The venerable axiom that the Bayou State's coastal wetlands were valued exclusively for their suitability for economic exploitation has endured to the present. Before Hurricane Katrina (2005), public policy polling commissioned by the State of Louisiana made

CHAPTER 5

S-NPP - VIIRS — I-Band 5 - 11µm — Hurricane Laura
27 August 2020, 2:51aam CDT (0751UTC)

Category 4 Hurricane Laura's eastern eyewall devastated southwestern Louisiana with maximum sustained winds of 150 miles per hour. The people, communities, and businesses that make up this section of the state's working coast were overwhelmed. (From CIMSS/NOAA, August 27, 2020.)

it painfully clear that residents of the American heartland had no interest whatsoever in proposed government subsidies for wetlands projects to protect New Orleans and other Louisiana coastal communities increasingly vulnerable to storm surge events intensified as a result of coastal subsidence, erosion, and environmentally destructive subsurface mineral exploitation.

The Louisiana shrimp industry's problems are those of the nation's endangered wetlands region in microcosm. First, like the rapidly disappearing Louisiana coastal plain, the region's major problems are invisible to the average Louisianan, much less the average American. This invisibility is hardly surprising, for these coastal residents are among the United States' most marginalized citizens. For more than 150 years, the cultural mainstream has alternately ignored and openly denigrated them—except during national emergencies, when their services and economic contributions were often crucially important. The miasma of ignorance and apathy surrounding the coastal population and their attendant businesses is compounded by the facts that the Bayou State's coastal parishes are popularly associated with industrial and commercial activities, not leisure, which has a far higher twenty-first-century

An unprecedented hurricane season and the COVID-19 pandemic have fundamentally damaged coastal Louisiana's economic well-being. Nationally, the staggering death toll aside, significant reductions in income, a dramatic rise in unemployment, and illness-related disruptions in the transportation, service, and manufacturing sectors are among the most noticeable economic consequences of the disease. In Louisiana, the seafood economy faced these issues, while also enduring a record number of hurricanes—Cristobal, Marco, Laura, Sally, Beta, Delta, and Zeta—whose trajectories affected all or part of Louisiana. Even storms such as Sally and Beta that threatened Louisiana before making landfall in neighboring states immobilized the state's shrimping fleet and negatively impacted shrimp habitats. When tropical systems made landfall in the Bayou State, coastal fishermen had small windows of opportunity to seek safe harbor in neighboring locations that often proved to be only marginally more secure than their respective home ports. With each landfall, shrimp boats were damaged or sunk, and the fishery's associated infrastructure decimated. In some communities repeatedly battered by the storms' relentless onslaughts of wind and waves, little survived. Yet a strong American demand for quality, wild-caught shrimp endures, and if the past is indeed prelude, Louisiana's fishermen from Cameron to Yscloskey will vigorously strive to rebound. However, major, perhaps insurmountable, challenges loom ahead, as the succinct post–Hurricane Laura report from Sea Grant agent Kevin Savoie makes painfully clear:

Monroe and Shirley owned and operated the shrimp boat, *Shirley Elaine*, for 36 years. He purchased the vessel in South Carolina and brought it over to Cameron, where it supported his family until now. An attempt to raise it this morning (9/16/2020), but it was too badly damaged.

National attitudes toward coastal issues began to change only in the wake of Hurricane Sandy (2012)—largely because the storm threatened the nation's most populous city. This slow national awakening, however, has prioritized safeguards for major metropolitan areas, at the expense of the undervalued rural multitudes and the sustainable coastal fisheries that employ many of them.

Image of a crane lifting the remains of the shrimp boat, *Shirley Elaine*, Lake Charles, 2020. (Photo from Kevin Savoie, Louisiana Sea Grant, Marine Agent, Cameron and Calcasieu Parishes, 2020.)

intrinsic value quotient, and that Americans have come to take the region's significant economic contributions for granted.

Louisiana's shrimpers are ultimately victims of their own success. Between the 1930s and the 1980s, Bayou State fishermen, consistent leaders in the nation's annual decapod harvest, were instrumental in cultivating and feeding an insatiable national appetite for shrimp. Despite the providential abundance of local resources, the shrimpers simply could not meet the surging domestic consumer demand by the 1990s. Their dilemma was compounded by steadily rising production costs and simultaneously falling market prices. The result is a pernicious existential threat to the venerable fishery's very survival.

The Louisiana shrimpers' plight is perhaps best articulated by Windell Curole, Darcy Kiffe, Andy Gibson, and Lance Authement—coastal Louisiana natives, members of shrimping families, and notable regional economic and/or political leaders. In recent interviews, they shared their accumulated memories and nuanced perceptions, and their reminiscences and observations provide a composite view of the root causes and effects of the industry's current distress. Kiffe, a former president of the Louisiana Shrimp Association, recalls that, as a child, "We fueled up diesel in Morgan City for three cents a gallon. We bought ice for $1.50. We were selling 20–25 [count] shrimp for $2.35, $2.40. You go today [March 28, 2019], [a] block of ice right now [sells for] about $16.00, $17.00 [and] fuel, $4.00 [a gallon], and you're getting $2.35 for the same shrimp."

The consistently low modern wholesale price for freshly caught Gulf shrimp contrasts with the market fluctuations commonplace before the mid-1980s, when the traditional laws of supply and demand paradoxically brought an element of economic stability to Bayou State shrimpers. Darcy Kiffe notes that "in the old days, when you didn't catch a lot of shrimp, the price went up, so you could make it. When there were a lot of shrimp, the price went down, but you [caught] a lot of shrimp. You made it." However, the influx of cheap foreign pond- or farm-raised shrimp subsumed the state's industry into the global shrimp marketplace, where regional market forces—and costly environmental regulations—did not apply. Kiffe

American shrimpers and the fishery's various ancillary services lobbied the federal government for protection from unfair foreign competition for nearly sixty years before the United States Department of Commerce finally imposed tariffs on imports from the world's six largest foreign shrimp exporters in retaliation for dumping in 2003. Shrimp imports nevertheless subsequently increased at the expense of domestic production, as crafty domestic corporate buyers shifted their acquisitions to third world countries excluded from the 2003 tariff. The Department of Commerce's limited levy on shrimp imports was further hamstrung by the tariff's inherent limitations. Numerous shrimp species and multiple forms of processed shrimp, particularly value-added shrimp products, were exempt from the new import duties. This glaring loophole continues to serve as a conduit for duty-free shrimp imports that undercut domestic production. Additional tariffs have been applied to China and Vietnam, but not to all Chinese and Vietnamese producers. Foreign-sourced shrimp—which account for roughly 90 percent of the shrimp consumed in this country—thus remains a persistent threat to the domestic fishery's viability.

The Southern Shrimp Alliance has consequently called for blanket tariffs on imported shrimp, ranging from 30 percent to more than 200 percent. The affected countries—in league with American retailers, restaurateurs, distributors, and related businesses in the shrimp processing chain—have mounted vocal opposition to the proposed duties under the banner of anti-protectionism. However, without aggressive protectionism, the upper Gulf Coast's shrimp fleet will become a quaint historical artifact, like lamplighters, ice delivery wagons, and uniformed elevator operators.

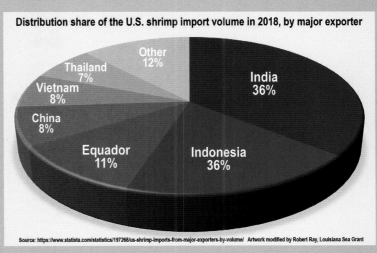

Distribution share of the U.S. shrimp import volume in 2018, by major exporter

Other 12%
Thailand 7%
Vietnam 8%
China 8%
Equador 11%
Indonesia 36%
India 36%

Source: https://www.statista.com/statistics/197268/us-shrimp-imports-from-major-exporters-by-volume/   Artwork modified by Robert Ray, Louisiana Sea Grant

The primary countries involved in the export of farm-raised shrimp to the United States, 2018.

notes that "once imports came in, . . . all the [established] economics just dropped out."

Cheap foreign imports initially proved particularly problematic for Louisiana shrimpers because some unscrupulous Gulf Coast processors packaged and sold foreign shrimp with "product of the United States" labels at prices undercutting domestic trawlers' bottom line. Darcy Kiffe remembers that "they caught a lot of people doing that, and they were fined . . . , but that was killing it and we weren't having new tariffs . . . put on the shrimp."

Although modest tariffs were subsequently imposed, imports have enjoyed an overwhelming price advantage to the present. The domestic industry has consequently been compelled to rely on the inherent advantages of their wild-caught product: better taste, better texture, and freedom from antibiotics, hormones, and, theoretically, harmful chemicals. The Louisiana shrimp industry's efforts to combat the influx have been thwarted by a variety of issues, the most significant of which hinged on conflicting political agendas on the national, regional, and local levels.

On the national level, politically powerful American animal-feed corporations lobbied effectively against crippling tariffs on imports to protect their significant financial interests in major Central American aquafarms during the 1980s, when these—particularly Panamanian aquafarmers and processors—dominated the shrimp-import industry. These shrimp farms naturally constituted a captive market for specialized aquaculture feed products.

In addition, the longstanding, often intense disputes between the diverse shrimper groups initially centered on season opening dates. Inshore fishermen—in tandem with processors—clamored for the earliest possible dates to take advantage of the initial surge of pent-up demand for fresh decapods. Offshore shrimpers, on the other hand, derived their biggest profits from larger shrimp that reached maturity near the end of the season and consequently promoted significantly later opening dates "to stop them from catching all the [juvenile] shrimp" (Kiffe, Curole and Kiffe interview). In 2020, Curole noted that "if you catch them smaller, you might catch even more shrimp, but the price tag's going to be smaller because you don't get much for that. [With] 100 count shrimp, [or] 80 count shrimp, you get a dollar, [or] eighty cents, compared to four or five dollars if you let them grow up as big as they can grow up."

The great political influence exerted by the animal-feed conglomerates through their state and national lobbyists has effectively thwarted American shrimpers' repeated efforts to stem the relentless tide of foreign shrimp imports. In Louisiana, anti-import campaigns were further constrained by internecine conflicts between inshore and offshore shrimpers, who obsessively focused their attention not on foreign competitors but on fundamentally antagonistic domestic agendas. Windell Curole recalls that Bayou State trawlers didn't hire lobbyists because "it was always competitive" between the industry's main constituent interests. "You basically had three [rival groups]," notes Curole. "You had the real small boat fishery, you had the big-boat industry, and the offshore [trawlers], and they all had different desires. There was always this crazy battle. How do you organize people that fight each other all the time?"

The unrelenting struggle among the various shrimper camps— and the consequent dissipation of their political influence—reached its crescendo at precisely the time that the feuding factions should have closed ranks against the unrelenting economic onslaught of cheap foreign shrimp. The catalyst for this economic and political cataclysm was the introduction and mandatory deployment of turtle excluder devices. In the late 1970s, the federal government added sea turtles, indigenous to the northern Gulf of Mexico, to the national endangered species list, and because shrimp trawls were widely presumed to be the principal threat to these aquatic chelonians, the National Oceanographic and Atmospheric Administration's (NOAA) Fisheries division launched a program to devise and test gear reducing the number of sea turtles inadvertently harvested and drowned in trawlers' nets. Early prototypes were inefficient; turtle captures were down by only 30 percent, while shrimp losses were reduced by up to 50 percent or more. By the early 1980s, improved experimental TEDs performed significantly better—reportedly turtle separation rates of 89 percent with a "minimal" loss of shrimp. In addition, new turtle excluder device designs included finfish

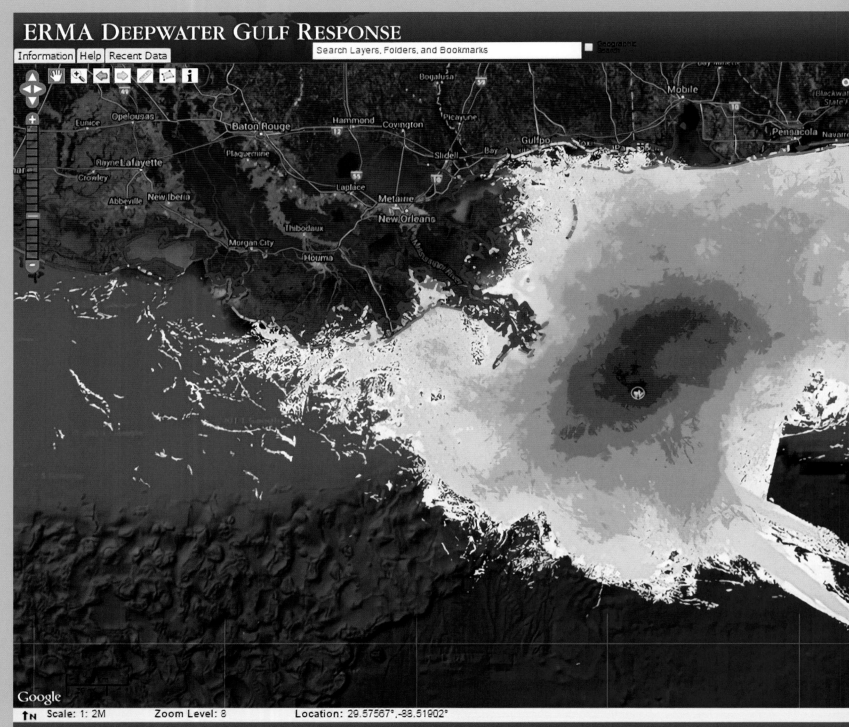

ERMA DEEPWATER GULF RESPONSE

Information | Help | Recent Data

Search Layers, Folders, and Bookmarks   Geographic Search

Google

↑N   Scale: 1: 2M   Zoom Level: 8   Location: 29.57567°, -88.51902°

National Oceanic and Atmospheric Administration | Environmental Protection Agency
U.S. Department of the Interior | U.S. Department of Homeland Security | University of New Hampshire | Privacy policy | Official Citation | Email Comments

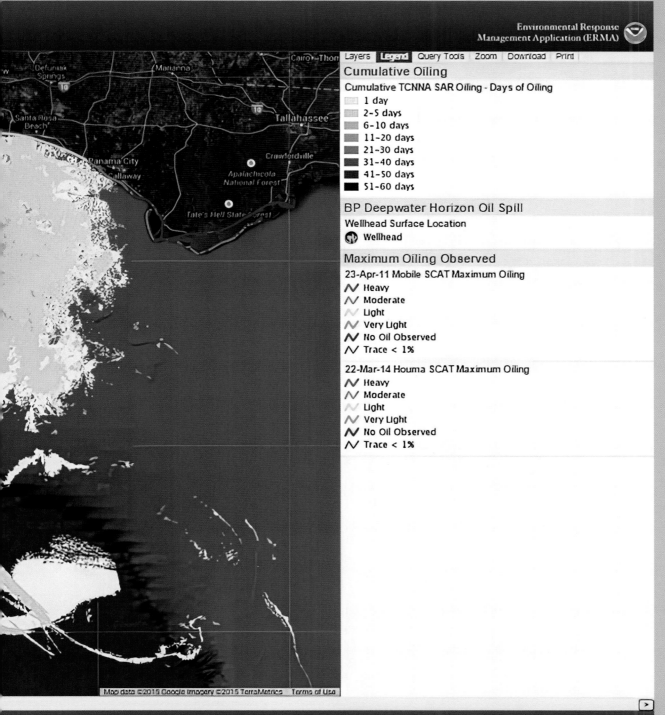

The spatial distribution of the Deepwater Horizon oil spill extended from Point Au Fer in Louisiana east to near Apalachicola, Florida. (From "In Mapping the Fallout from the Deepwater Horizon Oil Spill, Developing One Tool to Bring Unity to the Response," https://response.restoration.noaa.gov/about/media/mapping-fallout-deepwater-horizon-oil-spill-developing-one-tool-bring-unity-response.htm.)

diverters to reduce bycatch. Championing the new designs, NOAA Fisheries began urging Gulf Coast shrimpers to adopt TEDs on a voluntary basis, but most trawlers balked because the available devices were heavy (approximately one hundred pounds), cumbersome, and prone to increasing both drag and fuel consumption. By the mid-1980s, TED adoption on the northern Gulf Coast was limited to shrimpers seeking to reduce unwanted finfish in their nets. Litigation filed by various environmental groups in response to shrimpers' recalcitrance compelled the federal government to take a more aggressive stance regarding regulatory enforcement. On June 29, 1987, NOAA Fisheries ordered mandatory adoption of turtle excluder devices, but "an array of [retaliatory] lawsuits, injunctions, suspensions of law enforcement, legislative actions by several states, legislation by Congress, and temporary rules issued by NOAA Fisheries and the Department of Commerce" resulted in an ineffective patchwork of regulations and inconsistent levels of enforcement (NOAA Fisheries). This confused situation came to an end in 1989, when uniform federal TED regulations finally went into effect, resulting in more extensive use of commercial turtle excluder devices.

In Louisiana waters, federal enforcement of TED regulations was initially focused on the larger offshore trawlers, and this selective implementation effort widened the already broad gulf separating the feuding onshore and offshore shrimper camps. Once again, internal dissension obviated any chance of a cohesive regional response.

These persistent regulatory issues and their economic repercussions, which endured into the early twenty-first century, faded into relative insignificance following the Deepwater Horizon disaster in the Mississippi Canyon off the mouth of the Mississippi River. On April 20, 2010, a massive natural gas explosion aboard an offshore rig operated by the Transocean company and leased by British Petroleum (BP) triggered an oil spill of unprecedented size and breathtaking geographic scope. At its peak, the ruptured well spewed daily an estimated sixty thousand barrels of crude oil into the Gulf Stream. By the time the severely damaged wellhead was finally capped on July 22, the oil slick generated by the leakage covered an estimated 57,500 to 68,800 square miles of pristine open water—figures corresponding to the size of Illinois or Florida—contaminated approximately 1,100 miles of fragile wetlands and prime recreational coastline, and huge amounts of subaqueous toxic sludge polluted the nation's most productive shrimp and oyster fishing grounds.

The environmental impact of this unfolding cataclysm was compounded by a subtler menace. In a desperate attempt to mitigate the looming portable threat posed by the rapidly expanding oil spill, BP-approved contractors sprayed 1.8 million gallons of chemical dispersants to emulsify the surface accumulations of crude oil. These dispersants, which, according to ProPublica, had been banned by the United Kingdom for more than a decade because of their toxicity, immediately impacted the Gulf's regional food chain.

The most obvious initial result was a precipitous decline in the Bayou State's annual shrimp harvest. In May 2010 alone, Louisiana shrimpers harvested 65 percent fewer decapods than the previous year. Because of the petroleum-based sludge accumulating on the ocean bottom, the Louisiana oyster industry's falloff was even more calamitous. The United States Bureau of Ocean Energy Management estimated that the northern Gulf Coast fishing industry sustained losses variously reported at $94.7 million to $1.6 billion in gross revenue and from 740 to 9,315 jobs. Some areas of the Barataria estuary—North America's most productive shrimp nursery—were not reopened to commercial fishing until 2015. Consequently, according to a lower Bayou Lafourche shipyard operator, the area's shrimp fleet shrank by approximately 50 percent.

The short-term, direct impact of the unfolding environmental crisis was quickly overwhelmed by growing ancillary medical and consumer concerns about the chemicals—both petroleum droplets and chemical dispersants—ingested by commercially harvested shrimp in the seasons following the blowout. Invertebrates break down petroleum-based chemicals and dispersants very slowly, and consequently, shellfish tend to accumulate ever-higher concentrations of these toxic substances over time. This phenomenon was widely reported in the popular media, and mainstream consumers'

Every seasoned cook knows that any dish is only as good as its ingredients. Fresh ingredients are particularly critical to the success of any seafood dish. As with fresh vegetables, fresh seafood is more visually appealing, far more flavorful, and much healthier than frozen analogues, which are typically filled with preservatives, contaminants, and antibiotics. Freshness is particularly critical in restaurant settings, where success or failure is dictated by a kitchen's consistent ability to satisfy discerning consumer palates—particularly in coastal regions where fresh seafood is commonplace. Consumption of fresh local seafood is also economically advantageous for everyone in coastal regions. Steady demand keeps fishing fleets active, which, in turn, provides employment to hundreds of individuals in ancillary support industries. The circulation of seafood-generated revenue is particularly critical to coast communities along the northern Gulf of Mexico. (Photo from the authors' collections, sign on the outdoor wall of Elizabeth's Restaurant in New Orleans's Ninth Ward, 2011.)

resulting revulsion for tainted Gulf shrimp—formerly the gold standard for American shellfish aficionados—suppressed domestic demand for Louisiana decapods. The nation's major corporate seafood retailers responded by attempting to shift their domestic purchases to West Coast processors, who had far more limited inventory, and in the end, foreign pond-raised imports largely filled the temporary void in the supply chain, further solidifying their virtual stranglehold in the United States' commercial shrimp market.

Indeed, as the second decade of the twenty-first century drew to a close, globalization had become a seemingly implacable economic juggernaut. Between 1980 and 2016, foreign shrimp imports rose 650 percent, while Louisiana's dockside prices actually declined by 75 percent with adjustments for inflation. It is hardly surprising that Louisiana's shrimping fleet shrank by roughly half, as evidenced by the precipitous decline in commercial shrimp license sales, which, according to the Louisiana Department and Wildlife and Fisheries, fell from 12,590 in 2007 to 6,219 in 2017.

The Bayou State's shrimp fishery nevertheless doggedly endures. According to Rex H. Caffey, director of the Marine Extension for Louisiana Sea Grant based at Louisiana State University, as recently as 2016, "Louisiana ports led the Gulf region in landings of white shrimp (forty-six percent)." Louisiana Sea Grant programs have contributed in no small part to the vitality of the surviving shrimping fleet. Over the course of its fifty-two-year history, the agency has funded more than one thousand university research projects—more than 40 percent of which were designated for applied seafood research—but in recent years, the activities of Louisiana Sea Grant field agents have perhaps had a more profound effect on the state's shrimp industry during this past decade of disasters, disruptions, and distress.

Sea Grant's field agents have breathed new life into the regional shrimp fishery by bringing the industry full circle, back to its historic roots through the Louisiana direct seafood program. Reversing a century of precedent, this initiative seeks to turn shrimpers' focus from external markets to consumers in their own backyards. The pilot program, established in 2010 and hosted

In the second decade of the twenty-first century, the farm-to-table movement redefined and reinvigorated the American restaurant industry by rekindling mainstream consumers' appreciation for fresh local farm produce. The movement's success is predicated on local produce's inherent qualitative and nutritional superiority over virtually tasteless imports, whose safety remains suspect because federal agencies routinely inspect only 1 percent of all imported food.

The boat-to-table phenomenon followed closely on the heels of its terrestrial predecessor. In the Bayou State, the Louisiana Direct Seafood initiative, administered jointly by the Louisiana State University Agriculture Center and Louisiana Sea Grant, was in the movement's vanguard. Thomas Hymel, the program's director, and Rodney Emmer laid the foundation for the initiative by collaborating with the Port of Delcambre, the LSU Agriculture Center (known as the LSU AgCenter), and Louisiana Sea Grant to establish the Delcambre Direct Seafood project. After the devastation of Hurricane Rita, Rodney Emmer suggested the community rethink its redevelopment plan. The direct marketing program was a product of the community's vision with the aid and advice of Thomas Hymel, Michael Liffmann, Rodney Emmer, and others.

The initiative took a two-pronged approach to fishery revitalization: training and direct marketing. The LSU AgCenter and Sea Grant agents established instructional programs to train shrimpers in best practice business methods to ensure all participants delivered superior products to local consumers while using sustainable harvesting methods. Harnessing the power of the internet, the project administrators launched the DelcambreDirectSeafood.com website in May 2010. The site's centerpiece—a home page blog—permits shrimpers to post information regarding their onboard catch and their contact information. This allows consumers to contact a trawler directly, place an order online, and pick up their shrimp upon the boat's return to the Delcambre docks. The direct-marketing program created an immediate sensation in seafood-loving Acadiana (French-speaking southern Louisiana), where the benefits of freshly harvested *fruits de mer*—more nutrients, absence of additives and preservatives, and better taste—are deeply appreciated. The financial and nutritional benefits resulting respectively from the restored symbiosis between seafood harvesters and consumers demonstrated the potential benefits for other shrimping communities along the Louisiana coast. In 2012, the Delcambre model was copied in the creation of satellite programs in the Lafourche-Terrebonne, Cameron, and Southshore New Orleans areas. In 2021, the program is projected to expand beyond the Pelican State's boundaries. In addition, the program established Louisiana Direct Seafood, a marketing entity designed to facilitate direct distribution of Bayou State seafood to commercial markets. All of the aforementioned programs were flourishing until the onset of the COVID-19 pandemic in 2020.

at DelcambreDirectSeafood.com, was designed to allow active shrimpers to post online information about their current catch as well as contact information. This allowed fishermen to sell directly to consumers at more sustainable prices than those offered by local processors. Other regional shrimping communities profited from the success of the Delcambre experiment by establishing comparable programs in the Lafourche-Terrebonne, Cameron, and New Orleans areas. These programs have collectively allowed the industry to take a major step toward economic sustainability.

The marked success of the direct-to-consumer programs, however, did little nationally to blunt the unrelenting threat of foreign imports. In fact, the Global Aquaculture Alliance, an international special interest group, recently predicted a 5.7 percent increase in pond-raised shrimp exports by third world countries primarily to the United States between 2018 and 2020. Though this robust growth has undoubtedly been mitigated by both the Early Mortality Syndrome (EMS) that has decimated foreign pond-raised shrimp and the human ravages of the COVID-19 pandemic, the outlook for the Louisiana shrimp industry thus remains unquestionably bleak; a postmortem is also unquestionably premature. Will the unprecedented economic dislocation wrought by the COVID-19 crisis bring about the premature demise of the Louisiana shrimp industry? Or will the pandemic-driven national quarantines and the nationalist populism of the Trump era converge to at least temporarily interrupt the unbridled globalization that characterized the economic climate of the previous two decades and renew America's dependence on domestically harvested decapods? Will government-mandated restaurant closures and draconian seating restrictions, which have been particularly catastrophic for all-you-can eat buffet restaurants, suppress global demand for pond-raised shrimp sufficiently for the Asian export industry to implode? Only time will tell.

EPILOGUE

In many parts of the world, major natural disasters have traditionally constituted historical waypoints. During the nineteenth and twentieth centuries, destructive storms were generational benchmarks in Louisiana, but in this era of rapid global warming—and the resultant accelerated storm intensification patterns—they have become mere annual mileposts, as Category 3, 4, and 5 hurricanes become frighteningly commonplace along the northern Gulf Coast. In 2020 alone, Louisiana was struck or grazed by no less than five named storms. The most powerful of these tropical cyclones, Hurricane Laura—with sustained winds of approximately 140 mph—inflicted such catastrophic damage to the southwestern corner of the Bayou State that the entire region remains a disaster area a year after the storm made landfall. In an August 2021 email to the authors, a recent visitor to Lake Charles described the city as a virtual "sea of blue tarp roofs." In October, Hurricane Delta (in 2020, for the second time since the late nineteenth-century regularization of American weather records, United States forecasters were required to revert to the Greek alphabet for hurricane names after the English alphabet had been exhausted) retraced Laura's path of devastation, destroying in the process most of the region's valiant initial recovery efforts.

The 2021 hurricane season brought even more extensive devastation to the eastern nexus of the Louisiana shrimp fishery—the Lafourche-Terrebonne region and the economically interrelated coastal parishes to the east. On August 23, 2021, Hurricane Ida—now projected to become the sixth most costly Atlantic Basin storm on record—formed as a tropical wave in the Caribbean. Three days later, this wave morphed into a tropical depression (maximum sustained winds of 38 mph), then a tropical storm (sustained winds of 40–74 mph), and, finally, a hurricane (winds in excess of 75 mph) within a twenty-four-hour period. This rapid-intensification cycle, which is a twenty-first century hallmark of hurricane development in the Gulf of Mexico's superheated late-summer waters, foreshadowed the storm's explosive growth as it subsequently approached landfall on the northern Gulf Coast. Ida's continued maturation was temporarily interrupted as it crossed western Cuba on August 27, but, as it emerged into the southeastern Gulf of Mexico, the storm

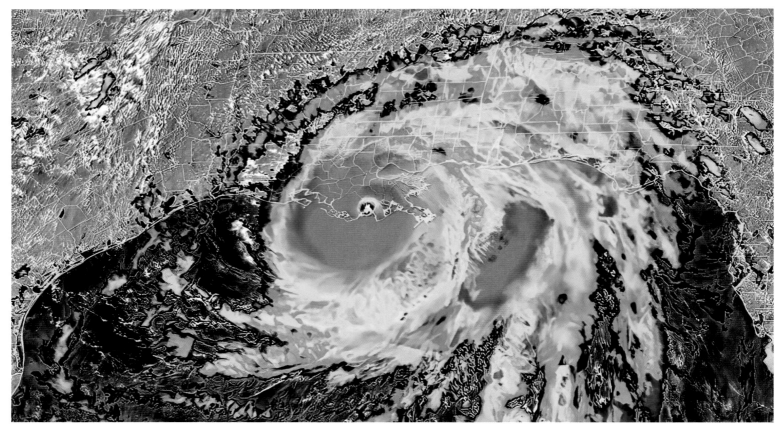

Radar image of Hurricane Ida as it made landfall on August 29, 2021.
(Courtesy of the National Oceanographic and Atmospheric Administration.)

initiated a second rapid-intensification cycle. Before making landfall near Port Fourchon (Lafourche Parish) on August 29—appropriately the sixteenth anniversary of Hurricane Katrina (the region's former benchmark storm), Ida mushroomed into a strong Category 4 monster with sustained winds officially just shy of the Category 5s 157 mph minimum sustained wind speed threshold. However, the official wind speed estimates, determined by hurricane-hunter aircraft, may have been overly conservative. Facebook posts by Lafourche Parish officials reported that state-of-the-art anemometers at the multi-billion-dollar offshore logistical center at Port Fourchon, on the boundary between the coastal marshes and the Gulf of Mexico, clocked sustained winds in the storm's northern eye wall at 180 mph. Wind gauges also measured sustained southern eye wall wind speeds of 192 mph and gusts of 218 to 228 mph.

As it moved inland, the storm's formidable winds and destructive tidal surge, estimated by the National Oceanographic and Atmospheric Administration (NOAA) at over ten feet, wrought unprecedented devastation to the low-lying coastal region between Port Fourchon and LaPlace, Louisiana. According to NOAA, Dulac,

Although the original building has been decimated, the site nevertheless served as a staging area for utility crews. (Photo by the authors.)

a shrimping village in Terrebonne Parish, experienced wind gusts of 138 mph on the afternoon of August 29, while Galliano, an unincorporated fishing community along lower Bayou Lafourche, endured winds of 121 mph. Numerous anecdotal reports, however, insist that these official figures underestimate the storm's windspeeds and destructive potential. While Ida's strongest winds were centered in the eye wall, the storm's strong wind field and intense rain bands extended far to the east, encompassing Jefferson, Plaquemines, and St. Bernard parishes in its widening path of destruction. Nearly sixty linear miles from the eyewall, Mandeville, in St. Tammany Parish across Lake Pontchartrain from New Orleans, experienced wind gusts of 110 mph during the evening of August 29. Following its initial onslaught, Ida stalled—like many other major storms of the climate-change era—near the coastline, where the storm maintained most of its initial strength as it continued to draw energy from the Gulf. Many coastal plain communities consequently faced relentless Category 3 force winds for four to five consecutive hours—with catastrophic consequences.

Shrimping communities in Lafourche and Terrebonne parishes were particularly hard-hit, but Jefferson, Plaquemines, and St. Bernard parishes also sustained significant damage. These parishes boast Louisiana's densest aggregate shrimping population and, over the past five years, their average annual landings account for 88.82 percent of the state's annual shrimp gross tonnage and 84.57 percent of its value. Because of its prodigious output, this coastal region is also home to much of the Louisiana shrimp industry's critical infrastructure, particularly shipyards, processors, and industrial ice factories. Loss or incapacitation of these facilities in conjunction with substantial storm-related damage to the region's fleet

Courtney Seafood was one of many processing companies that had to "gut" their building and move the debris to the street. The storm inflicted damage capriciously; some seafood docks and ancillary buildings were "hit" harder than others. (Photo courtesy of Thomas Hymel Marine Extension Agent, LSU AgCenter, Louisiana Sea Grant.)

AVERAGE LANDINGS AND VALUE, LOUISIANA, 2016-2021				
Parish	lbs	%	$	%
Cameron	948,864.80	1.05%	$931,074.98	0.76%
Iberia	10,515.60	0.01%	$22,870.15	0.02%
Jefferson	15,783,937.51	17.44%	$19,159,764.40	15.74%
Lafourche	12,041,071.77	13.31%	$18,353,898.53	15.07%
Plaquemines	21,695,984.58	23.98%	$29,288,874.59	24.06%
St. Bernard	3,907,046.15	4.32%	$5,550,794.03	4.56%
St. Mary	475,436.70	0.53%	$622,831.84	0.51%
Terrebonne	26,947,655.42	29.78%	$30,600,851.54	25.13%
Vermilion	8,682,135.24	9.59%	$17,222,138.82	14.15%
TOTALS	90,492,647.77		$121,753,098.87	

collectively constitute a crushing blow to the Louisiana shrimp industry.

Although authoritative estimates of the losses will not be available until mid-2022 at the earliest, Ida's cataclysmic passage is currently believed to have caused $18 to $20 billion in *insured* losses in coastal Louisiana. This staggering figure, however, is misleadingly deficient because it fails to reflect the actual scale of financial losses. For example, as a result of the narrow, often nonexistent profit margins and the stratospheric cost of insurance, virtually all of the inshore trawler fleet is uninsured. In fact, Louisiana fisheries experts now estimate that only 5 percent of the region's inshore shrimp boats—particularly marginally profitable fiberglass skimmers and Lafitte skiffs—have *any* insurance coverage. Destruction or incapacitation of these oft-ignored, yet indispensable resources consequently go unreported.

Even the more profitable large offshore trawlers—often called "slabs" in coastal communities—are, at best, underinsured. In recent years, only two or three insurance companies even offer coverage to big commercial boats, and, despite exponentially rising rates, coverage has declined steadily. According to Louisiana Sea Grant agent Thu Bui, a slab appraised at $600,000 can only be insured for roughly a third of its actual value. The limited benefit of this meager coverage is partially offset by high deductibles. Thus, in the aftermath of Hurricane Ida, boat owners with insurance often found that their limited coverage was only sufficient to refloat boats that had been sunk, overturned, "stacked" atop other vessels, or transported into the marshes.

When recovery costs are prohibitive, owners typically abandon stranded vessels either to the elements in the marshes or to government-funded demolition projects to clear navigable waterways as quickly as possible. Because of an as-yet-undetermined number of wrecked trawlers, underreported damages, and the pervasive chaos that inevitably follows in the wake of great natural disasters, one must look to recent past catastrophes to formulate reasonably sound estimates of the economic toll. Sea Grant agent Rusty Gaudé notes that after Hurricane Katrina, fully 85 percent of the fishing

More than ten ropes often proved insufficient to secure boats to their moorings. Unmoored vessels usually drifted onto levees or into marshes; others sank in navigable waterways. (Photo by Thomas Hymel Marine Extension Agent, LSU AgCenter , Louisiana Sea Grant.)

This large, steel-hulled-trawler, wrecked by Hurricane Ida, is no longer seaworthy. Photo from the authors' collections.) (Photo from the authors' collections.)

Throughout the region, hand-lettered signs expressed storm victims' gratitude to "line workers," electrical linemen from throughout the country who labored tirelessly to reconnect every household to the electrical grid. (Photo from the authors' collections.)

boats in the devastated parishes were disabled, and while Hurricane Ida's toll on the shrimp fishery is yet to be determined, Louisiana is using the Katrina experience as a preliminary model. In addition, major local hurricane landfalls entail very significant—usually catastrophic—damage to the regional electrical grid, water and sewerage systems, educational facilities, grocery stores, churches, and highways. Currently available figures fail to provide a complete picture of the infrastructure damage, but a snapshot of emerging data clearly shows the extent of devastation to the region's electrical grid and the magnitude of the efforts necessary to initiate routine post-hurricane recovery: 36,000 utility poles and 508 transmission structures were damaged or destroyed; 50,000 spans of electrical transmission cables were downed; and electrical service was interrupted to 1,098,433 customers.

Interruption and electrical- and fuel-delivery services are particularly crucial to recovery efforts in fishing villages and towns. For the boat owners and crews of boats spared by storms, these amenities

"Hurricane Ida . . . has been the most destructive hurricane in our area. It has hit the communities of the fishing industry. We have Dularge, Dulac, Pointe aux Chêne, Montegut, Chauvin, Cocodrie . . . ; all [have] been decimated. I mean these homes are like matchsticks. We have places that we were told were safe by our politicians that have been proven to be unsafe. That is from Robinson Canal to Boudreaux Canal, where people almost lost their lives. And some of them have lost their ability to fish because the boats have sunk or the boats are on levees. [Some] are way past the levee [i.e., in the marsh]. We have boats that we don't know where they are. So, it has been . . . I would say the devastation part is to see people still living in tents.

"The disaster plans that our officials have are not good enough. The disaster plans for the seafood industry is nonexistent. I didn't realize that there has been a task force for a disaster plan with UL [University of Louisiana, Lafayette]. There is a director there, and it is for businesses. The entire seafood industry, *the entire seafood industry* has been left out of it. That pisses me off. . . .

"[My husband] came here [Dulac] and didn't know what to do because it was overwhelming—the destruction here and at every one of our businesses. We have four businesses and five boats. And every single place has been touched by Ida. We are probably one of the only fishing docks in the entire state that was prepared for a disaster even before Ida came. We had two big generators, . . . and Ida took both of them out. We begged and pleaded . . . with . . . government officials to get generators. . . . Six days ago, we got one. We cannot freeze any shrimp. So we will be out because we don't have the capacity to do it until we get a generator for Bluewater, which is important because if I don't have shrimp . . . where does my work crew go, and we have a core group. So, that's a problem. I would say that [potable] water [is crucial]. We are without water for three weeks at this point. Wildlife and Fisheries was able to bring a tanker with 6,000 gallons of water here. But I have been begging my parish president for water every day. How you cannot get tankers of water here befuddles my mind because what we do . . . [for] water to make ice. . . .

"We are raising some of our grandkids. . . . As I said, every business has been touched here by Ida, our home has probably 75 percent [damage], but I can still live in it right now. So we are blessed on that part. It isn't a complaint that Ida has touched us. It is the lack of response.

"I am not asking for a generator and water for each of our ice houses, just one. When we look at that in the processing facility being able to continue on, in a manner [of speaking], I would think that it brings a safety issue not to have water here for the people. You know, hygiene-wise, but also fire. What do you do? How are you [going to survive] not having water

here? But there [was] water behind Holy Family Catholic Church for about a week, but they had to go away . . . It was not [that] Holy Family Catholic Church had anything to do with it. It is the government, and the National Guard was guarding it. And I am thinking, What? Why didn't you give it out to the people? . . . But . . . why didn't you [also] give us a little water so we can do a little bit [with it]? But we have to have pressure behind it. The state is also giving us an osmosis [machine] so we can take the bayou water. But we do not know if we will have enough pressure to do it. It will be the first time doing it, and it will do damage to our icehouse because no one can make those repairs but us. So it is a chance we are going to take to give ice to the fishermen. As of now, we are buying ice from Mississippi, and it is about $20 a block. Then we bought some in Bourg, which is very close by, which was $28 a block. We sell it for $16.50. We can't go up for the fishermen right now. They don't have money. So, what do you do? You give them ice.

"Then you have the work force that is coming to you, and you [are] trying to find campers [for them]. . . . We were able to get one camper for one of the guys. So they come to us for our [inaudible] facility. The thing we worry about right now is Wildlife and Fisheries went before the state and asked for a 50 percent increase in licenses for commercial fishing and 5 percent on recreational fishing. How does that make sense? Most of those guys will not be able afford their licenses come January. So guess where they're coming? When you look around here, the money being shelled out every single day for repairs, they are not going to have that come January. Guess what I have to do? I have to go to the SBA [Small Business Administration] and borrow money to make sure that my guys can get back out [on the water]. But there is no understanding of this. Our state, . . . our Wildlife and Fisheries, all the agencies do not understand our industry. I would say Sea Grant does because we have done a lot of work with Sea Grant, but the ones making the decisions do not understand this industry at all. The reason how I can tell you that, because Wildlife and Fisheries came to us and said, "What do you do here?"—after . . . having [had] a conversation with somebody else in Wildlife and Fisheries telling me they understood our industry. No, no, you don't. I would like you to, I really would. I would be happy to sit down with people to have them understand our industry and understand what we need to do in a disaster and understand what we need in economic development. But we don't have that, and it's sad because this is the [state's] third [leading] industry.

"So are you going to pull a magical bunny out of a hat? And, if you have that bunny, why aren't you using it now so we can add it to the tax base? There is no magical bunny." (Chauvin interview.)

With little or no water pressure and electrical lines down throughout the region after Hurricane Ida, southeastern Louisiana shrimper processors were compelled to transport ice from Biloxi and other distant communities. Imported ice was expensive, but the fishermen could not work without it. (Photo by the authors.)

are indispensable. Without fuel, vessels obviously cannot leave the docks, and additional fuel reserves are essential because, following hurricanes, waterborne storm debris forces trawlers to travel farther to find waters safe for net deployment. Without electricity, there is neither refrigeration nor ice production, and without ice, there is no way to preserve the catch, particularly aboard small boats.

It is hard to overstate the resulting toll in human misery levied by major storms. Because of the counterclockwise air flow generated by hurricanes, departing storms typically pump hot air from inland areas to the north and northwest into the impacted areas. The resulting unrelenting heat and humidity rapidly sap the energy of the battered populace seeking to initiate recovery and reconstruction efforts—particularly in areas impacted by successive disasters, now often recurring within a single calendar year. In Cameron Parish, ground zero for Hurricanes Laura and Delta in 2020, life

Within hours of Ida's departure, impacted homeowners were moving debris "to the road" for removal to landfills. (Photo by the authors.)

Throughout Ida's disaster area, many storm victims displayed the American flag as a symbol of hope and a can-do attitude. (Photo by the authors.)

has not returned to normal. Indeed, a modicum of normalcy is not expected for many months, perhaps years. Kevin Savoie, a Sea Grant agent residing in the parish, reports continued disruption of essential services—particularly lack of electrical power. Lack of electricity is crucial for local ice manufacturing and processing facilities that continue operating in a limited capacity with massive diesel-powered generators.

Like vital local businesses, the resident population still faces a daily struggle for survival. In the wake of Hurricanes Katrina and Rita (2005), thousands of coastal plain residents raised their homes—usually twelve to sixteen feet above ground level—to reduce the threat of tidal surge inundation. Elevated homes, however, are more vulnerable to wind damage, and a very substantial—though as yet untallied—number of homes were either pulverized into kindling or knocked from their pilings and destroyed. As a result, many displaced storm victims have literally lost all of their earthly possessions.

As one Hurricane Ida survivor recently noted, life in a storm-ravished community is a "hellish existence." Survivors face snakes, alligators, and clouds of voracious mosquitoes, and without electricity, water, and sewerage services the most modest initial efforts are often overwhelming. Even under the best of circumstances, there is an agonizingly slow pace of recovery, and momentum becomes nearly impossible to maintain as unrelenting heat and humidity sap the mental and physical strength of persons involved in the recovery effort. Savoie reports that many of his neighbors are still "living in campers." And already desperate post-storm living conditions are likely to be made considerably worse by the end of eviction moratoriums in shrimping communities.

The beleaguered disaster victims' goal—a return to "normalcy"—is thus highly uncertain. Many residents of hurricane-ravaged parishes privately wonder what the "new normal" will be and justifiably fear that it will be radically different from its predecessor. In the wake of unprecedented devastation, storm survivors initially pinned their hope of a rapid recovery on governmental assistance and private philanthropy during the small window of public sympathy that inevitably follows in the wake of modern disasters. The most opportune moment for capitalization on this outpouring of compassion is short because of the notorious brevity of American news cycle and the American public's acutely short attention span. In the aftermath of Hurricane Ida, rural storm survivors' ability to benefit is enormously complicated by the national news media's fixation on New Orleans—not the most seriously impacted areas outside the Crescent City—and the flooding subsequently caused in New York and New Jersey by Ida's remnants. These complications deflected public attention from Louisiana's desperate coastal plain communities, and much of the expected philanthropy did not materialize.

Storm-ravaged rural communities have consequently pinned their hopes on federal disaster assistance. But, even when resources are available, national relief and reconstruction efforts are hamstrung by the inherent limitations of the Federal Emergency Management Agency (FEMA). Established in 1978, the agency was designed to oversee the federal government's response to *occasional* natural disasters, which were expected to occur at appreciable intervals. The 2005 hurricane season stripped bare the agency's inadequacies during a highly volatile period of climatic transition. FEMA clearly lacked the leadership, resources, and perhaps willpower to handle the fallout from three major hurricanes—all with Category 5 intensity before landfall—that essentially destroyed broad swaths of the Gulf Coast, particularly in Louisiana, where Katrina and Rita leveled coastal communities and inundated a major American city. FEMA subsequently improved its responsiveness, but its overall effectiveness remains inadequate because of the myriad concurrent demands on its resources. As of late-September 2021, FEMA is currently managing federal responses to *seven* major natural disasters scattered across the United States.

There was a time not so long ago when Bayou State coastal residents could count on a three-to-four-year interval between "bad storms"—a window large enough for hurricane victims to recover physically, emotionally, and financially before a major new threat emerged from the Gulf. Now there is no longer breathing room between major hurricanes. Instead, coastal residents are confronted with the grim prospect of multiple major weather catastrophes each hurricane season. The resulting stress—compounded immeasurably by the COVID-19 pandemic—has depleted coastal denizens' formidable emotional and physical reserves, calling into question the region's well-deserved reputation for resiliency. This is particularly true of the end-of-the-road communities that literally sit on the front lines of global climate change. As journalist Jonathan Olivier so eloquently noted recently in the *Bitter Southerner* e-publication, "in Louisiana, we're tired of being resilient." One can only wonder just how much resilience remains in the depleted reserves of the Bayou State's oft-battered shrimpers.

However, reports of the Louisiana shrimp industry's imminent demise were also rampant after earlier crises, and yet the fishery

The U.S. Marine catchphrase "Improvise, Adapt, and Overcome" encapsulates the mindset of the most determined coastal residents during the post-Hurricane Ida recovery effort. (Photo by the authors.)

Within days of Ida's passage, still-operable boats returned to work. In the shrimp business, when a shrimp vessel is not pulling trawl, the captain is not making money. In Ida's aftermath, sustained income is crucial, for recovery bills are substantial. (Photo by Roy Kron, Louisiana Sea Grant, LSU.)

endures, though at a cost. Since Hurricane Katrina, each natural and manmade crisis has driven a substantial percentage of the region's fishermen from their livelihoods to safer and more dependable sources of income, but the most tenacious shrimpers triumphed over overwhelming odds. If this historical model perseveres—as expected—in the wake of Hurricane Ida's passage, the fishery will survive, though, as in the past, with reduced capacity and output. This remorseless paradigm, it would appear, is a cruel mistress with which the Louisiana shrimp industry must learn to dance.

GLOSSARY

Barataria Bay: The "Isle Barataria" is recorded on cartographer Jean Baptiste Bourguignon d'Anville's *Carte de la Louisiane* (1732); it is one of Louisiana's earliest place names. This marine feature is about fifteen miles long and twelve miles wide and is the cornerstone of the Barataria-Terrebonne estuary system. Most pre-1900 maps identify the northern section of the water body as "Grand Lake"—a term now lost to the mists of history.

Barataria Shrimp: The Dunbar company featured the term *Barataria Shrimp* prominently on their labels. The brand name, which implied consistent quality and good taste, became synonymous with the Dunbar brand until 1918 when the United States Department of Agriculture issued a circular banning geographic placenames from shrimp-can labels unless the processed crustaceans were caught in Barataria Bay ("Don't Label 'Em 'Barataria Shrimp'" 53).

Barrel: The customary unit of measurement—210 pounds—in the northern Gulf Coast shrimp industry. This standard is still universally applied even though physical barrels are no longer commonly used.

Barrier Island: Geomorphic features along Louisiana's gently sloping coastal plain, these elongated islands frame the southern boundary of the coastal lowlands. They are separated from the mainland by bays and marsh habitats.

Bassa Bassa: The use of terminology intimately linked to founders' respective cultural heritages is a salient feature of immigrants' geographic naming conventions. Because Bassa Bassa—translated as "wet, wet"—is derived from the Philippines-based Tagalog language, it is highly probable that Filipino émigrés established this remote platform community in Barataria Bay. *See* Manila Village.

Bayou: A bayou is the sluggish, often tidal waterways of the Louisiana coastal plain. The term *bayou* is a Louisiana francophone corruption of the Choctaw word *bayuk*.

Benevolent Society: America's first-generation immigrants have consistently sought to promote their cultural, social,

J. T. DESGRAIS,   V. SAUCIER.
V. SAUCIER,
COOPER,
3 Spain St., 3d Dist., New Orleans.

Molasses Whole and Half Barrels always on hand.   Out-door work punctually attended to at reasonable prices. All orders left at N. BARROIS, No. 74 Old Levee Street, will be promptly executed.

Wooden barrels were the mainstay of the nineteenth-century bulk-transportation industry. All kinds of bulk goods—nails, molasses, sugar, wine, shrimp, and many other commodities—reached their destinations in barrels. Unlike wooden crates, barrels could be rolled across ramps to vessels or boxcars. New Orleans's coopers and lumberyards made good on the barrel business's boast that its products were "always on hand." (Advertisement from A. Mygatt and Company 29.)

Canneries outside Louisiana also identified their canned products as "Barataria" shrimp. (Label from the Louisiana Historical Center, Louisiana State Museum, New Orleans, LA, date unknown.)

The *Lillian Malissie* is an early example of a Biloxi-type trawler built in a Mississippi shipyard. (Photo provided by Russell Barnes, a local historian in Biloxi, photographer and date unknown.)

and economic interests through benevolent societies. For example, in San Francisco, the Chinese Six Companies, a benevolent society, functioned as a savings and loan association, a labor brokerage, a health-care provider, a mentoring society, and a community defense league, battling racial stereotyping and prejudice. This groups continues to provide these services. On the Gulf Coast, Vietnamese benevolent groups often underwrite purchases of shrimp boats acquired by members of their respective founding communities.

Biloxien: Biloxi-class vessel. A larger variation of the upper Gulf Coast lugger, the Biloxien was designed for use in inshore waters. Ranging in size from thirty to forty-five feet in length, Biloxi-class shrimp boats featured aft-mounted cabins and engine rooms. After World War II, inshore Biloxiens were far less common than their Florida-class offshore cousins.

Bohemians: Eastern European immigrants recruited in Baltimore for employment as transient laborers in Louisiana and Mississippi seafood processing plants on a seasonal basis. Northern Gulf Coast residents collectively identified these laborers as Bohemians.

Breaded Shrimp: Peeled and deveined shrimp covered either by hand or machine with a batter mix, then flash frozen for supermarkets' frozen food sections.

Brown Shrimp: Louisiana's shrimp fishery is primarily based on two shrimp species—brown and white. Brown shrimp are identified by lateral grooves down both sides of their head and the last segment of their tails. These grooves typically feature purple to reddish-purple bands and green or red pigmentation. Brown shrimp spawn in relatively deep water and have a life span of less than two years.

Bucket: Before mechanization, shrimp processing was a labor-intensive industry requiring picking-shed employees—typically women and children—to dehead and wash the shrimp that accumulated in their "bucket." When a worker's bucket was heaping full, supervisors weighed it and paid the picker in either scrip that could only be redeemed at the company store or, less commonly, cash. Before minimum wage legislation, a worker rarely made more than five dollars a week. Depending on the time period, the pay for shrimp picking ranged from a penny to three cents a pound.

Bycatch: The unwanted catch caught in a fisherman's trawl.

Cabinash: This now forgotten placename was the United States Post Office's official designation for Manila Village from 1926 to 1949. Cabinash also appears on the 1948 United States Geological Survey, Ft. Livingston, 1:62500 scale map.

Cajuns: Descendants of Acadian colonists of present-day Nova Scotia who were expelled from the Bay of Fundy basin in a massive ethnic-cleansing exercise in 1755. The largest group of deportees ultimately made its way to the Bayou Country. In Louisiana, their descendants are now commonly known as Cajuns (an English corruption of the French contraction *Cadien*). Cajun communities have traditionally been distinguished by their Catholic faith, music, folkways, food, and *joie de vivre*—characteristics that set them apart from the state's Protestant, Anglo-Saxon population. In recent decades, however, many Cajuns have converted to Protestant—primarily evangelical—denominations.

Cannery: A seafood cannery—or factory—washed, processed, cooked, and packed shrimp and/or oysters in "tin" cans. Once packed in wooden boxes or, later, carboard containers, the canned products were shipped to markets throughout the United States and elsewhere.

Celestial Empire: *Celestial Empire* was a term nineteenth-century American journalists commonly applied to the portions of China under the control of the Chinese emperor. The term *Celestials*, on the other hand, referred to emigrants from imperial territories.

Champagne: A modern, seventy-pound basket measurement for raw shrimp.

Culling bycatch. (Photo from the authors' collections. Courtesy of Morgan City Archives, Morgan City, LA, photographer Melvin Hardee, date unknown.)

This is a representative example of the efficient machinery that replaced hand labor in the canning of seafood products. (Photo from the authors' collections. Courtesy of Louisiana Wildlife and Fisheries, New Iberia Office, photographer and date unknown. Right photo from the *Department of Wild Life and Fisheries Third Biennial Report of the Louisiana, 1948–1949* 55.)

The Dunbar Oyster and Shrimp Cannery in Lookout/Dunbar employed large numbers of Bohemian children. (Photo courtesy of the National Archives and Records Administration, Prints & Photographs Division, Department of Commerce and Labor, Children Bureau, 1912–1913, College Park, MD, photographer Lewis Hine, March 2, 1911, call number NWDNS-102-LH-2054.)

The final product is placed—and shipped—in water-resistant five-pound boxes, with the count clearly marked. (Photo from the authors' collections, 2019.)

Child Labor: In 1899, only two states processed canned shrimp: Louisiana and Mississippi. Canning facilities employed a low-wage labor force consisting primarily of women and children. Working in deplorable conditions, these often-illiterate children were subjected to egregious working conditions for as little as a nickel a day. In 1938, Congress passed the Fair Labor Standards Act that effectively outlawed child labor. Louisiana shrimp processing companies nevertheless continued to use significant numbers of child laborers until the mid-twentieth century.

Coastal Plain: Geographically, this geomorphic feature includes the low-lying, flat land adjacent to the coast.

Coolie: This pejorative term for an Asian person has come to mean the lowest class of unskilled or semiskilled laborers.

Count: The "count," based on the number of shrimp per pound, is a standard measurement universally used in the culinary trade. Restaurants base their bulk purchases on "uniform" tail sizes for incorporation into specific fried, boiled, broiled, grilled, baked, or sauce-based dishes. Breading and cooking plants and packers dealing in fresh-frozen shrimp typically demand a 21 to 30 count. Restaurants and fast food purveyors, on the other hand, prefer a 26 to 30 count. Individual cooks use a third standard; one typical Cajun shrimp étouffée recipe, for example, calls for a "16 to 20 count per pound." To satisfy the manifold requests, processors required flexible and precise grading and sorting machinery. In Louisiana, Laitram Machinery of Harahan has historically produced most of the necessary equipment.

Creole Cuisine: The simplest way to distinguish the difference between Cajun and Creole cuisine is Creole food typically uses tomatoes and tomato-based sauces such as *courtbouillon à la Créole*, *crabs à la Créole*, and *écrevisses gratinées à la Créole*. Cajun food incorporates tomato-based sauces less frequently.

Crescent City: A euphemism for New Orleans.

Double-Rig: The Florida-class shrimp trawler, when configured properly, could pull three small nets—one off the starboard, a second off the port sides, and a try net in-between. All nets in the double-rig could be pulled simultaneously. By the late 1950s, double-rigged trawlers had become the industry standard.

Drayage: The term originally was used to describe the movement of products by a sideless cart pulled by draft horses. In the twentieth century, the dray horse and cart were replaced by the delivery truck.

Estuary: A partially enclosed coastal water body whose connection to the sea allows freshwater to mix with salt water.

***Floridien* (a.k.a. *Floridiane, Floridienne*):** A Florida-class shrimping vessel, whose blueprint is derived from Mediterranean boat designs adapted by Greek immigrants for use in Florida's sponge and shrimp industries. Early models of these vessels typically ranged from fifty to seventy feet in length and initially featured wooden hulls and 150 to 200 horsepower diesel power plants. In the late 1930s, Florida resident Felice Golino relocated his trawler fleet to the Morgan City/Patterson area. This move introduced the Florida-type vessel into Louisiana's shrimp industry. Like the otter trawl, Golino's Floridiens revolutionized shrimping on the northern Gulf Coast. The Florida-class trawler featured a cabin-forward design, a six-thousand-gallon fuel tank, and a forty-five-ton ice storage capacity. Designed for use in deep-sea waters, the Florida-type boats could operate anywhere in the Gulf of Mexico—including the Bay of Campeche, where post–World War II discoveries extended the Gulf shrimp industry to Mexico's southeastern coast.

Folk Boats: Wooden watercraft built without plans and using traditional construction techniques as a part of a group's material culture.

Chinese "coolie" immigrants employed as laborers on the country's transcontinental railroad were vilified by America's non-Asian coworkers. *Labor World* (July 8, 1905, 1), one of the nation's oldest labor papers, was a mouthpiece of the movement to rid the country of foreign "interlopers."

Local mariners, who often built their own watercraft, used cypress whenever possible. Wooden boats required periodic caulking to keep the vessels' holds dry. One hardware store continues to carry this forgotten product to prevent seepage into the boats hull. (Photo from the Standard Oil (NJ) Collection, Photographic Archives, Archives and Special Collections, University of Louisville, photographer Martha Roberts, 1945, negative number 43345.)

Grand Isle: Louisiana's only inhabited barrier island, known for its world-class fishing and birding habitats. Grand Isle is the state's most popular beach resort. The island is about eight miles long and one mile wide. Caminada Pass constitutes the island's western boundary, while Barataria Pass serves as the eastern border. Both passes open into the Barataria estuary.

Grand Lake: *See* Barataria Bay.

Grand Terre: This uninhabited barrier island was once Jean Lafitte's stronghold and, later, the anchor point for Fort Livingston, designed to protect Barataria Pass. The fort was abandoned in 1889 and is a now a rapidly decaying ruin. The barrier island was designated as a state Wildlife and Fisheries reservation in 1955.

Hardware Stores: Marine equipment maintenance and repairs require locally available specialized parts. The following marine hardware stores apparently have the longest tenure of service to the Louisiana shrimp industry: Shannon (1872), Chauvin (1875), A. F. Davidson (1885), J. H. Menge (1900), Coast Gulf Supply (1956), Alario Brothers (1968), Touchard (1975), and Fishermans Net and Wholesale Marine Supply (1982).

Hold: The interior of a boat's hull, where shrimp are stowed and iced. The hold may be covered with a tarpaulin or moveable hatch composed of hatch boards.

Ice: For generations, commercially produced ice has sustained the upper Gulf Coast shrimp industry, for it allows coastal fishermen to extend their range exponentially. When used in adequate quantities, ice reduces the internal temperature of the catch to nearly 32 degrees Fahrenheit, which greatly retards both bacterial activity and enzymatic changes within the shrimp catch in the hold. For ice to be an effective deterrent to spoilage, crew members must ice the catch as quickly as possible. Aboard large, offshore vessels, ice usage has been replaced by flash-freezing equipment.

Inshore Shrimping: Inshore shrimpers—often condescendingly labeled "mom-and-pop" operators by their much more heavily invested offshore rivals—confine their trawling to coastal estuaries. In the spring, brown shrimp season normally runs from May to July. The fall white shrimp season generally dates from mid-August to mid-December. Some areas remain open into January. The Louisiana Department of Wildlife and Fisheries determines the season dates and selects the geographic zones that can be harvested.

Isleños: A Spanish-speaking ethnic minority in southeastern Louisiana. Isleños are descendants of Canary Island immigrants recruited between 1778 to 1783 in a failed attempt to Hispanicize the former French colony. Galveztown, Valenzuela, Barataria, and San Bernardo were the most notable immigrant settlements. The San Bernardo community (now St. Bernard Parish)—located along Bayou Terre-aux-Boeufs—has most successfully preserved its Hispanic identity. Isleños clashed with Louisiana's first Asian-immigrant shrimping community shortly before the Civil War.

Lafitte Skiff: The Lafitte skiff was developed in the early 1950s specifically for trawling in the Barataria-Terrebonne basins' shallow waters.

Lake Borgne: Located near the southeastern tip of Louisiana's "boot," Lake Borgne is an elongated saltwater bay that connects to Lake Pontchartrain through Chef Menteur Pass and the Rigolets. The lake's eastern waters coalesce with those of Mississippi Sound. Commercial fishing in this body of water has long been a source of friction between Mississippi and Louisiana, for Magnolia State fishermen often blatantly traversed the neighboring states' common offshore boundary and illegally harvested seafood from Lake Borgne.

Lazy Lines: Lazy lines connect a trawl's net bags or cod ends to a door. As the net is retrieved, the slack in the line allows crewmen to use a grappling hook to guide the net onboard using a winch.

Luggers (*Goélettes*): Louisiana's first commercial fishing vessel was the hand-built, eighteen- to nearly fifty-foot-long, shallow-draft, rounded-hull, sailing *goélette*. Manned by three- to six-man crews, these vessels were the mainstay of the Louisiana fishing industry from colonial times to the post–World War I era. Luggers transported crews to prime shallow, near-coast shrimping sites, where they waded in chest-deep water to play out and retrieve seines. In the second decade of the twentieth century, these vessels were mechanized with makeshift stern "wheelhouses." Louisiana shrimpers adapted these motorized former seine boats for trawling by adding a set of tow ropes and a stern-mounted trawl. Often the aft end was extended—locally identified as a "faux" fantail or false fantail—to provide additional room for the captain and a deckhand to retrieve a trawl net.

Manila Village: A 1937 *New Orleans Item* article by H. W. Franz suggests Manila Village was a Spanish colony established about 1770. However, modern research indicates that this isolated settlement dates from approximately the Spanish-American War (1898), hence the village's prominent geographic references to Camp Dewey, Manila/Cabinash, and Bassa Bassa. Manila Village was the largest shrimp-drying community in the state's once vast wetlands. The capitalization necessary to build this impressive facility remains a mystery. Local banks would not have taken the risk. Perhaps San Francisco's Chinese Six Companies served as the platform's financial benefactor, forging a partnership between two Pacific Rim communities half a continent apart. In its heyday, Manila Village was the nexus of considerable commercial activity, but its significance declined in importance over the course of the twentieth century. Hurricane Betsy destroyed many of its decaying structures in 1965.

Model A/Model T: In the first decade of the twentieth century, enterprising shrimpers mounted small gasoline, kerosene, and naphtha engines, often boasting only one or two cylinders and rated under five horsepower, in a lugger's stern. South Louisianans generally identified these underpowered

By the early 1960s, Manila Village—once the epicenter of the wetland-based dried shrimp business—had become a ghostly reminder of the industry's golden era. (Photo from the authors' collections. Courtesy of J. L. Risenden Jr., no date.)

watercraft as "gas boats." The introduction of Ford's Motel T automobile provided early twentieth-century boat owners another option as fishermen quickly learned to repurpose relatively cheap Ford engines for use on workboats. These motors were evidently obtained from Ford's Arabi, Louisiana satellite assembly plant or local automobile junkyards. Through a process known as expansion diffusion, Ford engines quickly replaced the single-cylinder engines aboard small folk boats. These practical and affordable twenty-horsepower Model T or forty-horsepower Model T Ford motors propelled luggers at sustained speeds of four to ten miles per hour. This is not fast by present standards, but a modest pace was considerably better than the alternatives—paddling a skiff or waiting helplessly for favorable winds.

Navigational Equipment: A compass is the most essential instrument on any shrimp vessel, but since the end of World War II, this centuries-old device no longer dominates the wheelhouse, having been eclipsed by new navigational aids. Eco-sounders, or fish finders, along with Sound Navigation and Ranging (SONAR), refined radar such as Automatic Radar Plotting Assisted technology and Electronic Chart Display and Information hardware, and Global Positioning System (GPS) have emerged as tools maximizing the shrimping fleet's efficiency.

NOAA: The National Oceanic and Atmospheric Administration, whose mission is to understand and predict changes in climate, weather, oceans, and coastlines; to share that knowledge and information; and to conserve and manage coastal and marine ecosystems and resources.

Northern Gulf Coast: This geographic province is generally recognized as the area between Florida's Suwannee River (in the state's panhandle) and Louisiana's Sabine River.

Office of Price Administration: Shortly after America's declaration of war in December 1941, President Franklin D. Roosevelt's administration established the Office of Price Administration (OPA) to prevent wartime inflation. The

The Ford Motor Company manufactured more than fifteen million Model T's between 1908 and 1927. Recyclable automobile engines were readily available for the transition from sail-powered watercraft to motorized luggers. (Photo courtesy of the National Archives and Records Administration, Prints & Photographs Division, College Park, MD, photographer Russel Lee, 1938, reproduction number LC-DIG-fsa-8a24201a.)

OPA administered two types of programs: First, the office limited the purchase of certain commodities such as tires, typewriters, bicycles, rubber shoes, and other metal and rubber goods. Second, it regulated the consumption of consumable items such as butter, coffee, sugar, and gasoline through price controls and a rationing process.

Offshore Oil: In the United States, underwater oil resources were first discovered in Ohio and California in the 1890s. In Louisiana, geologists found the Caddo Lake field in 1910. All these discoveries were well within sight of land. Two years after the conclusion of World War II, the American oil and gas industry established its first successful offshore oil and gas province, when Kerr-McGee, an Oklahoma-based independent oil company, completed a well ten and a half miles off southwestern Louisiana's coast.

Offshore Shrimping: Following the "discovery" of jumbo shrimp and the resulting deployment of steel-hulled Floridiens, Louisiana's shrimp fleet quickly moved beyond the state's inshore and nearshore waters. Far-offshore fishing afforded trawlers a major advantage: when operating beyond federal waters, the shrimpers were no longer subject to governmentally imposed seasons. In the 1950s, the United States Bureau of Commercial Fisheries, recognizing the volume and importance of Louisiana's offshore shrimping activities, deployed the research vessel *Oregon* to locate and assess new seafood resources throughout the Gulf of Mexico and the Caribbean Sea. The *Oregon*'s discoveries were complemented by those of the now wide-ranging shrimpers themselves. New harvesting sites off the coast of Texas, Louisiana, Key West, and Campeche were among the most significant of these postwar finds.

Otter Trawl: In 1917, the Louisiana-licensed "shrimp trawl" quickly replaced the seine net, which, for more than one hundred years, was the principal tool for catching decapods. Motorized boats pulled huge stern-mounted trawls held open with heavy, weighted, trawl boards (also called "doors" or "otter boards"). These trawl nets are tied to a boat by long ropes, bridled in such a manner that the webbing is pulled down and outward. The weight of the door aids the net's descent. As the net is dragged along the ocean floor, the doors act like a kite with wings that open the fishnet, and the trawl retains this configuration until the net is winched back onto the boat. This fishing innovation diffused throughout the shrimping community and dramatically changed Louisiana's fishing culture.

Parish: Louisiana is the only state in the union to use the term *parish* for its largest civil subdivisions. The role of the Bayou State's sixty-four parishes corresponds to that of counties in all other states, except Alaska. Louisiana's parish roots date back to the state's French colonial theocracy, in which the ecclesiastical and civil boundaries coincided. Usage of the colonial civil subdivisions persisted after the American acquisition of Louisiana in 1803. In 1807, the territorial legislature officially co-opted the ecclesiastical term.

Picker and Picker (Picking) Shed: When a load of shrimp arrived at a coastal factory, women and children began processing the crustaceans by removing the heads and outer shells. This "picking" process took place in a shed specifically outfitted to accommodate the labor force's needs.

Platforms: Louisiana's shrimp-drying platforms, consisting of undulating wooden surfaces elevated over the marsh surface, often encompassed an area larger than a modern football field. Platforms were typically ringed by sheds and residences whose roofs and walls were thatched with fan palm fronds, known locally as *latanier*. Wharfs, boiling vats, and shallow-water fishing gear were also defining visual elements of these isolated communities. Populated by three hundred or more residents, each platform was a self-contained factory town, where the daily catch—offloaded by returning seine crews—was processed for markets far beyond the marshes. Whenever the shrimp boats arrived at the platform dock, laborers used chinee baskets, capable of holding 105 pounds of raw

Like the winch, the otter trawl is an essential shrimp-harvesting tool. (Photo from the authors' collections, 2019.)

Before the advent of mechanical equipment, pickers were piecework laborers—they were paid according to the amount of product they processed. (Photo from the authors' collections. Courtesy of Morgan City Archives, Morgan City, LA, photographer and date unknown.)

shrimp, to offload the catch. Workers transferred the loaded baskets into a huge brick or copper, wood-fired vat, where the decapods were boiled. After the shrimp were cooked, workers moved the crustaceans from the super-saline brine tanks, placed them in wooden wheelbarrows to drain, and then spread them evenly in two- to three-inch-thick layers on the platform's surface. While the salt-infused shrimp were exposed to the sun, platform workers turned the crustaceans with wooden rakes at two- to three-hour intervals to ensure uniform dehydration. In the summer, depending on the weather, it normally took eighteen to thirty-six hours to cure the shrimp properly; in the winter, the dehydration phase extended to four to five days. Tarpaulins supported by A-frame structures erected on the crests of the undulating platform provided the curing decapods some protection from unfavorable weather conditions. In bad weather, platform residents hurriedly raked shrimp under the tarps because direct exposure to rainfall at this stage of the curing process inevitably resulted in catastrophic spoilage.

***Poupier*:** In coastal Louisiana, butterfly nets are also known as night trawls or *poupiers*. Shrimpers invented these nets to supply smaller, cheaper *chevrettes* for local consumption and, to a lesser extent, to shrimp driers. The poupier is a low-maintenance, standalone, barge- or shore-mounted, licensed device that does not require a crew.

Prohibition: The Eighteenth Amendment to the United States constitution, ratified in 1919, resulted in the imposition of alcohol prohibition from 1920 until the amendment's repeal in 1933. During this thirteen-year period, southern Louisiana's Catholics openly resisted the liquor ban, and Bayou State watermen became highly proficient at smuggling all types of liquor through the region's highly porous coast.

Refrigerated Trucks: With development of refrigerated railroad cars, seafood could be delivered to markets along any rail route. A second paradigm shift in seafood distribution occurred in the late 1930s when refrigerated trucks began to

(Photo courtesy of Dick Lafleur.)

appear on America's roads. These antecedents of the modern eighteen-wheelers were designed to carry perishable freight at specific temperatures to any community with road access. Demand for fresh seafood allowed the refrigerated truck to become a key element in the global distribution of perishable goods. In 1949, the Interstate Commerce Commission authorized unlicensed trucks to carry shrimp from packers to distributors or directly to markets, if the word *fish* was predominately displayed on the truck's trailer.

Rural Electrification Administration: For country folk, the Rural Electrification Administration was one of President Franklin D. Roosevelt's most important achievements. Through low-interest loans and creation of nonprofit cooperatives, the American electric grid gradually migrated from urban centers into rural farming communities. Louisiana's coastal parishes were beneficiaries, but in some cases, local electrical lines were not energized until after World War II.

Seabob: This coastal Louisiana idiom is an English corruption of the original French term *six barbes*, identifying the diminutive *Xiphopenaeus kroyer* decapod species. Cajun coastal communities are the primary consumers of seabobs.

Sea Grant: Congress passed the federal land-grant law in 1862. Known as the Morrill Act, this legislation created land-grant institutions that would focus on the teaching of practical agriculture, science, military science, and engineering. Congress established the Sea Grant College Program in 1966 as the land-grant program's maritime analogue with a focus on maintaining healthy coastal environments. The land-grant colleges have a long-established network of agricultural agents, while their sea grant counterparts function as marine extension agents. In both operations, field activities focus on applied science and outreach.

Seine: A seine is a fishing net with a vertical orientation. Designed for use in shallow waters, seines are commonly weighted on the bottom, with floats on the top. Seine

Before the Great Depression, Louisiana sawmills manufactured vast numbers of staves for use in barrel production by New Orleans cooperages. Extant documentation suggests that, in the pre–Civil War era, the Crescent City's stave yards collectively had an inventory of at least ten billion staves. (*Soards' New Orleans City Directory for 1895* 951.)

crews catch fish by pulling the net's ends together and then dragging the catch to shore. This work is quite hazardous, yet before power boats were introduced in the twentieth century, seines were the only method of commercially harvesting shrimp.

Shipyard: A ship- or boatyard is a site where watercraft are built or repaired. In Louisiana, the footprint of these industrial sites is quite small, for many are in the front- or backyards of self-taught shipwrights. These shipyards share a common element: a ramp extending from the shore into the water. This slipway (more commonly known as a "way"), identified by railroad-like steel tracks, is used to move a boat into or out of water. Vessels under construction or undergoing repairs are said to be "on the ways."

Shook and Staves: For nearly two thousand years, barrels were containers of choice for shipment and storage of bulk cargo. In New Orleans, the barrel was the mainstay of waterborne commerce, and barrel manufacturing businesses were distributed throughout the city. Barrel manufacturers used metal hoops to bind together shook (a set of staves) or staves—about thirty per barrel. Barrel makers, commonly called coopers, also usually constructed buckets, tubs, butter churns, hogsheads, kegs, and other wooden containers. In New Orleans, prior to the Civil War, the city's wood yards maintained a stave inventory that often exceeded ten billion pieces. In the late nineteenth century, coopers used "box shook" to assemble the boxes required by the canned shrimp business. Depending on the type of lumber used, and its thickness, the box could be nailed or manufactured with lock-corners.

Skimmer: In the early 1980s, the skimmer, or bay sweeper, was introduced into Louisiana's shrimp fishery. These nets, supported by a large rectangular steel frame attached to the boat's bow, are lowered from their standby position a little above the deck into the water column. Once deployed, the net is perpendicular to the port and starboard sides of the vessel. The top of the net stands slightly above the waterline to prevent shrimp from escaping by jumping over the webbing. Within ten years of its introduction, the net was used throughout coastal Louisiana. In 1991, Act 931 of the Louisiana legislature established skimmers' minimum mesh size, the maximum dimension of the skimmer's frame, and the maximum length of a net's lead line.

Shrimp Cocktail: This famous seafood appetizer, served in a cocktail glass, first made its appearance during the Probation era. The shrimp were aligned along the rim of the glass, with some type of piquant paste, fortified with a hot condiment, serving as a dipping sauce in the middle of the glass. For a half century, the shrimp cocktail was an important marketing tool for the shrimp industry. By the 1990s, however, this starter's popularity had waned, and the shrimp cocktail gradually disappeared from restaurant menus.

Tickler Chain: As a trawl net is pulled through the water column, a tickler chain, attached loosely between the two trawl net doors, penetrates the upper layer of sediment to disturb shrimp, forcing them to swim directly into the path of the net.

Timbalier Island: According to William A. Read's fanciful account (1931), Timbalier's roots extend to 1729, when a soldier beat a kettle drum to disperse a band of American Indians. The French combatant became known as Sieur Timbalier (Mr. Kettledrummer). A bay and a pass bear the name, as well as one of the region's barrier islands.

Tin Can Trust: The monopolistic "Tin Can Trust," dominated by the American Can Company, systematically acquired can-making companies and controlled 90 percent of tin container manufacturing in the United States. Once a company was absorbed by the trust, the former owners were compelled to sign an agreement banning their reentry into the can-making business for fifteen years.

An example of a try net used in the shrimping industry. (Photo from the Standard Oil (NJ) Collection, Photographic Archives, Archives and Special Collections, University of Louisville, photographer Martha Roberts, 1945, negative number 46358.)

Token: Cannery owners often paid their workers with metal or wooden coin-like objects called trade or barter tokens. The original value of these cannery tokens was based on a picker's individual dexterity. The token's value varied from a "quarter cup" to a "half cup." Use of these "shrimp tokens" (also known as "shrimp nickels") became an accepted practice at the factory's commissary and, in some cases, within the local community at large. Denominations varied, but the most common token was the "good for 5¢" iteration. Others were valued at 2½¢, 6¼¢, 10¢, 12½¢, 25¢, 50¢ and $1.00. These privately minted "coins" are now eagerly sought by collectors—a branch of numismatics called exonumia.

Trawl Board: *See* Otter Trawl.

Try Net: Try nets developed in tandem with large trawl nets. A shrimp boat usually tows a small try net from the boat's stern. The net is used to locate a school of shrimp before the trawl nets are lowered into the water. According to former shrimper Roland Guidry, watermen used a cast net, or a try net "made with a metal pipe for the lead line, with a cork line on top supporting an eight-foot net." Crewmen retrieved try nets by hand while the trawler was in motion.

Turtle Excluder Device: A turtle excluder device (TED) is a specialized metal grate inserted in a trawl net that allows a captured sea turtle to escape when caught in a commercial shrimper's net. Designed by NOAA in the 1970s and improved in the 1980s, these devices were fiercely opposed by commercial fishermen, particularly after NOAA implemented mandatory usage requirements in the United States shrimping industry in 1987. An array of lawsuits, injunctions, suspensions of law enforcement, legislative actions by several states, congressional legislation, and temporary rules issued by NOAA Fisheries and the Department of Commerce followed in the wake of the 1987 regulations. In 1989, federal regulations went into effect requiring the widespread use of TEDs, with NOAA's Office of General Counsel for Enforcement and Litigation assessing civil penalties on owners and operators of shrimp trawlers failing to comply with the law.

Twin City Fishermen's Cooperative Association: The Twin City Fishermen's Cooperative established the neighboring communities of Patterson and Morgan City as a nexus of the Louisiana shrimp industry. At least ten shrimp companies were based in these two communities. By 1954, the cooperative, headquartered at Morgan City where its major plant was located, also operated packing and freezing facilities in Port Isabel, Texas. These Lone Star facilities produced Texas Brand fresh-frozen shrimp. By the mid-1950s, the co-op was one of the South's leading shrimp producing organizations. The co-op facilitated the movement of numerous Cajun shrimpers to the south Texas coast.

White Shrimp: Unlike brown shrimp, white shrimp do not have grooves on their carapaces. Their bodies are light gray or green and have longer antennae than other shrimp species. They mature quickly, but their life span, like brown shrimp, is usually less than two years. White shrimp spawn in the Gulf of Mexico from March through September.

Winch: Although initially reluctant to adopt new innovations, shrimpers quickly saw the advantage of outfitting their boats with winches—machines used for lifting a load by winding a cable or rope around a spool. (Winch drums are commonly dubbed *catheads*.) On Floridiens, crewmen use two trawl-retrieval mechanisms mounted on the same winch frame. The main spools are used in the first operation: A crew member stands within inches of the rotating cathead drums and guides the incoming wire rope onto the main spools. In the second phase of the operation, lazy lines are wrapped multiple times around each of the two spinning catheads. Finally, the guarding ends are pulled by the operators to cinch the rope to the rotating spool, aiding trawl retrieval but posing a hazard for operators, who risk entanglement in the spinning cathead spools.

As the size of boats increased, the need for better and more powerful winches grew accordingly. In some cases, a boat's design began with the winch, as they were of paramount importance. (From the collection of F. C. Felterman Jr., Patterson, LA.)

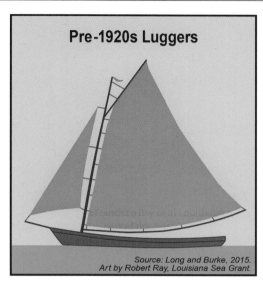

Pre-1920s Luggers

Source: Long and Burke, 2015.
Art by Robert Ray, Louisiana Sea Grant.

Vessel: Built by hand, the eighteen to nearly fifty-foot-long, flat-bottom, shallow draft, rounded-hull Louisiana luggers (often called a canot from the French canottes) were designed for shallow inside waters. The vessel, which dates from Louisiana's colonial period, probably has antecedents in Mediterranean watercraft. The state's luggers are easily identified by a four-corned, asymmetrical, often red "lugsail," suspended from a wooden pole (commonly called a spar) – hence the name, lugger. The center space was open and unobstructed for cargo. Geographer Richard Campanella reports in the early 1800s, up to 200 luggers, operating from the Big Easy. Each boat was manned by three to six men. Following the establishment of industrial ice plants on the northern Gulf Coast, luggers often featured covered, zinc-lined iceboxes for their perishable cargo, typically consisting of oysters and shrimp. At the turn of the twentieth century, Italian and Sicilians owned and operated most of the boats and organized their vessels into "fleets" to maximize the number of loads transported to New Orleans' French Market. In the second decade of the twenty century these vessels were mechanized, with a makeshift "wheelhouse" in the stern. These early seine boats were adapted for trawling by adding a set of tow ropes and a trawl from the stern. Often the aft end was extended to provide additional room for the captain and deck hand to physically pull in the net.

Construction Material: Developed in the "Golden Age of Cypress," the wood eternal was utilized by local and regional boatbuilders for lugger construction. The hull design was typically a semi-rounded-shaped, carvel planking, and well adapted for trawling in the wetland's shallow estuarine waters.

Engine: In the first decade of the twentieth century, small gasoline, kerosene and naphtha engines, often one or two cylinders rated under five horsepower, were mounted in the vessel's stern. The fish hold was located in the bow. Locally, these motorized watercrafts were often identified as "gas boats." Without a centerboard, the "new" lugger's speed improved the delivery time to canneries and other markets. Rigging: Before introduction of the otter trawl in 1917, sail-power luggers, the state's most common fishing type, contributed to the haul-seine fishery, that in the late nineteenth century annually produced more than 10,000,000 pounds of marketable seafood products. Luggers carried a seine crew of up to ten to a shallow water site. Often two luggers were required to meet the labor demands of the larger seines. Usually standing chest deep, the crew placed themselves between the catch and deep water. A seine 2,000 feet or longer was played out and slowly closed until the shrimp could be dipped out and placed in the lugger's hold. This process was repeated until the shrimp were depleted, or because of lack of ice, the boat had to sail to its home port.

With introduction of marine engines, and the otter trawl, the lugger could move without the aid of wind and became more efficient and operated with a two-man crew. For more than forty years luggers and seine crews dominated the industry; the boat was essentially a ferry. As advertising and marketing increased, the knowledge and availability of marine engines, along with the otter trawl, and ice, the lugger morphed into Louisiana's first mechanized shrimp boats.

Using a cast net, thrown ahead of the bow, the lugger captain looked for shrimp. When these evasive decapods were caught, the trawl was put overboard and dragged for up to two hours. Gradually, the rigging improved. Even so, up until the 1930's, few of these vessels were equipped with power-driven machinery. Hand operated gear was standard equipment.

Navigation Equipment: No navigation equipment was available. Fisherman sailed to a sight that often-produced shrimp. Local knowledge was the key to finding shrimp and considerable luck. Dead reckoning, that depended on estimating the direction and distance traveled, without astronomical observations or electronic navigation methods, was the rule.

Voltage: Not available.

Length of Trip: For nearly a half century, these boats made daily trips. Marine engines improved their efficiency, but the trips were still rarely longer than one day.

Accommodations: There were no beds or other amenities aboard these day boats. (Sleep was limited to quick naps.) A canvas covering provided shade.

Engine Manufacturers: Marine engines began to appear in the early 1900's in the region's hardware stores and New Orleans' chandleries. By 1917, Nadler, Fairbanks Morse, Globe Fairbanks-Morse and other motors were in use. Consequently, Louisiana's sail-boat-fishing fleet was rapidly replaced by powerboats that exploited expanded shrimping grounds. This transition constituted a fundamental first step toward expansion into deep water.

APPENDIX 1

Boat Information through Time

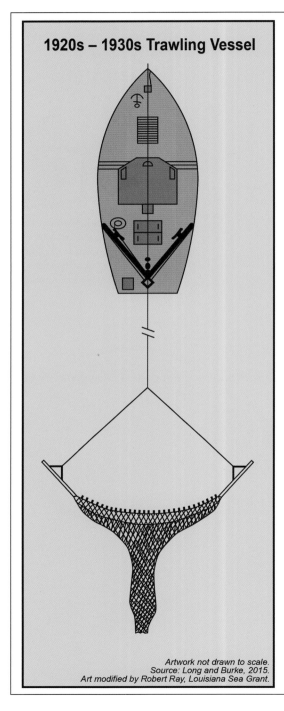

1920s – 1930s Trawling Vessel

Artwork not drawn to scale.
Source: Long and Burke, 2015.
Art modified by Robert Ray, Louisiana Sea Grant.

1920s – 1930s Trawling Vessel

Vessel: These vessels utilized in this time period were converted sail-powered luggers or Biloxi-type boats (also known as bow draggers), where the wheelhouse is in the back of the boat's aft section and the hold is in the foredeck. They are from eighteen to thirty-five feet in length. Unlike the flat-bottom lugger built in the first two decades of the nineteen century, Biloxi watercraft had more of a V-bottom and greater freeboard than their later cousin, the Floridien. This boat looked like a standard lugger, but was larger. They were reputedly designed by Mississippi shipyard owner, J.D. "Jackie Jack" Covacevich, and widely used in the shrimping industry, as they were more seaworthy than the traditional lugger. The engine closer to the propeller reduced strain on the propeller shaft and improved their efficiency.

The inshore lugger fleet was enlarged by the Lafitte skiff, designed by Schiro Perez or Emile Dufrene of Lafitte, Louisiana in the late 1930s. The indigenous eighteen to thirty-five-foot-long, smooth, flat hulled Lafitte skiff evolved into a sleek, fast, and shallow-draft folk boat, largely found between Vermilion Bay and the west bank of the Mississippi River.

Construction Material: Local boat builders preferred cypress planking, when it was available. If kept moist, cypress would last nearly indefinitely. Although the building material of choice, cypress was expensive; consequently, in the late 1930s, regional boat builders turned to marine plywood. The original relativity flat-bottom luggers partially modeled after the felucca, introduced into this country by Italian immigrants. There were few shipyards, and these traditional boats were built without blueprints in backyards or small boatyards scattered throughout the coastal zone and are an important element in Louisiana's folk landscape.

The Lafitte skiff, made largely of marine plywood or cypress planks, had a semi-flat hull and great sheer and flare in the bow section.

Engine: Gasoline engines, rated from ten-to-fifty horsepower, were commonplace. In the transition period, kerosene and naphtha engines were the pioneer powerplants used in the industry.

In the Lafitte skiff, small marine or modified water-cooled automobile engines provided propulsion. As automobile engines became more powerful, these engines, up to 400 horsepower, were adapted for marine use. As a result, a Lafitte skiff can "get on the step" and do at least thirty miles per hour.

Rigging: On a Biloxi trawler, nets were towed from a gallows-like structure, near the deckhouse, that supported a single 100-foot-wide net attached to six-foot otter doors. The otter doors were designed to drag the net downward and pull it outward as it descended into the coastal waters. Through time, the "gallows" supported two booms. Few winches were available. The two-man crew retrieved the net by hand using a ¾ to one-inch manilla tow rope. A drum of gasoline was on deck. If the boat was out for more than two days, a barrel to catch rainwater was also on deck.

The Lafitte skiff pulled a small trawl off the stern. Around 1983, a few Barataria fishermen outfitted their skiffs with

"skimmers," "bay sweepers," or "butterfly" nets. These nets, supported by a large rectangular steel frame attached to the boat's bow, were lowered from their horizontal position slightly above the deck into the water. In this position, the net was perpendicular to the port and starboard sides of the vessel, but slightly above the waterline to prevent the shrimp from escaping by jumping over the net. Skimmers are primarily used in the white shrimp fishery.

Navigation Equipment: Throughout this time period, limited availability of electronic navigation aids meant the wheelhouse had a small compass, a radio, and a few navigation maps.

Voltage: Six-volt systems were available; most engines were hand cranked.

Length of Trip: These boats made daily trips, unless they were working with an ice boat that could resupply them, then the trips could be up to a week in length.

Accommodations: On the Biloxi boats, rudimentary accommodations were available, with a bunk in the wheel-house or the forward extremity of the hold. A half-cabin on the aft section of a Lafitte skiff, with a tarpaulin covering the deck provided shade; there were no bunks on the boat.

Engine Manufacturers: By the 1930s, North America had more than 800 manufacturers of small marine engines. The companies most frequently mentioned in contemporary advertisements were Lathrop, Wolverine, Fairbanks Morse, Atlas, Globe, Palmer, Lockwood Ash, and hand-cranked, automobile engines repurposed for marine use.

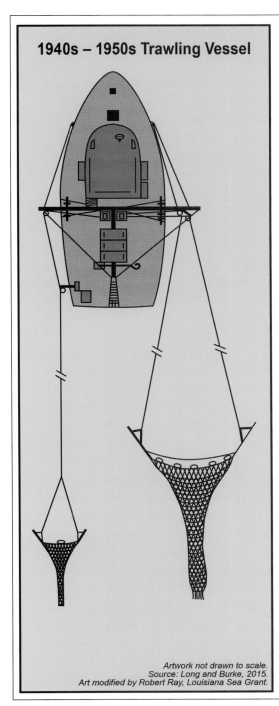

1940s – 1950s Trawling Vessel

Artwork not drawn to scale.
Source: Long and Burke, 2015.
Art modified by Robert Ray, Louisiana Sea Grant.

1940s – 1950s Trawling Vessel

Vessel Size: By the early 1940s, Biloxi-type watercraft was being rapidly replaced by Florida-type, or in the local vernacular, Floridianes, where the wheelhouse is in the boat's bow. The engine room is under the deckhouse and fish the hold is aft. The cabin-forward design allowed the captain far greater visibility than the Biloxi boats. These deep-hull trawlers are in the range of fifty to seventy feet in length. A few are up to eighty-five feet long and were often outfitted with refrigeration equipment or insulated holds; all permanently transformed the Louisiana shrimp industry from a "folk" occupation to a business. The hull has more of a round, or semi-V, shape and well adapted for trawling in the often-turbulent waters of the Gulf of Mexico. The boats are distinguished by their maneuverability.

There are two types: the inshore version was less than fifty feet in length and had a flat-bottom design and is often called a South Lafourche trawler; the offshore Floridians length varied from fifty to eighty feet.

Construction Material: Cypress planking was being used; marine plywood was readily available and steel hulls were being built at local shipyards. A Greek immigrant, Stathis Klonais, in Fernandina Beach Florida, designed and built these boats based on similar Mediterranean vessels. The boat, known as an "Atlantic Supertrawler" was introduced in coastal Louisiana in the late 1930s by Felice Golino who relocated his trawlers to the Morgan City-Patterson area and was rapidly followed by other opportunistic Floridians. The boat was adapted and copied by local fishermen and shipwrights. Immediately after World War II, fifty-five to sixty-five-foot all-steel trawlers were being introduced into the industry.

Engines: Gasoline engines, rated from eighty up to nearly 200 horsepower, were common and diesel-powered marine engines were expanding their market share. After World War II, fuel-efficient, diesel engines were being installed in the inshore and offshore trawler fleet and gasoline engines survived in some of the inshore folk boats.

Rigging: On the Floridianes, a wooden mast and boom outfitted with massive steel pipe outriggers, or towing booms, pulled a single 120-foot-wide net and the associated six- to eight-foot otter doors; however, by the late 1950's the trawler fleet was converting from a single-trawl to two-trawl rigs. Typically, winches, located behind the wheelhouse, powered from the main engines pulled cables connected to drum hoists were common. These power hoists were installed to make retrieving the net easier. In some cases, the boat's design begins with the proper placement of the winch. A small "try net," operated from an outrigger with a steel cable running to a drum hoist, was an efficient and time-saving tool. Operated from the vessel's stern, the try net was used to find shrimp before the larger net was employed.

Navigation Equipment: In the post-World War II era, fishermen learned quickly how to reconfigure surplus military long-range navigation (LORAN) systems for their use, as Loran grid lines are appearing on nautical charts in the 1950s.

Citizen band, or locally called come-back radios are readily available, as are depth finders and improved compasses.

Voltage: The new boats and engine configurations depended on six or twelve-volt electrical systems.

Length of Trip: The Floridianes became the industry's workhorse and was designed for day, a week or up to a month's use.

Accommodations: The cabin-forward wheelhouse was enlarged to accommodate a galley, small crew quarters, a liquid-petroleum-gas store and a twelve-volt efficiency refrigerator.

Engine Manufacturers: By the 1950s, Caterpillar, Gray Marine, Cummins, and Lathrop diesels are in use throughout the shrimp fleet.

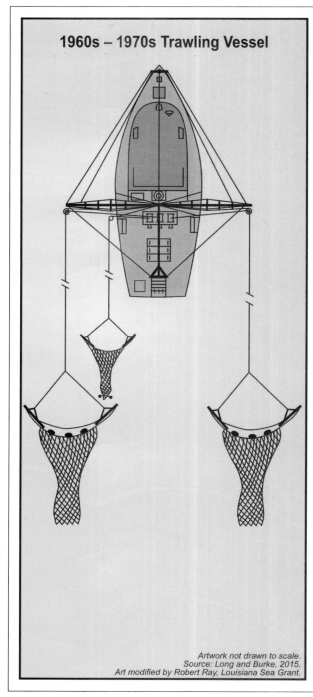

1960s – 1970s Trawling Vessel

Artwork not drawn to scale.
Source: Long and Burke, 2015.
Art modified by Robert Ray, Louisiana Sea Grant.

1960s – 1970s Trawling Vessel

Vessel Size: Floridianes typically extended from forty to eighty feet in length, with a width of from twelve to twenty-four feet.

Construction Material: A few boats were built from cypress planking, but steel and, to a lesser extent, fiberglass were the primary construction materials. Large boats were fabricated in shipyards, while their smaller cousins were built in a shipwright's bayouside yard. Other than size, Vietnam War-era boats differed little from the vessels constructed during the two previous decades.

Engines: Gasoline engines were available and used, but diesel power dominated the industry. During this period, diesel engines rated up to nearly 400 horsepower.

Rigging: Wooden masts and booms were no longer commonplace, having been replaced by steel counterparts. Dual outriggers were usually twenty-four feet long, each boom being outfitted to pull two forty to forty-two-foot nets and the associated six-to-nine-foot otter doors. (The horsepower of a vessel's power plant ultimately determined the trawl net and door size.) The two smaller nets configuration was considered more efficient over an uneven bottom. Further, the smaller nets caused let total towing resistance, and trawlers could therefore use faster towing speeds. Improved winches and cables were incorporated in deck designs. The try net was commonplace throughout the industry.

Navigation Equipment: By the mid-1960s, shrimp boats utilized more powerful commercial radios with broad band widths. LORAN-C (which was permanently discontinued in 2010), autopilots, depth finders, radar and air conditioning were added to the assembly of electronics that now dominated the wheelhouse.

Voltage: The new boats and engine configurations utilized twelve, thirty-two- and 110-volt systems to power the boat's electronics.

Length of Trip: Boats constructed in this period were designed for deployments of a week to a month in length.

Accommodations: The wheelhouse was enlarged to accommodate a captain's stateroom, crew quarters, a galley with freezer, television, heating and air conditioning units, and ice makers.

Engine Manufacturers: Caterpillar and Cummins diesels powered the fleet.

1980s – 2020s Trawling Vessel

1980s – 2020s Trawling Vessel

Artwork not drawn to scale.
Source: Long and Burke, 2015.
Art modified by Robert Ray, Louisiana Sea Grant.

Vessel Size: With development of new shrimp harvest sites, new steel-hull boats, from seventy-five to more than100 feet in length were built. They have deep drafts and include refrigeration systems and enormous fuel and water tanks

Construction Material: These steel and fiberglass "super trawlers" were fabricated in a few Louisiana shipyards; there was a slow shift to boatyards in Bayou La Batre, Alabama.

Engines: Diesel power dominated the industry, with engines rated up to nearly 600 horsepower. By the early twenty-first century, marine diesels generated up to 2600 horsepower, with a dozen engines rated between 650 and 1800 horsepower. Often two of these engines powered these new trawlers. Further, auxiliary generators, from thirty to forty kilowatts are part of the engine room.

Rigging: A steel mast and boom supported very long dual outriggers, often equipped with hydraulic systems. The outriggers dragged four sixty-five-foot nets and their otter doors, with a steel sled attached to the middle of the configuration. Large dual winches spooled in the steel cables connected to the nets. The try net continued to be used.

Navigation Equipment: Discovery after discovery benefitted the industry. Satellite navigation systems, improved radios, internet access, state-of-the art global positioning systems (GPS), better depth finders and dual radar units are incorporated into the electronics required to shrimp in open waters and beyond 200 miles from home ports.

Voltage: Along with the twelve, thirty-two, 110-volt systems, modern boats have 220-volt power supply, as well.

Length of Trip: The newer vessels are constructed to trawl for a week or up to two months. For these longer voyages, refrigeration units allow the catch to be individual quick freeze (IQF). Since these boats work in the Gulf of Mexico, they can operate year-round.

Accommodations: The wheelhouse continued to accommodate a captain's stateroom, crew quarters, galley with freezer, television, heat and air conditioning units, hot and cold showers, ice makers and phones.

Engine Manufacturers: Caterpillar and Cummins diesels continued to power the fleet with improved engines.

APPENDIX 2

Chin Seong Moon—One Man's Journey
from China, 1906–1909

Conversation between Interpreter, C.T.Coy, and
Chin Seong Moon, at the Parish Prison, New Orleans, La.,
Jan. 17, 1909.

Chin Seong Moon stated as follows:

That he left China on the 21st day of the second
--4th moon, KS 32nd (May 14, 1906); that he went from China
to Vancouver, B.C., arriving at Vancouver the last part of
the 5th moon; that he stayed in Vancouver one or two days
and then took the train to Montreal, Can. That he remained
in Montreal a few days, and took the steamer on the first part
of the 6th moon for Havana, Cuba. From Havana he went to
Merida, Mex. where he remained nearly two years. That
while in Merida he worked on a hemp farm; that he left Merida
for the United States on the 11th day, 7th moon,- KS 34 (Aug.
6, 1908); and that he reached New Orleans the 23rd day, 7th
moon,- KS 34 (Aug. 18, 1908). That he came on a lumber boat;
that there were 12 Chinese on the boat; that after their arrival off this coast they were changed twice to different boats;
that they were covered up with lumber when the officer came
on board to fumigate; that they were instructed by the sailors
to put out the light occasioned by fumigation after they went
away; that they put it out once, and the officer returned and
relighted same; that they were placed where they finally
landed at a pier where they could see a big building with lots
of electric lights, and other buildings all lighted up, which
were near the depot. That there was one building in which
there were lots of big wheels moving, but that he did not
know what the place was called. That as soon as they were
landed a few white men and a Chinaman was there waiting
to take them away; that they were taken from the boat, a few
in each party, and in different directions; that finally they
all met again in one house, but that they only remained in

this house for a little while, and that they were all taken away from there by different friends to different places. That Gee Den Shu, alias, Gee Guey, at Quong Yuen Chong Co. of New Orleans, is his friend, and it was this friend who paid Num Hing Co. at New Orleans, La. $450.00 to get him from Merida, Mex. to the United States. That he is very well acquainted with Chin Bing at Merida, and has had a great many meals with him. That Chin Bing and Jew Ping, alias, Jew Lin Kong, are the Chinese at Merida, Mex. who arranged for bringing the Chinamen from Mexico to the United States. That Chin Bing's address in Merida is Quong Hong Yick Co. That Jew Ping's address at Merida is Sum Hong On Co. That both of these stores at Merida ask $450.00 a head, and guarantee that the person sent by them will arrive at New Orleans, La. safely; that they ask $500.00 for each person who desires to go to New York, SanFrancisco, or elsewhere. That upon their arrival at New Orleans it was Chin Yon who was with the white man that met them. That he reached final landing place about 9:30 P.M.. ---- That since he has been in jail he has been visited by a Chinaman and a lawyer (Exhibited card of Howard & Hollander, Lawyers) who advised him not to talk to any one.

APPENDIX 3

Lafourche Parish Shrimp Boats and Their Owners

Shrimp boat names	Owners' names
[?]	Leon Lombas
A Jax	Percy Pitre
Albert B.	Albert Badeaux
Alberta R.	Leo Duet
Alice M.	Bruce
American Whitney	Charlie Louviere
Ann Martin	Eddie Martin
Annette Ann	Clophas Rousse
Anson T	Rémy Toups
Anthony T.	David Toups
Atom Bomb	Nolta Richoux
B 29	Louis " T-Man" Pitre
Baby Ruth	Ben Danos
B and J	Jefferson Guidry
Barbara Ann	Leonce Toups
Bayou Loures	Clovis Toups
Betty Kiff	Melvin "Pita" Kiff
Beverly Ann	Leonce Toups
Big D.	Dave Orgeron
Big Foot	Antoine Cheramie
Black Orchid	Menton Jambon
Bob and Steve	Alvin Cantrell
Bob and Wayne	Bienvenu "BM" Cheramie
Bob Jace	Eule Duet
Bobby Allen	Joe [surname unknown]
Boston Blackie	Maurice "Black" Vizier
Broadway	[?]
Buddy and Sherry	Otis Cantrell
C. W. Hudson	Louis «Red» Pitre
Capt. Nathan	Theo Cheramie
Cajun Lady	Mabry Guidry
Captain Buster	Louis Chabert
Captain Carl	Lawrence Falgout
Captain Chouest	Edison Chouest
Captain Curole	Bobby Curole
Captain Darcy	Tom Kiff
Captain Dave	Antoine Punch
Captain Day	[?]

Shrimp boat names	Owners' names
Captain Duet	Leo Duet
Captain Ed Sullivan	[?]
Captain Emery	Ernest Eymard
Captain Forest	[?]
Captain Guy	Guy Callais
Captain Harold	Gibson Collins
Captain Henry	Henry Charpentier
Captain Hubert L	Hubert Lafont
Captain Hurst	Ted Gisclair
Captain James	Alcide Hebert
Captain Jimmy	Beauregard Martin
Captain Lin	Linton [?]
Captain Lorraine	Edville Lorraine
Captain Nathan	Theo Cheramie
Captain Perry	Freddie Gisclair
Captain Pitre	Elphege Pitre
Captain Ray	Sylvest Cheramie
Captain Rickey	Edwin Kiff
Captain Rodney	Ted Gisclair
Captain Ronald	Ronald Cheramie
Captain Rusty	Foster Borne
Captain Steven	Steven Charpentier
Captain Sullivan	Morris Cheramie
Captain T.	[?]
Captain Troy	Felton Cheramie
Captain Vin	Lawrence "Vin" Cantrell
Captain Wallace	Wallace Chabert, Jr.
Captain Wayne	Ulysse Pitre
Captain Yo	Walter Anselme
Carlson Raider	Julien Boudreaux
Chabert Brothers	Harris Chabert
Cherbourg	Leon Bruce
Cindy Lou[?]	Ernest Eymard
CMW	[?]
Corregidor	Arthur Galjour
D and G	Elmo Guidry and Linton Duet
Daisy June	David Duet, Jr.
Dale and Gail	Lincoln Charpentier

Shrimp boat names	Owners' names
Dick	Preslic Smith
Dixie Queen	Leroy Chabert
Dorothy Marie L.	Vin Lafont
Dragnet	Leander Gaspard
Effie D	Clyde Galjour
Enola T.	[?] Theriot
Errold D.	David Duet, Sr.
Eveda	Leo Duet
Evening Star	Robert Champagne
Filton C.	Filton Cheramie
Five Daughters	Elo Charpentier
Freeway	T-Dud Galjour
General Mack	Mack Terrebonne
Gerald Anthony	Torris Guidry
Glendale	Lawrence Charpentier
Gloria	Arsène Lasseigne
Good Gulf	Tilman Melanson
Good Times	Lanny Rousse
Great Light	Louis Plaisance
Guiding Light	Eule Duet
Gulf Clipper	Derris Gisclair
Gulf Clipper 2	Sweetsay Gisclair
Gulf Kiss	Lodrigues Kiff
Gulf Stream	[?]
Gulf Wave	Harrison Rousse
Happy Gal	[?]
Helen A	[?]
Humming Bird	Leo Duet
Invader	Bruce
J. L.	Jefferson Lasseigne
J.L.D	Junis Duet
Jamaica	Bill Duet
Jan and Dennis	Norman Boudreaux
Janice D.	[?] Danos
Jewel R.	[?]
Jimmy and Johnny	Belonie Vizier
Jimmy M.	Beauregard Martin
Joan of Arc	Edgar Bouzigard

Shrimp boat names	Owners' names
Joey T.	David Toups
John Alan	Pershing Guidry
John Branasky	Walton "To To" Blanchard
John Kurt	John Lombas
Judy and Gary	Loveless Dantin
June Reed	[?]
Kelly G	Joseph Guidry
Key Largo	Merwin Ledet
L and F	Freddie Gisclair
L and L	[?]
L Dot 1	Frankie Lorraine
L Dot 2	Frankie Lorraine
L Dot 3	Frankie Lorraine
L. T.	[?] Theriot
Lady Anna	Essay Duet
Lady Catherine	Jessie Verdin
Lady Dee	Claude Blanchard
Lady Jo Ann	Jimmy Toups
Lady Luck	Godfrey Chabert
Lady Misty	Troy Sanamo
Lady of Fatima	Euclid Lafont
Lady of the Sea	Edison Chouest
Lady Phyllis	Ashton Cheramie
Lady Rayshell	Ray Dufrene
Lady Stephanie	Wylie Chabert
Lady Victoria	Emilien Gisclair
Lafourche Clipper	Adrien Danos
Lafourche Pride	Duffy Guidry
Lanny R	Clophas Rousse
Larose	Forest
Larry G.	Valance Gisclair
Leeville	Eddie Martin
Linda Sue	[?]
Lingalien Gulf	Victor Boudreaux
Little Bo Bo	Antoine Punch
Little Fox	Hewitt Ledet
Little Jeremy	Wilbert Galjour
Little Mark	Mark Terrebonne

Shrimp boat names	Owners' names
Little Pamela	[?]
Little Ray	Harris "Slim" Guidry
Little Roy	Harris "Slim" Guidry
Little Sunday	T. Rod Cheramie
Little Toot	Gerard Ledet
Loraina T.	Theriot
Love Boat	Herbert Cheramie
Lovenia S.	"Boy" St. Pierre
M and H	[?]
M. Goddessman	Levy Brunet
Madam Dean	Jack Filinich
Madam Drit	Tedman Collins
Marcel, Jr	Linwood Esponge
Mary Evelyn	Livingston Doucet
Master Burgess	Ellis Plaisance, Jr.
Master Dean	Spurgin Chouest
Mayflower	Fornest Callais
Melanie	Provis Esponge
Mermaid	Vendon Callais
Miami	Horace Guidry
Minnie Lee M.	Eddie Martin
Miranda	Oneal Galliano
Misfit	[?]
Miss Alvina	Edville Lorraine
Miss Bridgett	Louis Danos
Miss Carolyn	Eddie Martin
Miss Cathy L.	Jessie Ledet
Miss Emily	Eddie Orgeron
Miss Enola	Eroy Duet
Miss Gail	Eddie Bruce
Miss Genevieve	Clarence "Pank" Cheramie
Miss Geraldine	Harris "Slim" Guidry
Miss Janice	Emar Eymard
Miss Lola	Tilman Charpentier
Miss Mary	Alton Terrebonne
Miss Myann	Herman J. Crosby
Miss New Orleans	Euzèbe Pitre
Miss Pat	Roman Vega

Shrimp boat names	Owners' names
Miss Yvette	Jimmy Gisclair
Mister Clarence	Clarence Gisclair
Mister Fox	Calvin Fox Cheramie
Mister Keith	Roy Guidry
Mister Wood	Jimmy Wood
Muskrat	Armand Brunet
Mystery	Penelton Duet
Navy	[?]
Nellie Rose	Jeff Pitre
New Deal	[?]
Nice Bayhay	B. Ledet
O Henry	Alcess Charpentier
Oh Johnny	
Overseas	Leo Toups
Pappy's Gold	Jade Blanchard
Paris Minor	Etienne Louie Rousse
Paris T.	Theriot
Peter Paul	Penelton Duet
Petit Corporal	Theriot
Pioneer	Linton Duet, Jr.
Popeye	Madison St. Pierre
Radar	V. J. Martin
Rando D.	Firman Doucet
Raymond T	Rémy Toups
Rebel	Gilmo Pitre
Regal	[?]
Rhode Island	Alphonse "Bob" Lasseigne
Robert E. Lee	Joe-Joe Lee
Robert Frank	Robert and Frank Pitre
Rodney Anthony	[?]
Rosemary L	Louis Smith
Rosemary M	Wilson Richoux
Sable Island	Etienne Pitre
Saint Ann	Robert "Cobin" Evmard
Saint Lucy	Ernest Thibodaux
Saint Simon Island	Simon Island
San Antonio	Noon [full name unknown]
Santa Maria	Walton "To To" Blanchard
Sarah Jo	Collin Eymard

Shrimp boat names	Owners' names
Sea Drift	Gilman Cheramie
Sea Durbin	Herbert Charpentier
Sea Fox	Hewett Ledet
Sea Gypsy	[?] Lasseigne
Secret	Ray St. Pierre
Singapore	Ellis Plaisance, Jr.
Skipper G	Maurice Gisclair
Sonny Boy	Harrison Rousse
Southern Belle	Lodess Toups
Star Dipper	Steven Kiff
Star Dust	[?]
Stephen G	Joe Lorraine
Stormy Weather	Eddie Martin
Superior	Levy Charpentier
Ted Williams	Eddie Williams, Sr.
Tee Bayou Loures	Clovis Toups
Tee Jeff	Jefferson Lasseigne
Ten Commandments	Wylie Chabert
Terry	Freddy Bruce
Thunder Bay	Abdon Callais(?)
Tiger Lillie	Roy Guidry
Tiger Shark	[?]
T-Jim	Jimmy Melancon
T-Nol	Nolan Lasseigne
Todd Ann	Dudley Adams
Tony S.	André St. Pierre
Two Sons	Leonise Toups
Typhoon	Spurgin Chouest
Typhoon 2	Valcour Vizier
Ukraine	E. J. Rouse
Viking	Wylie Chabert
Virgin Island	Norey Dufrense
Walton	[?]
Wesco #4	Roberson Guidry
Young Emery	Ernest Eymard
Young Rudy	Leon Savoie
Young Stanley	Uderick Martin
Young Velma	Ocean Eymard
Zebella 1	Walton Kiff

UNITED STATES PATENT OFFICE.

YEE FO, OF GRAND LAKE, LOUISIANA.

PROCESS OF PRESERVING SHRIMPS.

SPECIFICATION forming part of Letters Patent No. 310,811, dated January 13, 1885.

Application filed July 2, 1884. (No specimens.)

To all whom it may concern:

Be it known that I, YEE FO, a subject of the Emperor of China, and a resident of Grand Lake, parish of Jefferson, and State of Louisiana, have invented a certain new and use- [5] ful Improvement in Processes of Preserving Shrimps; and I do hereby declare the following to be a full, clear, and correct description of the same.

This invention relates to a process for pre- [10] serving that class of shell-fish known as "shrimps;" and it consists, first, in placing the same in boiling water containing salt in the proportion of two or two and a half pounds of salt to each bushel of shrimps. The [15] vessel in which these are placed is then covered, and the boiling continued for about one and a half minute, when the cover is removed and the contents of the vessel thoroughly stirred with a paddle or other suitable appli- [20] ance, so as to thoroughly impregnate the shrimps with the salt. About one minute will suffice for this part of the process. The cover is next replaced and the boiling continued for one and a half or two minutes longer, [25] when the shrimps are removed by means of perforated skimmers or shovels, and spread out on a platform in open air, so as to expose them to the action of the sun. Here they are allowed to remain for two or three days, (ac- [30] cording to the heat of the sun,) during which time they are turned and re-turned, say, once in every two hours, so as to insure the removal of all moisture therefrom. When found to be sufficiently dry, they are treaded [35] or walked over by persons wearing moccasins, which process is continued until the heads and shells or heavy scales are detached from the main part of the flesh. By the same devices with which they were placed on the [40] platform, they are removed therefrom, the scales and light particles being fanned off by throwing them upward through the air to baskets or barrels, somewhat in the same style as that practiced with wheat, rice, and other [45] similar grain. The tails of the shrimps (which are the only edible portions thereof) are next removed and placed in canvas bags. These bags are then closed and beaten on boards or benches, so as to detach the small particles of [50] shell or scale still adhering to the flesh. About five minutes will suffice for this part of the process, when the bags are opened and their contents allowed to drop into sifters in which they are thoroughly agitated, so as to remove [55] any dust or scale still adhering thereto. The shrimps are next removed to a dry-house to await packing for shipment, or are immediately packed in barrels or other packages by placing the same therein in layers, and press- [60] ing down each layer until the package is finally filled, when it is headed and ready for shipment.

Having described my invention, what I claim as new, and desire to secure by Letters [65] Patent, is—

The herein-described process for preserving shrimps, the same consisting in first placing the shrimps in boiling water containing salt in the proportion stated, in thoroughly stir- [70] ring the same for the purpose described, and, finally, in successively drying, treading, beating, and packing the shrimps, substantially in the manner and for the purpose set forth.

In testimony whereof I affix my signature in [75] presence of two witnesses.

YEE FO.

Witnesses:
  P. N. JUDICE,
  R. C. HILL.

In 1885, nine years after seafood canning technology became viable, Yee Fo secured a United States patent for traditional Chinese shrimp drying techniques. (US Patent 310,811, 1885.)

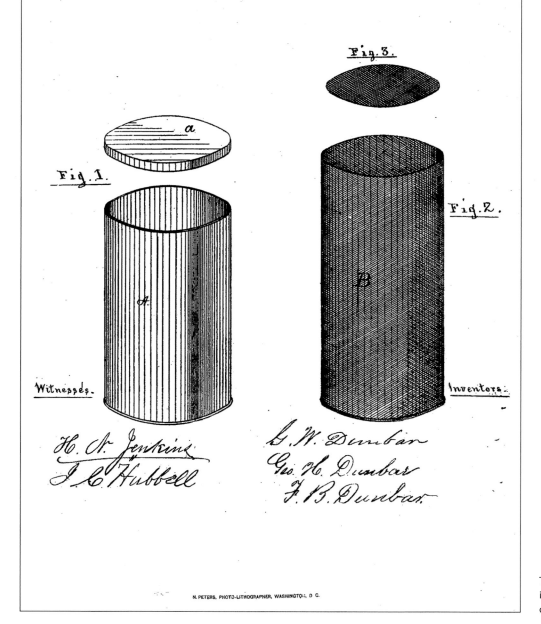

This diagram, drawn from a patent application, illustrates the Dunbar canning method's distinguishing features. (US Patent 178,916, 1876.)

An unofficial history of the Blum and Bergeron company notes the "rising cost of shrimp, health regulations, and competition from the canning and the frozen shrimp industries threatened all shrimp drying operations. Louis [Blum's] drying machine brought the drying process indoors and reduced the drying time to hours rather than days. It also eliminated spoilage due to weather, while keeping the drying process sanitary. All the inventions to produce (cook, dry, shell and clean) dried shrimp in Louisiana were invented and patented by members of the Blum and Bergeron families." (Document from the Blum and Bergeron Collection, Nicholls State University Archives, Thibodaux, LA.)

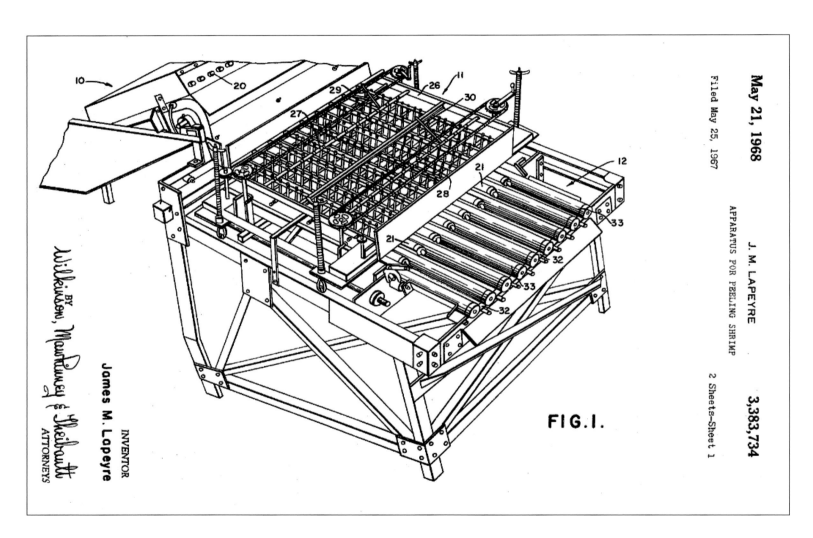

May 21, 1968   J. M. LAPEYRE   3,383,734

Filed May 25, 1967

APPARATUS FOR PEELING SHRIMP

2 Sheets—Sheet 1

FIG. I.

INVENTOR
James M. Lapeyre

BY
Wilkinson, Mawhinney & Theibault
ATTORNEYS

The "Model A" peeling machine patented in 1947 became a National Historic Mechanical Engineering Landmark in 2004. (Photo from the authors' collections. Courtesy of the Maritime and Seafood Industry Museum, Biloxi, MS, 2019.)

This compilation is drawn from numerous sources. Some references may be to a company's headquarters or a distribution company that was repacking shrimp under its own corporate label.

APPENDIX 5

Louisiana Canning Plants through Time

City	Label Names	Owner
Abbeville	Lusian Brand Oysters; Gulf Crown Brand Oysters; Gulf King Brand Oysters; Gulf King Brand Shrimp	Abbeville Packing Company
Abbeville	Dixie Brand	Distributed by Louisiana Coast Cannery
Algiers		Dunbar-Dukate Company
Algiers/New Orleans	Barataria Shrimp Timbalier Brand Louisiana Brand Barataria Shrimp	Louisiana Canning Company
Arabi		Devitt's Sons Incorporated
Avery Island	Last Island Cove Oysters; Neptune Brand Oysters; Peacock Brand Cove Oysters; Rainbow Cove Oysters; Silhouette Brand Oysters; Lugger Brand Superior Cove Oysters; Tabasco Standard Brand Oysters; Tabasco Fresh Gulf Shrimp Brand; Tabasco Brand Pickled Shrimp	McIlhenny Canning & Manufacturing Company and the Baltimore Packing Company
Berwick		J. R. Hardee Shrimp Company
Berwick		Brooks Seafood Corporation
Berwick		Colonial Shrimp Company
Berwick	Riverside Wet Shrimp	Riverside Company
Berwick	Riverside Brand Shrimp, Cooked, Peeled, Shrimp Perishable Keep On Ice	Riverside Packing Company
Berwick	Deep C Brand	Louisiana Oyster and Fish Company
Berwick		Purity Canning & Preserving Company
Braithwaite		Plaquemine Parish Canning Company
Braithwaite	Devitt's Brand Jumbo Shrimp; Devitt's Brand Wet Pack Shrimp	Distributed by Devitt's Sons
Boudreaux Canal		Indian Ridge Canning Co
Buras		Buras Union Packing Company
Buras		Crescent City Packing Company
Buras	Cotton Bale Brand Extra Fancy Selected Shrimp; Gulf Bay Brand Extra Fancy Selected Shrimp	Phoenix Packing Company

City	Label Names	Owner
Buras	Island Brand Barataria Shrimp	Lopez Packing Company
Caernarvon	Barataria Shrimp from the Gulf of Mexico; Fresh Shrimp Broadway Brand; Robinson's Fancy Selected Shrimp; Fresh Shrimp A Ready Lunch; Pride of Gulf Brand Cove Oysters; Barataria Shrimp, Pride of Gulf Brand	Caernarvon Canning Company
Caernarvon		Devitt Sons, Incorporation
Caernarvon		Plaquemine Parish Canning Company
Cameron		Steed's Shrimp Company
Cameron		Jumbo Shrimp Company
Cameron		Trosclair Canning Company
Cameron		Doxey's Canning Company
Chauvin/Houma	Oriento Brand Barataria Camarones; Rose Bud Shrimp; Rose Bud Prawns; Faborita Brand Shrimp; Pearl Brand Shrimp; Inrico Brand Timbalier Bay Shrimp	Indian Ridge Canning Company
Chauvin	Chauvin Brothers; Lucky Strike; Trout Brand Broken Shrimp; Trout Brand Shrimp	Louisiana Packing Company
Chauvin		Barre Seafood Company
Crown Point		General Seafood Company
Cut Off	Bayou Rose Brand Shrimp; Cotton Boll; Reel Brand Fancy Baby Shrimp	Henry J. Pitre
Cut Off	White Coast Brand Shrimp	White Coast Packing Company, Terrebonne and Pierce
Delcambre		Delcambre Packing Company
Dulac		Bourg and Voisin Canning Company
Dulac		Calvin J. Authement
Dulac		A.J. Authement Packing Company
Dulac		Gulf Coast Packing Company
Dunbar		G. W. Dunbar Sons
Empire	Battistella Brand Oysters	A. Battistella
Empire		Dunbar-Dukate Company
Empire	French Market Brand Shrimp	Empire Packing Company
Empire	French Market Brand Shrimp	Michel-Bougon Canning Company
Empire	New Deal Brand Shrimp	L.B. Galle Packing Company
Empire	Empire Brand Shrimp; Black Label Brand Shrimp	Galle & Stockfleth Packing Company

City	Label Names	Owner
Golden Meadow		American Packing Company
Golden Meadow		Desporte Packing Company
Golden Meadow		Dorgan McPhillips Packing Corporation
Golden Meadow		Dunbar-Dukate Company
Golden Meadow	Gomeco Brand Shrimp; Taste Good Brand Shrimp	Golden Meadow Packing Company
Golden Meadow		Green Wave Packing Company
Golden Meadow		Lafourche Packing Company
Golden Meadow		Pelican Seafood Packing Company
Golden Meadow		Schaffer-Sims Company
Golden Meadows	Dixie Brand Shrimp; Lisco Brand Medium Shrimp; U.S.A. Brand Medium Shrimp; Lisco-Pepper Brand Shrimp; Lafourche Brand Fresh Shrimp	Lafourche Ice and Shrimp Company
Golden Meadow		Bertoul Cheramie, Morgan City Packing Company.
Golden Meadow		Tamplain Packing House
Golden Meadow		Falgout Canning Factory
Golden Meadow		Picciola Packing Company
Golden Meadow		Pelican Seafood
Golden Meadow		Bob Collins Shrimp Company
Golden Meadow	D.B. Brand Shrimp	Timbalier Bay Packing Company
Golden Meadow		Hubert Lafont Shrimp Company
Golden Meadow		Devitt-Clark Packing Company also known as American Packing Company
Grand Isle		Dunbar & Sons
Grand Isle		Little Lake Oyster and Shrimp Company
Grand Isle		Jules Fisher Shrimp Company
Happy Jack	Boden Brand Fancy Shrimp	Fortuna Canning Factory
Happy Jack		Phoenix Packing Company
Harahan		Quong Sun Company
Harvey	Antler Brand Fancy Prawns; Beacon Brand Barataria Shrimp; Bouquet Marque Crevettes Roses; Palm Brand Barataria Shrimp; Fresh Prawns, Pride of the Gulf Brand; La Palma	Southern Shell Fish (also spelled Southern Shell Fish) Company
Harvey		Skrmetta Seafood Company

City	Label Names	Owner
Harvey	Savoy Brand Prawns	Seafood Company of Louisiana
Houma		St. Joseph Packing Company
Houma	Dulac Shrimp	Distributed by Aubin Buquet
Houma		Bay Packing Company
Houma		Bertoul Cheramie Canning Company
Houma		Buquet Canning Company
Houma	Bayou Rose Brand Shrimp; Chér-Amie Louisi-ana Cove Oysters	Daigleville Packing Company
Houma		Dularge Packing Company
Houma		Grand Caillou Packing Company
Houma		C. Cenec Company
Houma		Houma Fish and Oyster Company
Houma		Houma Packing Company
Houma	Rosado Pink Brand Cove Oysters	Gulf Oyster & Fish Company
Houma		John Labat & Brothers
Houma	Lake-View Brand Shrimp	Lake Oyster and Fish Company
Houma		Little Caillou Fish and Oyster Company
Houma		Lobes Oyster Packing Company
Houma	Cajun Louisiana Cove Oysters; Bayou Rose Brand Shrimp; Bayou Rose Brand Broken Shrimp; Chér-Amie Shrimp; Ho-Ma Brand Louisiana Cove Oysters; Ho-Ma Brand Small Size Shrimp	PeMorgan City Canning Company
Houma	Gulfine Brand Prawns	Packed for Louisiana Prawn Export Company
Houma		Houma Canning Company
Houma	Pelican Lake Brand Broken Shrimp; Creole Brand Oysters; Creole Barataria Shrimp; Lake-View Brand Shrimp; Blue Heron Brand Shrimp; Creole Brand Louisiana Shrimp	Pelican Lake Oyster Packing Company/ Pelican Lake Company
Houma		R. J. Younger & Company
Houma	Peacock Brand Dry Pack St. Martin's Pep-O-Brand Large Fancy Shrimp; Melrose Brand Broken Shrimp; Oriento Brand Shrimp; Peacock Brand Shrimp; Pep-O Brand Shrimp; Pepper Flavor Brand Shrimp	St. Martin Oyster Packing Company
Jeanerette	Queen of the South Cove Oysters	Murphy Canning Company

City	Label Names	Owner
Kenner		Kenner Canning & Packing Company
Lafitte		Dunbar-Dukate Company
Lafitte		Fisher Ice and Packing Company
Lafitte	Fisher Brand Delicious Barataria Shrimp	Fisher Packing Company
Lafitte		Johnson Seafood Canning Company
Lafitte		Lafitte Canning Company
Lafitte		Lafitte Packing Corporation
Lafitte		Lafitte Seafood Packing Company
Larose		Larose Canning Company
Lockport	L-C-C Brand Selected Shrimp	Lockport Canning Company
Lockport		Lockport Packing Company
Manila Village		Dunbar & Company
Manila Village		Jules Fisher Shrimp Company
Metairie		Fou Loy Company
Metairie		Robinson Canning Company
Montegut		Montegut Packing Company
Montegut		Frank LeBoeuf Packing Company
Morgan City		St. John's Shrimp Co
Morgan City		G. L. Palmer Shrimp Company
Morgan City		Patterson Shrimp Company
Morgan City		Ramon Shrimp Company
Morgan City		Versaggi Shrimp Company
Morgan City		Sea Shrimp Company
Morgan City		Brooks Seafood Corporation
Morgan City		Twin City Corporation.
Morgan City	Knotts Brand Crayfish Bisque	Knotts Packing Company
Morgan City		Aubin Buquett
Morgan City		Barre Seafood Company
Morgan City		Bourg & Voisin Seafood Company
Morgan City		Dunbar-Dukate Company
Morgan City	Dew Drop Brand Cove Oyster	Lopez & Dukate Company
Morgan City		Jumbo Shrimp Company
Morgan City		Leroy Chauvin, Inc.
Morgan City		Louisiana Packing Company

City	Label Names	Owner
Morgan City		Louisiana Syrup & Canning Company
Morgan City		Morgan City Packing Company – Bertoul Cheramie
Morgan City		V. Santos Shrimp Company
Morgan City		Conrad Fisheries
Morgan City		Pacetti Fish Company
Morgan City		
Morgan City		Louisiana Canning and Syrup Company
Morgan City		Booth Oyster and Shrimp Packing Company
Murphy	Queen of the South Cove Oysters	Murphy Canning Company
Myrtle Grove		Dunbar & Dukate Company
Myrtle Grove		Myrtle Grove Packing Company
Neptune		Dunbar-Dukate Company
Neptune	Dew Drop Brand Cove Oysters	Lopez & Dukate Company
New Iberia		Murphy Canning Company
New Iberia		New Iberia Canning Company
New Orleans		Curtice Brothers Company
New Orleans		Excelsior Packing Company
New Orleans	Panama Brand shrimp	United Milling Products Company
New Orleans		Louisiana Mavar Shrimp and Oyster Company
New Orleans		Lockport Canning and Packing Company
New Orleans		Anita Packing Company
New Orleans		"Golden" Gulf Packing Company
New Orleans		A. J. Bordelon Packing Company
New Orleans		Algiers Canning Company
New Orleans		American Packing Company
New Orleans		Antioch Canning and Packing Company
New Orleans		Barataria Canning Company
New Orleans		Biloxi Canning & Packing Company
New Orleans		Biloxi Fishermen's Packing Company
New Orleans		Garner Packing Company
New Orleans		Deepsouth Packing Company
New Orleans		Biloxi Seafood Packing Company

City	Label Names	Owner
New Orleans		Bouquet-Jordan Canning Company
New Orleans	Rose of New Orleans Brand Fresh Shrimp	Distributed by W. A. Gordon & Company
New Orleans		Braun Canning Company
New Orleans	Cooked, Peeler, Shrimp Burgess Brand Clean Jumbo Shrimp, Bayou King Brand; Humpty Dumpty Brand; Mother Goose Brand; Burgess Reprocessed Brand Dry Shrimp; Burgess Brand Broken Shrimp; Burgess Brand Shrimp; Burgess Brand Oysters	Distributed by Burgess Canning Company
New Orleans	Pirate Brand Shrimp	Burgess-Humphreys Canning Company
New Orleans		Central Canning Company
New Orleans		Chauvin Fishing & Packing Company
New Orleans		Devitt-Clark Packing Company
New Orleans		Deep South Packing Company
New Orleans	Dee-Dee Brand Broken Shrimp; Carnation Brand Barataria Prawns; Salad Dish Brand Shrimp; Dunbar Shrimp; Deer Head Brand Oysters; Dunbar Brand Small Salad Shrimp; Original Dunbar Shrimp; Carnation Brand Barataria Shrimp; Dunbar Brand Salad Shrimp	Dunbar-Dukate Company
New Orleans		E. C. Joullian Canning Company
New Orleans		Edgewater Canning Company
New Orleans		Fort St. Phillip Packing Company
New Orleans		G. W. Dunbar Food Products Company
New Orleans		G.W. Dunbar's Sons, Inc.
New Orleans	Magnolia Brand, Barataria Shrimp, Fresh from the Gulf	G.W. Dunbar' Sons, a Branch of Dunbars, Lopez & Dukate Company
New Orleans	Flora Reprocessed Small Dry Shrimp	Distributed by George E. Burgess
New Orleans		Gulf Shrimp Packing Company
New Orleans		Gussie Fountain Packing Company
New Orleans		H.L. Brignac Company
New Orleans		Howe Packing Company
New Orleans		Humphreys Canning Company
New Orleans	Jas. V.D. Shrimp; Jas V. D. Dunbar's Shrimp Pieces; Jas. V. D.. Dunbar's Prawns; Jas. V. D. Brand Oysters	Jas. V. Dunbar Incorporated

City	Label Names	Owner
New Orleans		Johnson Canning Company
New Orleans	Blue Gulf Shrimp; Empaque Seco Camarones; Seamaid Brand Shrimp dry pack; Miss-Lou Brand Cove Oysters; Miss-Lou Brand Shrimp; Señorita Marca Empaque Seco Camarones	Distributed by L. C. Mays Company
New Orleans		Lafourche Canning Company
New Orleans		Long Beach Canning Company
New Orleans		Matt Canning & Associates
New Orleans		Mexican Gulf Canning Company
New Orleans		New Central Canning Company
New Orleans		New Orleans Cuisine
New Orleans	Sunflower Brand	New Orleans Packing Company
New Orleans		Pascagoula Packing Company
New Orleans	Fort Bay Brand Oysters; French Brand Shrimp	Paul Bougon Fish and Oyster Company packed at Fort St. Phillip Cannery
New Orleans	Barataria Shrimp; French Market Brand Shrimp (a la Creole)	Michel Bougon Canning Company
New Orleans		Reuther's Seafood Company
New Orleans	Blue Knot Brand Oysters	Sancho Packing Company
New Orleans	Waldorf Brand Fancy Large Shrimp	Schaffer-Sims Packing Company
New Orleans		Southland Canning and Packing Company
New Orleans		Springfield Canning Company
New Orleans		Vieux Carre Canning Company
New Orleans	Eagle Brand Shrimp; Bull Dog Brand Barataria Shrimp	Waldmeier Packing Company
New Orleans	Bond Brand 35 Shrimp; Sea Hawk Brand Shrimp; Big Bill Shrimp; Sea Hawk Brand Oysters	Devitt & Sons, Incorporation
New Orleans	Gulfex Brand Barataria Shrimp	Packed for Gulf Export and Import Company
New Orleans	Orleans Brand Shrimp; Lou-Ezy-Ana Band Selected Large Shrimp; Rita Brad Shrimp; Starbrite Brand Fancy Shrimp	United Packing Company
New Orleans	French Market Brand Gulf Shrimp	H. Osborne Cannery
New Orleans	Sancho Panza Barataria Brand Camarones	J.W. Berengher
New Orleans	Gulf Baby Brand Shrimp; Braun's Fancy Shrimp	Braun Canning Company

City	Label Names	Owner
New Orleans	Dragon Brand Barataria Shrimp	Packed expressly for and guaranteed by Quong Sun Company
New Orleans	Barataria Brand Shrimp, Barataria Brand Camarones	Distributed by Fraering Brokerage Company
New Orleans	Bug Shrimp	Sea Food Distributing Company
New Orleans/Biloxi		Gulf City Packing Company
New Orleans/Biloxi		DeJean Packing Company
New Orleans – Bayou St. John		G.W. Dunbar's Sons
Ostrica		Neptune Canning Company
Patterson		Ramos Shrimp Company
Patterson		St. John Shrimp Company
Patterson		Versaggi Shrimp Company
Phoenix		Phoenix Packing Company
Point a la Hache		Dunbar & Dukate Company Shrimp and Rice Factory
Point a la Hache		Gravolet Canning Company
Point a la Hache	Gulf Coast Standard Oysters	Gulf Coast Products, Inc.
Rigolets	Dew Drop Brand Oysters	Lopez & Dukate Company
Rigolets		Louisiana Oyster Company
Slidell		Pearl River Canning Company
Slidell		White Kitchen Canning Company
St. Bernard Parish		Lopez-Desportes Packing Company
St. Bernard Parish		Lopez-Grenier Packing Company
Violet		Dunbar-Dukate Company
Violet		Southern Canning Company
Violet		E.C. Joullian Canning Company
Violet	Bumble Bee	Bumble Bee Foods,
Violet		C.B. Foster Packing Company
Violet		Canal Canning Company previously known as Vieux Canning Company
Violet		Deep Sea Canning & Packing Company
Violet		E. C. Joullian Canning Company
Violet		Louisiana Violet Packing Company
Violet		Vieux Carre Canning Company

City	Label Names	Owner
Violet	Sea Island Brand Shrimp	W.H. Foster/ also known as C. B. Foster
Violet	Dolphin Brand Shrimp	Deep Sea Canning and Packing Company
Westwego	Renis-Brand	Westside Commission Company
Westwego		Dunbar-Dukate Company
Westwego	Dew Drop Brand Cove Oysters	Lopez & Dukate Company
Westwego	Pride of Salad Brand Wet Shrimp; Humphreys Brand Broken Shrimp	Distributed by Humphreys Canning Company
Westwego	Pana Brand Shrimp	Panama Canning Company, Battistella and English
Westwego	Jefferson Brand Shrimp; Grand Isle Brand Shrimp; Grand-La-Co Brand Shrimp	Grand Isle Canning Company
Westwego	Cutcher Wet Pack Medium Shrimp; Cutcher Wet Shrimp; Cutcher Wet Pack Shrimp; Nearby Medium Wet Shrimp; Nearby Wet Shrimp; Nearby Jumbo Wet Shrimp; Nearby Dry Shrimp	Distributed by Cutcher Canning Company.
Westwego	Barataria Shrimp Labelle Brand; Wego Brand Shrimp; Labelle Brand Barataria Shrimp; La Bonita Brand Barataria Shrimp	Grand Lake & Gulf Shrimp Company
Westwego	La Bonita Brand Barataria Shrimp	Grand Lake & Gulf Shrimp Company
Westwego		Hudson Canning Corporation
Westwego		Panama Canning Company
Westwego	Cutcher Wet Shrimp; Nearby Wet Shrimp	Cutcher Canning Company
Westwego/New Orleans	Flagstaff Wet Shrimp; Jefferson Brand Fresh Shrimp; Salad Brand Medium Shrimp; Salad Brand Shrimp; Grand Isle Brand Shrimp; Fresh Shrimp Broadway Brand; Baby Shrimp	Robinson Canning Company
?	River Oaks Brands Shrimp	Oak River Canning
?	Kingfisher Brand Barataria Shrimp	Distributed by Koening & Schuster, New York
?	Pelican Brand Prawns – Barataria Prawns	Label may be from the Pelican Lake Oyster Packing Company, Houma.

SOURCES

Brasseaux, Carl A., and Donald W. Davis. *Ain't There No More.* Jackson, MS: University Press of Mississippi, 2017.

Breaux, J. M. *First Annual Report of the Oyster Commission of Louisiana to His Excellency, the Governor, and the General Assembly of the State of Louisiana, August 12, 1902 to January 21, 1904.* New Orleans: American Printing Company, 1904.

Canners Directory and Lists of Members of the Canning Machinery and Supplies Association and the National Food Brokers Association. Washington, DC: National Canners Association, 1922.

Chris Cenac personal collection.

Company Charters, Louisiana State Archives.

"Dunbar-Dukate Oyster Factory Re-Opens Here Next Week, 150 Men and Women Will Be Wanted at Once. Vegetable Canning to Follow Close of Oysters." *Daily Review* (Morgan City, LA), January 4, 1918.

"Fair Prices in 1938." *Biloxi Daily Herald* (Biloxi, MS), August 29, 1938.

Firms Canning Fish and Shellfish Specialties, 1955. Statistical List (SL)-107 Revised. Washington, DC: United States Fish and Wildlife Service, 1956, 1–7.

Firms Canning Shrimp, 1953. Statistical List (SL)-112 Revised April 1954. Washington, DC: United States Fish and Wildlife Service, 1955.

Food and Drug Administration. *Notices of Judgement Under the Food and Drugs Act; Given Pursuant to Section 4 of the Food and Drugs Act, Cases Numbers 24001–24025.* Washington, DC: Department of Agriculture, 1935.

Gorrell, Frank E. *Canners Directory and Lists of Members of the Canning Machinery and Supplies Association and the National Canned Foods and Dried Fruit Brokers Association.* Washington, DC: National Canners Association, 1922.

Industries of New Orleans. New Orleans: J. M. Elstner and Company, 1885.

Lafourche Parish Clerk of Court Records.

Lemmon, Alfred E., et al., eds. *Charting Louisiana: Five Hundred Years of Maps.* New Orleans: Historic New Orleans Collection, 2003.

Louisiana Secretary of State, Commercial and Business Directory.

"Murphy Canning Company, Jeanerette, Capital Stock." *Tensas Gazette* (St. Joseph, LA), July 7, 1905.

"The New Dunbar and Dukate Shrimp Factory at Myrtle Grove Canal Is Canning Large Quantities of Deep Sea Shrimp, Which Are Very Plentiful." *Le Meschacébé* (Lucy, LA), June 5, 1920.

"The New Dunbar Shrimp Factory on Grand Isle Is Being Overprovided with Large Sea Shrimp." *Rice Belt Journal* (Welsh, LA), September 18, 1920.

Paradise, Viola I. *Child Labor and the Work of Mothers in Oyster and Shrimp Canning Communities on the Gulf Coast*. Children's Bureau Publication 98. Washington, DC: Government Printing Office, 1922.

Report of the New Hampshire Board of Excise Commissioners for the Year Ending August 31, 1916. Manchester, NH: John B. Clarke Company, 1916.

"The Sea Coast Islands of Louisiana" *St. Landry Democrat* (Opelousas, LA), June 26, 1880.

"Sea Food Industry Is Growing Rapidly Here." *Houma (LA) Courier*, September 5, 1925.

Transfer of Certain Functions of the Fish and Wildlife Service to the Department of Agriculture: Hearings before the Committee on Merchant Marine and Fisheries. H.R., 78th Cong., 1st Sess., on H.R. 1766. Washington, DC: Government Printing Office, 1943.

Wood, Frank E. *Ninth Biennial Report of the Department of Commissioner of Labor and Industrial Statistics of the State of Louisiana, 1916–1918*. New Orleans: Hauser Printing Company, 1918.

Wurzlow, Helen Emmeline. *I Dug Up Houma Terrebonne*. 7 vols. Houma: Privately printed, 1984–1986.

APPENDIX 6

Louisiana Shrimp Harvest, 1881 to 2018

Year	Number of Barrels	Weight in pounds	Value	Number of Seines	Number of Trawls
				Not Available	Not Available
[1]1880	30,476	6,400,000	392,610	Not Available	Not Available
1881				Not Available	Not Available
1882				Not Available	Not Available
1883				Not Available	Not Available
1884				Not Available	Not Available
1885				Not Available	Not Available
1886	50,366	10,576,833		Not Available	Not Available
[2]1887	32,427	6,809,680	96,408	Not Available	Not Available
[2]1888	33,060	6,942,700	93,452	Not Available	Not Available
[3]1889	34,469	7,238,500	95,882	Not Available	Not Available
[3]1890	31,724	6,662,050	90,519	108[4]	Not Available
[4]1891	20,964	4,402,020	78,792	Not Available	Not Available
1892				Not Available	Not Available
[5]1893	31,724	6,662,050	90,519	Not Available	Not Available
1894				Not Available	Not Available
1895				Not Available	Not Available
1896				Not Available	Not Available
[4]1897	21,365	4,486,726	80,576	Not Available	Not Available
1898				Not Available	Not Available
1899				Not Available	Not Available
1900				Not Available	Not Available
1901				Not Available	Not Available
[6]1902	36,355	7,634,720	131,715	Not Available	Not Available
1903				Not Available	Not Available
1904				Not Available	Not Available
1905				Not Available	Not Available
1906				Not Available	Not Available
1907				Not Available	Not Available
[7]1908	42,146	8,851,000	212,500	Not Available	Not Available
1909				Not Available	Not Available
1910				Not Available	Not Available
1911				Not Available	Not Available
1912				Not Available	Not Available

Year	Number of Barrels	Weight in pounds	Value	Number of Seines	Number of Trawls
[8]1913	50,000	10,500,000	$ 525,000	131	Not Available
1914	52,381	11,000,010	550,000	131	Not Available
1915	57,143	12,000,030	650,000	268	Not Available
1916	85,714	17,999,940	900,000	Not Available	Not Available
1917	57,143	12,000,030	600,000	Not Available	Not Available
1918	110,288	23,160,586	649,804[9]	300	17
1919	76,190	15,999,900	880,000	...	66
1920	152,381	32,000,010	1,760,000	97	499
1921	163,012	34,232,520	1,029,979	135	983
1922	109,050	22,900,500	687,014	111	699
1923	156,749	32,917,290	968,682	128	1,021
1924	150,624	31,631,040	1,007089	143	905
1925	154,722	32,491,620	1,137,373	180	1,010
1926	123,967	26,033,070	911,158	143	692
1927	150,896	31,688,160	1,109,089	120	913
1928	195,303	41,013,630	1,378,455	261	1,454
1929	210,033	44,106,930	1,542,053	125	1,486
1930	197,550	41,485,500	1,351,994	172	1,176
1931	178,815	37,551,150	1,314,292	126	1,131
1932	152,273	31,977,330	1,119,944	66	699
[10]1933	166,058	34,872,180	1,220,525	67	1,045
[10]1934	226,576	47,580,960	1,665,333	107	1,441
[10]1935	252,981	53,126,010	1,859,412	125	1,433
[11]1936	254,427	53,429,800	Not Available	30	1,920
[12]1937	327,528	68,780,900	Not Available	35	2,313
[2]1938	387,518	81,378,900	Not Available	13	1,662
[12]1939	479,107	100,612,500	Not Available	26	1,621
[12]1940	471,361	98,986,000	[10]5,946,000	5	3,016
1941	554,354	116,414,340	Not Available	5	3,028
1942	489,173	102,726,330	Not Available	4	2,380
1943	441,445	92,703,450	Not Available	4	2,101
1944	544,378	114,319,380	Not Available	4	1,866
1945	495,994	104,158,740	Not Available	4	2,373
1946	464,981	97,646,010	Not Available	4	3,030
1947	365,617	76,779,570	Not Available	4	3,408
1948	376,605	79,087,050	Not Available	4	3,200

Year	Number of Barrels	Weight in pounds	Value	Number of Seines	Number of Trawls
1949	376,040	78,968,400	Not Available	4	3,310
1950	361,365	75,886,650	16,338,425	4	2,819
1951	396,980	85,365,800	19,022,485	9	2,248
1952	398,952	83,779,920	17,440,236	…	2,277
1953	437,340	91,841,400	17,871,955	10	3,543
1954	451,647	94,845,870	16,512,855	4	3,442
1955	365,542	76,763,820	14,317,049	5	3,276
1956	318,130	66,807,300	16,292,557	7	3,072
[13]1957	162,394	34,102,800	10,232,900	9	2,419
1958	195,274	41,007,700	13,533,273	Not Available	Not Available
1959	273,109	57,353,000	13,066,935	Not Available	Not Available
1960	294,085	61,757,900	15,881,197	Not Available	4,135
1961	147,747	31,027,000	8,912,840	Not Available	2,267
1962	178,386	37,461,213	4,946,059	Not Available	5,952
1963	384,633	80,773,098	19,779,557	Not Available	5,286
1964	282,780	59,384,005	18,785,939	[10]5,946,000	5,871
1965	296,468	62,258,300	19,530,520	Not Available	5,476
1966	292,327	61,388,772	24,155,951	Not Available	6,122
1967	344,650	72,376,642	23,804,439	Not Available	6,148
1968	322,626	67,751,515	25,604,451	Not Available	6,254
1969	394,254	82,793,508	33,327,198	Not Available	6,595
1970	432,289	90,780,769	34,551,924	Not Available	6,254
1971	440,114	92,424,039	43,242,115	Not Available	7,871
1972	395,405	83,035,100	47,063,955	Not Available	7,756
1973	279,269	58,646,500	44,511,087	Not Available	9,711
1974	283,732	59,583,800	32,203,049	Not Available	6,201
1975	253,021	53,134,500	40,968,175	Not Available	7,307
1976	392,168	82,355,400	79,688,243	Not Available	9,000
1977	495,453	104,045,200	87,183,214	Not Available	8,803
1978	497,762	104,530,217	100,847,849	[10]5,946,000	Not Available
1979	373,568	78,449,456	122,681,495	Not Available	Not Available
1980	429,059	90,102,408	120,979,896	Not Available	Not Available
1981	534,546	112,254,721	136,390,563	Not Available	Not Available
1982	430,679	90,442,723	143,484,579	Not Available	Not Available
1983	370,223	77,746,868	132,312,635	Not Available	Not Available
1984	507,972	106,674,161	143,058,235	Not Available	Not Available

Year	Number of Barrels	Weight in pounds	Value	Number of Seines	Number of Trawls
1985	554,878	116,524,462	135,324,303	Not Available	Not Available
1986	700,083	147,017,618	206,654,425	Not Available	Not Available
1987	560,606	117,727,433	184,198,106	Not Available	Not Available
1988	488,541	102,593,811	149,572,177	Not Available	Not Available
1989	455,169	95,585,682	130,152,201	Not Available	Not Available
1990	568,817	119,451,718	152,981,271	Not Available	Not Available
1991	452,792	95,086,464	141,457,586	Not Available	Not Available
1992	464,905	97,630,202	92,863,355	[10]5,946,000	Not Available
1993	417,589	87,693,821	113,882,731	Not Available	Not Available
1994	430,153	90,332,186	157,143,841	Not Available	Not Available
1995	468,417	98,367,677	167,140,630	Not Available	Not Available
1996	431,468	90,608,480	128,030,131	Not Available	Not Available
1997	443,973	93,234,396	149,894,267	Not Available	Not Available
1998	533,312	111,995,607	159,176,385	Not Available	Not Available
1999	576,208	121,003,770	171,481,148	Not Available	Not Available
2000	692,308	145,384,688	253,032,194	Not Available	Not Available
2001	594,343	124,812,114	187,967,593	Not Available	Not Available
2002	513,309	107,794,921	141,213,327	Not Available	Not Available
2003	598,715	125,730,160	135,152,868	Not Available	Not Available
2004	586,878	123,244,445	128,613,478	Not Available	Not Available
2005	484,685	101,783,934	132,404,818	Not Available	Not Available
2006	657,868	138,152,350	147,817,815	[10]5,946,000	Not Available
2007	540,359	113,475,414	143,851,638	Not Available	Not Available
2008	458,040	96,188,482	141,479,538	Not Available	Not Available
2009	544,264	114,295,498	118,550,784	Not Available	Not Available
2010	352,383	77,000,459	105,764,491	Not Available	Not Available
2011	431,199	90,551,891	131,393,066	Not Available	Not Available
2012	477,059	100,182,446	145,102,736	Not Available	Not Available
2013	469,545	98,604,499	181,053,231	Not Available	Not Available
2014	546,640	114,794,451	235,420,034	Not Available	Not Available
2015	430,985	90,506,869	113,710,991	Not Available	Not Available
2016	460,277	96,658,310	135,828,136	Not Available	Not Available
2017	448,693	94,225,646	133,055,849	Not Available	Not Available
2018	431,778	90,673,434	112,015,761	Not Available	Not Available

SOURCES

1. Fiedler, R. H. "Fisheries of Louisiana." *Louisiana Conservation Review* 2, no. 4 (1932): 7–8, 26. (The value is for all the state's production, not just shrimp; from Smith, 1894.)

2. Collins, Joseph William. "Statistical Review of the Coast Fisheries of the United States." *Bulletin of the United States Fish Commission.* Vol. XVI, 1888. Washington, DC: Government Printing Office, 1892, 270–378.

3. Collins, Joseph William, and Hugh M. Smith. "A Statistical Report on the Fisheries of the Gulf States." *Bulletin of the United States Fish Commission.* Vol. XI, 1891. Washington, DC: Government Printing Office, 1893, 94–108.

4. Townsend, Charles Haskins. "Statistics of the Fisheries of the Gulf States." In *Report of the Commissioner for the Year Ending June 30, 1899.* Vol. XXV, 1899. Washington, DC: Government Printing Office, 1900, 105–69.

5. Smith, Hugh M. "Statistics of the Fisheries of the United States." *Bulletin of the United States Fish Commission.* Vol XIII, 1893. Washington, DC: Government Printing Office, 1894, 389–417.

6. Alexander, A. B. "Statistics of the Fisheries of the Gulf States, 1902." In *Report of the Commissioner for the Year Ending June 30, 1903.* Vol. XXIX, 1903. Washington, DC: Government Printing Office, 1905, 411–81.

7. Alexander, M. L. *Biennial Report of the Louisiana Department of Conservation, 1916–1918.* New Orleans, LA: Palfrey-Rodd-Pursell Company, 1918.

8. Clement, F. L. *Seventh Biennial Report of the Louisiana Department of Wild Life and Fisheries, 1956–1957.* New Orleans, LA: Department of Wild Life and Fisheries, 1958. [From 1913 to 1957.]

9. "Fisheries of Louisiana." In Lewis Radcliff. *Fishery Industries of the United States: Report of the Division of Statistics and Methods of the Fisheries for 1919.* Bureau of Fisheries Document No. 892. Washington, DC: Government Printing Office, 1920, 170–80.

10. Guillot, James P. "Statistical Summary of Natural Resources of Louisiana." *Louisiana Conservation Review* 5, no. 3 (1936): 6–7.

11. Peterson, G. E. "Seasons, Sources, and Sizes of Gulf Shrimp." *Fishery Market News* 5, no. 2 (1943): 1–4.

12. Sandberg, Arthur M. "The Relative Productivity and Value of the Fisheries of the United States and Alaska." *Fishery Market News* 5, no. 12 (1943): 5.

13. NOAA Fisheries. "Landings for Brown and White Shrimp from 1950–2018." Accessed May 9, 2020. https://www.st.nmfs.noaa.gov/commercial-fisheries/commercial-landings/annual-landings/index.

BIBLIOGRAPHY

PRIMARY SOURCES

Artifacts

Cenac, Christopher. Personal Collection of Historic Artifacts and Memorabilia from the Louisiana Oyster and Shrimp Industries, Houma, LA.

Manuscripts

Archives Nationales, Archives des Colonies, Paris, France, Série B, volumes 64–65.

Archivo General de Indias, Papeles Seville, Spain, Procedentes de Cuba, legajos 187A–220B.

Bergeron, Shelly J., and Fred Chauvin. Shrimp-Shelling Machine. US Patent 1,493,425, filed September 2, 1922, issued May 6, 1924, and expired May 6, 1941.

Blum, Louis. Dried Shrimp Industry. Typescript. Blum and Bergeron Inc., Houma, LA.

Blum, Louis. Untitled typescript. Louisiana State Library, Baton Rouge, LA.

Cheramie, P. "Bertoul Cheramie: Louisiana Seafood Pioneer." Unpublished term paper, April 1988. Document in the authors' possession.

Corporate Charters, Louisiana State Archives, Baton Rouge, LA.

Curole, Hector. "The Shrimp Canning Plant." Typescript. Copy in the authors' possession.

Dunbar, George, George H. Dunbar, and Francis B. Dunbar. Method of Preserving Shrimp and Other Shellfish. US Patent 178,916, issued June 20, 1876.

Fo, Yee. Processing of Preserving Shrimp. US Patent No. 310,811, filed July 2, 1884, and issued January 13, 1885.

Guidry, Velton. "Shrimping." Unpublished manuscript in the authors' possession.

Lapeyre, Fernand S., James M. Lapeyre III, and Emile M. Lapeyre. Machine for Peeling Shrimp. US Patent 2,537,355, filed December 9, 1947, and issued January 9, 1951.

Letter from the Louisiana Department of Wild Life and Fisheries, August 16, 1949. New Orleans, LA. Copy provided by the agency's New Iberia office.

Loose, Henry. "My Life Story." Typescript. Archives and Special Collections, Nicholls State University, Ellender Memorial Library, Thibodaux, LA.

Merrick, Wallace N. Shrimp Deheading Machine. US Patent 2,958,896, filed September 19, 1957, and issued November 8, 1960.

NOAA. "Shrimp Fishery of the Gulf of Mexico, Plan Approval and Proposed Regulations." *Federal Register* 45, no. 218 (1980): 74178–308.

Wing, C. B. Untitled typescript. 5 pp. Archives and Special Collections, Nicholls State University, Ellender Memorial Library, Thibodaux, LA.

Books

Berquin-Duvallon. *Vue de la colonie espagnole du Mississipi, ou des provinces de Louisiane et Floride Occidentale, en l'année 1802.* Paris: Imprimerie Expéditive, 1803.

Canners Directory and Lists of Members of the Canning Machinery and Supplies Association and the National Canned Foods and Dried Fruit Brokers Association. Washington, DC: National Canners Association, 1917.

Cobb, John N. *The Canning of Fishery Products.* Seattle: Miller Freeman, 1919.

Crocker-Langley San Francisco City Directory. San Francisco: R. L. Post and Company, 1929.

Davis, Jack E. *The Gulf: The making of an American sea.* Liveright Publishing, 2017.

Descourtilz, Michel Etienne. *Voyage d'un naturaliste et ses observations.* 2 vols. Paris: Dufart, Père, 1809.

Dictionnaire raisonné universel d'histoire naturelle. 2 vols. Paris: Jean-Marie Bruyset, Père et Fils, 1776.

Dumont de Montigny. *Mémoires historiques sur la Louisiane.* 2 vols. Edited by Jean-Baptiste Le Mascrier. Paris: Claude J. B. Bauche, 1753.

Dunbar, George W. *Original Dunbar Shrimp.* New Orleans: Dunbar-Dukate Company, 1915.

Edwards' Annual Directory of New Orleans' Businesses. [Tucson?]: W. C. Cox and Company, 1873.

Everything for Canning for Homes, Farms, Clubs and Factories. LaGrange, IL: National Canning Supply Co., n.d.

Falls, Rose C. *Cheniere Caminada, or The Wind of Death: The Story of the Storm in Louisiana.* New Orleans: Hopkins' Printing Office, 1893.

Fauconnet, Charles Prosper. *Ruined by This Miserable War: The Dispatches of Charles Prosper Fauconnet, a French Diplomat in New Orleans, 1863–1868.* Edited by Carl A. Brasseaux and Katherine Carmines Mooney. Translated by Carl A. Brasseaux. Knoxville: University of Tennessee Press, 2012.

Federal Writers' Project, Works Progress Administration. *New Orleans City Guide: American Guide Series.* Boston: Houghton Mifflin Company, 1938.

Field, Martha Reinhard Smallwood, ed. *Louisiana Voyages: The Travel Writings of Catharine Cole.* Jackson: University Press of Mississippi, 2006.

Gorrell, Frank E. *Canners Directory and Lists of Members of the Canning Machinery and Supplies Association and the National Canned Foods and Dried Fruit Brokers Association.* Washington, DC: National Canners Association, 1922.

Gross, George B. *Shrimp Industry of Central America, Caribbean Sea, and Northern South America.* [Washington, DC?]: United States Department of Commerce, NOAA, National Marine Fisheries Service, 1973.

Guilbert, Aristide. *Histoire des villes de France.* Paris: Furne et Compagnie, Perrotin, et H. Fournier, 1845.

Hallowell, Christopher. *People of the Bayou: Cajun Life in Lost America.* New York: E. P. Dutton, 1979.

Hicks, John. "Unrest in California." In *The American Nation: A History of the United States from 1865 to the Present.* New York: Houghton Mifflin Company, 1937.

Hobbs, A. B. *Sixth Biennial Report of the Factory Inspection to Mississippi State Board of Health.* Jackson: Mississippi State Board of Health, 1921.

Hooton, Charles. *St. Louis' Isle, or Texiana: With Additional Observations Made in the United States and Canada.* London: Simmonds and Ward, 1847.

Illustrated Guide and Sketch Book to New Orleans and Environs. New York: W. H. Coleman, 1885.

Jackson, Charles Tenney. *The Fountain of Youth.* New York: Outing Publishing Company, 1914.

Kammer, Edward Joseph. *A Socio-Economic Survey of the Marshdwellers of Four Southeastern Louisiana Parishes.* Washington, DC: Catholic University of America Press, 1941.

Kane, Harnett T. *The Bayous of Louisiana.* New York: William Morrow and Company, 1943.

Kane, Harnett T. *Deep Delta Country.* New York: Duell, Sloan and Pearce, 1944.

Kimball, Charles P. *The San Francisco City Directory.* San Francisco: Journal of Commerce Press, 1850.

Knight, Edward Frederick. *Sailing.* London: G. Bell and Sons, 1889.

Landreth, John. *The Journal of John Landreth Surveyor.* Edited by Milton B. Newton Jr. Baton Rouge, LA: Department of Geography and Anthropology, Louisiana State University, 1985.

Le Page du Pratz, Antoine Simon. *Histoire de la Louisiane.* 2 vols. Paris: De Bure, Veuve Delaguette, et Lambert, 1757.

Mémoires sur la Louisiane et la Nouvelle-Orléans. Paris: Ballard, 1904.

Morrison, Andrew. *Industries of New Orleans.* New Orleans: J. M. Elstner and Company, 1885.

Morrison, Andrew. *New Orleans and the New South.* [New Orleans?]: Metropolitan Publishing Company Guide, 1888.

National Canners Association. *Canners Directory and List of Members of the Canning Machinery and Supplies Association and the National Food Brokers Association, Washington.* Washington, DC: National Canners Association, 1922.

National Canners Association. *The Canning Industry: Its History, Importance, Organization, Methods, and the Public Service Values of Its Products.* Washington, DC: National Canners Association, 1963.

The New Orleans Book. New Orleans: Orleans Parish School Board, 1919.

Osborne, John. *Guide to the West Indies, Madeira, Mexico, New Orleans, Northern South-America, &c.* London: Royal Mail Steam Packet Company, 1845.

Putney, Bryant. "Problems of Tin and Rubber Supply." In *Editorial Research Reports 1940* 2:129–44. Washington, DC: CQ Press, 1940.

Ramsey, Carolyn. *Cajuns on the Bayous.* New York: Hastings House Publishers, 1957.

Réclus Elisée. *The Earth and Its Inhabitants, North America.* 3 vols. New York: D. Appleton and Company, 1893.

Robson, John B. *Louisiana's Natural Resources: Their Use and Conservation.* Morristown, NJ: Silver Burdett Company, 1966.

Rudloe, Jack, and Anne Rudloe. *Shrimp: The endless quest for pink gold.* FT Press, 2009.

Smith, T. Lynn. *The Population of Louisiana: Its Composition and Changes,* Bulletin 293. Baton Rouge: Louisiana Agricultural Experiment Station, 1937.

Soards' New Orleans City Directory for 1895. Vol. 22. New Orleans: L. Soards, 1896.

Soards' New Orleans City Directory for 1915. Vol. 43. New Orleans: Soards Directory Company, Limited, 1915.

Soards' New Orleans City Directory for 1935. New Orleans: Soards Directory Company, Limited. 1935.

Stephens, Deanne Love. *The Mississippi Gulf Coast Seafood Industry: A People's History.* Univ. Press of Mississippi, 2021.

Sweetser, Moses Foster. *King's Handbook of the United States.* London: Osgood McIlvaine, 1891.

United States Bureau of the Census, Department of Commerce. *Compendium of the Seventh Census: 1850.* Washington, DC: Government Printing Office, 1854.

Journals and Magazines

Abbott, Edith. "A Study of the Early History of Child Labor in America." *American Journal of Sociology* 14 (1908): 15–37.

Adkins, Gerald. "Shrimp with a Chinese Flavor." *Louisiana Conservationist* 25, nos. 7–8 (1973): 20–25.

"Advantages of Wooden Boxes." *Barrel and Box* 24, no. 2 (1915): 5.

"Advertisement." *Louisiana Conservation Review* 1, no. 6 (1931): 144, 147.

"Air Lines Carry Louisiana Seafood." *Louisiana Conservationist* 3, no. 1 (1945): 1.

"Among the Fish Canners." *The Canner* 44 (1919): 55.

Anchor Cap and Closure Corporation. "Packing a De Luxe Grade Shrimp." *Canning Age* 7, no. 7 (1926): 559–63.

Anderson, William Wyatt, et al. "The Shrimp Fishery of the Southern United States." *Commercial Fisheries Review* 11 (February 1949): 1–17.

Antunovich, John. "Regulations Assure Shrimp Industry Future." *Louisiana Conservationist* 4, no. 6 (1952): 21–22.

Armentrout-Ma, L. Eve. "The Chinese in California's Fishing Industry, 1850–1941." *California History* 60, no. 2 (1981): 152–57.

Barde, Robert, and Gustavo J. Bobonis. "Detention at Angel Island: First Empirical Evidence." *Social Science History* 30, no. 1 (2006): 103–36.

"Bird's-Eye Survey by Parishes of Louisiana Fishing Conditions." *Louisiana Conservation Review* 8, no. 3 (1939): 12.

"Blessed Are the Shrimp." *Louisiana Conservationist* 1, no. 2 (1948): 6–7, 24.

Brown, Martin, and Peter Philips. "Craft Labor and Mechanization in Nineteenth-Century Canning." *Journal of Economic History* 46, no. 3 (1986): 743–56.

Brown, M. J. "Broad Aspects of Louisiana's Wild Life Restoration Program." *Louisiana Conservation Review* 10, no. 2 (1941): 6–12.

Bullis, Harvey R., and Hilton Floyd. "Double-Rig Twin Shrimp-Trawling Gear Used in Gulf of Mexico." *Marine Fisheries Review*, 28 no. 34 (1976): 8–12.

"Building for the Future." *Jefferson Parish Yearly Review* (1946): 15, 17.

Busch, Jane. "An Introduction to the Tin Can." *Historical Archaeology* 15, no. 1 (1981): 95–104.

Cameron, E. J. "Canning Technology." *Industrial and Engineering Chemistry* 35, no. 1 (1943): 38–42.

Cameron, E. J., and C. C. Williams. "Procedures in Shrimp Canning that Will Eliminate Spoilage." *Canning Age* 15, no. 10 (1934): 443–45.

Campbell, Carlos. "Commercial Canning. What Does the Future Hold?" *Journal of Marketing* 26, no. 2 (1962): 44–47.

"Canning Machinery and Supplies Exhibit." *Canning Age* (February 1922): 28–46.

"Cans, Shipment for Fishery Products, January–March 1954." *Commercial Fisheries Review* 16, no. 7 (1954): 24.

Carlson, Carl B. "Increasing the Spread of Shrimp Trawls." *Commercial Fisheries Review* 14, no. 7 (1952): 13–15.

Chesney, Edward J., et al. "Louisiana Estuarine and Coastal Fisheries and Habitats: Perspectives from a Fish's Eye View." *Ecological Applications* 10 (2000): 350–66.

Chinn, Thomas W. "The Chinese in California." *California History* 57, no. 1 (1978): 2–7.

Clay, Cassius, L. "The Louisiana Seafood Industry." *Louisiana Conservation Review* 7, no. 3 (1938): 45–47.

Clifford, D. M. "Marketing and Utilization of Shrimp in the United States." *Proceedings of the Indo-Pacific Fisheries Council, 6th Session.* (1955): Section III, 438–43.

"Contract Awarded for New Navigation Lock at Empire." *Louisiana Conservationist* 3, no. 1 (1945): 1, 8.

Cunningham, Glenn. "The Tin Can Industry in California." *Yearbook of the Association of Pacific Coast Geographers* 15 (1953): 11–16.

Daniels, Rodger. "No Lamps Were Lit for Them: Angel Island and the Historiography of Asian American Immigration." *Journal of American Ethnic History* 17 (Fall 1997): 3–18.

Dassow, John A. "Freezing Gulf of Mexico Shrimp at Sea." *Commercial Fisheries Review* 16, no. 7 (1954): 1–9.

Dauenhauer, John B., Jr. "Louisiana Fisheries Benefited by Newly Created Scientific Bureau." *Louisiana Conservation Review* 4, no. 4 (1930): 20–21.

Dauenhauer, John B., Jr. "Shrimp: An Important Industry of Jefferson Parish." *Jefferson Parish Yearly Review* (1938): 109–31.

"A Day with a Shrimper." *Rural Louisiana* no. 2 (March 1954).

Dechter, Aimée R., and Glen H. Elder Jr. "World War II Mobilization in Men's Work Lives: Continuity or Disruption of the Middle Class?" *American Journal of Sociology* 110, no. 3 (2004): 761–93.

Denham, S. C. "Fisheries Review, Gulf States, 1947." *Commercial Fisheries Review* 10, no. 7 (1948): 1–8.

Denham, S. C. "Gulf Coast Shrimp Fisheries, January–June, 1948." *Commercial Fisheries Review* 10, no. 10 (1948): 11–18.

Denham, S. C. "Skiffs Used for Shrimp Fishing in Inside Waters of Gulf of Mexico." *Commercial Fisheries Review* 17, no. 3 (1955): 39–41.

"Department Cracks Down on Violators in Drive to Protect Shrimp Industry." *Louisiana Game, Fur, and Fish* 5, no. 4 (1947): 7.

"Development of the [Shrimp] Industry." *Commercial Fisheries Review* 11 (February 1949): 2, 4–5, 9, 16–17.

"Don't Label 'Em 'Barataria Shrimp' Unless Caught in Barataria Bay." *The Canner* 49, no. 4 (1919): 53.

Dormon, Caroline. "Save, Oh, Save!" *Louisiana Conservation Review* 9, no. 4 (1940–1941): 19–26.

"Do You Know What Is Being Done in Washington to Safeguard the American Table?" *Ladies' Home Journal* (February 1920): 69.

"Draft Deferment in the [Fishing] Industry." *Fishery Market News* 4, no. 7 (1942): 2–5.

Dunn, Harry H. "Putting the Power Boat on the Gulf." *Power Boating* 22 (January 1920): 20, 82.

"85 Shrimp Haul a Record." *Louisiana Conservationist* 38, no. 3 (1986): 29.

Estaville, Lawrence E., Jr. "Changeless Cajuns: Nineteenth-Century Reality or Myth?" *Louisiana History* 28, no. 2 (1987): 117–40.

Ferleger, Louis. "The Problem of 'Labor' in the Post-Reconstruction Louisiana Sugar Industry." *Agricultural History* 72 (Spring 1998): 140–58.

Fiedler, R. H. "Fisheries of Louisiana." *Louisiana Conservation Review* 2, no. 4 (1932): 7–8, 26.

Firms Canning Shrimp, 1953. Statistical List (SL)-112, Revised April 1954. Washington, DC: Fish and Wildlife Service, 1955.

Fisher, Jos. L. "Crabs Solve Morgan City's Unemployment." *Louisiana Conservation Review* 2, no. 2 (1931): 18.

Fisk, Henry A. "The Fishermen of San Francisco Bay." *Railroad Trainmen's Journal* 23, no. 5 (1906): 394–400.

"Freezing Gulf-of-Mexico Shrimp at Sea." *Commercial Fisheries Review* 16 (July 1954): 1–2.

Gayarré, Charles Etienne. "A Louisiana Sugar Plantation of the Old Régime." *Harper's New Monthly Magazine* 74 (March 1887): 606–21.

Gowanloch, James Nelson. "Biological Natural Resources." *Louisiana Conservation Review* 6, no. 3 (1936): 63.

Gowanloch, James Nelson. "Give a Little Shrimp a Chance." *Louisiana Conservationist* 1, no. 1 (1948): 16–17.

Gowanloch, James Nelson. "Problems Retarding Development of South's Marine Assets." *Louisiana Game, Fur, and Fish* 6, no. 2 (1948): 3, 6.

Gramling, Bob, and Ronald Hagelman. "A Working Coast: People in the Louisiana Wetlands." Special issue, *Journal of Coastal Research* 44 (Spring 2005): 112–33.

Graves, Ralph A. "Louisiana, Land of Perpetual Romance." *National Geographic Magazine* 57, no. 4 (1930): 393–482.

Griffin, Wade L., and John P. Nichols. "An Analysis of Increasing Coasts to Gulf of Mexico Shrimp Vessel Owners, 1971–75." *Marine Fisheries Review* 28, no. 3 (1976): 8–12.

Groth, Philip. "The Human Ecology of Louisiana Shrimping." *Journal of Applied Sociology* 18, no. 1 (2001): 150–74.

Guillot, James P. "Statistical Summary of Natural Resources of Louisiana." *Louisiana Conservation Review* 5, no. 3 (1936): 6–7.

"Gulf States Marine Fisheries Commission." *Commercial Fisheries Review* 15 (December 1953): 24–25.

Gunter, G. "Should Shrimp and Game Fishes Become More or Less Abundant as Pressure Increases in the Trash Fish Fishery of the Gulf of Mexico?" *Louisiana Conservationist* 8, no. 4 (1956): 11, 14–15, 19.

Gunter, G. "Studies of the Destruction of Marine Fish by Shrimp Trawlers in Louisiana." *Louisiana Conservation Review* 5, no. 4 (1936): 45.

Hansen, Lawrence Douglas Taylor. "The Chinese Six Companies of San Francisco and the Smuggling of Chinese Immigrants across the U.S.-Mexico Border, 1882–1930." *Journal of the Southwest* 48, no. 1 (2006): 37–61.

Harris, Wendy Elizabeth, and A. Pickman. "Towards an Archaeology of the Hudson River Ice Harvesting Industry." *Northeast Historical Archaeology* 29, no. 1 (2000): 4.

Haskell, Winthrop A. "Gulf of Mexico Trawl Fishery for Industrial Species." *Commercial Fisheries Review* 23, no. 2 (1961): 1–6.

Hawkins, Robert A. "Advertising and the Hawaiian Pineapple Canning Industry, 1929–39." *Journal of Macromarketing* 29, no. 2 (2009): 172–92.

Hearn, Lafcadio. "Saint Malo, A Lacustrine Village in Louisiana." *Harper's Weekly* 27 (March 31, 1883): 89–102.

"Heavy Tax Put on Out-of-State Fishing Boats." *Louisiana Game, Fur, and Fish* 4, no. 9 (1946): 5.

Hebert, A. O. "Terrebonne's Oyster Industry: Rapid Growth of Industry During the Past Decade, Houma Oyster Enjoys Wide Reputation." Magazine edition, *Houma (LA) Courier*, September 13, 1906.

Hedgpeth, Joel. "San Francisco Bay." Edited by Harley J. Walker. *Coastal Resources*. Baton Rouge: School of Geoscience, Louisiana State University (1975): 25–30.

Hein, Stephen, and Paul Meier. "Skimmers: Their Development and Use in Coastal Louisiana." *Marine Fisheries Review* 47, no. 1 (1995): 17–24.

Higgins, Elmer. "A Story of the Shrimp Industry." *Scientific Monthly* 38, no. 5 (1934): 429–43.

Hine, Lewis Wickes. "Child Labor in Gulf Coast Canneries: Photographic Investigation Made February 1911." *Annals of the American Academy of Political and Social Science* 38 (February 1911): 118–22.

Holston, J. "Is Salt a Problem in Brine-Frozen Fish?" *Fishing Gazette* 72, no. 1 (1955): 62–63.

"An Ideal in Cannery Construction." *Canning Age* 3, no. 1 (1922): 1–11.

Idyll, Clarence P. "A New Fishery for Grooved Shrimp in Southern Florida." *Marine Fisheries Review* 12, no. 3 (1950): 10–16.

"Importance of Vast Louisiana Marine Resources Stressed in Congressional Fight for Tidelands." *Louisiana Game, Fur, and Fish* 6, no. 4 (1948): 5.

International Tin Research and Development Council. *Tin Plate and Tin Cans in the United States*. No. 4. 1936.

"Interstate Commerce Commission." *Commercial Fisheries Review* 11 (April 1949): 65.

"Irradiation Preservation." *Commercial Fisheries Review* 25 (January 1963): 37–38.

Jacobson, Phyllis L. "The Social Context of Franco-American Schooling in New England." *French Review* 57, no. 5 (1984): 641–56.

Jarvis, Norman D. "Curing and Canning of Fishery Products: A History." *Marine Fisheries Review* 50, no. 4 (1988): 180–85.

Jones, Edgar R. "The Empire Canning Industry." *Journal of the Royal Society of Arts* 78 (1960): 651–61.

Juhl, Rolf. "A Study of Vessel and Gear Usage in the Shrimp Fishery of the Southeastern United States." *Commercial Fisheries Review* 23, no. 8 (1961): 8.

Jurado, C. T. "The Power Work Boats of New Orleans." *Power Boating* 15, no. 4 (1916): 26–32.

Jurado, Ramon. "Along the Gulf Coast." *Power Boating* 18, no. 5 (1917): 68.

Jurado, Ramon. "With the Bread Winners at New Orleans." *Power Boating* (September 1917): 31–32.

Kenny, Jim. "Dancing the Shrimp." *Philippine Studies* 42, no. 3 (1994): 385–90.

Landes, Ruth. "A Visitor Gives Her Views on Louisiana's Bayou People." *Louisiana Conservationist* 1, no. 1 (1943): 4–6.

"A Large Importation of Labor." *Louisiana Planter and Sugar Manufacturer* (October 7, 1905): 230.

Larned, W. L. "The 'Face Value' of the Label." *Canning Age* (November 1922): 11–13.

Lassiter, Roy L., Jr. "Utilization of U.S. Otter-Trawl Shrimp Vessels in the Gulf of Mexico, 1959–1961." *Commercial Fisheries Review* 26, no. 2 (1964): 1–6.

"Latin America." *Commercial Fisheries Review* 30 (January 1968): 55–59.

Lee, Charles F., and F. Bruce Sanford. "Handling and Packing of Frozen Breaded Shrimp and Individually Frozen Peeled and Deveined Shrimp." *Commercial Fisheries Review* 25, no. 11 (1963): 1–10.

Lee, Erika. "Enforcing the Borders: Chinese Exclusion along the U.S. Borders with Canada and Mexico, 1882–1924." *Journal of American History* 89, no. 1 (2002): 54–86.

Lee, Erika. "The 'Yellow Peril' and Asian Exclusion in the Americas." *Pacific Historical Review* 76, no. 4 (2007): 537–62.

"Legislation in 1930." *Louisiana Conservation Review* 1, no. 6 (1931): 15.

"Licenses Show Increase in Shrimp Trawls." *Louisiana Conservationist* 1, no. 9 (1943): 5.

Lindner, M. J. "A Discussion of the Shrimp Trawl-Fish Problem." *Louisiana Conservation Review* 5, no. 4 (1936): 12–17, 51.

Lindsey, Ben B., and George Creel. "Children in Bondage: The Sacrifice of Golden Boys and Girls." *Good Housekeeping* (July 1913): 20–21.

"Louisiana." *Commercial Fisheries Review*, 16 (November 1954): 33–34.

"Louisiana Shrimp Production." *Louisiana Conservationist* 11, no. 9 (1959): 19.

"Louisiana's 1944 Seafood Output Shows Decreases." *Louisiana Conservationist* 3, no. 4 (1945): 4.

Love, T. D. "Survey of the Sun-Dried Shrimp Industry of the North-Central Gulf of Mexico." *Commercial Fisheries Review* 29, no. 4 (1967): 58–61.

Ma, Xiaohua. "The Sino-American Alliance during World War II and the Lifting of the Chinese Exclusion Acts." *American Studies International* 38 (June 2000): 39–61.

Major, Harlan. "The Delectable Shrimp: Once a Culinary Stepchild, Today a Gulf Coast Industry." *National Geographic* 86, no. 4 (1944): 501–12.

Marks, Brian. "The Political Economy of Household Commodity Production in the Louisiana Shrimp Fishery." *Journal of Agrarian Change* 12, nos. 2–3 (2012): 227–25.

Mayfield, M. A. "The Great Gulf Storm of 1893." *Nickell Magazine* 6 (1896): 76.

McConnell, B. "Child Labor and Youth Employment in the Nation's Third Year of War." *Social Service Review* 18, no. 4 (1944): 444–50.

McKelway, A. J. "Child Labor in the South." *Annals of the American Academy of Political and Social Science* 35, no. 1 (1910): 156–64.

Miller, George Blane. "Louisiana's Tidelands Controversy: The United States of America v. State of Louisiana Maritime Boundary Cases." *Louisiana History* 38, no. 2 (1997): 203–21.

"The Miracle on Your Table." *Good Housekeeping* 70, no. 2 (1920): 102.

Morgan, Robert. "Motor Boats Boost the Shrimp Industry." *Motor Boat* 18 (February 1921): 27–29.

Mukundan, M. "The Design and Construction of Flat Rectangular Otter Boards for Bottom Trawling: A Review." *Fishery Technology* 7, no. 1 (1970): 1–19.

Murphy, C. "Shrimp Cocktails by the Million." *Louisiana Conservationist* 8, no. 9 (1956): 11–12.

Myers, Hu B., and James Gowanloch. "Cooperative Shrimp Investigations Shed Important Light on South's Most Valuable Fishery." *Louisiana Conservation Review* 4, no. 1 (1934): 19–20.

"The Mysterious but Productive Shrimp." *Louisiana Conservation Review* 6 (Autumn 1936): 11–17.

"New Orleans, Forest Products Export Center: The Geography of the Timber Holdings Surround It." *Barrel and Box* 24, no. 11 (1919): 32–32a.

"New Shrimp Law Gives Big Boost to Shrimp Industry." *Louisiana Game, Fur, and Fish* 4, no. 8 (1946): 6, 8.

"New Snapper Bank Found by Accident." *Louisiana Conservationist* 4, nos. 11–12 (1952): 21.

Ogden, John T. "Counter Publicity." *Canning Age* 3, no. 8 (1922): 24.

Ong, Paul. "An Ethnic Trade: The Chinese Laundries in Early California." *Journal of Ethnic Studies* 8, no. 4 (1981): 95.

Orr, Arthur. "Shrimp Canning at Biloxi, Mississippi." *Canning Age* (1921): 36–39.

"Oyster Industry Gets Continued Use of Tin Cans." *Louisiana Conservationist* 1, no. 2 (1943): 4.

"Oyster Packers Seek Containers." *Louisiana Conservationist* 1, no. 1 (1942): 8.

Padgett, Herbert R. "Physical and Cultural Associations of the Louisiana Coast." *Annals of the Association of American Geographers* 59, no. 3 (1969): 481–93.

Padgett, Herbert R. "The Sea Fisheries of the Southern United States: Retrospect and Prospect." *Geographical Review* 53, no. 1 (1963): 22–39.

Padgett, Herbert R. "Some Physical and Biological Relationships to the Fisheries of the Louisiana Coast." *Annals of the Association of American Geographers* 56, no. 3 (1966): 423–39.

Pérez, Louis A., Jr. "Cuba and the United States: Origins and Antecedents of Relations, 1760s–1860s." *Cuban Studies* 21 (1991): 57–82.

Perret, William S., et al. "Louisiana's Brown Shrimp Monitoring and Management Program." *Proceedings of the Annual Conference, Southeast Association of Fish and Wildlife Agencies* 47 (1993): 502–10.

Petrick, Gabriella M. "An Ambivalent Diet: The Industrialization of Canning." *Magazine of History* 24, no. 3 (2010): 35–38.

Pillsbury, Richard. "The Production of Sun-Dried Shrimp in Louisiana." *Journal of Geography* 63 (1964): 254–58.

Postel, Mitchell. "A Lost Resource Shellfish in San Francisco Bay." *California History* 67, no. 1 (1988): 26–41.

Postgate, J. C. "History and Development of Swamp and Marsh Drilling Operations." *Oil and Gas Journal* 47, no. 48 (1949): 87.

Quinn, D. L. "Fibre Boxes as Shipping Containers." *Canning Age* (November 1922): 27–36.

Quinn, D. L. "Rediscovering the Packing Case." *Canning Age* (May 1922): 25–30.

Radcliff, Lewis. "Canned Fishery Products and By-Products South Atlantic Gulf States." *Louisiana Conservation Review* 1, no. 13 (1931): 29, 35.

Radcliffe, Lewis. "Fisheries Progress." *Louisiana Conservation Review* 12, no. 3 (1932): 4.

Rathjen, Warren F., and B. C. C. Hsu. "Sea Bob Fishery of the Guianas." *Commercial Fisheries Review* 32, no. 11 (1970): 38.

Reardon, C. M. "Chicago Receipts of Fishery Products, 1948." *Commercial Fisheries Review* 10, no. 12 (July 1949): 10–16.

Reilly, Joe. "Big Bayou Pigeon Makes It Pay." *Oil and Gas Journal* 54 (July 23, 1956): 136–39.

"Repeal of Chinese Exclusion Acts." *American Journal of International Law* 38, no. 1 (1944): 1–2.

"Revenue from Shrimp." *Louisiana Conservation Review* 1, no. 6 (1931): 74.

"A Review of Conditions and Trends of the Commercial Fisheries." *Fishery Market News* 1, no. 8 (August 1939): 1–19.

"Right Off the Ocean Floor [Advertisement]." *Saturday Evening Post* 190, no. 13 (September 29, 1917): 43.

Rinderle, P. J. "Louisiana Leads in Production of Shrimp." *Louisiana Conservation Review* 1 (November 1930): 11–13.

Robinson, H. R. "Handling Shrimp in the Canning Plant." *Southern Fisherman Yearbook* 125 (March 1954): 65–66.

Rock, James T. "Cans in the Countryside." *Historical Archaeology* 18, no. 2 (1984): 97–111.

Roedel, Philip M. "Shrimp '73: A Billion Dollar Business." *Marine Fisheries Review* 35, nos. 3–4 (1973): 1–5.

Ryo, Emily. "Through the Back Door: Applying Theories of Legal Compliance to Illegal Immigration during the Chinese Exclusion Era." *Law and Social Inquiry* 3, no. 1 (2006): 109–46.

Sampsell, Lorillard Dudley. "Pleasure Yachting 'Way Down South, Part 2." *Outing* 35, no. 5 (1900): 463–72.

Sanford, F. Bruce, et al. "Gulf States Shrimp Canning Industry." *Commercial Fisheries Review* 25, no. 2 (1963): 7–14.

Saxon, Lyle. "Their Faces Tell the Story." *Jefferson Parish Yearly Review* (1940): 32–58.

Scharf, J. Thomas. "The Farce of the Chinese Exclusion Laws." *North American Review* 166, no. 494 (1989): 85–97.

Schoonover, Frank E. "In the Haunts of Jean Lafitte." *Harper's Monthly Magazine* 124, no. 739 (1911): 80–81.

Schulz, Peter D., and Frank Lortie. "Archaeological Notes on a California Chinese Shrimp Boiler." *Historical Archaeology* 19, no. 1 (1985): 86–95.

Scofield, N. B. "Shrimp Fisheries of California." *California Fish and Game* 5, no. 1 (1919): 1–12.

"Shrimp." *Commercial Fisheries Review* 16, no. 7 (1954): 30–31.

"The Shrimp Catch." *Louisiana Conservation Review* 8, no. 1 (1939): 7.

"Shrimp Catch Increases as Prices Soar." *Louisiana Conservationist* 1, no. 8 (1943): 1–2.

"The Shrimp Fishery in San Francisco Bay." *Scientific American* 39 (December 7, 1878): 356.

"Shrimp King Killed in Wreck." *Louisiana Conservationist* 11, no. 4 (1959): 11.

"Shrimp Production for South Atlantic and Gulf States, 1952." *Commercial Fisheries Review* 15 (March 1953): 39–40.

"Shrimp Production Up." *Louisiana Conservationist* 5, no. 10 (1953): 11.

"Shrimp Rail-Freight Rates Reduced." *Commercial Fisheries Review* 17, no. 10 (1953): 70.

Simoneaux, N. E. "The Commercial Fisheries of Louisiana." *Louisiana Conservation Review* 4, no. 4 (1934): 22.

"Southern Canners' Association." *Canning Age* 3, no. 2 (1922): 45.

"Speak Your Piece." *Louisiana Conservationist* 8, no. 1 (1955): 20.

Springer, Stewart. "Expansion of Gulf of Mexico Shrimp Fishery, 1945–50." *Commercial Fisheries Review* 13, no. 9 (1951): 1–6.

Springer, Stewart, and Harvey R. Bullis. "Exploratory Shrimp Fishing in the Gulf of Mexico, 1950–51." *Commercial Fisheries Review* 14 (July 1952): 1–17.

Starr, Paul D. "Troubled Waters: Vietnamese Fisherfolk on America's Gulf Coast." *International Migration Review* 15, nos. 1–2 (1981): 226–38.

Still, William. "A Nickel a Bucket: A History of the Shrimping Industry in North Carolina." *American Neptune* 47, no. 3 (1987): 257–74.

Tettey, Ernest O., and Wade L. Griffin. "Investment in Gulf of Mexico Shrimp Vessels, 1965–77." *Marine Fisheries Review* 46, no. 2 (1984): 49–52.

Theriot, Jason P. "Cajun Country During World War II." *Louisiana History* 51, no. 2 (2010): 133–70.

Thomas, J. Stephen, et al. "Independence and Collective Actions: Reconsidering Union Activity among Commercial Fishermen in Mississippi." *Human Organization* 54, no. 2 (1995): 143–52.

Thompson, John. "The People of the Sacramento Delta. Golden Notes." *Sacramento County Historical Society* 28, nos. 3–4 (1982): 1–45.

Toledano, W. R. "Jefferson Builds." *Jefferson Parish Yearly Review* (1940): 5–6.

Trudgen, B. "The Naphtha Launch: The Forgotten Boats that Spanned the Gap Between Steam and Gasoline-Powered Vessels." *The Ensign* 96, no. 6 (2008): 18–22.

Tulian, E. A. "The Present Status of the Louisiana Shrimp Industry." *Transaction of the American Fisheries Society* 53 (1923): 110–21.

"Twenty Years for Fishery Market News." *Louisiana Conservationist* 12, no. 1 (1960): 16.

Underhill, Ruth M. "Indians of the Louisiana Bayous." *Indians at Work* 6 (January 1939): 5–8.

"United States: Repeal of Chinese Exclusion Acts." *American Journal of International Law* 38, no. 1 (1944): 1–2.

"U.S. Adopts 12-Mile Fishery Zone." *Commercial Fisheries Review* 29, no. 1 (January 1967): 5.

"Use Floating Cannery in Alaska Trade." *Marine Review* 52, no. 1 (1922): 349.

"U.S. Pack of Canned Shrimp, 1950." *Commercial Fisheries Review* 13, no. 5 (1951): 42–43.

"U.S. Pack of Canned Shrimp, 1948." *Commercial Fisheries Review* 11, no. 5 (1949): 30–31.

"Value and Take of Fresh and Salt Water Fisheries of Louisiana." *Louisiana Conservationist* 1, no. 6 (1943): 3.

"Value and Take of Fresh and Salt Water Fisheries of Louisiana." *Louisiana Conservationist* 2, no. 6 (1944): 4.

"Value and Take of Fresh and Salt Water Fisheries of Louisiana." *Louisiana Conservationist* 3, no. 9 (1945): 7.

Viosca, Percy, Jr. "Is the Sea Exhaustible?" *Louisiana Conservationist* 10, no. 12 (1958): 6–7.

Viosca, Percy, Jr. "New Research Lab." *Louisiana Conservationist* 10, nos. 7–8 (1958): 17–18.

Viosca, Percy, Jr. "Observations on the Life History and Habits of the Lake Shrimp." *Louisiana Conservationist* 5, no. 4 (1953): 2–5, 18.

Viosca, Percy, Jr. "Oyster, Water Bottoms and Seafood Division." *Seventh Biennial Report of the Louisiana Department of Wild Life and Fisheries,*

1956–1957. New Orleans: Department of Wild Life and Fisheries, 1958: 96–106.

Viosca, Percy, Jr. "Shrimp Comeback." *Louisiana Conservationist* 11, no. 2 (1959): 2–4.

Viosca, Percy, Jr. "Shrimp Potpourri." *Louisiana Conservationist* 9, no. 7 (1959): 19–22, 29.

"Voters to Decide on November 7th Future Destiny of Conservation Department." *Louisiana Conservationist* 2, no. 11 (1944): 1.

Waldo, E. "From Cattle to Shrimp Boats." *Louisiana Conservationist* 17, nos. 7–8 (1965): 18–21.

Walsh, Robert F. "Chinese and the Fisheries." *Californian Illustrated Magazine* 4, no. 6 (1893): 835–36.

Washburn, M. "Federation for Wildlife Commission." *Louisiana Conservationist* 4, no. 6 (1952): 6–8.

"Water Pollution." *Louisiana Conservation Review* 1, no. 6 (1931): 74.

"W. B. Morgan's New Connection." *Barrel and Box* 24, no. 4 (1919): 44.

Weymouth, F. W. "Shrimp Investigation on the South Atlantic and Gulf Coasts." *Louisiana Conservation Review* 1, no. 13 (1931): 11–13.

Whitaker, Donald R. "The U.S. Shrimp Industry: Past Trends and Prospects for the 1970's." *Marine Fisheries Review* 35, nos. 5–6 (1973): 23–30.

"Who Eats Shrimp?" *Marine Fisheries Review* 35, nos. 3–4 (1973): 3–5.

Williams, Neil. "Drilling for Oil in the Out of the Way Marshlands of Terrebonne Parish, Louisiana." *Oil and Gas Journal* 28 (December 1929): 40–41.

Winston, James E. "Notes on the Economic History of New Orleans, 1803–1836." *Mississippi Valley Historical Review* 11, no. 2 (1924): 200–226.

"World's Largest Shrimp Cannery." *Louisiana Conservation Review* 7/8 (Spring 1938): 21–24.

Newspapers

"Abbeville To Be Headquarters for Shrimping Fleet in Gulf." *Abbeville (LA) Meridional*, January 13, 1940.

"About 75 of New Iberia's Leading Business Men Sunday Made a Special Trip Over the Proposed New Iberia-To-Gulf Highway." *Morgan City (LA) Daily Review*, September 24, 1917.

"About 200 Bohemians Employed at the Pelican Lake Oyster Packing Plant in Houma Returned to Baltimore. *Colfax (LA) Chronicle*, May 9, 1908.

"A. F. Roberts & Co. [Advertisement]." *Windham County Performer* (Brattleboro, VT), February 21, 1902.

"Agents Fired Upon in Raid on Opium Den in Marsh." *New Orleans Times-Picayune*, April 5, 1934.

"Agitation for Immigration of Coolies Stirs Western Labor Men to Action." *Labor World* (Duluth and Superior, MN), July 8, 1905.

"A. J. Rapp Wholesale and Retail Dealer and Shipper of All Kinds, Including Shrimp." *St. Tammany Farmer* (Covington, LA), July 28, 1900.

"Alexander Freidenrich Co. [Advertisement]." *Idaho County Free Press* (Grangeville, ID Territory), February 25, 1909.

"All Quiet at Lake Borgne Between the Chinese and Spanish." *New Orleans Daily Crescent*, July 17, 1860.

"All Races Mix Freely in Louisiana Shrimperies." *New York Sun*, August 30, 1903.

"A. M. & C. W. West's [Advertisement]." *Savannah Morning News*, January 9, 1886.

"American Can Company to Erect Great Industrial Establishment, Attracted by the Growth of the Oyster Trade Here." *New Orleans Times-Picayune*, July 15, 1905.

"A. Moll Grocer Co. [Advertisement]." *St. Louis Republic*, August 17, 1900.

"The Anti-Chinese Bill." *Ouachita Telegraph* (Monroe, LA), February 14, 1879.

"A. P. Nelson & Co. Grocers [Advertisements for Shrimps]." *Canyon City (CO) Record*, July 26, 1900.

"Arrival of Chinese." *Knoxville Weekly Chronicle*, July 20, 1870, 6.

"As a Result of Bounteous Supply, the Shrimp Canning Industry Was Early Developed in Louisiana." *Argonaut* (San Francisco), July 18, 1914.

"Assembly Passes Bill to Bar Shrimp Drying." *San Francisco Morning Call*, March 21, 1911.

"At Manila Village." *New Orleans Daily Picayune*, September 24, 1909.

"Bauer and Weill Groceries [Advertisement]." *Louisiana Democrat* (Alexandria, LA), 1888.

"B. F. Nicholas Company [Advertisement]." *Colfax (WA) Gazette*, August 16, 1907.

"Big Factory as Tribute to the Oyster Industry." *New Orleans Times-Picayune*, July 15, 1905.

"Big Shrimp Catch Clogs Canneries: Meeting Called at Biloxi to Limit Haul—Prices Still High." *New Orleans Times-Picayune*, September 19, 1921.

"Big Tin Can Factory Here to Employ New Process." *New Orleans Daily Picayune*, November 17, 1905.

"Biloxi." *New Orleans Daily Picayune*, October 29, 1910.

"Blue Point Fish and Oyster Co. [Advertisement]." *El Paso Herald*, February 25, 1918.

"Boats in Marsh Looking for Storm Survivors." *Biloxi Daily Herald*, September 29, 1917.

Branan, Will A. "The Dual Life of Chinatowns." *New Orleans Daily Picayune*, August 14, 1910.

"Buxton's [Advertisement]." *Arizona Republican* (Phoenix), November 18, 1901.

"Canned Food." *Greenville (MS) Times*, August 9, 1884.

"Canned Foods Are a Danger: People Who Eat Them Are in Peril of Poisoning by Metals." *Washington Evening Star*, September 2, 1893.

"Canned Shrimp and Oyster May Bring Millions to the State." *St. Landry Democrat* (Opelousas, LA), March 15, 1890.

"Canneries Closed When Boats Held Up." *New Orleans Times-Picayune*, August 27, 1915.

"The Canning Business in New Orleans." *New Orleans Daily Picayune*, November 25, 1877.

Carmichael, Joe. 1954. "Let's Go Visiting Manila Village: Town of Wet Stilts and Dried Shrimp." *New Orleans Times-Picayune*, November 21, 1954.

"Celestial Gotham." *Lafayette (LA) Gazette*, May 6, 1893.

"Chas. H. Kelly [Advertisement]." *Carson City Morning Appeal*, May 24, 1889.

"Chas. Lehman and Co., Salad Days [Advertisement]." *Fergus County Democrat* (Lewiston, MT), August 18, 1908.

"Cheniere Caminada Hotel Open." *Thibodaux (LA) Minerva*, November 18, 1854.

"Chinatown Inspected by Immigration Agents and All Chinese Without Papers, Even Though Accidentally Lost, Will Be Deported." *New Orleans Times-Picayune*, December 15, 1904.

"Chinese Business Woman." *Washington Morning Times*, February 2, 1896.

"Chinese Community Hub Shifting to Jeff[erson Parish]." *New Orleans Times-Picayune*, December 6, 1981.

"Chinese Devastating the Bay: Our Stock of Fish Being Exhausted to Supply China." *San Francisco Call*, June 27, 1892.

"Chinese Devastating the Bay: They Are Killing All the Young Fish in the Bay." *San Francisco Call*, June 29, 1892.

"A Chinese Emigration Agent Has Had Contracts for the Delivery of 20,000 Chinese Laborers at New Orleans for Next Year's Crops." *Natchitoches (LA) Semi-Weekly Times*, October 10, 1866.

"Chinese Emigration Company [Advertisement]." *New Orleans Republican*, January 21, 1871.

"Chinese Enter Fish Bribes as 'Wasted Money.'" *San Francisco Morning Call*, February 25, 1911.

"Chinese Exclusion Convention Opens Fight in Defense of American Labor." *San Francisco Morning Call*, November 22, 1901.

"Chinese Exporting Shrimp from Barataria Bay." *Pascagoula (MS) Democrat-Star*, September 29, 1882.

"Chinese Fishermen Caught Red Handed, Crew of a 'Junk' Placed Under Arrest by Constable Creed of Sausalito for Using Prohibited Nets." *San Francisco Morning Call*, March 3, 1899.

"Chinese Immigration." *Opelousas (LA) Journal*, August 7, 1869.

"Chinese Immigration into Louisiana." *Planters' Banner* (Franklin, LA), February 9, 1870.

"Chinese Immigration into the United States." *New Orleans Daily Democrat*, August 31, 1879.

"Chinese Immigration Statistics." *New Orleans Republican*, November 9, 1870.

"Chinese in the National Census." *New Orleans Semi-Weekly Louisianan*, December 3, 1871.

"Chinese Junks at San Francisco." *Hopkinsville (KY) Kentuckian*, July 7, 1896.

"Chinese Junks in San Francisco Bay." *Weekly Thibodaux (LA) Sentinel*, September 5, 1895.

"Chinese Laborers are not Welcome in Louisiana." *New Orleans Daily Democrat*, March 10, 1880.

"Chinese Labor in Louisiana." *Planter's Banner* (Franklin, LA), September 21, 1870.

"A Chinese Laundry Is One of Donaldsonville's Latest Acquisitions." *Donaldsonville (LA) Chief*, February 24, 1883.

"Chinese Must Go!" *Donaldsonville (LA) Chief*, April 17, 1886.

"Chinese Not Allowed to Land at the Port of New Orleans." *South-Western* (Shreveport, LA), May 26, 1869.

"The Chinese Problems in California and Labor Issues." *New Orleans Daily Democrat*, April 5, 1879.

"Chinese Railroad Workers Arrive in New Orleans to Work in Texas." *South-Western* (Shreveport, LA), January 5, 1870.

"Chinese Ruining the Fishing in San Francisco Bay." *New Orleans Daily Picayune*, September 13, 1892.

"Chinese Shrimpers in Louisiana and the Orient Market." *New Orleans Daily Picayune*, January 1, 1909.

"Chinese Shrimpers: Odd Occupation Which Supports a California Colony." *Daily Arizona Silver Belt* (Globe, AZ), November 16, 1899.

"Chinese Shrimp Fishermen of Barataria Bay Shipped About $300,000 Worth of Shrimp to China." *St. Landry Clarion* (Opelousas, LA), August 14, 1909.

"Chinese Smuggler Arrested." *Lower Coast Gazette* (Pointe à la Hache, LA), November 27, 1909.

"Chinese Tong Troubles." *New Orleans Daily Picayune*, August 20, 1907.

"Chin Kum and Joe Toy Hand, Directors of the Chinese Shrimp Drying Industry at Grand Lake Are Leaving for a Trip to China." *New Orleans Daily Picayune*, December 11, 1890.

"Citizens Rally to the Cry for Help from the Recent Storm." *New Orleans Daily Picayune*, October 6, 1893.

"City Fed by the World's Largest Motor Fleet." *Dearborn (MI) Dearborn Independent*, October 23, 1920.

Cole, Catherine. "An Island Outing: The Rich Fisheries of the Barataria Country." *New Orleans Daily Picayune*, September 25, 1892.

"Community Life of a Chinese Shrimp Fishers Village." *San Francisco Call*, November 7, 1897.

"A Company of Chinese Are Exporting Shrimp from Barataria Bay to China." *Donaldsonville (LA) Chief*, September 23, 1882.

"The Conservation Commission Visits a Chinese Shrimp Drying Platform at Manila Village and Bayou Du Fon [Defond]." *New Orleans Daily Picayune*, June 25, 1913.

"Cost of a Small Cannery." *Weekly Thibodaux (LA) Sentinel*, May 26, 1888.

"The Country a Sea of Corpses Below New Orleans." *Los Angeles Herald*, October 5, 1893.

"C. Tatum [Advertisement]." *Chicago Daily Tribune*, April 19, 1876.

"A Curious Colony: The Shrimpers Who Live Not Far from New Orleans Are a Mixed Lot." *Colfax (LA) Chronicle*, February 25, 1899.

"C. Wm. Ramsay [Advertisement]." *Alexandria (VA) Gazette and Virginia Advertiser*, September 12, 1890.

"Cyclone in the South: Its Destructive Path in Louisiana and Alabama." *Abbeville (SC) Press and Banner*, October 18, 1893.

"The Damage Along the Gulf Coast: A Picayune Man Makes a Trip from the Rigolets to Biloxi." *New Orleans Daily Picayune*, October 6, 1893.

"Daniel Dennett Wanted Chinese Laborers Because They Would Work for Eight Dollars Per Month." *New Orleans Republican*, August 8, 1872.

"Davis & Kelley [Advertisement]." *Cheyenne (WY) Daily Sun-Ledger*, April 7, 1900.

"Death List from Storm Still Grows, Many Towns Washed Away." *Anderson (SC) Intelligencer*, October 2, 1915.

"Developing the Oyster Trade: Movement of the Bayou Cook Oyster Company." *New Orleans Daily Picayune*, December 5, 1890.

"Died as Heroes: Pathetic Incidents of the Storm in the Bay of Barataria." *New York Evening World*, October 9, 1893.

"Dixie Oyster Company Will Build a Cannery in St. Bernard." *New Orleans Daily Picayune*, March 6, 1906.

"D. McKinnon [Advertisement]." *Madison (SD) Daily Leader*, August 28, 1899.

"Donaldsonville Ice Company, Ice and Cold Storage, Free Auto Truck Delivery to Any Part of the City." *Donaldsonville (LA) Chief*, August 19, 1922.

"Donaldsonville Ice Company Purest and Best Quality Ice [Advertisement]." *Donaldsonville (LA) Chief*, January 14, 1911.

"Doullut Canal Connects Oyster Bed East and West of the Mississippi River." *New Orleans Daily Picayune*, August 31, 1903.

"Down Among the Island of the Sea." *Weekly Thibodaux (LA) Sentinel*, June 19, 1880.

"Dried Shrimp Firm Seeks Asian Buyers." *New Orleans Times-Picayune*, November 2, 1986.

"Dried Shrimps at Bass' at 40 Cents Per Gallon [Advertisement]." *Attakapas Register* (Morgan City, LA), May 19, 1877.

"Dried Shrimp, Very Fine, at the Italian Store [Advertisement]." *Arizona Sentinel* (Yuma County, AZ), March 16, 1878.

"Dunbar-Dukate General Office Moved from Biloxi to New Orleans." *New Orleans Times-Picayune*, July 29, 1925.

"Dunbar-Dukate Gives Bonus." *Biloxi Daily Herald*, December 23, 1916.

"Dunbar-Dukate Oyster Factory Re-Opens Here Next Week, 150 Men and Women Will Be Wanted at Once. Vegetable Canning to Follow Close of Oysters." *Morgan City (LA) Daily Review*, January 4, 1918.

"Dunbar-Dukate Shipyard, Globe Engine for Sale." *Biloxi Daily Herald*, October 2, 1919.

"Dunbar, Lopez & Dukate [Advertisement]." *Herald* (New Orleans, LA), December 16, 1915.

"Dunbar Okra [Advertisement]." *New Orleans Times-Picayune*, August 22, 1925.

"Dunbar's Barataria Shrimp [Advertisement]." *San Francisco Morning Call*, May 25, 1896.

"E & B Jacobs, Groceries [Advertisement]." *South-Western* (Shreveport, LA), February 9, 1859.

"Eight Chinese Fishermen Were Catching, Curing and Shipping Fish from Their Base on Caillou Island. Three Hundred Barrels of Dried Product Were Shipped to San Francisco and Then Transshipped to China." *Rayne (LA) Signal*, February 5, 1887.

"1898 Pack Barataria Shrimps." *Seattle Post-Intelligencer*, April 22, 1898.

"Ellefsen's [Advertisement]." *Fargo (ND) Forum and Daily Republican*, March 8, 1906.

"The Empire Canal Will Cut a 50 Feet Wide Canal Leading into Bay Adam and a Modern Shrimp Factory Will Be Built." *Weekly Iberian* (New Iberia, LA), March 5, 1921.

"Enforce Chinese Rights." *Lower Coast Gazette* (Pointe à la Hache, LA), September 4 1909.

"E. N. Ratcliff Mercantile Co. [Advertisement]." *Daily Chieftain* (Vinita, Indian Territory), March 8, 1901.

"E. P. Adams Fresh Groceries [Advertisement]." *Pacific Commercial Advertiser* (Honolulu, HI), October 20, 1880; November 23, 1878.

"E. Strauss, Oysters, Shrimp, Rice Birds," [Advertisement]. *Daily Citizen* (Asheville, NC), September 10, 1899.

"Edw. E. Hallston [Advertisement]." *Morning Journal and Courier* (New Haven, CT), November 10, 1880.

"Exclusion Laws Wiping Out Chinatown." *Colfax (LA) Chronicle*, January 30, 1909.

"Excursion to Grand Isle." *New Orleans Republic*, July 16, 1872.

"Factory Owners Face Commission." *Biloxi Daily Herald*, December 19, 1908.

"Fair Prices in 1938." *Biloxi Daily Herald*, August 29, 1938.

"F. D. Ladd, Leading Cash Grocer [Advertisement]." *Daily Times* (Barre, VT), November 30, 1904.

"Federal Legislation Proposed to Limit the Number of Chinese Coming to the United States." *St. Landry Democrat* (Opelousas, LA), March 2, 1878.

"Ferro Gasoline Engines Available at D. Ohlmeyer [Advertisement]." *Donaldsonville (LA) Chief*, October 24, 1908.

Field, Flo. "Coy Shrimps Are Worth Untold Wealth to Louisiana." *New Orleans Times-Picayune*, November 1, 1914.

"Figs Wanted, Write Us, Barataria Canning Company [Advertisement]." *Pascagoula (MS) Democrat-Star*, August 9, 1901.

"Filipinos Settled in America About 1710." *Philippine-American Observer* (Stockton, CA), August 1943, 14.

"The Finish of the New Iberia Southern Canal, May 30th, 1911." *Weekly Iberian* (New Iberia, LA), July 29, 1911.

"The Fishing-Shrimping Season." *New Orleans Republic*, April 1, 1871.

"Fish Laws." *Rice Belt Journal* (Welsh, LA), February 6, 1914.

"Five Chinese from Canada Arrested on the Charge of Being in the Country in Violation of the Chinese Exclusion Law." *New York Sun*, April 19, 1903.

"Forty-Five Dead in Storm in the Barataria Section." *Sunday Gate City* (Keokuk, IA), October 3, 1915.

"400 Cases of Shrimp Exported from the Port of New Orleans." *New Orleans Daily Democrat*, May 7, 1879.

Franz, H. W. "Manila Village Is Subject of Official Survey." *New Orleans Item-Tribune*, March 14, 1937.

Frazer, Tom. "Brogans: Lafitte Girl's First Pair of Shoes Used for 'Dancing the Shrimp.'" *New Orleans Times-Picayune*, October 19, 1980.

"Fresh Arrivals . . . At the Teapot Grocery [Advertisement]." *Ocala (FL) Evening Star*, July 21, 1904.

"Fresh Barataria Shrimp [Advertisement]." *Rio de Janeiro Rio News*, April 11, 1899.

"Fresh Barataria Shrimps [Advertisement]." *San Francisco Pacific Commercial Advertiser*, November 23, 1878.

"Fresh Groceries Just Received from San Francisco and Europe [Advertisement]." *Hawaiian Gazette* (Honolulu, HI), December 3, 1879.

"Fresh Shrimp Daily [Advertisement]." *Biloxi (MS) Daily Herald*, August 15, 1922.

"The 'Frisco' Chinaman, the Open-Air, Cobbler, Sugar-Cane Vendor, Pork Butcher, and Pipe Mender." *Dallas Daily Herald*, November 11, 1887.

"Funeral of Strike Victim During a Labor Clash at a Violet Seafood Packing Plant." *New Orleans Times-Picayune*, August 28, 1939.

"Gas, Gasoline and Oil Engines available at Wilmot Machinery Company." *Donaldsonville (LA) Chief*, October 24, 1908.

Gateway, W. Boyd. "Most of World's Roads Still to Be Constructed." *New Orleans Times-Picayune*, December 9, 1928.

"Geo. C. Shaw & Co. [Advertisement]." *Portland Daily Press*, July 9, 1880.

"George Rettig, Just Received Dried and Canned Shrimp [Advertisement]." *Bayou Sara (LA) True Democrat*, December 12, 1914.

"G. G. Cornwell and Son [Advertisement]." *Washington Evening Star*, March 3, 1898.

"Give Us Shrimp." *Daily Herald* (Dallas, TX), February 22, 1880.

"Godfrey's Grocery [Advertisement]." *Ottawa (IL) Free Trader Journal*, May 18, 1917.

"Goldberg Bowen & Co. [Advertisement]." *San Francisco Call*, October 10, 1898.

"Golden Meadow Crowded for Fleet Blessing." *Lafourche Comet* (Thibodaux, LA), August 11, 1938.

"Good Things to Eat [Advertisement]." *Pullman (WA) Herald*, April 2, 1904.

"Government Sues American Can Co. Seeks Dissolution of $88,000,000 Corporation." *New York Times*, November 30, 1913.

"Grand Isle Hotel Open for the Season of 1872." *New Orleans Republican*, July 12, 1873.

"Grand Isle Sighs as World Begins Rapping at Door: Great Changes Expected to Follow Building of Highway." *New Orleans Times-Picayune*, July 19, 1931.

"The Great Storm." *Washington Bee*, September 30, 1893, 2.

"Great Tragedy at Mouth of Mississippi Where Storm Took Half Thousand Lives." *Sunday Gate City* (Keokuk, IA), October 3, 1915.

"Great Traveling Menagerie: Chinese Jugglers and Artist." *New Orleans Daily Crescent*, October 23, 1866.

"Grinager's Sunshine Grocery [Advertisement]." *Bemidji (MN) Daily Pioneer*, December 23, 1919.

"A Growing Colony of Philippine Emigrants in Louisiana." *Arizona Republican* (Phoenix, AZ), March 9, 1902.

"The Gulf Coast of Mississippi." *New Orleans Daily Picayune*, July 6, 1896.

"G. W. Dunbar & Son." *New Orleans Daily Picayune*, February 20, 1869.

"G. Wm. Ramsay [Advertisement]." *Alexandria (VA) Gazette and Virginia Advertiser*, January 22, 1886.

"Hanscom's [Advertisement]." *Evening Journal* (Wilmington, DE), May 9, 1899.

"Hard to Keep the Chinese Out of the United States." *St. Mary Banner* (Franklin, LA), December 12, 1914.

"Health Officers Find Conditions Shocking at Barataria Fisheries." *New Orleans Daily Picayune*, September 24, 1911.

"Hendrix Mercantile Co. [Advertisement]." *Roundup (MT) Record*, April 7, 1911.

"Herpolsheimer and Co. [Advertisement]." *Lincoln (NE) Courier*, November 19, 1898.

"Herrington and Tobin [Advertisement]." *North Platte (NE) Semi-Weekly Tribune*, July 20, 1900.

"H. H. Lee [Advertisement]." *Indianapolis Journal*, May 10, 1883.

"Highbinders, An Outgrowth of Chinese Life in San Francisco." *St. Martinville (LA) Weekly Messenger*, April 28, 1888.

"Highlights and Sidelights on the History of Our Commercial Fishing Industry." *Morgan City (LA) Daily Review*, Special Seafoods Edition, 1951.

"Highly Perishable Salt Water Fish Were Once Brought to Market Alive in 'Well' in Specially Constructed Fishing Boats." *New York Tribune Illustrated Supplement*, April 1, 1900.

"The Hitchins Bros. Co. [Advertisement]." *Frostburg (MD) Mining Journal*, February 14, 1891.

"Hotel Dacotah Café [Advertisement]." *Grand Forks (ND) Evening Times*, September 20, 1912.

"Houx's Big Cash Grocery and Meat Market [Advertisement]." *Rocky Ford (CO) Enterprise*, December 19, 1902.

"How Chinese Catch Shrimp." *Tionesta (PA) Forest Republican*, August 3, 1892.

"How Shrimp Are Caught in San Francisco Bay." *New York Home Journal*, December 26, 1878.

"How Shrimp Are Caught in San Francisco Bay." *Saline County Journal* (Salina, KS), January 2, 1879.

"H. R. Neblett [Advertisement]." *Forest City (AR) Times*, May 20, 1910.

"H. W. Hackett [Advertisement]." *Worcester (MA) Daily Spy*, September 2, 1888.

"Importers and Dealers in Fine Groceries [Advertisement]." *Washington Evening Star*, October 23, 1878.

"In Grand Isle Shrimp Are Selling for $5 a Box to Canning Factories and Drying Platforms." *Abbeville (LA) Progress,* October 30, 1920.

"The Independent Market [Advertisement]." *Rock Island (IL) Argus*, January 24, 1919.

"Inhabitants of the Storm Ravaged Region of Louisiana." *St. Landry Democrat* (Opelousas, LA), January 13, 1894.

"Jack's Store [Advertisement]." *Morgan City (LA) Daily Review*, March 5, 1917.

"Jaffa Grocery [Advertisement]." *Albuquerque Daily Citizen*, October 3, 1900.

"The Jake Biederman Grocery Co. [Advertisement]." *Paducah (KY) Sun*, December 20, 1901.

"Jas. Carroll & Co. [Advertisement]." *Daily Morning Alaskan* (Skagway, AK), February 17, 1900.

"Jasper and Levy [Advertisement]." *Seattle Post-Intelligencer*, September 6, 1900.

"Jeanerette Man Shoots Striking Longshoremen in Biloxi." *New Iberia (LA) Enterprise and Independent*, September 4, 1915.

"Jim Lee's Chinese Laundry [Advertisement]." *Rice Belt Journal* (Welsh, LA), August 3, 1906.

"John Chinaman Out West." *New York Sun*, January 25, 1891–October 16, 1893.

"John K. Renaud and Company, Family Groceries for Summer [Advertisement]." *New Orleans Democrat*, July 21, 1876.

"Johnston's Grocery [Advertisement]." *Washington Morning Times*, October 31, 1895.

"John T. Connor Co. [Advertisement]." *Barre (VT) Times*, January 1916.

"Jos. R. Peebles' Sons Groceries [Advertisement]." *Cincinnati Daily Star*, December 7, 1876.

"J. S. Budd and Sons [Advertisement]." *St. Landry Clarion* (Opelousas, LA), December 18, 1909.

"Jury Discharged; Unable to Agree on Violet Clash." *New Orleans Times-Picayune*, October 6, 1939.

"J. Waterman and Brothers [Advertisement]." *New Orleans Daily Crescent*, January 4, 1859.

"Kilgore and Tracy Grocery [Advertisement]." *Sacramento Record-Union*, November 29,1899.

"The Lake Borgne Murders." *New Orleans Daily Picayune*, October 7, 1860.

"Lake Shrimp: Why Conservation Should Operate in Their Behalf." *Weekly Iberian* (New Iberia, LA), July 29, 1911.

"Large Quantities of River Shrimp." *Rapides Gazette* (Alexandria, LA), April 6, 1872.

"The Large Shrimp Factory at Myrtle Grove Will Afford a New Market for Grand Isle Shrimp Industry." *New Orleans Times-Picayune*, March 10, 1920.

"The Largest Packets of Oysters and Shrimp in the World, Dunbar-Dukate Co. Bid A Welcome to Southern Wholesale Grocers." *New Orleans Times-Picayune*, May 7, 1919.

"La. Seafood Industry: Growing Up." *New Orleans Times-Picayune*, November 2, 1986.

"A Latent Source of Wealth." *New Orleans Times-Picayune*, June 25, 1881.

"Lead Poison Most Prevalent of All Industrial Diseases." *Labor World* (Duluth and Superior, MN), September 3, 1921.

"Lee Yat Chinese Pioneer in Shrimp Packing Head of Company, Passes Away." *New Orleans Times-Picayune*, May 29, 1925.

"A Legal Battle for Vast Oyster Tract." *New Orleans Times-Picayune*, June 16, 1905.

"L. F. Hughes Groceries [Advertisement]." *Dallas Daily Herald*, December 19, 1880.

Litwin, Sharon. "The Last of the Chinese Laundries." *New Orleans Times-Picayune*, August 1, 1982.

"L. M. Kinsey [Advertisement]." *Log Cabin Democrat* (Conway, AR), March 28, 1917.

"Lobsters, Salmon and Shrimp for Sale at L. W. Arthur & Co. [Advertisement]." *New Orleans Daily Crescent*, September 25, 1850.

"The Lopez-Dukate Canning Company at Morgan City is Nearly Complete." *Donaldsonville (LA) Chief*, August 31, 1907.

"Lopez, Dunbar [S]ons & Co. and Barataria Canning Company [Advertisement]." *Sea Coast Echo* (Bay St. Louis, MS), March 16, 1895.

"Louch, Augustine & Co. [Advertisement]." *Seattle Post-Intelligencer*, April 17, 1898.

"Louisiana Canning Co., Packers Shrimp, Pumpkins, Okra, etc. in Algiers, La. [Advertisement]." *New Orleans Herald*, December 13, 1917.

"Louisiana Exporting Shrimp to China." *Wood River Times* (Hailey, ID), September 18, 1882.

"Louisiana Legends: Dancing the Shrimp." *New Orleans Times-Picayune*, October 1, 1987.

"Louisiana Motorboats Hunt the Last Pirates in the World." *St. Landry Clarion* (Opelousas, LA), May 22, 1920.

"Louisiana's Chinese Population reported as 387." *New Iberia (LA) Enterprise*, August 20, 1921.

"Louisiana Shrimp as a Lenten Special [Advertisement.]" *Alpena (MI) Weekly Argus*, March 28, 1888.

"Louisiana's Shrimp Industry Profitable and Picturesque: Season Opens for Crustaceans Which Bring Nearly Two Million Dollars into State Yearly." *New Orleans Times-Picayune*, August 31, 1930.

"Lower Ship Landing." *New Orleans Daily Picayune*, January 24, 1878.

"Lucien Casso Is the Place to Go for River Shrimp [Advertisement]." *Donaldsonville (LA) Chief*, January 14, 1911.

"Magic Surf Pauses to Listen for Expected Shouts of Tourist Throng: Photo of Wharves and Shrimp Platform in Barataria Bay." *New Orleans Times-Picayune*, December 15, 1904.

"Maguire and Schneider [Advertisement]." *Lake Providence (LA) Banner-Democrat*, April 8, 1899.

Maiolo, John R. "Hard Times and a Nickel a Bucket." *Carteret County News Times* (Morehead City, NC), October 11, 1955.

"Many Filipinos in Louisiana." *Wichita (KS) Daily Eagle*, March 13, 1902.

"Many Lives Lost." *Mower County Transcript* (Lansing, MN), August 20, 1893.

"The Markets in General." *San Francisco Elevator*, January 17, 1868.

"Maryland Oyster War: Battle Between the Dredgers and a Virginia Police Schooner." *New Orleans Daily Picayune*, March 3, 1893.

"McBride, The Grocer. [Advertisement]." *Mower County Transcript* (Lansing, MN), May 9, 1888.

McCann, C. C. "Louisiana's Shrimp Industry Profitable and Picturesque." *New Orleans Times-Picayune*, August 31, 1930.

"Millions for Louisiana Good Roads." *New Iberia (LA) Enterprise*, September 2, 1916.

"Mississippi Cotton Planter's Association Has Open Correspondence with the Chinese Six Companies." *New Orleans Democrat*, July 8, 1879.

"The Mohican Co. [Advertisement]." *Norwich (CT) Bulletin*, June 30, 1909.

"M. P. Dowling [Advertisement]." *Press and Daily Dakota* (Yankton, SD), January 13, 1886.

"M. Quinn Wholesale and Retail Grocer [Advertisement]." *Kansas City Journal*, July 23, 1899.

"Murphy Canning Company, Jeanerette, Capital Stock." *Tensas Gazette* (St. Joseph, LA), July 7, 1905.

"M. W. Hansen Grocer [Advertisement]." *Grand Forks (ND) Daily Herald*, August 6, 1915.

"The Navigation Canal along the Rear of Grand Isle for Deep Water Purposes Will Be Begun in a Few Weeks." *Abbeville (LA) Progress*, October 30, 1920.

"The Neptune and Crescent Canning Factories Are Now in Operation." *Rice Belt Journal* (Welsh, LA), October 20, 1905.

"New Alhambra Restaurant Serves Shrimp [Advertisement]." *Ouachita Telegraph* (Monroe, LA), June 7, 1878.

"The New Chinese Bill." *Lake Charles (LA) Echo*, November 24, 1893.

"The New Dunbar and Dukate Shrimp Factory at Myrtle Grove Canal Is Canning Large Quantities of Deep Sea Shrimp, which Are Very Plentiful." *Le Meschacébé* (Lucy, LA), June 5, 1920.

"The New Dunbar Shrimp Factory on Grand Isle Is Being Overprovided with Large Sea Shrimp." *Rice Belt Journal* (Welsh, LA), September 18, 1920.

"New Iberia Ice and Bottling Works [Advertisement]." *Weekly Iberian* (New Iberia, LA), September 25, 1920.

"New Orleans." *Weekly Eastern Argus* (Portland, ME), December 2, 1803.

"New Orleans' Chinese Captains of Industry." *New Orleans Daily Picayune*, June 2, 1911.

"The New Shrimp Factory Belonging to Dunbar-Dukate, at Myrtle Grove, Began Operation Yesterday." *New Orleans Times-Picayune*, March 31, 1920.

"Next to Agriculture the Largest and Most Import Industry in Louisiana and Mississippi Is the Fisheries." *Rice Belt Journal* (Welsh, LA), September 13, 1919.

"Ninth Infantry to Leave for Islands." *San Francisco Morning Call*, March 16, 1910.

"No Flat-Irons in China: How the Chinaman Took to the Laundry Business." *St. Tammany Farmer* (Covington, LA), June 27, 1885.

"None of the Chinese Fishermen Who Are Dealers in Dried Shrimp Attended Yesterday's Meeting of the Board of Commissioners." *New Orleans Daily Picayune*, February 4, 1909.

"Notice: It Having Become Necessary for the Lessees to Repair the Barataria and Lafourche Canal No. 2." *New Orleans Democrat*, August 22, 1879.

"One Chinaman Held, Two Still on Trial, for Holding White Men in Peonage at Shrimp Camps." *New Orleans Daily Picayune*, September 7, 1911.

"100 Cases of Dunbar's Shrimp Shipped to New York." *New Orleans Daily Picayune*, April 1, 1883.

"150 Cases of Shrimp Exported from the Port of New Orleans." *New Orleans Democrat*, January 21, 1880.

"150 Chinese Revolt on a Plantation Near New Orleans." *Bossier Banner* (Bellevue, LA), July 30, 1870.

"Opelousas Railroad and a Shipment of Shrimp." *Thibodaux (LA) Minerva*, September 15, 1855.

"The Ostrica Oyster and Shrimp Factory Is Being Dismantled and Removed to Myrtle Grove by the Dunbar and Dukate Company." *New Orleans Times-Picayune*, November 28, 1919.

"Our Bay Fish Supply." *San Francisco Merchant* 11 (October 12, 1883–January 18, 1884): 240.

"Our Filipino Settlements." *Inter Mountain* (Butte, MT), November 8, 1899.

"Over 2,000 Chinese Arrived in San Francisco." *New Orleans Republican*, July 12, 1873.

"The Oyster and Shrimp Cannery at Morgan City Has Resumed Operations." *Lower Coast Gazette* (Pointe à la Hache, LA), January 29, 1910.

"Oyster Commission of Louisiana Survey of Oyster Leases." *New Orleans Daily Picayune*, April 22, 1909.

"Oyster Pirates Chased." *New Orleans Daily Picayune*, March 1, 1908.

"Oyster Pirates: The Commission's Patrol Yields Results in Court." *New Orleans Daily Picayune*, February 10, 1905.

"Oyster Saloon [Advertisement]." *Plaquemine (LA) Gazette and Sentinel*, December 15, 1860.

"Oyster Shipments have been Heavy During the Week." *Biloxi Daily Herald*, December 24, 1913.

"The Packing Plant at Violet, La." *New Orleans Times-Picayune*, August 9, 1927.

"Painte [Pointe] a la Hache." *Patriot* (Glenmore, LA), August 18, 1922.

"Parish Suffers Little Damage from Hurricane." *Abbeville (LA) Meridional*, September 27, 1941.

"Passing of the Shrimp Metropolis." *San Francisco Call*, May 17, 1908.

"People Arrive for Oyster Season." *Biloxi Daily Herald*, October 16, 1919.

"Peoples Oyster Depot [Advertisement]." *Painesville (OH) Journal*, September 31, 1871.

"The Peoples That Suffered in the Louisiana Storm." *New York Sun*, October 16, 1893.

"The Peoples Warehouse [Advertisement]." *East Oregonian* (Pendleton, OR), June 21, 1912.

Perry, James A. 1984. "Louisiana's Filipino Heritage." *New Orleans Times-Picayune*, February 19, 1984.

"Pirates: How They Operate at the San Bruno Camp." *San Francisco Call*, July 7, 1892.

"Placard in San Francisco Cigar Store: 'White Labor Only.'" *New Orleans Republican*, July 12, 1873.

"Pomeroy and Stewart [Advertisement]." *Harrisburg Star-Independent*, October 16, 1914.

Poole, Carleton F. "Catching of Shrimp Important Industry." *New Orleans Times-Picayune*, April 30, 1922.

Poole, Carleton F. "Forty-Five Dead in Storm in the Barataria Section: Twenty-Eight Lose Lives at Quong Sang's 'New' Platform." *New Orleans Times-Picayune*, October 2, 1915.

Poole, Carleton, F. "Gulf Coast Oyster Puffs Out His Chest: Big Canning Industry Never Really Employs Girl Shuckers Who Form Majority of Operative." *New Orleans Times-Picayune*, May 8, 1927.

"Poole's New Grocery. [Advertisement]." *Washington Evening Star*, April 30, 1894.

"Power Co. Holds Banquet at Montegut." *Houma (LA) Courier*, January 2, 1930.

"Practically All the Chinese in New Orleans Are Members of One of Three Powerful Native Societies: Have Administrative in 'Frisco and Branches All over the United States." *Opelousas (LA) Journal*, April 6, 1901.

"Premium Fruit Syrups Are Made by G. W. Dunbar & Son [Advertisement]." *New Orleans Daily Picayune*, June 11, 1869.

"The Price of Shrimp Is Simply Outrageous." *New Orleans Republican*, May 27, 1875.

"Probe in Shrimp Union Death to Be Resumed Today." *New Orleans Times-Picayune*, October 5, 1935.

"A Quiet Feud Has Existed for Years among the Spanish and Chinese Fishermen at Lake Borgne." *New Orleans Daily Crescent*, July 17, 1860.

"Quong Wo, Louisiana Businesswomen." *Sacramento Record-Union*, April 19, 1896.

Ragusin, Anthony V. "Everything's Changed But the Taste." *New Orleans Times-Picayune*, January 15, 1946.

"A Real New Women Fight from China: Romance and Reality in a Colony Down in the Gulf of Mexico." *Philadelphia Inquirer*, February 2, 1896.

"Receipts at the New Basin." *New Orleans Daily Picayune*, December 19, 1878.

"Recipe for a Shrimp Salad." *Tensas Gazette* (St. Joseph, LA), January 20, 1911.

"Recommendations of Game Commission Endorsed." *St. Tammany Farmer* (Covington, LA), May 14, 1910.

"Refusal to Admit Several Filipino Students to the Louisiana State University." *Turner County Herald* (Hurley, SD), September 13, 1906.

"Revival of the River's Traffic, Including the Movement of Shrimp." *New Orleans Daily Picayune*, September 1, 1913.

"R. Gordon, Pilot Town, Cushman Gasoline Motors in Stock. [Advertisement]." *Lower Coast Gazette* (Pointe à la Hache, LA), January 29, 1910.

"Richardson and Robbin's Groceries. [Advertisement]." *Lancaster (PA) Daily Intelligencer*, May 14, 1880.

"River Shrimp Eat Oakum in the Seams of Boats." *Bossier Banner* (Bellevue, LA), December 19, 1889.

"R. J. Smyth [Advertisement]." *Wheeling (WV) Register*, May 28, 1878.

"R. S. Ligon, Wholesale and Retail Grocer [Advertisement]. *Anderson (SC) Intelligencer*, January 1, 1891.

"Sail Makers [Advertisement]." *New Orleans Daily Picayune*, October 18, 1865.

"Saint & Co. [Advertisement]." *Albuquerque Morning Journal*, November 12, 1882.

"Salad Days, Barataria Shrimps [Advertisement]." *Fergus County Democrat* (Lewiston, MT), August 18, 1908.

"Salade aux Chevrettes a la Mayonnaise [Advertisement]." *New Iberia (LA) Enterprise*, September 2, 1916.

"Sanitary Cash Grocery. [Advertisement]." *Great Falls (MT) Daily Tribune*, January 25, 1919.

"S. B. Jones [Advertisement]." *Newberry (SC) Herald and News*, October 22, 1901.

"Schooner North America's Crew Jailed by Oyster Patrol in St. Bernard." *New Orleans Daily Picayune*, January 5, 1905.

"The Sea Coast Islands of Louisiana." *St. Landry Democrat* (Opelousas, LA), June 26, 1880.

"Seafood Big Industry in Terrebonne Parish." *Lafourche Comet* (Thibodaux, LA), February 20, 1941.

"The Sea Food Company Is Chartered." *New Orleans Herald*, July 31, 1913.

"Sea Food Industry Is Growing Rapidly Here." *Houma (LA) Courier*, September 5, 1925.

"Self-Defense Plea Offered in Killing Shrimper at Bayou Rigaud." *New Orleans Times-Picayune*, August 31, 1930.

"A Serious Charge: Chinese Arraigned for Illegal Fishing on the Pacific Coast." *Roanoke (VA) Times*, June 16, 1893.

"$771,842 Paid at M. [Morgan] City for Shrimp Catch." *Abbeville (LA) Meridional*, February 10, 1940.

"Shellfish Law to Move Dunbar-Dukate Plants into Louisiana." *New Orleans Times-Picayune*, May 13, 1926.

"Shellfish to Save Meat." *Cincinnatian: Official Organ of the Cincinnati Chamber of Commerce*, December 15, 1917.

"Shipment of Louisiana Sun-Dried Shrimp to Markets in the Philippine Islands, Is Being Planned by Citizens of Bayou Defon [Defond] and Bayou Barataria." *Assumption Pioneer* (Napoleonville, LA), August 1, 1931.

"Shrimp as Lenten Food [Advertisement]." *St. Landry Clarion* (Opelousas, LA), March 31, 1906.

"Shrimp Brand Used as Hog Feed." *Vernon Parish Democrat* (Leesville, LA), March 30, 1922.

"Shrimp Canners of South Atlantic and Gulf Coast Form Organization." *Biloxi Daily Herald*, October 18, 1921.

"Shrimp Canning Plant Planned in St. Tammany and Site Bought: New Louisiana Law Seen as Influencing Move of Company." *New Orleans Times-Picayune*, November 4, 1926.

"'Shrimp Dance' Passes Away: Use of Machinery Brings an End to Picturesque Custom." *Grand Forks (ND) Herald*, September 7, 1921.

"Shrimper to Build Platform to Compete with the Chinese in Barataria Bay." *New Orleans Daily Picayune*, August 23, 1912.

"Shrimp Fishing Is Resumed by Chinese, The Ancient Junks Are Not To Be Used Any More." *San Francisco Morning Call*, November 24, 1913.

"Shrimp Fishing: Work of the Chinese Fishermen Along the Pacific Coast." *Abilene (KS) Reflector*, June 3, 1886.

"Shrimp for Five Cents a Gallon." *Donaldsonville (LA) Chief*, September 1, 1877.

"Shrimp for Sale." *New Orleans Republican*, November 16, 1873.

"Shrimp Give St. Mary Parish Much Prosperity." *Lafourche Comet* (Thibodaux, LA), November 13, 1941.

"The Shrimp Industry in Barataria Bay and the Chinese Settlement at Cabanage." *New Orleans Daily Picayune*, November 2, 1883.

"The Shrimp Industry in Louisiana Waters." *New Orleans Daily Picayune*, November 25, 1900.

"The Shrimp Industry of Louisiana Employs More than 20,000 People." *Washington Evening Star*, November 12, 1921.

"Shrimp Nets for Sale [Advertisement]." *New Orleans Daily Crescent*, October 4, 1850.

"Shrimp Packers Agree to Abide by State Rules: Port of Entry at Biloxi Favored at Orleans Conference." *New Orleans Times-Picayune*, September 6, 1928.

"Shrimp Packers Fined as Users of Child Labor: Three Firms Plead Guilty in Federal Court." *New Orleans Times-Picayune*, October 1, 1940.

"The Shrimp Packing Season." *Lafourche Comet* (Thibodaux, LA), September 8, 1938.

"Shrimp Pie at a New Orleans' Restaurant [Advertisement]." *New Orleans Daily Crescent*, July 25, 1849.

"Shrimp Salad Served on the Rail-Ride Up the Valley of Minnesota." *St. Paul Daily Globe*, July 9, 1884.

"Shrimps Are Caught and Dried by the Fishermen and Sent in Barrels to Market." *New Orleans Daily Picayune*, August 27, 1844.

"Shrimps Condemned." *San Francisco Call*, October 26, 1899.

"Shrimp Seines for Sale [Advertisement]." *New Orleans Daily Crescent*, September 24, 1860.

"Shrimps, Oliver Finnie and Company [Advertisement]." *Memphis Public Ledger*, December 22, 1877.

"Shrimps. Only Two Places in the United States Possessing Shrimp Canning Factories Are New Orleans and Biloxi, Miss." *Lafayette (LA) Advertiser*, November 16, 1889.

"Shrimp Trawl Boats Has [*sic*] Also Taken the Place of the Old Sail Schooner." *New Orleans Times-Picayune*, January 1, 1946.

"Siegel-Cooper Co. [Advertisement]." *Jersey City (NJ) News*, July 12, 1897.

"Siegel-Cooper Co [Advertisement]." *New York Evening World*, April 2, 1901.

Simmons, T. C. "Terrebonne Parish Shrimp Drying Alive and Well." *New Orleans State-Times*, June 9, 1983.

"Sims Grocery [Advertisement]." *Daily Arizona Silver Belt* (Globe, AZ), December 20, 1908.

"Slidell Will Get a New Dunbar-Dukate Dual-Purpose Canning Plant." *New Orleans Times-Picayune*, June 25, 1927.

"Smith & McClatchie [Advertisement]." *Washburn (WI) Times*, December 25, 1902.

"Some Chinamen Happened to See That Shrimp Were Remarkably Large and Fine in Barataria Bay." *Jackson (MI), Weekly Citizen*, October 10, 1882.

"Something about Shrimps." *New York Sun*, October 17, 1883.

"Southern Scenes: Barataria Bay and Grand Isle—The Seaside Health Resorts of the Southern People." *Memphis Daily Appeal*, August 21, 1881.

"South's Oldest Colony Composed of Chinese and Other Oriental Shrimp Fishermen." *Winnsboro (SC) News and Herald*, January 14, 1899.

"State Revenue Filed Tax Liens Against E. A. Dunbar." *New Orleans Times-Picayune*, May 9, 1925.

"St. Bernard and Plaquemine Citizens Have Organized the Pointe a la Hache Oak River Canal and Development Company." *New Orleans Daily Picayune*, February 15, 1913.

"St. Bernard Parish Approved Railroad Spur the Dunbar-Dukate Factory at Violet." *New Orleans Times-Picayune*, September 6, 1928.

"Steamboats Still Big Trade Feeders." *New Orleans Daily Picayune*, September 1, 1911.

"Stevenson Bros. Co. [Advertisement]." *Imperial (CA) Press*, July 14, 1905.

"Stewart & Dawson [Advertisement]." *Wichita (KS) Daily Eagle*, December 24, 1899.

"The Store of Ike Davis [Advertisement]." *Las Vegas (NV) Optic*, April 11, 1911.

"Storms in the East." *Evening Bulletin* (Marysville, KY), August 30, 1893.

"Storm Sweeps Gulf Coast." *St. Tammany Farmer* (Covington, LA), September 15, 1909.

"Strike Situation Remains Same." *Biloxi Daily Herald*, September 13, 1917.

"Strong & Chase [Advertisement]." *Daily Weekly Alert* (Jamestown, ND), February 8, 1894.

"Stuart House [Advertisement]." *Raleigh State Chronicle*, May 6, 1886.

"Suit for Damages in Labor Shoot Dismissed." *New Orleans Times-Picayune*, June 11, 1941.

"The Teapot Grocery [Advertisement]." *Evening Star* (Ocala, FL), April 17, 1901.

"Terribly Stricken Grand Isle as It Was." *New Orleans Daily Picayune*, October 5, 1893.

"T. H. Cook & Co. [Advertisement]." *Lyon County Times* (Silver City, NV), August 20, 1890.

"There Is a Shrimp Famine in Baton Rouge." *Rice Belt Journal* (Welsh, LA), June 25, 1909.

"Things in Canned Goods." *Saint Paul Daily Globe*, November 27, 1887.

"Three New Shrimp Factories." *Assumption Pioneer* (Napoleonville, LA), March 8, 1924.

"Three Oyster Canneries to Be Built at the Rigolets." *New Orleans Daily Picayune*, November 17, 1905.

"Tons of Fish Wasted, Caucasians Are Aiding the Chinese Devastators." *San Francisco Call*, June 30, 1892.

"Trabing Brothers [Advertisement]." *Laramie (WY) Daily Sentinel*, November 24, 1877.

"Traffic in Washed Clothes, Men Who Buy Uncalled for Parcels at Chinese Laundries." *Opelousas (LA) Courier*, August 17, 1901.

"Traffic on Vermilion Is Growing." *Abbeville (LA) Meridional*, November 2, 1940.

"A Trip to the Upper and Suburban Portion of the City." *New Orleans Daily Crescent*, November 9, 1866.

"Truman Pacetti. [Advertisement]" *Abbeville (LA) Meridional*, June 15, 1940.

"200 Women to Pick Shrimp at Dunbar-Dukate Factory in Violet." *New Orleans Times-Picayune*, August 23, 1929.

"250 Bohemians from Baltimore Arrived at Houma." *Donaldsonville (LA) Chief*, October 24, 1908.

"Two New Canning Plants Will Be Erected in the New Orleans Industrial Zone This Fall by the Dunbar Dukate Company." *New Orleans Times-Picayune*, June 19, 1927.

"Union and Non-Union Longshoreman Trouble: Protected by the Louisiana Conservation Commission." *New Iberia (LA) Enterprise and Independent Observer*, September 4, 1915.

Van Pelt, Arthur W. "Fishing Fleets Ready to Ease Food Pinch: Young Men Gone to War, Oldsters and Boys Will Bring Catch Home." *New Orleans Times-Picayune*, May 16, 1943.

"Veto of the Anti-Chinese Bill." *St. Landry Democrat* (Opelousas, LA), April 29, 1882.

"Violet Plant Bought by Dunbar and Dukate." *New Orleans Times-Picayune*, August 9, 1927.

"Violet Seafood Worker's Association." *New Orleans Times-Picayune*, August 24, 1939.

"Wallace D. Coburn [Advertisement]." *Montanian* (Choteau, MT), June 9, 1899.

"Warner's [Advertisement]." *True Northern* (Paw Paw, MI), December 23, 1904.

"Waters Recede in New Orleans Coastal Section: Chen Tung Sing Drowned in Bayou Barataria." *New Orleans Times-Picayune*, August 8, 1940.

"W. B. Reed's Sons [Advertisement]." *Washington Evening Star*, October 23, 1878.

"Welsh Bakery and Grocery [Advertisement]." *Rice Belt Journal* (Welsh, LA), April 21, 1916.

"What! Shrimp Dance to Go Before Jellybeans and Vamps Get Chance at It?" *Galveston Daily News*, October 16, 1921.

"A White Waif Rescued from Chinaman." *Lafayette (LA) Advertiser*, August 24, 1889.

"W. K. M. Dukate Dies: Banker and Business Man Was Pioneer Shrimp and Oyster Packer." *New Orleans Times-Picayune*, March 30, 1916.

"The Wonderful Story of the Tin Can [Advertisement]." *Evening Public Ledger* (Philadelphia, PA), January 10, 1920, 5.

"The Wonderful World of the Tin Can [Advertisement]." *Los Angeles Herald*, January 10, 1920.

"Woodward and Lothrop [Advertisement]." *Washington Evening Star*, February 11, 1898.

"W. R. Bennett Co. [Advertisement]." *Omaha Daily Bee*, May 4, 1902.

"W. S. Henderson [Advertisement]." *Salt Lake Herald*, January 24, 1897.

"W. W. Henderson, Green and Fancy Groceries [Advertisement]." *Salt Lake Herald*, January 31, 1897.

"Yellow Fever in Joss House." *Evening Telegram* (St. John's, Newfoundland), September 30, 1905.

"Young's Market Co. [Advertisement]." *Los Angeles Herald*, December 14, 1907.

Government Documents

State Materials

Alexander, M. L. *Biennial Report of the Louisiana Department of Conservation, 1916–1918*. New Orleans: Palfrey-Rodd-Pursell Company, 1918.

Alexander, M. L. *Fifth Biennial Report of the Louisiana Department of Conservation, 1920–1921*. New Orleans: Palfrey-Rodd-Pursell Company, 1922.

Alexander, M. L. *Fourth Biennial Report of the Louisiana Department of Conservation, 1916–1918*. New Orleans: Palfrey-Rodd-Pursell Company, 1920.

Barnett, Barney B., and Marilyn C. Gillespie. *Environmental Conditions Relative to Shrimp Production in Coastal Louisiana*. Technical Bulletin 15. New Orleans: Louisiana Wildlife and Fisheries Commission, 1975.

Berwick, D. *Sixth Biennial Report of the Louisiana Department of Conservation, 1922–1923*. New Orleans: Hyatt Printing Company, 1922.

Bonnot, Paul. *The California Shrimp Industry*. Fish Bulletin No. 38. Sacramento: Division of Fish and Game of California, Bureau of Commercial Fisheries, 1931.

Bouchereau, Louis. *Statement of the Sugar and Rice Crops Made in Louisiana*. New Orleans: Young, Bright and Company, 1869–1871.

Bourgeois, Marty, et al. *Louisiana Shrimp. Fishery Management Plan*. Baton Rouge: Louisiana Department of Wildlife and Fisheries, 2015.

Breaux, J. M. *First Annual Report of the Oyster Commission of Louisiana to His Excellency, the Governor, and the General Assembly of the State of Louisiana, August 12, 1902 to January 21, 1904*. New Orleans: American Printing Company, 1904.

Christmas, J. Y., and David J. Etzold, eds. *The Shrimp Fishery of the Gulf of Mexico United States: A Regional Management Plan*, Technical Report Series, No. 2. Ocean Springs, MS: Gulf Coast Research Laboratory, 1977.

Clement, F. L. *Seventh Biennial Report of the Louisiana Department of Wild Life and Fisheries, 1956–1957*. New Orleans: Department of Wild Life and Fisheries, 1958.

Conservation of the Natural Food Resources of the State of Louisiana. Report of the Board of Commissioners for the Protection of Birds, Game and Fish, State of Louisiana. New Orleans: [Dameron-Pierson Company?], 1912.

Dauenhauer, John B., Jr. *Fisheries Division*. Thirteenth Biennial Report of the Louisiana Department of Conservation, 1936–1937. New Orleans: Department of Conservation, 1938.

Edwards' Annual Directory to the Inhabitants, Institutions, Incorporated Companies, Manufacturing Establishments, Business, Business Firms, Etc. in the City of New Orleans. New Orleans: Southern Publishing Company, 1873.

Guillot, James P. "Statistical Summary of Natural Resources of Louisiana." *Louisiana Conservation Review* 5, no. 3 (1936): 6–7.

A Hand-Book of Louisiana. Baton Rouge: Louisiana State Board of Agriculture and Immigration, 1917.

Irion, V. K. *Seventh Biennial Report of the Department of Conservation of the State of Louisiana, 1924–1926*. New Orleans: Louisiana Department of Conservation, 1926.

Lee, Robert L. *Report of the Bureau of Statistics for the State of Louisiana, 1906–1907*. Baton Rouge: Daily State Publishing Company, State Printers, 1908.

Leovy, R. S. *Report of the Division of Fisheries*. State of Louisiana Department of Conservation Ninth Biennial Report, 1928–1929. New Orleans: Department of Conservation, 1930, 41–69.

Louisiana Board of Commissioners for the Protection of Birds, Game and Fish. *Fish, Diamond-Back Terrapin and Shrimp Laws*. New Orleans: Press of Walle and Company, 1910.

Louisiana Bureau of Immigration. *An Invitation to Immigrants. Louisiana: Its Products, Soil and Climate*. Baton Rouge: Baton Rouge *Advocate*, 1894.

Louisiana Bureau of Statistics of Labor. *Ninth Biennial Report of the Department of Commissioners of Labor and Industrial Statistics of the State of Louisiana*. New Orleans: Hauser Printing Company, 1918.

Louisiana Department of Conservation. *Ninth Biennial Report of the Department of Conservation of the State of Louisiana, 1928–1929*. New Orleans: Department of Conservation, 1930.

Louisiana Department of Conservation. *Twelfth Biennial Report of the Department of Conservation of the State of Louisiana, 1934–1935*. New Orleans: Department of Conservation, 1936.

Louisiana Department of Public Works, in Cooperation with Cameron Parish Planning Board and Vermilion Parish Planning Board. *Louisiana Proposed Coastal Highway and Why It Should Be Built*. Baton Rouge: Louisiana Department of Public Works, 1948.

Louisiana Department of Wild Life and Fisheries. *First Biennial Report*. New Orleans: Louisiana Department of Wild Life and Fisheries, 1946.

Louisiana Oyster Commission. *First Annual Report of the Oyster Commission of Louisiana*. New Orleans: American Printing Company, 1904.

Louisiana Public Service Commission. *Annual Report*. New Orleans: Ramies-Jones Printing Company, 1951.

McHugh, J. L. *Sixteenth Biennial Report of the Louisiana Department of Conservation, 1942–1943*. New Orleans: Department of Conservation, 1944.

Montoucet, Jack. *Louisiana Department of Wildlife and Fisheries, 2015–2016 Annual Report*. Baton Rouge: Office of State Printing, 2017.

Peteet, Walton, et al. *Community Canning Plants*. Bulletin of the Texas Agricultural Extension Service, No. B-48. College Station: Texas A&M University, 1919.

Reddings, B. B., et al. *Report of the Commissioners of Fisheries of the State of California, for the Years 1870 and 1871*. Sacramento, CA: T. A. Springer, State Printer, 1872.

Report of the New Hampshire Board of Excise Commissioners for the Year Ending August 31, 1916. Manchester, NH: John B. Clarke Company, 1916.

Scofield. William Lance. *Trawling Gear in California*. Fish Bulletin No. 72. Sacramento: California State Printing Office, 1948.

Skinner, J. E. *An Historical Review of the Fish and Wildlife Resources of the San Francisco Bay Area*. Water Projects Branch Report No. 1. Sacramento:

Resources Agency of California Department of Fish and Game Water Projects Branch, 1962.

Terrebonne Parish Development Board. *Terrebonne Parish Resources and Facilities*. Baton Rouge: State of Louisiana Department of Public Works, 1953.

Viosca, Percy, Jr. *The Louisiana Shrimp Story*. New Orleans: Louisiana Department of Wildlife and Fisheries, 1962.

Washburn, Mel. *Seventh Biennial Report of the Louisiana Department of Wild Life and Fisheries, 1956–1957*. New Orleans: Department of Wild Life and Fisheries, 1958.

Werlla, W. S. *Fresh and Salt Water Fisheries*. Department of Wild Life and Fisheries Third Biennial Report, 1948–1949. New Orleans: Department of Wild Life and Fisheries, 1950.

Wood, Frank E. Ninth Biennial Report of the Department of Commissioner of Labor and industrial Statistics of the State of Louisiana, 1916–1918. New Orleans: Hauser Printing Company, 1918.

Wood, Frank E. Tenth Biennial Report of the Department of Commissioner of Labor and Industrial Statistics of the State of Louisiana, 1919–1920. New Orleans: Hauser Printing Company, 1920.

Federal Materials

Abbot, Frederic V. *Report of the Board of Engineers for Rivers and Harbors on Survey*. H.R. Document No. 200, 65th Cong., 1st Sess., 3–4. Washington, DC: Government Printing Office, 1917.

Alperin, Lynn M. *History of the Gulf Intracoastal Waterway: Alexandria, Va.* US Army Corps of Engineers Water Resources Support Center, National Waterways Study NWS-83-9, 1983. [Fort Belvoir, VA?]: Institute for Water Resources, 1983.

Alexander, A. B. *Statistics of the Fisheries of the Gulf States, 1902*. Report of the Commissioner for the Year Ending June 30, 1903, Volume. XXIX, 1903. Washington, DC: Government Printing Office, 1905, 411–81.

American Canners Association. *Can-venient Ways with Shrimp*. Fishery Market Development Series No. 2. Washington, DC: Government Printing Office, 1975.

Anderson, Andrew Wallace, and C. E. Peterson. *Fishery Statistics of the United States, 1950*. Statistical Digest 27. Washington, DC: Government Printing Office, 1953.

Anderson, Andrew Wallace, and C. E. Peterson. *Fishery Statistics of the United States, 1953*. Statistical Digest No. 36. Washington, DC: Government Printing Office, 1956.

Anderson, Andrew Wallace, and E. A. Power. *Fishery Statistics of the United States, 1947*. Washington, DC: Government Printing Office, 1950.

Anderson, William Wyatt. *Recognizing Important Shrimps of the South*. Fishery Leaflet 536. Washington, DC: Government Printing Office, 1962.

Anderson, William Wyatt. *Shrimp and the Shrimp Industry of the Southern United States*. US Fish and Wildlife Service, Fishery Leaflet No. 472, Revision of Leaflet No. 319. [Washington, DC?]: [Government Printing Office], 1958.

Annual Report of the Chief of Engineers, United States Army, to the Secretary of War, for the Year 1880. 46th Cong., 3d Sess., H.R. Executive Document 1, Part 2, Vol. 2. Washington, DC: Government Printing Office, 1880.

Annual Report of the Chief of Engineers, United States Army, to Secretary of War, for the Year 1881. 47th Cong., 1st Sess., H.R. Executive Document 1, Part 2, Vol. 2. Washington, DC: Government Printing Office, 1881.

Annual Report of the Chief of Engineers, United States Army, to the Secretary of War, for the Year 1888. 4 parts. Washington, DC: Government Printing Office, 1888.

Atchafalaya Basin Floodway System, Louisiana: Feasibility Study. Vol. 3. New Orleans: US Army Corps of Engineers, 1982.

Athens, William P., et al. *Cultural Resources Survey of Gretna, Phase 2 Levee Enlargement Item M-99, 4 to 95.5-R, Jefferson Parish Louisiana*. Cultural Resources Series, Report Number: DACW29-88-D-0121, COELMN/PD-90/04. New Orleans: US Army Corps of Engineers, New Orleans District, 1990.

Austin, Diane E. *History of the Offshore Oil and Gas Industry in Southern Louisiana. Volume III: Morgan City's History in the Era of Oil and Gas—Perspectives of Those Who Were There*. Gulf of Mexico OCS Region. OCS Study MMS 2008-044, New Orleans: Minerals Management Service, US Department of the Interior, 2008.

Austin, Diane E., et al. *History of the Offshore Oil and Gas Industry in Southern Louisiana. Volume I: Papers on the Evolving Offshore Industry*. Gulf of Mexico OCS Region, OCS Study MMS 2008-042. New Orleans: Minerals Management Service, US Department of the Interior, 2008.

Barataria Bay, La. and Connecting Waters: Letter from the Secretary of War. 65th Cong., 1st Sess. H.R. Document No. 200. House Documents, Vol. 33, 1917, Serial set 7298. Washington, DC: Government Printing Office, 1917.

Bitting, Avrill Wayne. *The Canning of Foods: A Description of the Methods Followed in Commercial Canning*. Nos. 151–160. Washington, DC: Government Printing Office, 1912.

Bullis, Harvey Raymond. *Gulf of Mexico Shrimp Trawl Designs*. Fishery Leaflet 394. Washington, DC: Fish and Wildlife Service, 1951.

Burtis, Jean, and Rose G. Kerr. *How to Cook Shrimp*. Test Kitchen Series, No. 7. Washington, DC: Fish and Wildlife Service, 1952.

Butler, Charles, et al. *Refrigeration of Fish, Part One: Cold Storage Design and Refrigeration Equipment*. Fishery Leaflet No. 427. Washington, DC: Fish and Wildlife Service, 1956.

"Canning." *Bulletin of the United States Fish Commission*. Volume XVII, 1897. Washington, DC: Government Printing Office, 1898, 294.

"Cans and Boxes." *Bulletin of the United States Fish Commission*. Volume XVIII, 1898. Washington, DC: Government Printing Office, 1899, 33–34.

Carson, Rachel. *Fish and Shellfish of the South Atlantic and Gulf Coasts*. Bulletin, No. 37. Washington, DC: Government Printing Office, 1944.

"Chinese Fishing Craft." *Bulletin of the United States Fish Commission*. Volume X, 1890. Washington, DC: Government Printing Office, 1892, 46–49.

Chinese Shrimp Fishery of San Francisco Bay. United States Fish and Fisheries, Part XXVI Report of the Commissioner for the Year Ending June 30, 1900. Washington, DC: Government Printing Office, 1901, 182–84.

Clark, Ernest Dunbar, and Leslie MacNaughton. *Shrimp: Handling, Transportation, and Uses*. Bulletin No. 538. Washington, DC: Government Printing Office, 1917.

Clem, Joe P. and Spencer Garret. *Sanitation Guidelines for the Breaded-Shrimp Industry*. Circular 308. Washington, DC: Fish and Wildlife Service, 1968.

Collins, Joseph William. "The Fishing Vessels and Boats of the Pacific Coast." *Bulletin of the United States Fish Commission*. Volume X, 1890. Washington, DC: Government Printing Office, 1892, 13–48.

Collins, Joseph William, and Hugh M. Smith. "A Statistical Report on the Fisheries of the Gulf States." *Bulletin of the United States Fish Commission*. Volume XI, 1891. Washington, DC: Government Printing Office, 1893, 94–108.

Dawson, William L. *Hearings Before a Subcommittee of the Committee Government Operations House of Representatives, 91st Cong., 1st Sess., August 20 and 21, 1969*. Washington, DC: Government Printing Office, 1970.

"Decision of the Commissioner of Patents and the United States in Patent Cases." *Official Gazette of the United States Patent Office*, vol. 73 no. 5, 811–15.

Elliott, Henry Wood, et al. *The History and Present Condition of the Fishery Industries*. Washington, DC: Government Printing Office, 1884.

Excise Tax Exemptions Granted to Fishermen. Fishery Leaflet No. 468. Washington, DC: Fish and Wildlife Service, 1958.

Fiedler, R. H. *Fisheries Statistics of the United States, 1939*. Statistical Digest No. 1. Washington, DC: Department of the Interior, 1942.

Fiedler, R. H. *Fishery Industries of the United States, 1930. Report of the United States Commissioner of Fisheries, 1931*. Appendix II, Report of the Division of Statistics and Methods of Fisheries for the Fiscal Year 1931. Washington, DC: Government Printing Office, 1931, 109–552.

Firth, Frank E., and Carl B. Carlson. *Preservation and Care of Fish Nets*. Fishery Leaflet No. 66. Washington, DC: Fish and Wildlife Service, 1949.

Firms Canning Fish and Shellfish Specialties, 1955. Statistical List (SL)-107 Revised. Washington, DC: Fish and Wildlife Service, 1956, 1–7.

Fisheries for the Fiscal Year, 1937. Washington, DC: Government Printing Office, 1939.

"Fisheries of Louisiana." In Lewis Radcliff, *Fishery Industries of the United States: Report of the Division of Statistics and Methods of the Fisheries for 1919*. Bureau of Fisheries Document No. 892. Washington, DC: Government Printing Office, 1920, 170–80.

"Fishery Statistics of the United States, 1973." In National Marine Fisheries Service, *Statistical Digest No. 67*. Washington, DC: Government Printing Office, 1976.

Food and Drug Administration. *Notices of Judgement Under the Food and Drugs Act; Given Pursuant to Section 4 of the Food and Drugs Act, Cases Numbers 24001-24025*. Washington, DC: Department of Agriculture, 1935.

Goode, George Brown, ed. *The Fisheries and Fishery Industries of the United States*. 8 vols. Washington, DC: Government Printing Office, 1887.

Goode, George Brown, ed. *The Shrimp and Prawn Fisheries: The Fisheries and Fishery Industries of the United States, Section V*. History and Methods of the Fisheries. 8 vols. Washington, DC: Government Printing Office, 1887, vol. 2, 799–810.

Hamilton and Associates. *The Cajuns: Their History and Culture*. Report submitted to the National Park Service, 1987.

How to Make and Mend Fish Nets. Fishery Leaflet No. 125. Washington, DC: Fish and Wildlife Service, 1952.

Immigration Records. National Archives at Fort Worth, Texas.

Immigration Records. National Archives at San Francisco, San Bruno, California.

Improvement of Rivers and Harbors in the New Orleans, La., District. Report of the Chief of Engineers, US Army, 1916 in Three Parts, Part 2. Washington, DC: Government Printing Office, 1916.

Jarvis, Norman D. *Canning Crabs, Lobster and Shrimp*. Fisheries Leaflet No. 85. Washington, DC: Fish and Wildlife Service, 1943.

Jarvis, Norman D. *Curing of Fishery Products*. Washington, DC: Government Printing Office, 1950.

Jarvis, Norman D. *Historical Outline of the Canning of Fishery Products*. Fishery Leaflet No. 78. Washington, DC: Fish and Wildlife Service, 1943.

Jarvis, Norman, D. *Principles and Methods in the Canning of Fishery Products*. Research Report, No. 7. Washington, DC: Fish and Wildlife Service, 1943.

Johnson, Fred F., and Milton J. Lindner. *Shrimp Industry of the South Atlantic and Gulf States*. United States Bureau of Fisheries, Investigational Report, No. 21. Washington, DC: Government Printing Office, 1934.

Jordan, D. S. *The Fisheries of the Pacific Coast: The Fisheries of San Francisco County*. Fisheries and Fishery Industries of the United States. Washington, DC: Government Printing Office, 1887, 612–18.

Josselyn, Michael. *The Ecology of San Francisco Bay Tidal Marshes: A Community Profile*. No. FWS-/OBHS-83/23. San Francisco, CA: San Francisco State University Tiburon Center for Environmental Studies, 1983.

Knake, Boris O. *Assembly Methods for Otter-Trawl Nets*. Fishery Leaflet No. 437. Washington, DC: Fish and Wildlife Service, 1956.

Knake, Boris O. *Operation of North Atlantic Type Otter Trawl Gear*. Fishery Leaflet No. 445. Washington, DC: Fish and Wildlife Service, 1958.

Knake, Boris, O., et al. *Double-Rig Shrimp Trawling in the Gulf of Mexico*. Fishery Leaflet 470. Washington, DC: Fish and Wildlife Service, 1958.

Knake, B. O., and R. T. Whiteleather. *Otter Trawl Net for Small Fishing Boats*. Fishery Leaflet 49. Washington, DC: Fish and Wildlife Service, 1944.

Kutkuhn, Joseph H. *Gulf of Mexico Commercial Shrimp Populations, Trends and Characteristics, 1956–59*. Fishery Bulletin 212. Washington, DC: Fish and Wildlife Service, 1962.

Larson, D. K., et al. *Mississippi Deltaic Plain Regional Ecological Characterization: A Socioeconomic Study, Volume 1: Synthesis Papers*. Report FWS/OBS-79/05. Washington, DC: Fish and Wildlife Service, 1980.

Lemon, J. M., and Carl B. Carlson. *Freezing Fish at Sea*. Fishery Leaflet No. 278. Washington, DC: Fish and Wildlife Service, 1948.

Leonard, John R. *The Fish Car Era*. Washington, DC: Fish and Wildlife Service, 1979.

Letter from the Secretary of the Army, Transmitting a Letter from the Chief of Engineers, Department of the Army, Dated January 21, 1945, Submitting a Report, Together with Accompanying Papers and Illustrations, on a Review of Reports on, and Preliminary Examinations and Surveys of, Bayou Segnette Waterway, La., Made Pursuant to Several Congressional Authorizations Listed in the Report. Washington, DC: Government Printing Office, 1954.

"Louisiana: Interior Waters Fishery." *Bulletin of the United States Fish Commission*. Volume XXI, 1895. Washington, DC: Government Printing Office, 1896.

Maygarden, Benjamin, and Jill Karen Yakubik. *Bayou Chene: The Life Story of an Atchafalaya Basin Community*. New Orleans: Army Engineers District, 1999.

McGuire, Tom. *History of the Offshore Oil and Gas Industry in Southern Louisiana: Interim Report; Volume II: Bayou Lafourche—An Oral History of the Development of the Oil and Gas Industry.* OCS Study MMS 2004. New Orleans: Minerals Management Service, US Department of the Interior, Gulf of Mexico OCS Region, 2004.

McMullin, Leslie D. *List of Fishery Cooperatives in the United States, 1960–1961.* Fishery Leaflet No. 292. Washington, DC: Fish and Wildlife Service, 1961.

McMullin, Leslie D. *List of Fishery Cooperatives in the United States, 1961–62."* Fishery Leaflet No. 545. Washington, DC: Fish and Wildlife Service, 1962.

New Orleans Fishing Lugger. United States Fish and Fisheries, Part XXVII, Report of the Commissioner for the Year Ending June 30, 1901. Washington, DC: Government Printing Office, 1902, 697–701.

Ninth Census—Volume I: The Statistics of the Population of the United States. Table I. Population of the United States, (By States and Territories,) in the Aggregate, and as White, Colored, Free Colored, Slave, Chinese, and Indian, at Each Census. Washington, DC: Government Printing Office, 1872.

"Notes on Fishing Products Exported from San Francisco, California During the Year 1883." *Bulletin of the United States Fish Commission.* Volume IV, 1884. Washington, DC: Government Printing Office, 1884, 125–26.

Osborn, Kenneth W., et al. *Gulf of Mexico Shrimp Atlas.* Circular 313. Washington, DC: Fish and Wildlife Service, 1969.

Paradise, Viola I. *Child Labor and the Work of Mothers in Oyster and Shrimp Canning Communities on the Gulf Coast.* Children's Bureau Publication 98. Washington, DC: Government Printing Office, 1922.

Pearson, Charles E., et al. *A History of Waterborne Commerce and Transportation within the U.S. Army Corps of Engineers New Orleans District and an Inventory of Known Underwater Cultural Resources.* Final Report No. AR-223; COELMN/PD-88/11. Baton Rouge: Coastal Environments, 1989.

Peterson, G. E. "Seasons, Sources, and Sizes of Gulf Shrimp." *Fishery Market News* 5 no. 2 (1943): 1–4.

"Preparation of Shrimps in China." *Bulletin of the United States Fish Commission.* Volume VI, 1886. Washington, DC: Government Printing Office, 1887.

"Preservation of Fishery Products for Food, Canning Shrimp." *Bulletin of the United States Fish Commission.* Volume XVIII, 1898. Washington, DC: Government Printing Office, 1899, 523–24.

"Preservation of Fishery Products for Food, Chinese Shrimp and Fish Drying." *Bulletin of the United States Fish Commission.* Volume XVIII. Washington, DC: Government Printing Office, 1898, 414–17.

"Production and Value of Shrimp." *Bulletin of the United States Fish Commission.* Volume XLVIII, 1940. Washington, DC: Government Printing Office, 1940, 2–3.

Report of the Commissioner for the Year Ending June 30, 1903. US Commission of Fish and Fisheries, Part 19. Washington, DC: Government Printing Office, 1905.

Sandberg, Arthur M. "The Relative Productivity and Value of the Fisheries of the United States and Alaska." *Fishery Market News* 5, no. 12 (1943): 5.

"Shipment of Marine Products from San Francisco to China." *Bulletin of the United States Fish Commission.* Volume VI, 1886. Washington, DC: Government Printing Office, 1892, 46–49.

"The Shrimp and Prawn Fishery of the Pacific Coast." *Bulletin of the United States Fish Commission.* Volume II. Washington, DC: Government Printing Office, 1883, 150–52.

The Shrimp and the Shrimp Industry of the South Atlantic and Gulf of Mexico. Fishery Leaflet No. 319. Washington, DC: Fish and Wildlife Service, 1948.

The Shrimp Industry of the South Atlantic and Gulf of Mexico. Fishery Leaflet No. 310. Washington, DC: Fish and Wildlife Service, 1948.

Shrimp Packing Industry in the South Atlantic and Gulf States. Department of the Interior, Information Service, Public Notice 112184. Washington, DC: Department of the Interior, 1940.

Shrimp Tips from New Orleans. Circular 41. Washington DC: Fish and Wildlife Service, 1956.

Slavin, Joseph W., and Martin Heerdt. *Refrigeration of Fish, Part Five: Distribution and Marketing of Frozen Fishery Products.* Fishery Leaflet No. 431. Washington, DC: Fish and Wildlife Service, 1956.

Smith, Hugh M. "The Fyke Nets and Fyke-Net Fisheries of the United States, with Notes on the Fyke Nets of Other Countries." *Bulletin of the United States Fish Commission.* Volume XII. Washington, DC: Government Printing Office, 1894, 299–355.

Smith, Hugh M. "Notes on a Reconnoissance [sic] of the Fisheries of the Pacific Coast of the United States in 1894." *Bulletin of the United States Fish Commission.* Volume XIV, Document 293. Washington, DC: Government Printing Office, 1895, 223–387.

Smith, Hugh M. "Statistics of the Fisheries of the United States." *Bulletin of the United States Fish Commission.* Volume XIII. Document 276. Washington, DC: Government Printing Office, 1894, 388–417.

"The Southern States. Gulf Coast, Shrimp Canning." *Bulletin of the United States Fish Commission.* Volume II, 1882. Washington, DC: Government Printing Office, 1883, 146–50.

Stansby, Maurice E., et al. *Refrigeration of Fish, Part Three: Factors to be Considered in the Freezing and Cold Storage of Fishery Products.* Fishery Leaflet No. 429. Washington, DC: Fish and Wildlife Service, 1956.

"Statistical Report on the Fisheries of the Gulf States." *Bulletin of the United States Fish Commission.* Volume XI, 1891. Washington, DC: Government Printing Office, 1893, 94–108.

Stearns, S. *Fisheries of the Gulf of Mexico: The Fishery Interests of Louisiana.* Fisheries and Fishery Industries of the United States. Washington, DC: Government Printing Office, 1887, 575–82.

Stevenson, Charles H. "The Oyster Industry of Maryland." *Bulletin of the United States Fish Commission.* Volume XII, 1892. Washington, DC: Government Printing Office, 1894.

Survey of the United States Shrimp Industry Vol. 1. Special Scientific Report-Fisheries, No. 277. Washington, DC: Fish and Wildlife Service, 1958.

Survey of the United States Shrimp Industry Vol. 2. Special Scientific Report, Fisheries No. 308. Washington, DC: Government Printing Office, 1959.

Townsend, Charles Haskins. *Statistics of the Fisheries of the Gulf States.* Report of the Commissioner for the Year Ending June 30, 1899. Vol. XXV, 1899. Washington, DC: Government Printing Office, 1900, 105–69.

Transfer of Certain Functions of the Fish and Wildlife Service to the Department of Agriculture: Hearings before the Committee on Merchant Marine and Fisheries. H.R. 78th Cong., 1st Sess., on H.R. 1766. Washington, DC: Governbment Printing Office, 1943.

Unemployment Insurance Information for Fishermen and Allied Workers: Gulf States, Alabama, Mississippi, Louisiana Texas. Fishery Leaflet No. 154. Washington, DC: Fish and Wildlife Service, 1945.

United States Bureau of Fisheries. *Canned Fishery Products and By-products of the United States and Alaska, 1935.* Statistical Bulletin No. 1185. Washington, DC: Bureau of Fisheries, 2001.

United States Census Bureau. *Fourteenth Census of the United States Taken in the Year 1920.* Vol. 5. Washington, DC: Government Printing Office, 1922.

United States Census Bureau. *Twelfth Census of the United States Taken in the Year 1900,* Census Reports, Vol. 1, Population, Part 1. Washington, DC: United States Census Office, 1901, 756–57.

United States Code, 1964 Edition, Containing the General and Permanent Laws of the United States, in Force on January 3, 1965. Volume 11, Title 50, War and National Defense and Tables. Washington, DC: Government Printing Office, 1965.

United States Commission of Fish and Fisheries. *Report of the Commissioner for the Year Ending June 30, 1903, Part XXIX.* Washington, DC: Government Printing Office, 1905, 414.

United States Congress. *A Bill to Prevent Interstate Commerce in the Products of Child Labor, and for Other Purposes: Hearings on H.R. 8234, United States Document 550.5 before the Committee on Labor, House of Representatives.* 64th Cong., 1st Sess. Washington, DC: Government Printing Office, 1916.

United States Congress. 67th Cong., 2nd Sess., December 5, 1921–September 22, 1922. Washington, DC: Government Printing Office, 1922.

United States Department of the Interior, Information Service, Fish and Wildlife Service. *Packing Industry, Atlantic and Gulf States. August 26, 1940.* Public Notice 1121184. Washington, DC: Fish and Wildlife Service, 1941.

United States Department of the Interior. *The Statistics of the Wealth and Industry of the United States, Ninth Census, Volume III.* Washington, DC: Government Printing Office, 1872.

United States Fish Commission. *Bulletin of the United States Fish Commission, Volume XVIII, for 1898.* Washington, DC: Government Printing Office, 1899.

United States General Services Administration, National Archives and Records Services. Federal *Records of World War II, Volume 1, Civilian Agencies.* Publication No. 51-7. Washington, DC: Government Printing Office, 1950.

United States House of Representatives. *Hearings Before the Committee on Ways and Means.* House of Representatives. 80th Cong., 1st Sess. Washington, DC: Government Printing Office, 1950.

United States Tariff Commission. *Shrimp.* Report on Investigation No. 332–40, Under Section 332 of the Tariff Act of 1930. Washington, DC: United States Tariff Commission, 1961.

United States War Department, Corps of Engineers, US Army and United States Shipping Board. *Port Series, No. 5.* New Orleans: Port of New Orleans, 1924.

Various Issues. Fishery Industries of the United States, Report of the Division of Statistics and Methods of the Fisheries for 1918–1978. Washington, DC: Bureau of Fisheries, Government Printing Office.

Ward, John. *Vessel Operating Behavior in the Gulf of Mexico Shrimp Fishery: An Annotated Bibliography.* NOAA Technical Memorandum NMFS-SEFE-212. Washington, DC: Government Printing Office, 1988.

Whiteleather, R. T. *Kite Rigs for Otter Trawl Gear.* Fishery Leaflet No. 302. Washington, DC: Fish and Wildlife Service, 1948.

Wilcox, William A. *The Commercial Fisheries of the Pacific Coast States in 1904.* Bureau of Fisheries Document No. 612. Washington, DC: Government Printing Office, 1907.

Wilcox, William A. *Notes on the Fisheries of the Pacific Coast in 1899.* Washington, DC: US Commission of Fish and Fisheries, 1902.

Interviews and Personal Communications

Authement, Lance. Interviewed by Donald W. Davis, Terrebonne Parish, June 19, 2019. Interview archived at Louisiana Sea Grant, Louisiana State University, Baton Rouge, LA.

Benge, Dorothy, and Michael Benge. Interviewed by Carl A. Brasseaux, Donald W. Davis, Roy Kron, and Paul Ouder, Orleans Parish, July 13, 2013. Interview archived at Louisiana Sea Grant, Louisiana State University, Baton Rouge, LA.

Blanchard, Arthur. Interviewed by Earl Robichaux, Grand Isle, LA, August 5, 2009. Interview archived at Louisiana Sea Grant, Louisiana State University, Baton Rouge, LA.

Blanchard, Philip. Interviewed by Carl A. Brasseaux, Lafourche Parish, July 2019. Interview archived at Louisiana Sea Grant, Louisiana State University, Baton Rouge, LA.

Blum, Louis. Interviewed by the authors, Terrebonne Parish, November 4, 2009. Interview archived at Louisiana Sea Grant, Louisiana State University, Baton Rouge, LA.

Blum, Louis. Personal communications, November 20, 2008. In the authors' possession.

Blum, Louis. Personal communications, May 19, 2009. In the authors' possession.

Bouquet, Sandra. Interviewed by the authors, Terrebonne Parish, December 29, 2010. Interview archived at Louisiana Sea Grant, Louisiana State University, Baton Rouge, LA.

Brassieur, C. Ray. Letter to Donald W. Davis, January 25, 2007. In Donald W. Davis's possession.

Carihnas Family. Interviewed by the authors, St. Mary Parish, June 20, 2010. Interview archived at Louisiana State University, Baton Rouge, LA.

Chauvin, Kimberley. Interviewed by Donald W. Davis, David Chauvin's Seafood Company Dock, Dulac, Louisiana, September 24, 2021. Transcripts in the authors' possession.

Curole, Windell, and Darcy Kiffe. Interviewed by Donald W. Davis, Lafourche Parish, March 28, 2018. Interview on deposit at Louisiana Sea Grant, Louisiana State University, Baton Rouge, LA.

Ensminger, Allan. Interviewed by the authors, Cameron Parish, May 28, 2010. Recording archived at Louisiana Sea Grant, Louisiana State University, Baton Rouge, LA.

Foret, Houston. Interviewed by the authors, Terrebonne Parish, May 20, 2010. Recording archived at Louisiana Sea Grant, Louisiana State University, Baton Rouge, LA.

Gibson, Andy. Interviewed by Donald W. Davis, Terrebonne Parish, June 19, 2019. Recording archived at Louisiana Sea Grant, Louisiana State University, Baton Rouge, LA.

Guidry, Roland. Personal communications, August 3, 2006. Copies in the authors' possession.

Guidry, Roland, and Lou Anna Guidry. Interviewed by Carl A. Brasseaux, Golden Meadow, July 24, 2019. Interview on deposit at Louisiana Sea Grant, Louisiana State University, Baton Rouge, LA.

Hoy, Robert. Interviewed by the authors, Jefferson Parish, January 19, 2011. Interview on deposit at Louisiana Sea Grant, Louisiana State University, Baton Rouge, LA.

Isaac, J. Personal communications, January 20, 2011. Copies in the authors' possession.

Pellegrin, M. Personal communications, August 8, 2006. Copies in the authors' possession.

Price, Norris. Interviewed by Donald W. Davis, Terrebonne Parish, ca. 2010. Recording archived at Louisiana Sea Grant, Louisiana State University, Baton Rouge, LA.

Skrmetta Family. Interviewed by the authors, Jefferson Parish, October 15, 2010. Interview archived at Louisiana Sea Grant, Louisiana State University, Baton Rouge, LA.

Theriot, Joseph D. Interviewed by Glen Pitre, Terrebonne Parish, March 7, 1982. Transcript in the authors' possession.

Thibodeaux, Brenda Bertrand, and Michael Thibodeaux. Interviewed by Carl A. Brasseaux, Vermilion Parish, ca. 2009. Interview archived at Louisiana Sea Grant, Louisiana State University, Baton Rouge, LA.

SECONDARY SOURCES

Books

A. Mygatt and Company. *New Orleans Business Directory with a Map Compiled and Arranged by W. H. Rainey to Be Published Annually Containing the Name and Address of Every Business or Professional Man in the City, Classified According to Their Respective Avocations*. New Orleans: A. Mygatt and Company, 1858.

Anderson, Oscar Edward, Jr. *Refrigeration in America*. Princeton, NJ: Princeton University Press, 2015.

Barone, Michael. *Our Country: The Shaping of America from Roosevelt to Reagan*. New York: Free Press, 1990.

Bentley, Amy. *Eating for Victory: Food Rationing and the Politics of Domesticity*. Chicago: University of Illinois Press, 1998.

Bernard, Shane K. *The Cajuns: Americanization of a People*. Jackson: University Press of Mississippi, 2003.

Bitting, A. W. *Appetizing, or The Art of Canning: Its History and Development*. San Francisco: Trade Pressroom, 1937.

Boudreaux, Edmond. *The Seafood Capital of the World: Biloxi's Maritime History*. Charleston, SC: Arcadia Publishing Company, 2011.

Boutwell, A. P., and G. Folse. *Terrebonne Parish: A Pictorial History, Then and Now*. Houma, LA: Courier, 1997.

Brasseaux, Carl A., and Donald W. Davis. *Ain't There No More*. Jackson: University Press of Mississippi, 2017.

Burger, Michael. *Breaker Boys: How a Photograph Helped End Child Labor*. Mankato, MN: Capstone Publishers, 2012.

Butler, J. Thomas. *The Lafitte Skiff: Workboat of the Bayou Country*. Thibodaux, LA: Center for Traditional Louisiana Boatbuilding, Nicholls State University, 1985.

Campanella, Richard. *Geographies of New Orleans: Urban Fabrics Before the Storm*. Lafayette: Center for Louisiana Studies, 2006.

Case, Gladys C. *The Bayou Chene Story: A History of the Atchafalaya Basin and Its People*. Detroit, MI: Harlo Press, 1979.

Cenac, Christopher, and Claire Domangue Joller. *Eyes of an Eagle: Jean-Pierre Cenac, Patriarch. An Illustrated History of Early Houma Terrebonne*. Houma, LA: JPC LLC, 2011.

Chan, Sucheng. *This Bitter-Sweet Soil: The Chinese in California Agriculture, 1860–1910*. Berkeley: University of California Press, 1986.

Chenier Hurricane Centennial. *Réfléchir II: Les Décades: 1860–1960*. Cut Off, LA: Chenier Hurricane Centennial, 1995.

Chiang, Connie Y. *Boom and Bust in Wartime Monterey*. Seattle: University of Washington Press, 2008.

Chung, Sue Fawn. *In Pursuit of Gold: Chinese American Miners and Merchants in the American West*. Champaign: University of Illinois Press, 2011.

Clark, John G. *New Orleans, 1718–1812: An Economic History*. Baton Rouge: Louisiana State University Press, 1970.

Clipp, Amy. *Shrimping in Louisiana: Supporting Innovation in the Face of Coastal Change*. Baton Rouge: Coalition to Restore Coastal Louisiana, 2018.

Cohen, Lucy M. *Chinese in the Post-Civil War South: A People Without a History*. Baton Rouge: Louisiana State University Press, 1984.

Collins, James H. *The Story of Canned Foods*. New York: E. P. Dutton and Company, 1924.

Comeaux, Malcolm L. *Atchafalaya Swamp Life: Settlement and Folk Occupations*. Vol. 2. Baton Rouge: School of Geoscience, Louisiana State University, 1972.

Coolidge, Mary R. *Chinese Immigration*. New York: Henry Holt and Company, 1909.

Crété, Liliane. *Daily Life in Louisiana, 1815–1830*. Translated by Patrick Gregory. Baton Rouge: Louisiana State University Press, 1981.

Davis, Donald W. *Washed Away? The Invisible Peoples of Louisiana's Wetlands*. Lafayette: University of Louisiana at Lafayette Press, 2010.

Davis, Edwin Adams. *Louisiana the Pelican State*. Baton Rouge: Louisiana State University Press, 1959.

Decuers, Leonora. *The Story of Shrimp*. New Orleans, LA: National Shrimp Canners Association, 1949.

Delfino, Susan, and Michelle Gillespie, eds. *Technology, Innovation, and Southern Industrialization: from the Antebellum Era to the Computer Age*. Vol. 1. Columbia: University of Missouri Press, 2008.

Dicker, Laverne M. *The Chinese in San Francisco, A Pictorial History*. New York: Dover Publications, 1980.

Din, Gilbert C. *The Canary Islanders of Louisiana*. Baton Rouge: Louisiana State University Press, 1988.

Din, Gilbert C., and John E. Harkins. *The New Orleans Cabildo: Colonial Louisiana's First City Government, 1769–1803*. Baton Rouge: Louisiana State University Press, 1996.

Ditto, Tanya Brady. *The Longest Street: A Story of Lafourche Parish and Grand Isle*. Baton Rouge, LA: Moran Printing, 1980.

Dore, Ian, ed. *An Illustrated Guide to Shrimp of the World*. New York: Springer, 2012.

Edenfield, Gray. *Amelia Islands: Birthplace of the Modern Shrimping Industry*. Charleston, SC: Fonthill Media, 2014.

Edwards, George Wharton. *Brittany and the Bretons*. New York: Moffat Yard and Company, 1910.

Edwards, Jay. *Creole Lexicon: Architecture, Landscape, People*. Baton Rouge: Louisiana State University Press, 2004.

Espina, Marina E. *Filipinos in Louisiana*. New Orleans: A. F. LaBorde and Sons, 1988.

Evans, Amanda M., ed. *The Archaeology of Vernacular Watercraft*. New York: Springer, 2016.

Falgoux, Woody. *Rise of the Cajun Mariners: The Race for Big Oil*. Ann Arbor, MI: Edwards Brothers, 2007.

Federal Writers Project, Works Projects Administration. *The WPA Guide to Mississippi: The Magnolia State*. Reprint, San Antonio, TX: Trinity University Press, 2013.

Freedman, Russell. *Kids at Work: Lewis Hine and the Crusade Against Child Labor*. Boston: Houghton-Mifflin, 1994.

Fritchey, Robert. *Let the Good Times Roll: Louisiana Cashes In Its Chips with the 1995 Net Ban*. Golden Meadow, LA: New Moon, 2017.

Gilliam, Harold. *San Francisco Bay*. Garden City, NJ: Doubleday and Company, 1957.

Gomez, Gay M. *The Louisiana Coast: Guide to an American Wetland*. College Station: Texas A&M University Press, 2008.

Grayson, Stan. *American Marine Engines, 1885–1950*. Marblehead, MA: Devereux Books, 2008.

Greenberg, Paul. *American Catch: The Fight for Our Local Seafood*. New York: Penguin Press, 2015.

Gumina, Deanna Paoli. *The Italians of San Francisco, 1850–1930*. Bilingual edition. New York: Center for Migration Studies, 1978.

Gutierrez, C. Paige. *The Cultural Legacy of Biloxi's Seafood Industry*. Biloxi, MS: City of Biloxi, 1984.

Hardee, T. S. *Topographical and Drainage Map of New Orleans and Surroundings from Recent Surveys and Investigations By T. S. Hardee, Civil Engineer, 1878*. N.p., 1878.

Harris, W. H. *Louisiana Products, Resources, and Attractions, with a Sketch of the Parishes: A Hand Book of Reliable Information Concerning the State*. New Orleans: New Orleans Democrat, 1881.

Harrison, Jill Ann. *Buoyancy on the Bayou: Shrimpers Face the Rising Tide of Globalization*. Ithaca, NY: Cornell University Press, 2012.

Herman, Arthur. *Freedom's Forge*. New York: Random House, 2012.

Historical Sketch Book and Guide to New Orleans and Environs, with Map. New York: Will H. Coleman, 1885.

History of the Jews of Louisiana. New Orleans: Jewish Historical Publishing Company of Louisiana, n.d.

Horst, Jerald, and Glenda Horst. *The Louisiana Seafood Bible: Shrimp*. Gretna, LA: Pelican Publishing Company, 2009.

Hubert-Robert, Régine. *L'Histoire Merveilleuse de la Louisiane française*. New York: Editions de la Maison française, 1941.

Jackson, Harvey H. *The Rise and Decline of the Redneck Riviera: An Insider's History of the Florida-Alabama Coast*. Athens: University of Georgia Press, 2012.

Jaffe, Maureen E., et al. *By the Sweat and Toil of Children: The Use of Child Labor in US Agricultural Imports and Forced and Bonded Child Labor*. Vol. 2. Collingdale, PA: Diane Publishing, 1997.

Johnson, Jeff. *Shrimp Highway: Savoring U.S. 17 and Its Iconic Dish*. Jefferson, NC: McFarland and Company, 2017.

Jung, John. *Chinese Laundries: Tickets to Survival on Gold Mountain*. Charleston, SC: Yin and Yang Press, 2007.

Jung, Moon-Ho. *Coolies and Cane: Race, Labor, and Sugar in the Age of Emancipation*. Baltimore, MD: Johns Hopkins University Press, 2006.

Kemp, John R., ed. *Lewis Hine: Photographs of Child Labor in the New South*. Jackson: University Press of Mississippi, 1986.

Kovel, Ralph, and Terry Kovel. *The Label Made Me Buy It: From Aunt Jemima to Zonkers: The Best Dressed Boxes, Bottles, and Cans from the Past*. New York: Crown Publishers, 2007.

Kurlansky, Mark. *Cod: A Bibliography of the Fish that Changed the World*. New York: Penguin Putnam, 1997.

Kurlansky, Mark. *Frozen in Time: Clarence Birdseye's Outrageous Idea about Frozen Food*. New York: Delacorte Press 2014.

Lane, Yvette Florio. *Shrimp: A Global History*. London: Reaktion Books Ltd., 2017.

Lee, Erika A., and Judy Yung. *Angel Island Immigrant Gateway to America*. New York: Oxford University Press, 2010.

Leet, William. S. *California's Living Marine Resources: A Status Report*. Berkeley: University of California, Division of Agriculture and Natural Resources, California Sea Grant Program, 2001.

Lemmon, Alfred E., et al., eds. *Charting Louisiana: Five Hundred Years of Maps*. New Orleans: Historic New Orleans Collection, 2003.

Lippert, Ellen J. *George Ohr: Sophisticate and Rube*. Jackson: University Press of Mississippi, 2013.

Long, E., and B. Burke. *Shrimp Boat City: 100 Years of Catching Shrimp and Building Boats in St. Augustine, the Nation' Oldest Port*. St. Augustine, FL: St. Augustine Lighthouse and Museum, 2016.

López, Kathleen. *Chinese Cubans: A Transnational History*. Chapel Hill: University of North Carolina Press, 2013.

Lydon, Sandy. *Chinese Gold: The Chinese in the Monterey Bay Region*. Santa Cruz, CA: Capitola Book Company, 1985.

Ma, Eva Armentrout. *Hometown Chinatown: A History of Oakland's Chinese Community, 1852–1995*. New York: Routledge, 2014.

Magruder, Harriet. *A History of Louisiana*. Boston: D. C. Heath and Company, 1909.

Maiolo, John R. *Hard Times and a Nickel a Bucket: Struggle and Survival in North Carolina's Shrimp Industry*. Chapel Hill, NC: Chapel Hill Press, 2004.

Margavio, Anthony V. and Craig J. Forsyth. *Caught in the Net: The Conflict between Shrimpers and Conservationists*. College Station: Texas A&M University Press, 1996.

Markham, Edwin, et al. *Children in Bondage: A Complete and Careful Presentation of the Anxious Problem of Child Labor*. New York: Hearst's International Library Company, 1914.

May, Earl Chaplin. *The Canning Clan: A Pageant of Pioneering Americans*. New York: Macmillan Company, 1937.

Melendy, Howard Brett. *Asians in America: Filipinos, Koreans, and East Indians*. Boston: Twayne Publishers, 1977.

Mémoires sur la Louisiane et la Nouvelle-Orléans accompagnés d'une dissertation sur les avantages que le commerce de l'empire doit tirer de la stipulation faite par l'article VII du traité de cession du 30 Avril 1803. Paris: Ballard, 1804.

Mercene, Floro L. *Manila Men in the New World: Filipino Migration to Mexico and the Americas from the Sixteenth Century*. Quezon City: University of the Philippines Press, 2007.

Mine, Sarah, Rui Chen, et al. *Louisiana Shrimp Value Chain: Price Dynamics, Challenges, and Opportunities*. Baton Rouge: Coalition to Restore Coastal Louisiana, 2016.

Monterrey Bay Seafood Watch. *Warmwater Shrimp: Brown shrimp, Pink Shrimp, Rock Shrimp, Royal Red Shrimp, Seabob Shrimp, White Shrimp: U.S. Gulf of Mexico and Western Central Atlantic Ocean, Bottom Trawls, Pushed Skimmer Nets*. Monterey, CA: Monterey Bay Aquarium, 2013.

Nolan, Charles E. *The Catholic Church in Mississippi, 1865–1911*. Lafayette: Center for Louisiana Studies, 2002.

Norton, Henry Kittredge. *The Story of California, from the Earliest Days to the Present*. Chicago: A. C. McClurg and Company, 1913.

Okamoto, Ariel Rubissow, and Kathleen M. Wong. *Natural History of San Francisco Bay*. Vol. 102. Berkeley: University of California Press, 2011.

O'Neil, Ted. *The Muskrat in the Louisiana Coastal Marshes.* New Orleans: Louisiana Wild Life and Fisheries Commission, 1949.

Pitre, Vernon. *Grandma Was a Sail-Maker: Tales of the Cajun Wetlands*. Thibodaux, LA: Blue Heron Press, 1991.

Read, William A. *Louisiana-French*. University Studies No. 5. Baton Rouge: Louisiana State University Press, 1931.

Rees, Jonathan. *Refrigeration Nation: A History of Ice, Appliances, and Enterprise in America*. Baltimore, MD: Johns Hopkins University Press, 2013.

Reeves, William Dale, and Pat Legendre. *Westwego from Cheniere to Canal*. Mr. & Mrs. D. Alario, Sr. under the aegis of the Jefferson Parish Historical Commission, 1996.

Rightor, Henry. *Standard History of New Orleans*. Chicago: Lewis Publishing Company, 1900.

Rodrigue, John C. *Reconstruction in the Cane Fields: From Slavery to Free Labor in Louisiana's Sugar Parishes, 1862–1800.* Baton Rouge: Louisiana State University Press, 2001.

Rosenberg, Chaim M. *Child Labor in America: A History*. Jefferson, NC: McFarland and Company, 2013.

Rudloe, Jack, and Ann Rudloe. *Shrimp: The Endless Quest for Pink Gold*. Upper Saddle River, NJ: Financial Times Press, 2014.

Rushton, William Faulkner. *The Cajuns: From Acadia to Louisiana*. New York: Farrar Straus Giroux, 1979.

Schaefer, Richard T. *Racial and Ethnic Groups*. Boston: Pearson, 2015.

Sears, Jane. *Baltimore's Packing & Canning Industry: Directory of Individuals & Companies Engaged in the Oyster, Fruit & Vegetable Industry from 1840 to 1940*. San Bernardino, CA: [Creative Space Independent Publishing Platform?], 2015.

Senette, Julana M. *Images of America: St. Mary Parish*. Charleston, SC: Arcadia Publishing, 2012.

Sheffield, David A., and Darnell L. Nicovich. *When Biloxi Was the Seafood Capital of the World*. Biloxi: City of Biloxi, 1979.

A Sketch of the Louisiana Inter-Coastal Canal Route from Morgan City to New Orleans via Houma and Lockport. New Orleans: Southern Manufacturer, 1910.

Skinner, John E. *An Historical Review of the Fish and Wildlife Resources of the San Francisco Bay Area (No. 1)*. Sacramento: California Department of Fish and Game, Water Projects Branch, 1962.

Smith, Andrew F., ed. *Oxford Encyclopedia of Food and Drink in America, Volume 1*. 2nd ed. New York: Oxford University Press, 2013.

Soulé, Frank, et al. *The Annals of San Francisco: Containing a Summary of the History of . . . California, and a Complete History of . . . Its Great City: To which are Added, Biographical Memoirs of Some Prominent Citizens*. New York: D. Appleton and Company, 1855.

Spitzer, Nicholas. *Louisiana Folklife: A Guide to the State*. Baton Rouge: Louisiana Folklife Program, 1985.

Swedberg, Harriett. *Tins'n Bins*. Lombard, IL: Wallace-Homestead Book Company, 1985.

Szabo, A. J., et al. *Dissolved Air Flotation Treatment of Gulf Shrimp Cannery Wastewater*. Cincinnati: Industrial Environmental Research Laboratory, 1979.

Theriot, Clifton P. *Images of America: Lafourche Parish*. Charleston, SC: Arcadia Publishing Company, 2014.

Thoede, Henry J. *History of Jefferson Parish and Its People*. Gretna, LA: Privately printed, 1976.

Triana, Mauro Garcia, and Pedro Eng Herrera. *Chinese in Cuba, 1847–Now*. Lanham, MD: Lexington, 2009.

Uzee, Philip D., ed. *The Lafourche Country: The People and the Land*. Lafayette: Center for Louisiana Studies, 1985.

Van Sickle, Virginia R. *Barataria Basin: Salinity Changes and Oyster Distribution*. Baton Rouge: Center for Wetland Resources, Louisiana State University, 1976.

Visitor's Guide to New Orleans. New Orleans: J. Curtis Waldo, 1875.

Walton, Shana, and Barbara Carpenter, eds. *Ethnic Heritage in Mississippi: The Twentieth Century*. Jackson: University Press of Mississippi, 2012.

Warne, Darian. *Manual on Fish Canning*. No. 285. Rome, Italy: Food and Agriculture Organization of the United Nations, 1988.

Wurzlow, Helen Emmeline. *I Dug Up Houma Terrebonne*. 7 vols. Houma, LA: Privately printed, 1984–1986.

Yun, Lisa. The Coolie Speaks: Chinese Indentured Laborers and African Slaves in Cuba. Philadelphia: Temple University Press, 2008.

Zacharie, Jas S. Hansell's Illustrated New Orleans Guide. New Orleans: F. F. Hansell and Bros, 1893.

Journal Articles and Book Chapters

"Advertisement." *Lumber Trade Journal* 69, no. 2 (January 15, 1916): 51.

Alexander, A. B. "Statistics of the Fisheries of the Gulf States, 1902." *Report of the Commissioner for the Year Ending June 30, 1903, Vol. 29*. Washington, DC: Government Printing Office, 1905, 411–81.

Alverson, Dayton L. "Fishing Gear and Methods." In *Industrial Fishery Technology*. edited by Maurice E. Stansby and John A. Dassow, 41–60. New York: Reinhold Publishing Corporation, 1963.

Bentz, Linda, and Robert Schwemmer. "The Rise and Fall of the Chinese Fisheries in California." In *The Chinese in America: A History from Gold Mountain to the New Millennium*, edited by Susan Lan, 140–55. Walnut Creek, CA: AltaMira Press, 2002.

Busch, Jane. "An Introduction to the Tin Can." *Historical Archaeology* 15, no. 1 (1981): 95–104.

"Canned Foods: The Miracle on Your Table." *Literary Digest* 64, no. 10 (1920): 91.

Comeaux, Malcolm. L. "Folk Boats of Louisiana." In *Louisiana Folklife a Guide to the State*, edited by Nicholas R. Spitzer, 161–78. Baton Rouge, LA: Moran Color Graphics, 1985.

Condrey, Richard, and Deborah Fuller. "The U.S. Gulf Shrimp Fishery." In *Climate Variability, Climate Change, and Fisheries*, edited by Michael H. Glantz, 89–119. Cambridge, UK: Cambridge University Press, 1992.

Dassow, John A. "Handling Fresh Fish." In *Industrial Fishery Technology*, edited by Maurice E. Stansby and John A. Dassow, 275–287. New York: Reinhold Publishing Corporation, 1963.

Davidson, William V. "Research in Coastal Ethnogeography: The East Coast of Central America." In *Research Techniques in Coastal Environments*, edited by Harley J. Walker, 277–84. Baton Rouge: School of Geoscience, Louisiana State University, 1977.

Dubofsky, Melvyn. "Labor Unrest in the United States, 1906–90." *Review (Fernand Braudel Center)* 18, no. 1 (1995): 125–35.

Harris, Wendy h, and Arnold Pickman. "Towards an Archaeology of the Hudson River Ice Harvesting industry." *Northeast Historical Archaeology* 29, no. 1 (2000): 4.

Idyll, Clarence P. "The Shrimp Fishery." In *Industrial Fishery Technology*, edited by Maurice E. Stansby and John A. Dassow, 160–85. New York: Reinhold Publishing Corporation, 1963.

Keithly, Walter R., et al. "The Impacts of Imports, Particularly Farm-Raised Shrimp Product, on the Southeast US Shrimp Processing Sector." *Project Final Report to the Gulf and South Atlantic Fisheries Foundation, Tampa, FL.* N.p., 2006.

Kenny, Jim. "Dancing the Shrimp." *Philippine Studies* 42, no. 3 (1994): 385–90.

Kniffen, Fred Bowman. "To Know the Land and Its People." In *Environment and Culture*, edited by Harley J. Walker and Milton B. Newton Jr. Baton Rouge, LA: School of Geoscience, Louisiana State University, 1978.

Landgraf, R. G., Jr. "Canned Fishery Products." In *Industrial Fishery Technology*, edited by Maurice E. Stansby and John A. Dassow, 309–22. New York: Reinhold Publishing Corporation, 1963.

Magnaghi, R. M. "Louisiana's Italian Immigrants Prior to 1870." *Louisiana Historical Quarterly* 27, no. 1 (1986): 43–68.

Orr, Arthur. "The American Shrimp Industry." In *Marine Products of Commerce: Their Acquisition, Handling, Biological Aspects and the Science and Technology of Their Preparation and Preservation*, edited by Donald Kiteley Tressler and Ward Taft Bower, 548–60. New York: Chemical Catalog Company, 1923.

Read, William A. "Louisiana Place-Names of Indian Origin." *University Bulletin, Louisiana State University and Mechanical College* 19, no. 2 (1927): 1–72.

Slavin, Joseph W. "Freezing and Cold Storage." In *Industrial Fishery Technology*, edited by Maurice E. Stansby and John A. Dassow, 286–308. New York: Reinhold Publishing Corporation, 1963.

Wilcox, W. "The Wartime Use of Manpower on Farms." *Journal of Farm Economics* 28, no. 3 (1946): 723–41.

Theses and Dissertations

Barnes, Russell E. "Impact of Industrialization on Work and Culture in Biloxi Boatbuilding, 1890–1930." MA thesis, University of Southern Mississippi, 1997.

Becnel, Thomas A. "A History of the Louisiana Shrimp Industry, 1867–1961." MA thesis, Louisiana State University, 1962.

Donaldson, Gary A. "A History of Louisiana's Rural Electric Cooperatives, 1937–1983." PhD diss., Louisiana State University, 1983.

Finley, Mary C. "The Tragedy of Enclosure: Fish, Fisheries Science, and U.S. Foreign Policy, 1920–1960." PhD diss., University of California, San Diego, 2007.

Haddad, Nicholas Alan. "Evaluation of Post-Harvest Procedures for Quality Enhancement in the Louisiana Commercial Shrimp Industry." MS thesis, Louisiana State University, 2019.

Kaitin, Noah Karr. "How It Worked When It Worked: Electrifying Rural America." Senior Honors thesis, Cornell University, 2013.

Knipmeyer, William Bernard. "Settlement Succession in Eastern French Louisiana." PhD diss., Louisiana State University, Baton Rouge, 1956.

Nash, Robert Allan. "The Chinese Shrimp Fishery in California." PhD diss., University of California at Los Angeles, 1974.

Pacetti, Derald, Jr. "Shrimping at Fernandina, Florida, Before 1920: Industry Development, Fisheries Regulation, Maritime Maturation." MA thesis, Florida State University, 1980.

Padgett, Herbert Ryals. "The Marine Shellfisheries of Louisiana." PhD diss., Louisiana State University, 1960.

Pearson, Gregg S. "The Democratization of Food: Tin Cans and the Growth of the American Food Processing industry, 1910–1940." PhD diss., Lehigh University, 2016.

Whitfield, K. R. "Canning Foods and Selling Modernity: The Canned Food Industry and Consumer Culture, 1898–1945." PhD diss., Louisiana State University, 2012.

Internet Resources

"A. F. Davidson Hardware and Supply." Accessed August 2, 2018. https://www.davidsonhardware.com.

Allario Brothers Hardware and Fisherman Supplies." Accessed August 2, 2018. https://www.alariobros.com.

"Al's Shrimp Company." Accessed September 1, 2020. https://americanshrimp.com/suppliers/als-shrimp-company/.

"Alviso—Bayside Canning Company." Accessed June 29, 2018. https://en.wikipedia.org/wiki/Alviso,_San_Jose,_California.

"An Amendment to the Constitution Is Needed to Give the United States Power to Safeguard the Child Life of the Nation." VCU Libraries Gallery. Accessed September 12, 2020. https://gallery.library.vcu.edu/items/show/82555.

"American Can Company." Accessed August 10, 2018. https://en.wikipedia.org/wiki/American_Can_Company.

"American Shrimp Processors Association." Accessed February 20, 2019. https://www.americanshrimp.com/association/about/.

"Annual Commercial Landing Statistics, California and Louisiana." 2017. Accessed March 10, 2019. https://www.st.nmfs.noaa.gov/commercial-fisheries/commercial-landings/annual-landings/index.

Bellande, Ray L. "Seafood." Biloxi Historical Society. Accessed January 29, 2019. https://biloxihistoricalsociety.org/seafood.

"Bertoul Cheramie's Conviction of Bootlegging." Accessed October 3, 2018. http://www.laed.uscourts.gov/sites/default/files/200th/notablecases/31%20Cheramie%20-%205th%20Cir.pdf.

Besson, Eric. "Blums Maintain 100-Years of Trafficking Dried Shrimp." 2014. Accessed March 7, 2018. https://www.houmatimes.com/business/blums-maintain--years-of-trafficking-dried-shrimp/article_3ca274f8-9f1b-11e3-8aac-0019bb2963f4.html.

"Bibliography on Boat Building." Accessed April 17, 2018. http://www.folkstreams.net/film-context.php?id=82.

"Blum and Bergeron, Incorporated, Our History." Accessed July 31, 2018. http://blumandbergeroninc.com/?page_id=56.

Bourgeois, David A. "Sun-Dry Shrimp Has Long History." 2001. Accessed December 1, 2017. http://www.houmatoday.com/news/20010930/fisheries-news-sun-dry-shrimp-has-long-history.

Brassieur, C. Ray. "Louisiana Boatbuilding: An Unfathomed Fortune." 1989. Accessed April 4, 2007, http://www.louisianafolklife.org/LT/Articles_Essays/creole_art_boatbuild_unfat.html.

"Brrr. The Secret History of Frozen Food." 2017. Accessed February 6, 2019. https://www.wired.com/2017/05/brrrr-secret-history-frozen-food/.

Burke, Brendon. "Life on the Beautiful Lower Atchafalaya." 2016. Accessed October 1, 2020. https://www.staugustinelighthouse.org/2016/11/02/life-on-the-beautiful-lower-atchafalaya/.

California Department of Fish and Wildlife. "Final California Commercial Landings for 2017, Table 10—Monthly Landing in Pounds in the San Francisco Area During 2017." 2018. Accessed March 13, 2019. https://www.wildlife.ca.gov/fishing/commercial/landings#260042120-2017.

Campanella, Richard. "Lugger Culture: Distinctive Sail Boats Once Defined Coastal Louisiana's Oyster Trade. Geographers' Space." Fall 2016. Accessed July 24, 2020. http://richcampanella.com/wp-content/uploads/2020/02/article_Campanella_LCV_Fall2016_LuggerCulture.pdf.

Campanella, Richard. "185-Year-Old New Basin Canal Continues to Affect Thousands of New Orleanians Every Day." 2020. Accessed May 23, 2020. http://www.richcampanella.com/assets/pdf/Picayune_Cityscapes_2017_12_The%20New%20Basin%20Canal.pdf.

Campanella, Richard. "When St. Bernard Made Cars: Arabi Assembly Plant Represented a Little Bit of the Motor City in the Crescent City." 2014. Accessed November 2, 2018. https://www.nola.com/entertainment_life/home_garden/article_0784844f-0eef-5c07-80d5-238a576e7ea6.html.

Can Manufacturers Institute. "Rapid Growth of Industry." Accessed February 11, 2019. http://www.cancentral.com/can-stats/history-of-the-can/rapid-growth-industry.

"Canning Through the World Wars." Accessed August 2, 2019. https://www.nal.usda.gov/exhibits/ipd/canning/exhibits/show/wartime-canning/world-war-ii.

"Capt. Blair Seafood. Accessed October 1, 2020. https://www.mapquest.com/us/louisiana/capt-blair-seafood-355057430.

Carlsson, Chris. "Chinese Shrimp Village." Accessed July 25, 2020. https://www
.foundsf.org/index.php?title=Chinese_shrimping_village.

"Chauvin Brothers." Accessed August 2, 2018. http://chauvinbrothers.com/.

"China Camp." 2006. Accessed November 3, 2006. http://www.cr.nps.gov/
history/online_books/5views/5views3h19.html.

"Chinese Exclusion Act and the Geary Act." Accessed January 3, 2013. http://
en.wikipedia.org/wiki/Geary_Act.

"Chung Fat Platform." 2006. Accessed November 3, 2006. http://www.nutrias
.org/photos/grandisle/8.html.

Comeaux, Malcolm. "Folk Boats of Louisiana." 1985. Accessed April 17, 2018.
http://www.louisianafolklife.org/lt/virtual_books/guide_to_state/comeaux
.html.

Comeaux, Malcolm. "Louisiana Folk Boats." Accessed July 26, 2020. http://
www.louisianafolklife.org/lt/virtual_books/guide_to_state/comeaux.
html#:~:text=Photograph%3A%20Malcolm%20Comeaux.,(Padgett%20
1960%3A%20190).

"Covacevich Shipyard, Biloxi Mississippi." 2019. Accessed March 1, 2020. http://
shipbuildinghistory.com/shipyards/small/covacevich.html.

"David Chauvin's Seafood Company." Accessed October 1, 2020. https://
americanshrimp.com/suppliers/david-chauvins-seafood/.

"Dean Blanchard Seafood, Inc." Accessed October 1, 2020. https://americans
hrimp.com/suppliers/dean-blanchard-seafood/.

"Definition and History: Turtle Excluder Device (TED)." Accessed August 6,
2020. https://www.seagrantfish.lsu.edu/management/TEDs&BRDs/teds.htm.

Demetri, Justin. "Changes in Navigation and Communication." New Bedford
Fishing Heritage Center. 2016. Accessed February 3, 2020. https://
fishingheritagecenter.org/wp-content/uploads/2016/04/Changes-in
-Navigation-and-Communication.pdf.

DeSantis, John. "Processors Have Tradition, Legacy." 2003. Accessed October 1,
2020. https://www.houmatoday.com/news/20030129/processors-have
-tradition-legacy.

Dunaeva, Aleksandra, and Don Mathews. "How the Shrimp Tariff Backfired."
2007. Accessed April 20, 2020. https://mises.org/library/how-shrimp-tariff
-backfired.

Elzey, Bill. "Photos and Memories: 1881 Article Describes Oyster Luggers."
April 8, 2018. Accessed July 27, 2020. https://www.houmatoday.com/
news/20180408/photographs-and-memories-1881-article-describes-oyster
-luggers."

Enriquez, Nestor Palugod. "Manila Village in New Orleans, 1895–1965." Accessed
October 15, 2018. http://members.tripod.com/Philippines/reggie/manilav
.html.

"Entergy, Company History." 2020. Accessed October 15, 2020. https://www
.entergynewsroom.com/history/.

Explore Beaufort. "Our History: The Deadly Sea Island Hurricane of 1893." 2019.
Accessed October 2, 2020. https://explorebeaufortsc.com/the-deadly-sea
-island-hurricane-of-1893/.

"Faith Family Shrimp Company, Chauvin, La." Accessed October 1, 2020.
https://americanshrimp.com/suppliers/faith-family-shrimp-company/.

FEFCO Corrugated Packaging. "History of Corrugated Paper." Accessed July 30,
2018. http://www.fefco.org/corrugated-packaging/history-corrugated.

Felterman, E. "Who Says You Can't Water Ski Behind Eight Horsepower?"
Gas Engine Magazine (June/July 1991). Accessed March 1, 2019. https://
www.gasenginemagazine.com/gas-engines/who-says-you-cant-water-ski
-behind-eight-horsepower.

Fisherman's Wholesale Marine Supply." Accessed September 4, 2020. https://
fishermanswholesale.net/.

"The 5 Key Flavors of Chinese Food." Accessed February 4, 2019. https://www
.chinahighlights.com/travelguide/chinese-food/food-flavors.html.

"Five Views: An Ethnic Historic Site Survey for California, China Camp, Point
San Pedro, Marin County." 2004. Accessed November 3, 2006. http://www
.cr.nps.gov/history/online_books/5views3h19.html.

"Ford Motor Company, Plant Construction, New Orleans, Louisiana, 1922–1933."
Accessed September 10, 2018. https://www.thehenryford.org/collections
-and-research/digital-collections/artifact/376648/.

Ganzler, Maisie. "Will Trade Tariffs Cause The American Fish Industry
To Flop?" 2018. Accessed May 13, 2020. https://www.forbes.com/sites/
maisieganzler/2018/08/16/will-trade-tariffs-cause-the-american-fish
-industry-to-flop/#473f0c71e8c0.

Gilbert, Jay. "When Did Rural Louisiana Get Electricity? *eNotes Editorial*,
February 16, 2018. Accessed May 23, 2020. https://www.enotes.com/
homework-help/when-did-rural-louisiana-get-electricity-1165618.

"Rev Fr Yves F. Grill." Find a Grave. Accessed January 15, 2019. https://www
.findagrave.com/memorial/194564550/yves-grall.

"Gulf Crown Seafood Company." Accessed February 26, 2020. http://gulfcrown.us/.

Gyory, Andrew. *Journal of American Ethnic History* 20, no. 1 (2000): 100–102.
Accessed May 3, 2020. www.jstor.org/stable/27502658.

"Handling and Processing Shrimp." Accessed January 22, 2020. http://www.fao
.org/3/x5931e/x5931e01.html.

Hebert, Julie Elizabeth. "Identifying Cajun Identity: Cajun Assimilation and
the Revitalization of Cajun Culture." 1984. Accessed January 3, 2014. http://
www.loyno.edu/~history/journal/1999-2000/Hebert.html.

Hein, Stephen. "Skimmers: Their Development and Use in Coastal Louisiana."
2006. Accessed November 3, 2006. http://aquaticcommons.org/9845/.

Heisig, Eric. "Before Fridges, Ice House Kept It Cool." Accessed February 3, 2019. http://www.houmatoday.com/article/20110101/ARTICLES/101239937.

History.com. "Child Labor." 2009. Accessed March 1, 2019. https://www.history.com/topics/industrial-revolution/child-labor.

"History and Development of The [Louisiana Electric Power] Industry." Accessed June 3, 2020. http://www.dnr.louisiana.gov/sec/EXECDIV/TECHASMT/electricity/electric_vol1_1994/002.htm.

"The History of Lithography." Accessed March 3, 2019. https://web.tech.uh.edu/digitalmedia/materials/3350/History_of_Litho.pdf.

"History of Maritime Radio." Accessed February 19, 2020. http://www.arlomaritime.com/history-of-marine-radio/.

"History of SLECA, First Lines Energized on April 14, 1939." Accessed March 5, 2020. http://www.sleca.com/AboutSleca/history.ASP.

Hoag, Christina. "The Shrimp Wars." 2004. Accessed April 20, 2020. https://yaleglobal.yale.edu/content/shrimp-wars.

"Ice Trade." Accessed August 5, 2018. https://en.wikipedia.org/wiki/Ice_trade.

"Illinois Central Railroad, Main Line of Mid-America." Accessed July 31, 2018. https://www.american-rails.com/illinois-central.html.

"Inboard Motor." Accessed August 1, 2018. https://en.wikipedia.org/wiki/Inboard_motor.

Ives, Colta. "Lithography in the Nineteenth Century." Accessed March 2, 2019. http://www.metmuseum.org/toah/hd/lith/hd_lith.html.

"J. H. Menge and Sons Letterhead." Accessed July 30, 2018. http://southeasternarchitecture.blogspot.com/2013/03/more-building-letterheads.html.

Kilbourne, Kathy. "Vietnamese Folklife in New Orleans." 2007. Accessed January 3, 2007. http://www.louisianafolklife.org/LT/Articles_Essays/creole_art_vietnamese_folk.html.

"The Lafitte Skiff." Accessed July 31, 2018. https://www.nicholls.edu/boat/lafitteSkiff.html.

"Laitram, Built On Innovation." 2020. Accessed October 3, 2020. https://www.laitram.com/.

Landry, Laura. "Shrimping in Louisiana: Overview of a Tradition." 1999. Accessed November 3, 2006. http://www.louisianafolklife.org/LT/Articles_Essays/creole_art_shrimping_overv.html.

Leduc, Martin. "The Diesel Engine and Its Development: A Historical Timeline." 2019. Accessed March 5, 2019. http://www.dieselduck.info/historical/01%20diesel%20engine/prime_movers.html#.XIKvhU3sap0.

"Let There Be Ice: In 1868, New Orleans Taught the World a New Way to Deep Cool." Accessed February 28, 2019. https://www.nola.com/300/2017/05/louisiana_ice_works_company_05102017.html.

Library of Congress. "Who Invented Frozen Food?" Accessed August 3, 2018. http://www.loc.gov/rr/scitech/mysteries/frozenfood.html.

"Light Up the Navajo Nation." Accessed March 5, 2020. https://www.publicpower.org/LightUpNavajo.

"List of Ford Factories." Accessed July 26, 2019. https://en.wikipedia.org/wiki/List_of_Ford_factories.

Long, Tony. "Dec. 1, 1942: Mandatory Gas Rationing, Lots of Whining." 2009. Accessed January 24, 2020. https://www.wired.com/2009/11/1201world-war-2-gasoline-rationing/.

"Louisiana Seafood: A Life's Work." Accessed March 13, 2019. https://www.louisianaseafood.com/industry.

"Louisiana Seafood Industry Tokens." Accessed August 22, 2018. https://www.louisiana-trade-tokens.com/seafood.html.

"Marine VHF Radio." Accessed February 19, 2020. https://en.wikipedia.org/wiki/Marine_VHF_radio.

Mattern, Shannon. "Community Plumbing." 2018. Accessed February 26, 2019. http://doi.org/10.22269/180717.

Mitenbuler, Reid. "The Stubborn American Who Brought Ice to the World." 2013. Accessed November 9, 2018. https://www.theatlantic.com/national/archive/2013/02/the-stubborn-american-who-brought-ice-to-the-world/272828.

"New York Hurricane, 1893." Accessed October 2, 2020. https://en.wikipedia.org/wiki/1893_New_York_hurricane.

NOAA Fisheries. "Landings for Brown and White Shrimp from 1950–2018." Accessed May 9, 2020. https://www.st.nmfs.noaa.gov/commercial-fisheries/commercial-landings/annual-landings/index.

NOAA Office of Science and Technology. "Commercial Fisheries Statistics, Commercial Fishery Landings at an Individual U.S. Port for All Years after 1980, San Francisco Area, California." 2019. Accessed March 13, 2019. https://www.st.nmfs.noaa.gov/commercial-fisheries/commercial-landings/other-specialized-programs/total-commercial-fishery-landings-at-an-individual-u-s-port-for-all-years-after-1980/index.

"Notices of Judgment Under the Food and Drug Act." Accessed September 10, 2018. https://archive.org/stream/CAT11088278131/CAT11088278131_djvu.txt.

Nuwer, Deanne Stephens. "The Seafood Industry in Biloxi: Its Early History, 1848–1930." Mississippi History Now: An Online Publication of the Mississippi Historical Society. 2006. Accessed April 23, 2020. http://www.mshistorynow.mdah.ms.gov/articles/209/the-seafood-industry-in-biloxi-its-early-history-1848-1930.

Nuwer, Deanne Stephens. "Shipbuilding Along the Mississippi Gulf Coast." Mississippi History Now: An Online Publication of the Mississippi Historical Society. Accessed April 23, 2020. http://mshistorynow.mdah.state.ms.us/articles/351/shipbuilding-along-the-mississippi-gulf-coast.

Office of the Historian, Foreign Service Institute, US Department of State. "Repeal of the Chinese Exclusion Act, 1943." Accessed August 3,2018. https://history.state.gov/milestones/1937-1945/chinese-exclusion-act -repeal.

Ostrander, Jack. "Child Labor." February 7, 2016. Accessed August 29, 2020. https://sites.google.com/a/k12.wcsdny.org/jack-o-s-magical-website/teen -activism--child-labor.

"Packaging Matters." Accessed February 6, 2019. https://www.npr.org/sections/ thesalt/2012/05/18/152743718/clarence-birdseye-and-his-fantastic-frozen -food-machine.

"The Paranzella." Accessed October 15, 2019. https://oac.cdlib.org/view?docId =kt709nb229;NAAN=13030&doc.view=frames&chunk.id=d0e323&toc .id=d0e206&brand=oac4.

"The Pelican State Goes to War: Louisiana in World War II." Accessed August 2, 2019. http://www.nationalww2.museum.org.

"Post-WWII Construction by Other Gulf Coast Boatbuilders in Louisiana." Accessed March 1, 2020. http://shipbuildinghistory.com/shipyards/other/ gulflapostwar.html.

"Quong Son Platform." 2006. Accessed November 3, 2019. http://www.nutrias .org/photos/grandisle/9.html.

Perugini, Nick. "Navigating Waters Before GPS: Why Some Mariners Still Refer to Loran-C." Accessed July 22, 2020. https://www.nauticalcharts.noaa.gov/ updates/navigating-waters-before-gps-why-some-mariners-still-refer-to -loran-c/.

Quikan, W., et al. "Investigation of Dried Fishery Products in the Chinese Market." Report submitted to the Dalian Fisheries University, Dalian, Peoples Republic of China (1997–1998). Accessed May 16, 2020. http:// aquaticcommons.org/23055/2/062_opt.pdf.

"Richmond to Point Richmond: Abandoned Rails." Accessed September 2, 2018. http://www.abandonedrails.com/Richmond_to_Point_Richmond.

Rkasnuam, Hataipreuk, and Jeanne Batalova. "Vietnamese Immigrants in the United States." Migration Policy Institute. Accessed February 29, 2020. http://www.migrationpolicy.org/article/vietnamese-immigrants-united -states.

"Robert Samanie, Jr." Accessed October 1, 2020. https://www.legacy.com/ obituaries/name/robert-samanie-jr-obituary?pid=188060775.

Rock, James T. "Can Chronology." 1993. Southern Oregon Digital Archives. Accessed August 2, 2018. https://digital.sou.edu/digital/collection/ p16085coll5/id/1948/.

Roth, David. "Louisiana Hurricane History." Accessed January 23, 2019. National Weather Service, Camp Springs, MD. https://www.weather.gov/media/lch/ events/lahurricanehistory.pdf.

San Francisco Fisherman's Wharf Merchants Association. "The Wharf's Fishing Fleet." Accessed June 2, 2019. http://www.fishermanswharf.org/wharf-s -fishing-fleet.html.

Sartore, Melissa. "Hell on Water: The Brutal Misery of Life on Slave Ships." Accessed August 9, 2018. https://www.ranker.com/list/what-life-was-like -on-slave-ships/melissa-sartore.

Schaber, Stephen. "Why Napoleon Offered a Price for Inventing Canned Food." 2012. Accessed August 2, 2018. https://www.npr.org/sections/money/2012/ 03/01/147751097/why-napoleon-offered-a-prize-for-inventing-canned-food.

Schumm, Laura. "Food Rationing in Wartime America." 2017. Accessed September 13, 2017. https://www.history.com/news/food-rationing-in -wartime-america.

"Seafood Industry Landings in the United States in 2017, By State (in Million Pounds)." 2019. Accessed March 12, 2020. https://www.statista.com/ statistics/195214/total-us-seafood-industry-landings-by-state/.

"Sea Island Hurricane, 1893." 2020. Accessed October 2, 2020. http://www .hurricanescience.org/history/storms/pre1900s/1893/.

"Selective Training and Service Act of 1940." Accessed January 24, 2020. https:// en.wikipedia.org/wiki/Selective_Training_and_Service_Act_of_1940.

"Seventeen States Put Gasoline Rationing into Effect." Accessed January 24, 2020. https://www.history.com/this-day-in-history/seventeen-states-put -gasoline-rationing-into-effect.

Sheehan, R. (1955). "Continental Can's Big Push." *Fortune*. Accessed February 11, 2019. http://fortune.com/1955/04/01/continental-cans-big-push/.

"Southern Pacific Railroad." Accessed July 31, 2018. https://www.american-rails .com/southern-pacific.html.

"Southern Shrimp Alliance." Accessed February 20, 2018. http://www.shrimp alliance.com/about/.

Spring, K. S. "Food Rationing and Canning in World War II." 2017. Accessed August 2, 2019. https://www.womenshistory.org/articles/food-rationing -and-canning-world-war-ii.

"The St. Johns Shrimp Co." Accessed October 30, 2020. https://www.pinterest .com/pin/350858627212423395/?nic_v2=1a1ZIy5Gk.

"St. John Shrimp Company Boats." Accessed October 30, 2020. https://www .wisconsinhistory.org/Records/Image/IM65974.

"Steel and Tin Cans." 2018. Accessed August 2, 2019. https://en.wikipedia.org/ wiki/Tin_can#History.

"The Strange History of Frozen Food." Accessed February 6, 2019. https://www .eater.com/2014/8/21/6214423/the-strange-history-of-frozen-food-from -clarence-birdseye-to-the.

Strohl, D. "The Houses that T Built (and that Built the T): Tracking Down the Assembly Plants of Ford's First Distributed Production Effort." December

13, 2018. Accessed February 10, 2019. https://www.hemmings.com/
blog/2018/12/13/the-houses-that-t-built-and-that-built-the-t-tracking
-down-the-assembly-plants-of-fords-first-distributed-production-effort/.

Sutton, Trevor, and Avery Siciliano. "Seafood Slavery: Human Trafficking in the
International Fishing Industry." December 15, 2016. Accessed March 6, 2019.
https://www.americanprogress.org/issues/green/reports/2016/12/15/295088/
seafood-slavery/.

Swanson, Paul D. "Antitrust Monopolization Considerations in Licensing
Cutting-Edge Food Technology Patents." 2012. Accessed November 30,
2014. http://www.earthandtablelawreporter.com/2012/12/05/antitrust
-monopolization-considerations-in-licensing-cutting-edge-food-tech
nology-patents-2/.

"This Is Our Story." Accessed February 26, 2020. http://www.paulpiazza.com/
our-story/.

"Tidelands Seafood Company." Accessed August 3, 2020. https://american
shrimp.com/suppliers/tideland-seafood-company-inc/.

Touchard Marine Supply. "Touchard Marine and Netting." 2012. Accessed
August 2, 2018. www.touchardmarine.com.

"The Unsung Hero." 2018. Accessed October 1, 2020. https://www.houmatimes
.com/opinion/an-unsung-hero/.

"The Versaggi Family, Florida's Shrimp Pioneers." Accessed January 21, 2020.
https://www.shrimpalliance.com/stories/the-versaggi-family-floridas
-shrimp-pioneers/.

VHF Channel Information. "Navigation Center: The Navigation Center of
Excellence." 2018. Accessed February 19, 2020. https://www.navcen.uscg
.gov/?pageName=mtvhf.

"The Walle Company: Humble History, Proud Reputation." Accessed August 2,
2018. http://walle.com/about-walle/History.aspx.

"War History of Canned Fish." United States War Food Administration, Office
of Distribution. Unpublished manuscript. 1945. https://archive.org/details/
CAT31070760/mode/2up and the U.S.

Warner, Kimberly, et al. "Shrimp: Oceana Reveals Misrepresentation of
America's Favorite Seafood." Oceana. 2014. Accessed January 7, 2020.
https://usa.oceana.org/news-media/publications/reports/shrimpfraud\.

"When Did Louisiana Get Electricity." Accessed March 5, 2020. https://www
.enotes.com/homework-help/when-did-rural-louisiana-get-electric
ity-1165618.

You, Palm. "Hicks Marine Engine Archival Collection." 2015. Accessed March 2,
2019. https://www.nps.gov/safr/learn/historyculture/hicksengine.html.

INDEX

236, 239, 240, 242; Laura (2020), 4, 5, 218, 231, 238–39; Marco (2020), 219; Rita (2005), 4, 5, 229, 239, 240; Sally (2020), 219; Sandy (2012), 219; Storm of 1893, 38, 61, 104–5; Storm of 1915, 66, 105; Zeta (2020), 5, 219

Hymel, Thomas, 229

I

Iberia Parish, 234; and St. Mary Drainage Canal, 78

ice, 4, 27, 84, 96, 100–101, 159, 168, 176, 196, 220, 237, 238; boats, 68, 110; crushers, 69; electrification of factories, 193; imported block, 68; increased lugger range resulting from usage, 66; manufacturing in Louisiana's coastal plain, 66; transfer of blocks to shrimp boats, 85

I'm Alone incident (1929), 139

Imperial brand shrimp, 87

India, 209

Indian Ridge Canning Company, 109–10, 113, 116, 152

Interstate Commerce Commission, 156

Interstate Highway System, 156, 202

Intracoastal City, Louisiana, 202, 211

Invader, 273

Isleños (Canary Island immigrants), 21–23, 67

J

J. C. Julian cannery, 110

J. L., 273

J. L. D., 273

J. Waterman and Brothers, 23

Jackson, Michigan, 132

Jamaica, 273

Jambon, Menton, 271

James, Buckner, and Company, 36

James, Samuel L., 36

Jan and Dennis, 273

Janice D., 273

Jastremski, Leon, 123

Jeanerette, Louisiana, 78

Jefferson: brand shrimp, 86; Parish, 104, 120, 233, 234

Jewel R., 273

Jews, 120, 122–26

Jimmy and Johnny, 273

Jimmy M., 273

Joan of Arc, 273

Joey T., 274

John Alan, 274

John Branasky, 274

John Kurt, 274

John R. Hardee Company, 153

Jones, S. L., 44, 123

Jones Express, 22

Judy and Gary, 274

June Reed, 274

K

Kee, Chen, 40

Kelly G., 274

kerosene engines, 132

Kerr-McGee Corporation, 179

Key Largo, 274

Kiff, Edwin, 272

Kiff, Lodrigues, 273

Kiff, Melvin "Pita," 271

Kiff, Steven, 277

Kiff, Tom, 271

Kiff, Walton, 277

Kiffe, Darcy, 220, 222

Korean War, 155, 201

L

L. T., 274

L and F, 274

L and L, 274

L Dot 1, 274

L Dot 2, 274

L Dot 3, 274

La Palma brand shrimp, 114

La Place, Louisiana, 232

La Rochelle, France, 11

Lady Anna, 274

Lady Catherine, 274

Lady Dee, 274

Lady Jo Ann, 274

Lady Luck, 274

Lady Misty, 274

Lady of Fatima, 274

Lady of the Sea, 274

Lady Phyllis, 274

Lady Rayshell, 274

Lady Stephanie, 274

Lady Victoria, 274

Lafitte, Louisiana, 120, 188

Lafont, Euclid, 274

Lafont, Hubert, 272

Lafont, Vin, 273

Lafourche Clipper, 274

Lafourche Ice and Shrimp Company, 100–101

Lafourche Parish, 190, 229, 231–34

Lafourche Pride, 274

Laitram Machinery, Inc., 91

Lake Charles, Louisiana, 219, 231

lake shrimp, 7–8

lakes: Barre, 152; Borgne, 10, 12, 17, 19, 21–23, 27, 31; Felicity, 120; Pelto, 152; Pontchartrain, 10, 19–20, 233

Lamoureux, J. J., 22

Lancaster, Pennsylvania, 73

Lanny R., 274

Lapeyre, Emile, 191

Lapeyre, J. M., 191

Lapeyre Automatic Shrimp Peeling Machine, 195, 199

Larose, 274

Larry G., 274

Lasseigne (shrimp boat owner), 277

Lasseigne, Alphonse "Bob," 276

Lasseigne, Arsène, 273

Lasseigne, Jefferson, 273, 277

Lasseigne, Nolan, 277

Lathrop Marine Engines, 133

Lawrence, D. W. C., 129

Le Page du Pratz, Antoine-Simon, 10, 12

Ledet, B., 276

Ledet, Gerard, 275

ABOUT THE AUTHORS

CARL A. BRASSEAUX, former director of the Center for Louisiana Studies, has spent a lifetime studying the peoples and cultures of the Louisiana coastal plain. He is author or coauthor of more than three dozen books and more than one hundred scholarly articles, including *Ain't There No More: Louisiana's Disappearing Coastal Plain*; *Acadian to Cajun: Transformation of a People, 1803–1877*; and *Creoles of Color in the Bayou Country*, all published by University Press of Mississippi. He is a former Louisiana Writer of the Year.

DONALD W. DAVIS has been involved for more than fifty years in coastal-related research on the wide array of renewable and nonrenewable resources vital to the use of the wetlands. His professional career has concentrated on the people and economic drivers in the state's coastal plain. His publication record reflects his human-centric focus. His work has appeared in numerous journals including *Annals of the American Association of Geographers*, *Shore & Beach*, *Journal of Soil and Water Conservation*, *Louisiana Conservationists*, and *Louisiana History*. He is coauthor of *Ain't There No More: Louisiana's Disappearing Coastal Plain*, published by University Press of Mississippi, and author of *Washed Away? The Invisible Peoples of Louisiana's Wetlands*.